Securitization

Founded in 1807, John Wiley & Sons is the oldest independent publishing company in the United States. With offices in North America, Europe, Australia, and Asia, Wiley is globally committed to developing and marketing print and electronic products and services for our customers' professional and personal knowledge and understanding.

The Wiley Finance series contains books written specifically for finance and investment professionals as well as sophisticated individual investors and their financial advisors. Book topics range from portfolio management to e-commerce, risk management, financial engineering, valuation, and financial instrument analysis, as well as much more.

For a list of available titles, visit our Web site, www.WileyFinance.com.

Securitization

Structuring and Investment Analysis

ANDREW DAVIDSON
ANTHONY SANDERS
LAN-LING WOLFF
ANNE CHING

WILEY

John Wiley & Sons, Inc.

Library of Congress Cataloging-in-Publication Data:
  Securitization: structuring and investment analysis / Andrew Davidson . . . [et al.].
    p. cm.
  Includes bibliographical references.
  ISBN 0-471-02260-8 (CLOTH/CD-ROM)
  1. Mortgage-backed securities—United States.   2. Asset-backed financing—United States.
3. Portfolio management—United States.
4. Mortgage-backed securities—Europe.   5. Asset-backed financing—Europe.   6. Portfolio
management—Europe.   I. Davidson, Andrew S.
HG4655.S43 2003
332.63′2044—dc21   2003001698

Printed in the United States of America.

10   9   8   7   6   5   4   3

Acknowledgments

This book draws on the work of Andrew Davidson and Michael Herskovitz in their previous books on mortgage-backed securities. In addition to the work of the other authors—Anthony Sanders, Lan-Ling Wolff, and Anne Ching—the book draws on the expertise of current and former analysts at Andrew Davidson & Co., Inc. In particular, Alex Levin is responsible for much of the material on interest rates and interest-rate models. William Storms is responsible for much of the credit risk analysis. Sections on prepayments draw on work performed by Sanjeeban Chatterjee, Howard Stern, and Eknath Belbase.

We would like to thank all of the organizations that have allowed us to incorporate their information into the book and the accompanying CD. We would also like to thank those who have reviewed all or parts of the text and who provided comments and encouragement. Special thanks to Nancy Davidson who was responsible for coordinating the preparation and editing of the manuscript.

Preface

Since the early 1980s, as the field of securitization has grown, the practice of securitization has become increasingly specialized. Some participants focus on issuing securities, while others focus on investing in the resulting products. On the issuance side, bankers, structurers, and ratings analysts have become narrowly specialized in certain products and types of structures. On the investing side, knowledge of prepayments, valuation models, and investment strategies has also become highly specialized. For the new participant in the market, this fragmentation is frustrating because it is difficult to get an overall view of the market.

This book, *Securitization: Structuring and Investment Analysis*, moves beyond these divisions and brings together many ideas and issues that are frequently segmented in the marketplace. The book moves back and forth between the structural and investment characteristics of securitization. It establishes frameworks for evaluating the securitization and structuring process across many different products. It also identifies common elements in the investment analysis process that cross product boundaries. In this way the book differs from the current practice of securitization, where terminology and practices have become segmented as the market has grown.

We believe that participants who can bridge the gap between the various disciplines in the securitization business will have a fuller understanding of the risks and opportunities that are available to them. Too often we have seen that development of the market that has focused too narrowly on a particular aspect of the securitization process leads to problems down the road. For example, some securities that were highly rated exhibited extreme levels of risk that caught issuers and investors unaware; and accounting treatment has lead in some instances to bankruptcy as securitization created illusory profits. Participants with a broad perspective across structuring and investment analysis and across a broad range of products may be able to avoid some of these pitfalls.

The book is intended for participants in the securitization market who are issuers, bankers, structurers, rating analysts, and investors. In a complex field like securitization, a book such as this cannot provide a complete picture of the issues that you will face. In fact, the models and analyses in the book have been simplified to facilitate the learning process. This book is intended as a road map to guide the reader into the world of securitization. Once in the market, it is necessary to continue to explore and ask probing questions to get to the heart of securitization. The accompanying CD not only contains information supporting the book, but also contains a list of Web sites that can provide additional information.

BOOK ORGANIZATION

This book spans the securitization market in all its breadth and variety. The book is organized into seven parts. The first part has four chapters that introduce securitization and the foundation for all of the concepts in the book. Chapters 5 through 10, the second part, discuss agency mortgage-backed securities (MBS), the foundation for the securitization market. Advanced MBS and analytics are presented in Part Three, Chapters 11 through 18, and Part Four, Chapters 15 through 18, covers non-agency MBS and analyzing credit risk. The main types of asset-backed securities are covered in Part Five, Chapters 19, 20, and 21. Part Six encompasses securities in Chapters 22, 23, and 24. Finally, securitization in Europe is discussed in Part Seven, Chapters 25 through 28.

The book was written such that each chapter builds on ideas discussed in the previous chapters. However, the chapters were also written to be relatively self-contained so that they can be read separately. This means that there may be a certain repetition of underlying ideas.

Every chapter contains exercises to help the reader understand the concepts in each chapter. Some of the questions may not have answers and are intended to lead the reader into topical questions of debate in the securitization market. Supporting material for each chapter, such as data, documents, spreadsheets, and answers to some exercises, are included on the CD, as indicated by the disk icon.

In most cases the mathematics in the book is at a level that we would expect most college graduates and business students would find accessible. In some cases, we utilize continuous time mathematics that may be beyond those who have not taken or wish they hadn't taken calculus and statistics. Many of the more advanced mathematical sections are found within shaded boxes, so those who are not comfortable with the mathematical notation can identify and skip those parts before becoming frustrated or disillusioned. Those who are comfortable with the math will find that these sections provide additional insight into understanding complex securities.

Categorization of asset classes and instruments is a complex subject in securitization that reflects history and the organization of the investment banking function. We have chosen to classify subprime residential mortgages as mortgage products, rather than as asset-backed products. We save the asset-backed designation for other nonmortgage receivables such as credit cards and auto loans. Manufactured housing (MH) could easily fall into the residential mortgage category, but since many of these loans are not true mortgages, we leave MH in the asset-backed category.

This book does not address the growing field of collateralized bond obligations and collateralized debt obligations. While these are interesting instruments that utilize some of the same structuring technology described in this book, they require an evaluation of portfolio strategy, capital adequacy, and diversification of credit risk that is outside of the scope and framework developed here.

ANDREW DAVIDSON
ANTHONY SANDERS
LAN-LING WOLFF
ANNE CHING

Contents

Introduction to Securitization

CHAPTER 1

The Role of Securitization

Every time a person or a firm makes a promise to pay, a financial asset is born. The promise can take the form of a verbal agreement or a written contract. The promise can involve the purchase of an asset or a service. The promise can also be to repay a loan used to acquire assets or services. In each case, the value of the promise as a financial asset will depend on the ability and willingness of the person or firm to make good on the promise. Some loans are backed solely by the general credit of the borrower, while others are backed by legal obligations that would force payment or the forfeiture of a specific asset. Such collateralized promises include mortgages, leases, and auto loans.

It is the full collection of these promises that provide the raw material for the massive securitization market. Some of these promises will remain, for the entire life of the transaction, an agreement that involves only the original two parties. Others will be packaged with other similar promises, passed through a variety of legal structures, and may ultimately be bought and sold by hundreds or even thousands of investors. The process of packaging financial promises and transforming them into a form whereby they can be freely transferred among a multitude of investors is **securitization**.

The raw promises often are not in a form that is desirable to investors. The size of the transactions may be too small or too large. The promises may contain a mixture of risks that are undesirable to many investor groups. Investors may fear that they lack understanding of crucial aspects of the underlying transactions. For all these reasons and more, many financial promises are transformed through the securitization process. This transformation of the raw assets into a form that is more desirable for investors often involves segmenting cash flows and risks, through a process called **structuring**.

Financial markets consist primarily of three types of instruments:

1. Direct obligations of corporations and sovereigns.
2. Derivatives, such as swaps and futures.
3. Securitized and structured assets.

Direct obligations include equities, treasuries, corporate debt, and convertibles. These instruments represent obligations created by the issuer for investors. Derivatives, such as swaps and futures, represent a zero-sum game. They are created when two parties agree to take opposite sides of a transaction. While each side takes on certain risks and obligations, if the two sides were combined they would cancel each other out. Securitization transforms raw assets into tradable units. Structuring rearranges the cash flows and risks of the real financial assets to meet investor needs. In this way, securitization and structuring transactions reflect the characteristics of the original promises from which they were created. Combined, these three tools create the myriad of financial instruments in the markets today.

This book focuses on U.S. mortgage-backed securities, the largest and most developed securitization market, but it also describes securitization of other assets, including commercial mortgages, auto loans, credit-card loans, and securitization outside the United States.

SUMMARY OF MAJOR ASSET CLASSES

Table 1.1 shows the volume of outstanding mortgage-backed securities (MBS) and asset-backed securities (ABS) by collateral type from 1995 to 2002. MBS are by far the most dominant sector in the securitization market. The outstanding volume of MBS in 2002, including both agency and private label, was $4.7 trillion dollars. (A detailed discussion of agency and private-

TABLE 1.1   Mortgage-Backed and Asset-Backed Securities Outstanding (in billions)

	MBS ($)	Credit Cards ($)	Auto ($)	Home Equity Loans ($)	Manu-factured Housing ($)	Student Loans ($)	Equip-ment Leases ($)	Total ($)
1995	2324.5	153.1	59.5	33.1	11.2	3.7	10.6	2595.7
1996	2488.3	180.7	71.4	51.6	14.6	10.1	23.7	2840.4
1997	2692.5	214.5	77.0	90.2	19.1	18.3	35.2	3146.8
1998	2997.0	236.7	86.9	124.2	25.0	25.0	41.4	3536.2
1999	3371.4	257.9	114.1	141.9	33.8	36.4	51.4	4006.9
2000	3602.7	306.3	133.1	151.5	36.9	41.1	58.8	4330.4
2001	4169.9	361.9	187.9	185.1	42.7	60.2	70.2	5077.9
2002	4709.0	397.9	221.7	286.5	44.5	74.4	68.3	5802.3

Source: 2003 *Mortgage Market Statistical Annual* and The Bond Market Association.

label MBS is contained in Chapters 6 and 15, respectively.) This volume represented 81 percent of the entire securitization market as shown in Figure 1.1. Credit-card ABS were in a distant second place with $398 billion outstanding or 7 percent of the market at the end of 2001, followed by auto loans ($222 billion or 4 percent), home equity loans ($286 billion or 5 percent), equipment leases ($68 billion or 1.2 percent), student loans ($74 billion or 1.3 percent) and manufactured housing ($44 billion or 1 percent).

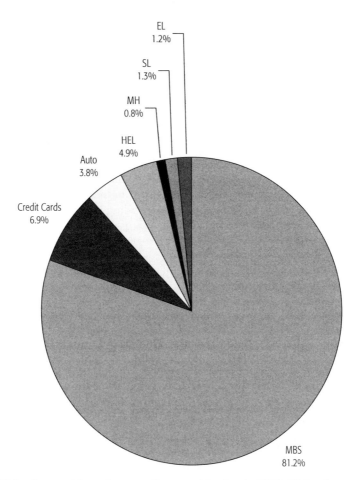

FIGURE 1.1   Composition of outstanding securitization in 2002. HEL = home equity loans, MH = manufactured housing, SL = student loans, and EL = equipment leases. *Sources*: Bond Market Association and *Federal Reserve Bulletin*.

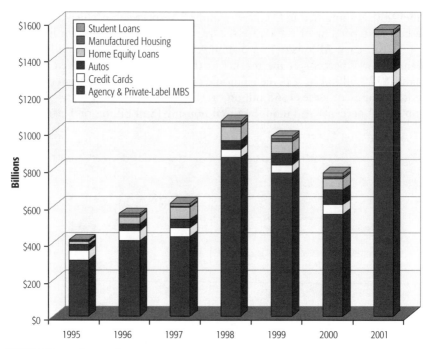

FIGURE 1.2   Volume of MBS and ABS issuance, 1995–2001.
Source: *2003 Mortgage Market Statistical Annual*. The Bond Market Association.

Figure 1.2 shows the volume of newly issued MBS and ABS transactions on an annual basis from 1995 to 2001. Not only has the volume of outstanding MBS eclipsed all other sectors in the U.S. securitization market, but MBS also continue to dominate the volume of annual issuance. In 2001, newly issued MBS reached a record $1.2 trillion as shown in Figure 1.2. MBS issuance has more than quadrupled since 1995. However, the volume of new issuance declined in 1999 and 2000. Origination of mortgage loans during this period declined mainly because of rising mortgage rates.

Figure 1.3 shows a detailed view of ABS issuance by collateral group between 1995 and 2001. The home equity loan (HEL) sector represents the largest sector in terms of newly issued deals in 2001. HEL ABS issuance reached $104 billion in 2001. The HEL sector also experienced explosive growth during the 5-year period shown. Since 1995, issuance of HEL ABS has increased sixfold. However, like the MBS market, HEL ABS issuance volume also declined in 1999 and 2000.

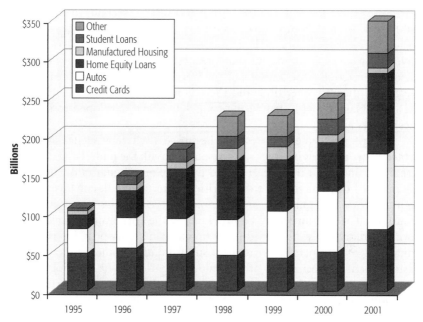

FIGURE 1.3 Volume of ABS issuance, 1995–2001.
Source: 2002 Mortgage Market Statistical Annual.

Auto loan ABS represent the second largest sector in terms of issuance, followed by credit cards, student loans, and manufactured housing. In 2001, $98 billion of auto loan ABS were issued, which has increased by more than fourfold since 1995. Credit card, student loan, and manufactured housing ABS issuance in 2001 was $79 billion, $18 billion, and $7 billion, respectively.

KEY CONCEPTS

Several key concepts permeate the world of securitization. **Collateral** represents the raw promises that underlie the transaction. The cash flow and credit characteristics of the collateral will determine the performance of the securities and drive the structuring process. There are a wide variety of assets that could be the collateral for securitization. Residential mortgages are the most widely used form of collateral. This derives from two fundamental features of these loans: First, they are plentiful and, second, there is a well-established legal structure for transferring ownership of mortgages and ensuring the enforceability of lien on the property. Credit-card receivables have also been securitized, but they present significant challenges for structuring transactions; the amount of the borrower's loan can increase or decrease significantly over time and there is no specific collateral supporting the loan. Nevertheless, structuring tools have been developed to securitize these assets as well.

Credit enhancement represents the process whereby securities may be protected from losses or other risks associated with the underlying collateral. Credit enhancement may be provided by an external guarantor, or may be the result of the structure of the securities. External credit enhancement can be in the form of a guaranty on all or part of the promised payments of the securities. The guaranty may be provided by the corporate issuer of the security, or more likely, by a third-party financial guaranty firm. Internal credit enhancement is generally created by **subordinating** some of the bonds or cash flows of the security to other **senior** obligations. These senior/subordinated structures may have very complex rules to describe the distribution of cash flow. Generally, rating agencies are responsible for establishing the appropriate levels of credit enhancement for each transaction.

Standardization is a general term that represents the process of taking disparate loan types and terms and moving toward a common framework. Consistent documents and underwriting are important aspects of standardization. Standardization facilitates investor understanding of the collateral. Without standardization, investors have a great deal of difficulty understanding the cash flows and risks of the underlying loans. If the loan diversity is too great, investors may feel the need to analyze each of the loans individually. At that level of effort, securitization is no longer economical and investors would prefer to invest in individual loans or other products. In the mortgage market, the mortgage agencies—Ginnie Mae, Fannie Mae, and Freddie Mac—have been a very powerful force in standardizing loan terms, loan documents, and underwriting requirements.

Liquidity is one of the goals of securitization and reflects the degree to which the securities can be transferred from one investor to another. While liquidity is an important characteristic of securities, it is difficult to measure. Some measures of liquidity look at the bid–ask spread, the difference in the price where dealers would buy or sell that security. Other measures of liquidity reflect the amount of time to sell a position, without having to price at a significant discount to a price that could be realized if more time were allowed. By packaging loans in standardized packages, with credit enhancement that protects investors, loans can be sold more readily, hence improving liquidity.

There may be many motivations for an issuer to seek to securitize assets. The primary economic motivation is that securitization allows an issuer to sell loans in an efficient manner, that is, to receive the maximum value for the loans. The issuer is then free to utilize the proceeds of the sale of the loans to originate more loans. Without securitization, an originator would be forced to build a large portfolio of loans. The originator would need to finance that portfolio through the issuance of debt and equity. The originator would also bear the risk of changes in value of the loans. Securitization allows the **segmentation** of the origination and investment functions.

There are several key tax, accounting, and legal issues in securitization. The fundamental **tax** issue in securitization is whether there will be taxation at the level of the trust; that is, will the interest payments of the borrowers be considered taxable income to the trust? The fundamental **accounting** issue is whether the securitization will be treated as a sale or a financing. The fundamental **legal** issue in securitization is whether the trust or other legal entity, created for the purpose of holding the collateral, has sufficient title to the assets and is protected from bankruptcy or other disruptions at the issuing firm.

KEY PLAYERS IN SECURITIZATION

Securitization involves a number of players. Let us look at the case of MBS. First, there is the **borrower** who wants a to buy a home. The borrower goes to the **mortgage broker**, who arranges with a **mortgage banker** to originate the loan. The mortgage banker (who also in many cases acts as the **issuer**) will securitize the loan with other similar loans. The security is sold to a **dealer** who will structure the MBS into a collateralized-mortgage obligation (CMO) or sell the MBS outright to a number of investors. In the course of the securitization, the mortgage banker and the dealer will work with a number of parties including **lawyers, accountants**, and **rating agencies**. Each of these parties will receive compensation for its services. Generally, they are paid up-front fees that effectively come from the difference between the sale price to the investors and the proceeds to the borrowers. A portion of these expenses may be paid out of "points" paid by the borrower. Points represent a reduction in the amount paid to the borrower relative to the amount owed on the loan. The allocation of proceeds is shown in Figure 1.4.

Once the loan has been originated, the proud home owner will make a monthly payment of principal and interest as required by the loan contract. The loan **servicer** receives this payment and distributes it to the appropriate parties. The distribution of the interest payment is shown in Figure 1.5. The servicer handles the paperwork for the loan and is responsible for collections in the event of a default. In case of default, a **guarantor** may be called on to

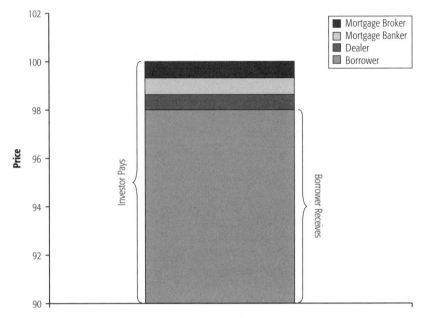

FIGURE 1.4   Allocation of proceeds.

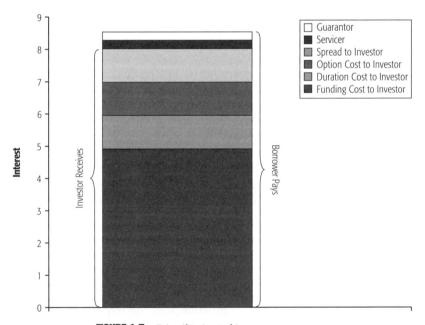

FIGURE 1.5   Distribution of interest payments.

cover any losses. The servicer passes the payments to the **trustee**, who provides for the distribution of the payment to the appropriate bondholders. Generally, the servicer, guarantor, and trustee will all take a slice of the interest payment as compensation for their services.

KEY INVESTMENT CHARACTERISTICS OF SECURITIES (BONDS)

The goal of securitization is to transform the promises of individuals and corporations to make future payments into freely transferable securities that are appealing to investors.

Financial instruments, and bonds in particular, can be viewed as having three general features, which will determine their investment characteristics:

1. Timing of repayment of **principal**.
2. The amount and form of **interest** paid on the amount of outstanding principal.
3. The **credit** quality of the instrument.

The timing of the principal payment determines how long the investor bears the risk of the investment. Principal can be outstanding for months or years. Principal can be returned all at once, in a bullet bond, or can be paid back in monthly increments. Maturity represents the time of the final payment on the bond, while average life is the weighted-average time that principal is received. In securitizations, the amount and timing of principal payments are often driven by the cash flows of the collateral. Because the collateral may have variable payoff schedules, such as prepayments on mortgages, the principal payment schedule of the bonds can also vary.

Interest payments can come in many forms, but generally are either a **fixed** rate or a **floating** rate. Fixed-rate bonds pay a constant rate of interest on the outstanding principal balance. Floating-rate bonds pay a coupon that varies over time. Usually the floating-rate coupon is linked to a particular index such as LIBOR.

The credit quality of the instrument reflects the likelihood that principal and interest payments will be paid in full and on schedule. The credit quality of the bonds will be a result of the credit quality of the collateral and the degree and form of credit enhancement. Credit quality is frequently described by a rating agency, such as Standard & Poor's or Moody's.

Investment characteristics are analyzed by investors who seek to analyze the **value** and the **risk** of the securities. Measures of value include **yield** and various **spreads**, relative to other instruments. Yield is the calculated internal rate of return of the investment. Spread represents the difference between the yield on the investment and the yield on another instrument. Most investors in securities are primarily interested in relative value, which is whether the instrument offers a more or less attractive return for its risk. Therefore, spread is an important consideration for investors.

Rating is one measure of risk. The rating agencies' highest rating (AAA or Aaa) represents securities with the least risk of default. Securities down to BBB or Baa, are considered investment grade. Securities with lower ratings are considered speculative.

Another measure of risk is **duration**. Duration is a measure of the sensitivity of the price of the instrument to changes in interest rates. A related measure is **convexity**, which represents the change in duration as interest rates change and is a measure of the imbedded option features of the instrument.

There are many ways to calculate these value and risk measures. Various measures have strengths and weaknesses. The choice of appropriate measures and calculations will depend on the instrument being analyzed and the objectives of the investors. There are also additional measures of risk and value that may be appropriate for different instruments depending on the collateral and the structure of the security.

EXERCISES

Exercise 1.1   Make a list of types of financial transactions. Indicate which are the most likely candidates for securitization. Which are the least likely?

Exercise 1.2   Figure 1.5 shows the allocation of interest cash flows. What factors are likely to lead to higher monthly fees? What does that mean about the rate charged to the borrower? Is the market more likely to accept a lower rate on an investment to cover higher fees or is the borrower more likely to pay?

Exercise 1.3   Borrowers generally receive the face amount of the loan or less when they borrow. Points reflect receiving less than the face amount as proceeds. If the loan can only be sold at a price well below the face amount, what will be the economics to the originator? If a loan can be sold at a premium price, what does that say about the coupon on the loan?

Exercise 1.4   Suppose a $100,000 loan has a maturity of 5 years. If the borrower makes a $20,000 principal payment at the end of each year, in addition to any interest due, the average life of the loan is 2.5 years. (Average life is the weighted-average time until the receipt of principal.)

a. What is the average life of the loan if the borrower pays $50,000 per year for the first 2 years?

b. What is the average life if the borrower makes no principal payments until the maturity date?

CHAPTER 2

Fundamentals of Structuring

Regardless of the credit quality of the collateral, the flexibility of the structure, or the appetite of investors, securitization only occurs when the owner of the loans chooses to do so. The owner of the loans technically may not end up as the legal issuer of the security, and in most cases it does not, but it is the owner who decides whether or not to utilize securitization. For the time being, we speak interchangeably about the original owner of the loans and the issuer of the securitization. In the second half of this chapter, we clarify the nature of the legal entities involved in the securitization.

ISSUER'S MOTIVATIONS: LEGAL, ACCOUNTING, AND TAX CONSIDERATIONS

From the point of view of the issuer, securitization may be viewed as a **sale** or a **financing,** and in many ways securitization has features of both. Because of this dual nature, securitization reflects many motivations of the issuer, including **financial, regulatory, tax, accounting,** and **strategic** considerations.

Financial or economic motivations will reflect whether the securitization represents the best use of corporate resources. One of the first decisions the issuer faces is whether to sell the assets outright or to securitize them (presuming that the issuer decided to buy or originate the assets in the first place). The main advantage to selling the assets is that risks are transferred to the buyer (with the seller retaining responsibility for the representations and warranties). Another advantage to selling is that the costs of the transactions are generally lower than securitization. In a securitization, several classes of securities may be created and sold to investors. The issuer may retain other classes. Frequently, the issuer retains the most junior class, or the **residual interest,** in the transaction. This retained class can be thought of as the equity of the transaction.

Viewing the transaction as a **sale,** the issuer must determine whether the proceeds from the securitization, after taking into account the value and risk of the retained classes, represents greater value than an outright sale of the loans. Improvements in standardization and liquidity could lead to better values for a securitized sale versus a loan sale.

Viewing the transaction as a form of **financing**, the issuer must determine whether the all-in cost of issuing securities, including the coupons paid to investors and the associated underwriting costs and administrative fees, is a more attractive source of funding compared to corporate debt and equity. In this regard, the issuer should also assess how the transaction alters the risk profile of the institution.

If the bonds created in the securitization have a higher credit rating or are otherwise perceived to have less risk than the issuer's general obligations, there may be a cost savings from the securitization. Thus, firms with high-quality assets may be able to reduce their financing costs through securitization.

Securitization may also impact the firm's capital. Firms are generally limited to the amount of leverage they can have, which is the amount of debt financing on their balance sheet. Securitization may allow issuance of a greater amount of debt than otherwise possible. In this fashion, securitization may allow firms to increase their leverage or free equity for other investments. When pursuing greater leverage, firms should closely evaluate the risks remaining on their balance sheet as a result of the securitization process.

The residual or equity interests retained by the issuer generally are illiquid, complex investments. They may bear much of the prepayment risk and credit risk of the original loan portfolio. However, the issuer generally does not bear any risk beyond the residual class, so that the total amount of potential risk may be greatly reduced. For example, suppose an issuer retains a residual of $2 million on a $100 million loan portfolio. If there are credit losses of $1 million, the issuer may lose half the value of the residual. However, if losses climb to $3 million, the issuer's losses are capped at the original $2 million investment.

Securitization may have a **regulatory** component as well. Most financial institutions are regulated in one way or another. Regulated financial institutions have various capital requirements. Rated securities generally have lower capital requirements than unrated loan portfolios. Securitization may allow a firm to reduce its capital requirements. Recent changes in regulatory requirements have made the capital treatment of securitization more akin to the economic characteristics. While the rated classes may have lower capital requirements than the loans, the residual interests may have increased capital requirements. (See CD.)

From a **tax** standpoint, issuers generally desire to treat securitization as a financing. Sale treatment from a tax standpoint would generally accelerate taxable income. Issuers are also concerned that the securitization is tax efficient and does not result in nondeductible interest costs or double taxation of residual income. Some securitization strategies even provide additional tax benefits to the issuer.*

Selling assets generally requires immediate recognition of gain or loss on the transaction. The sale may also affect the accounting treatment of other similar assets as it may become necessary to treat those assets as **trading** or **available for sale**. Assets in a trading account must be held at market value or fair value. Available-for-sale assets are held on the books at the lower of cost or market value. Loans in portfolio can generally be accounted for as **held to maturity**. Held-to-maturity assets generally can be held at original cost, with some adjustments.

From an **accounting** point of view, firms generally seek to record a securitization as a sale. Based on the proceeds of the sale of the bonds and the value of retained interests, firms may record a **gain on sale** when completing a securitization transaction. While firms generally seek to increase reported income, gain-on-sale accounting may lead to income instability as additional transactions may be required to maintain income levels. Also, if the value of the residual interests declines, firms would be required to show the reduction in value. How those changes flow through the income and balance sheets would depend on whether the residual assets were classified as available for sale or trading.

A firm may enter into securitizations as part of a strategic effort to increase origination of a loan product that it would otherwise be unable to sell or keep on its balance sheet. Securitization may broaden the range of investors for a particular type of loan. Thus, a firm can utilize its strength in underwriting and origination without growing its balance sheet excessively. For some loans, there may already be an active securitization market, and there may be other institutions that would purchase the assets to securitize them. An issuer that sells its assets avoids the costs of securitization, but loses control over the securitization process. Strategically, it may make sense to continue to securitize assets even if securitization currently offers little economic benefit versus a sale of the loans.

---

*See James Peaslee and David Z. Nirenberg, *Federal Income Taxation of Securitization Transactions*, 3rd ed. (New Hope, PA: Frank Fabozzi Associates, 2001) for more detailed discussion of tax considerations of securitization.

ISSUES IN BALANCE-SHEET ANALYSIS

Assets held by the firm must be funded with a mix of debt and equity. Since the assets are generally held on the balance sheet of the firm, they usually are viewed as being supported by the same debt/equity mix as all other balance-sheet items. (This view is not theoretically correct, and can lead to inappropriate evaluation of the economics of securitization.)

Let us take a look at the balance sheet of a simple financial institution that is considering securitization. In Table 2.1, XYZ has total assets of $300 million, of which $200 million is a loan portfolio that it seeks to sell or securitize. XYZ has equity equal to 10 percent of its assets. XYZ estimates its cost of capital by taking the weighted average of the components of its liabilities. On this basis, XYZ might be encouraged to sell or securitize whenever the cost of securitization is less than the cost of capital.

After the securitization, the size of XYZ's balance sheet is greatly reduced as proceeds from the securitization are used to pay down debt (see Table 2.2). The securitization of $200 million in loans will result in cash

TABLE 2.1 Sample Balance Sheet: XYZ Corporation

Assets ($000)		Liabilities ($000)	
Cash	10,000	Short-term debt	45,000
Loans	200,000	Long-term debt	225,000
Investments	50,000		
PP&E	40,000	Equity	30,000
Total assets	300,000	Debt + Equity	300,000

TABLE 2.2 Cost of Capital

Liabilities ($000)		Percentage	Cost of Capital (%)
Short-term debt	45,000	15	4
Long-term debt	225,000	75	7
Equity	30,000	10	25
Debt + Equity	300,000	WACC[a]	8.35

[a]Weighted average cost of capital.

proceeds of $190 million. The bonds issued had an all-in cost of 6.5 percent (based on the yields of the bonds and expenses). XYZ will retain a residual (equity-like component) interest in the securitization. XYZ values that component at $15 million. This valuation results in a **gain on sale** of $5 million. The resulting balance sheet is shown in Table 2.3.

XYZ sees the securitization as being profitable using two separate analyses. First, the securitization resulted in a profit of $5 million. Second, the all-in cost of the bonds of 6.5 percent was less than XYZ's cost of capital of 8.35 percent as calculated in Table 2.2. Even if XYZ blends in the cost of equity of 25 percent on the $10 million not received as cash in the securitization, the blended cost of securitization is 7.43 percent.

The XYZ analysis is too simplistic, however, because it fails to take into account the risk of the retained residual. The residual bears much of the credit risk of the original loan portfolio and might even have substantial interest-rate and prepayment risk. Investors in the company's debt may require higher yields or a higher amount of capital to maintain the same yield. Moreover, given the illiquid nature of the market for residuals, it may be difficult for the firm to verify the value of the residual. If the appropriate value of the residual should have been $9 million rather than $15 million, then the firm actually lost money on the securitization transaction.

If XYZ retains most of the risk that it had before the securitization and the securitization did not add to income, then, from a theoretical standpoint, the amount of equity required by XYZ should not have been reduced through the securitization process. In practice, whether or not the securitization was economically beneficial will depend on a variety of institutional regulatory, tax, and accounting factors.

In general, in most markets, securitization will offer, at best, relatively modest advantages to other forms of financing or sale of the assets. Whenever firms record a large gain on sale using securitization, but otherwise cannot

TABLE 2.3 Post-Securitization Balance Sheet of XYZ Corporation

Assets ($000)		Liabilities ($000)	
Cash	10,000	Short-term debt	30,000
Residuals	15,000	Long-term debt	50,000
Investments	50,000		
PP&E	40,000	Equity	35,000
Total assets	115,000	Debt + Equity	115,000

find investors to purchase the underlying loans or resulting residuals for cash, it is likely that some part of the transaction is being incorrectly analyzed or mispriced. Securitization exists as one tool in a family of financial strategies and is likely to provide similar value as other strategies. Firms that aggressively pursue securitization without regard to other financial strategies frequently end up underperforming in the long run.

THE STRUCTURING PROCESS

As discussed earlier in the chapter, securitization requires balancing financial, regulatory, tax, accounting, and strategic considerations. Tax considerations are one of the driving forces behind the choice of legal structure for the transaction. No issuer would want to incur additional tax obligations for simply acting as a conduit between individual borrowers and investors in asset-backed securities. Asset-backed securities and mortgage-backed securities are usually issued by trusts because income is not generally subject to taxation at the trust level. In a typical securitization, the owner of the pool of receivables deposits them to a trust, which, in turn, issues securities backed by these assets. Not only does the existence of a trust serve to minimize the issuer's tax burden, the trust also establishes a legal separation between the issuer and the pool of assets deposited into the trust. That way, in the case of a corporate bankruptcy, the **bankruptcy-remote** trust cannot be consolidated with the other assets of the insolvent company. This structure allows investors to continue to receive proceeds without interruption from the underlying loan pool.

ISSUING VEHICLES

Several types of issuing vehicles are commonly used in securitizations. A **grantor trust** is the simplest type of trust because principal and interest from the underlying loan pool is simply "passed through" to investors. Investors, commonly referred to as **certificate holders**, are treated as owners of the underlying collateral and are entitled to a pro rata share of cash flow generated from the underlying loan pool. A grantor trust can be structured as a single- or multiple-class security. In the case of grantor trusts, principal payments cannot be accelerated to any one class of securities. All classes must receive principal payments at the same rate, except in the case whereby a subordinate class is written down due to credit losses. Therefore, the average life is the same for all classes, assuming that no losses have occurred. Grantor trusts can be used for just about any debt instrument and are most commonly used for automobile loans.

Owner trusts are more flexible structures because they allow for the creation of multiple-class securities with varying maturities, which appeal to a broader range of investors. Unlike grantor trusts, principal payments can be accelerated or delayed with respect to specific classes and do not have to mirror the underlying cash-flow patterns of the collateral. In the case of a "fast-pay" class, principal payments are made until the class with the earliest stated maturity is fully retired, even though the underlying collateral may have loan terms of up to 30 years. Owner trusts tend to be used most commonly for auto, student, home equity, and equipment loans.

Revolving trusts are typically used for credit-card receivables and home equity lines of credit because of the revolving nature of the collateral. For example, the balance on any given loan fluctuates as charges (or draws, in the case of home equity loans) are made and some percentage of the balance is paid off. There are two distinct phases of a revolving trust: a revolving period and a principal amortization period. In the revolving period, investors only receive interest payments. Any principal that is repaid by credit-card holders during the revolving period is used to purchase additional receivables. During the amortization period, the principal is either repaid in equal installments over a predetermined period of time or in one lump sum.

A **master trust** is a subset of the revolving-trust category, which has been adopted as the preferred vehicle for credit-card securitizations. The master trust allows issuers to use one collateral pool to support multiple transactions. For example, an issuer might create a multitranche security supported by $1 billion of receivables. At some later date, the issuer might issue another transaction supported by an additional $1 billion in receivables that are deposited into the trust. All of the securities that have been issued up to this point are now supported by the entire $2 billion in receivables. Now, principal and excess spread may be shared among securities issued from the same trust. The master revolving-trust structure is advantageous because it reduces the cost of setting up and maintaining multiple stand-alone trusts. In addition, the pool of receivables can be larger and more diversified in terms of demographic characteristics.

A **real estate mortgage investment conduit** (REMIC) is another important vehicle used for securitizations. REMICs were created primarily as a means of issuing multiple-class securities backed by mortgages or real property not subject to tax at the trust or entity level as long as they are in compliance with REMIC requirements as stated in the Tax Reform Act of 1986. REMICs can take many legal forms including corporations, partnerships, and trusts, or as a segregated pool of assets. REMICs are the vehicle of choice for multiple-class, sequential-pay mortgage-backed securities.

Financial asset securitization investment trusts (FASITs) were created in 1996 at the request of credit-card sponsors to provide similar tax relief for

revolving nonmortgage assets as do REMICs. A FASIT generally represents
a pool of debt instruments (e.g., credit-card receivables) that issues a single
class of ownership interests and one or more classes of regular interests.
Ownership interests must be held by a single domestic corporation while
regular interests must be held by taxable domestic corporations. A FASIT is
not a separate tax entity because its assets and liabilities are treated as the assets and liabilities of the holder of the ownership interest. Therefore, the
holder is subject to taxation on the resulting net income, which cannot be
offset by non-FASIT losses. To date, FASITs have not been used widely even
by the groups that sponsored the legislation in 1996.

Types of Securities Issued

Various types of securities can be issued from the issuing vehicles described
previously. The main features of the issuing vehicles are summarized in
Table 2.4, and brief descriptions of the various types of securities are contained in Table 2.5.

TABLE 2.4   Features of Issuance Vehicles

Issuing Vehicle	Type of Securities Listed	Qualifying Collateral
Grantor trust	Pass-through certificates Stripped pass-through certificates (IOs & POs) Senior-sub pass-through certificates Callable pass-through certificates	Fixed pool of mortgages or medium-term or long-term debt
Owner trust	Pay-through bonds CMOs	Any securitizable asset Mortgages, auto loans, student loans, home equity loans, equipment loans
REMIC	Regular interest Residual interest	Real property Mortgage loans
FASIT	Regular interest Residual interest	Any debt instrument Credit-card receivables

TABLE 2.5 Securities Descriptions

Pass-through certificates	Pass-through certificates are treated as owners of the trust and entitle holders to a pro rata share of principal and interest payments. The composition of the asset pool cannot change over time and the trust cannot reinvest any payments received from the asset pool.
Stripped pass-through certificates	Interest-only (IO) and principal-only (PO) strips are examples of stripped pass-through certificates in which ownership rights to interest and principal are completely separated. IO and PO strips entitle investors to 100 percent ownership of either interest or principal, respectively. POs are similar to zero-coupon bonds because they are purchased at substantial discounts and repay principal in one bullet payment. Investors typically purchase POs because they either expect a high rate of prepayments or wish to hedge against declining interest rates. IOs are purchased by investors who expect low prepayments and who want to hedge against losses resulting from rising interest rates.
Senior/subordinated pass-through certificates	Pass-through certificates can have both senior and junior classes, in which the rights of the junior classes to receive principal is subordinated to senior classes.
Callable pass-through certificates	Pass-through certificates can also have an embedded call option, which entitles the holder to purchase the trust assets for cash.
Pay-through bonds	Pay-through bonds represent debt obligations of a legal entity rather than ownership interests and are most commonly issued by owner trusts. One of the main advantages of pay-through bonds is that the cash flows of the underlying collateral can be rearranged to create bonds with various maturities and different payment priorities.
REMIC interests	Regular interests are treated as ownership interests in the underlying mortgages. Only one residual interest allowed per REMIC.
FASIT interests	Single class of ownership interest and one or more class of regular interests.

Credit Enhancement and the
Role of Rating Agencies

Once the type of issuing vehicle has been established, the issuer will face the decision of how to structure the resulting class of securities. A driving force behind this decision will be the level of credit enhancement necessary to achieve a given credit rating (AAA, AA, A, BBB, etc.) for each of the various classes of the security. The basis for the required credit enhancement is the estimated losses for each of the classes under a range of modeling assumptions. At this point, the credit rating agencies (e.g., S&P, Moody's, Fitch) enter into the process.

Rating agencies, generally, seek to determine the financial strength of the securitization to make promised payments to the certificate holders. They determine the required credit enhancement to ensure that certificate holders will be paid in full. Each rating level requires a different degree of assurance. AAA certificates require the highest level of assurance that promised payments will be made. Lower-rated classes require a lower level of assurance. In practical terms, this rating translates into a particular forecast for losses that the certificate must be able to withstand.

In general for mortgage-backed securities (MBS) and asset-backed securities (ABS) transactions, the rating agencies will forecast loss coverage amount as a product of **foreclosure frequency** and **loss severity**. Foreclosure frequency represents the percentage of the loans that will default over the life of the transaction. Loss severity represents the losses experienced by the transaction and consists of any loan amounts not recovered as a result of foreclosure or other sale of the loan. Severity includes all costs of liquidation as well as any accrued interest not paid by the borrower. The rating agencies will establish different levels of foreclosure frequency and loss severity for the various rating levels. The rating agencies will also establish a pattern of timing that describes when the losses will occur. Generally, the rating agencies seek to be conservative, using loss amounts and timing that are more severe than expected under stable market conditions.

The rating process first begins with a financial and corporate overview of the originator and servicer to determine the company's track record. The rating agencies then conduct an in-depth review of the underlying receivables to be sold. For example, in the case of mortgage loans, rating agencies generally will evaluate each mortgage loan against certain criteria, which may include geographic diversification, property type, loan type, loan purpose, presence of mortgage insurance, and owner occupancy. Rating agencies will conduct a careful weighting of each of these loan characteristics for the overall pool in order to determine the ultimate credit enhancement level.

Based on the loan level characteristics, the rating agencies can determine an overall base case amount of required loss coverage as a product of the foreclosure frequency and loss severity. This determination may be an iterative process between the issuer and rating agency, because the collateral composition, sizing of the tranches, and credit enhancement levels may be adjusted several times in order to achieve the issuer's desired ratings.

Rating agencies also examine the structural underpinnings of the transactions, as described in the contractually binding documents of the transaction, such as the deal prospectus and pooling and servicing agreements. While the level of required credit enhancement is a function of the risk of the underlying collateral, the form of credit enhancement can vary, depending on the structure of the securitization. Credit enhancement can either be internal or external to the transaction. Excess interest, subordination, overcollateralization, and spread accounts are all examples of internal credit enhancement. Corporate guarantees, bond insurance, and letters of credit (LOC) are all examples of external credit enhancement.

Excess Interest   Excess interest represents the difference between the coupon or interest rate paid by the borrowers and the coupon or interest rate paid to the certificate holders. Generally the interest rate paid by borrowers is higher than the interest rate paid to the certificate holders. This difference, called the excess interest, is available to cover any losses that occur during that period. Thus, if a loan defaults, the excess interest could be used to make payments to the certificate holders.

Subordination   In a typical subordinated transaction, the rights of junior classes of investors to receive principal and interest are subordinated to the rights of the senior classes. More importantly, the junior classes are in a "first-loss" position and shield senior classes from potential principal and interest shortfalls resulting from defaults or credit losses.

Overcollateralization   Overcollateralization (OC) is a form of subordination and represents the difference between the certificate balance (sometimes referred to as bond balance) and the underlying loan balance. An original OC amount is established when the transaction is issued. For example, if $100 million of bonds were secured by $102 million of collateral, the OC amount would be equal to $2 million ($102 million minus $100 million). In other words, the transaction is overcollateralized by 2 percent. What this means is that this transaction can withstand losses equal to the OC, plus any excess spread available before senior certificate holders incur any losses.

In a typical transaction, in addition to the initial OC level, an OC target level is set. Additional OC can be created while the securities are outstanding by accelerating the amortization of the certificate balance relative to the underlying collateral balance. In any given period, excess interest is used to pay down the certificate balance until the desired target level is reached. As long as the OC target is maintained, excess interest is paid to the holder of the residual interest. If at any time the OC level falls below the target, excess interest is used to pay down the certificate balance to restore the OC level.

Spread Accounts   In contrast to OC, excess interest/spread is deposited into an account that accumulates over time to cover any current losses of the underlying pool. Once a deal has reached its target level, any remaining excess spread is distributed to the residual holders.

External Credit Enhancement   Credit enhancement can also be provided by an external guarantor. The primary sources of external credit enhancement are corporate guarantees or monoline insurers. A corporation can guarantee full and timely payment of interest and principal on a transaction, regardless of the performance of the collateral. While this guarantee is generally viewed as atypical, it is actually the most prevalent form of credit enhancement; the Federal Home Loan Mortgage Corporation (Freddie Mac) and the Federal National Mortgage Association (Fannie Mae), which are government-sponsored enterprises (GSEs), issue corporate guarantees for the timely payment of interest and ultimate repayment of principal for all of the mortgages and collateralized-mortgage obligations (CMOs) they issue. The Government National Mortgage Association (GNMA) issues MBS with the full faith and credit guarantee of the U.S. government.

Bond insurance underwritten by monoline insurers is another form of external guarantee. Bond insurers review the collateral and structure of a transaction to determine the level of risk they are willing to accept. They charge the issuer a fee to provide their guaranty on the certificates.

The structure of a securitization requires balancing a variety of potentially conflicting factors. Creation of a securitization requires the involvement of a number of parties including the issuer, the underwriter, legal counsel, tax counsel, rating agencies, bond insurance companies, trustees, and others. The cost to create a first-time securitization of a new asset can be prohibitive. Over time, standard structures evolve and the cost of issuance declines.

EXERCISES

Exercise 2.1 Suppose a $500 million given set of assets has the following foreclosure frequency and severity assumptions:

Rating	Foreclosure Frequency (%)	Loss Severity (%)
AAA	5	60
AA	3	50
A	2	40
BBB	1	30

a. What is the loss coverage requirement at each rating level?
b. What is the size of each class?
c. If the yields for the respective classes are 6.0 percent, 6.25 percent, 6.5 percent, 7 percent, and 18 percent for the unrated/residual class, what is the all-in cost of funding?
d. If the AAA class pays off and the other classes are still outstanding in the same proportions as the original deal, what is the all-in cost of funding?

Exercise 2.2 How do up-front costs affect the all-in cost of funding?

CHAPTER 3

Fundamentals of Investment Analysis

Financial instruments created through securitization, particularly those such as mortgage-backed securities (MBS) that derive from loans made to individuals, present unique requirements for investment analysis. These securities present investors with complications not found in other markets. These complications are a source of opportunity and a source of difficulty. The main difficulty arises from the combination of the complexity of the structuring of the transaction coupled with the unpredictability of human behavior.

From a purely academic standpoint, collateral can be viewed as a pool of loans with a specific set of **embedded options**. The value and performance of these loans could be calculated based on optimal exercise of the embedded options and the results for each loan could be combined to produce overall value and performance measures for the security. To evaluate the security, one would only need to examine the underlying loan documents to determine the contractual obligations of the borrower.

Unfortunately, this procedure would fall far short. Borrower behavior is driven by the interaction of a number of complex factors; many not directly observable. For mortgages, the debt is secured by real estate, and for many borrowers, this real estate is their primary residence as well as their most valuable asset. The borrower's decisions on how and when to exercise his or her options are driven by many factors, in addition to pure mathematics. For this reason, many securitization transactions are "warm-blooded securities," where the dynamics of human life interplay with the mechanisms of the financial markets.

Choosing the Right Solution

For many years, market participants have struggled with the idea of finding the perfect model to analyze all investment decisions. They hoped to find one method whereby they could input all securities currently available and the correct choice would pop up on the computer screen. This model would somehow take into account all the risks and the likely performance of all securities. The model would analyze the current holdings, the desired outcomes, and find the bond or bonds that would make everything right. The model would review history and forecast the future. The model would produce the perfect portfolio.

For better or for worse, such a model does not exist. Not that analysts have not tried. Some felt that simulation-based, option-adjusted spread (OAS) would be the answer. Since OAS considers hundreds of future possibilities, analysts thought that OAS would definitely answer the question of which bond to buy. However, even OAS, with its broad exploration of the future, cannot by itself provide a clear investment recommendation. OAS analysis, if performed well, can tell you which bonds are cheap, but it does not tell you which bonds are appropriate for your portfolio.

Some market participants have turned to optimization methods to find the perfect black box. Optimization methods involve setting up an objective and a set of constraints and then finding the bonds that maximize the objective function. While optimization often leads to good solutions for simple portfolio problems, when applied to complex problems, optimization is more likely to demonstrate the shortcomings of your assumptions than to provide a viable prescription for investing.

Given the complexity of the investment decision and the variety of methods of analysis, how should an investor determine which method is appropriate. The answer is a bit unsatisfying if you are looking for a quick solution, but is something like the following: Choose an analysis method that reflects your investment objectives and the complexity of the instruments you are considering. A few examples may demonstrate this point.

It is easy to see that the nature of your investment objectives is important in determining the appropriate level of analysis. For example, if you have a targeted income level and duration, the income and duration of each potential investment are minimum requirements of any analysis. The complexity of these requirements may increase if, as portfolio manager, you are also required to evaluate based on periodic earnings and portfolio market value. Also, more and more portfolio managers are being asked to manage more complex investment targets that more closely reflect the nature of the liabilities. For example, many insurance products contain embedded options and the investment portfolios need to be structured to offset these risks.

The complexity of the assets also determines the level of analysis required. Suppose you are evaluating two double-A-rated corporate bonds. Both are 5-year, noncallable bullet-maturity bonds. To determine which is cheaper, you need only calculate the yield and affirm that they both bear the same amount of credit risk. If they both have the same coupon, you need only compare their prices. No amount of scenario analysis, total-return analysis, or OAS analysis could change the conclusion.

However, if you are comparing a callable agency bond, with a collateralized-mortgage obligation (CMO) support bond, comparing the yields of the two securities will give you only limited information about the relative value of the two securities. Some type of option analysis will be required to distinguish between the two bonds. In this case, the option analysis may become quite complex because the methods typically used for evaluating callable agencies and the methods used for evaluating CMOs are usually different and not always compatible. Table 3.1 outlines some examples of bond comparisons of increasing complexity.

In addition, even if you determine that the agency bond is cheaper than the CMO, you might still purchase the CMO if it produces better performance in certain environments. For example, you may be more interested in higher income if rates are stable or if the prepayment behavior of the support bond offsets the risk of other bonds in your portfolio.

It might seem that the safest course is to perform the most complex analysis to ensure that the risks of the securities are captured and that the investments match the objectives. While it may be appealing, this approach is dangerous. More complex analysis generally requires more

TABLE 3.1 Analytical Problems of Increasing Complexity

Bond	Versus Bond	Description
High-grade, noncallable corporate	High-grade, noncallable corporate	Same market, bullet maturity, same maturity, same coupon
High-grade, noncallable corporate	High-grade, noncallable corporate	Different maturities, coupons, types of companies
MBS pass-through	MBS pass-through	Callable (prepayments), same markets
Callable corporate	MBS pass-through	Callable (prepayments), same markets
CMO inverse floater	MBS pass-through	Leveraged, same markets
ARM + IO	Perpetual floater	Leveraged, different markets

assumptions. In a complex analysis, these assumptions are hidden from the decision maker. It then becomes very difficult to evaluate the impact of changing assumptions on the result. A slight change in assumptions could produce a significant change in investment decisions. Therefore, it is advisable to keep the analysis as simple as possible while addressing all of the relevant risks.

A corollary to the rule that the investment analysis should reflect your investment objectives and the complexity of the instruments you are considering is that the judgment of the investment manager is an important ingredient in the investment process. In this book, we do not provide prescriptions that eliminate the need for judgment; rather we hope to alert managers to issues to consider and to provide an outline of the tools that are available to assist in these complex decisions.

TYPES OF INVESTORS

While there are innumerable types of investors, each with their own unique investment requirements and objectives, they can generally be grouped into three categories: **trading, net interest spread**, and **total return**. Each category of investor can be defined by the fundamental investment objective. Investors may seek to define risk in different ways and may perform different types of investment analysis. In reality, most investors represent a combination of these three categories, as they face multiple investment objectives.

The trading firm has a relatively simple objective: Buy instruments at a low price and sell at a higher price. The trading firm generally operates on a short time horizon for each transaction. The amount of time that a position is held by the firm increases its risk, so it seeks to minimize that time. The trading firm has two fundamental sources of income. The trading firm benefits from its position as market maker and earns a spread on transactions. The price at which a firm will buy a security is called the **bid**. The price at which it will sell, or offer, a security is called the **ask**, or asking price. The difference between the two is called the **bid–ask spread**. That spread times the volume of transactions represents the firm's profits from its market-making function.

Trading firms also seek to profit from identifying value. The firm seeks to buy securities for which it believes others in the market will be willing to pay a higher price. The trading firm takes advantage of its active participation in many markets to identify these opportunities. Securitization is one tool that trading firms can use to profit from relative value opportunities. At times, traders may discover that if they transform certain assets through the securitization and structuring process, they can sell the assets at a higher price.

Traders seek to reduce their risk through hedging. For a trader, the ideal hedge is to sell the position, thereby eliminating all risk. However, not all positions can be sold immediately at the most attractive prices. Traders will assess whether a hedging vehicle can reduce the risk of a position. Most traders in fixed-income securities will reduce the risk of their position associated with changes in the level of yield curve, that is, the duration risk of their positions. Traders may also seek to reduce some of the sector risks of their holdings by selling short instruments similar to those they hold.

Traders refer to the situation when certain assets can be purchased and resold at a higher price, or purchased and structured to be sold at a higher price, as an *arbitrage* opportunity. While arbitrage may have certain specific meanings to economists and financial theorists, traders use the term broadly to reflect a broad range of profit opportunities. Often traders cannot simultaneously execute all portions of a trade and may lack appropriate vehicles to fully hedge their risks. Such situations are not truly arbitrage transactions, and in many cases have led to significant losses when market conditions changed rapidly.

Wall Street firms, with their large trading desks and their associated broker/dealer operations, are the typical traders. However many other firms may operate like traders. Mortgage bankers, who originate loans primarily to sell to the market, essentially operate as traders, buying loans from individual borrowers and selling them as securities into the market. Some investment vehicles, such as hedge funds, which operate with high turnover seeking short-term relative value opportunities, also act like traders.

Net-interest investors seek to earn a steady stream of income based on the difference between what they earn on the assets they own versus what they pay on liabilities they have incurred. The spread differential should be sufficient to provide an adequate return on the equity required by the strategy. Banks and other depository institutions are generally net-interest investors.

The typical bank will take money it raised from deposits and make loans to a variety of borrowers. The differential between the interest income from the assets and the interest expense paid to the depositors represents the net-interest income or spread. Regulators require banks to have a certain amount of equity, based on the risk of the assets. Banks will measure the profitability of an investment strategy by computing a return on assets, which equals the spread divided by the total assets, or a return on equity that equals the spread divided by the total equity. An essential aspect of the investment management process is balancing the risk of the strategy with the amount of equity. Reducing the amount of equity through greater leverage will not only increase the return on equity, but will also increase the risk of failure.

While banks are the primary example of spread investors, virtually any investor who borrows to acquire assets and holds positions for extended time periods acts as a spread investor and must be concerned with an evaluation of leverage and risk. Many recently structured collateralized-bond obligations (CBOs) and collateralized-debt obligations (CDOs) are essential securities that represent structured spread investors.

The **total return** manager seeks to outperform a set of benchmarks on a total return basis. Total return means the sum of income and changes in value over a specified time horizon. The classic total return manager is a pension or retirement fund manager. Many mutual funds also operate principally on a total rate of return basis. Total return managers are generally considered to be unleveraged, in that they do not utilize borrowing in their strategies.

Total return managers are generally measured against the performance of either other managers with similar investment objectives, or against an *index* of the performance of a certain set of securities. Lehman Brothers, Citigroup (formerly Salomon Brothers), and Merrill Lynch are the major providers of index performance for fixed-income securities. (The Dow Jones Index, Standard & Poor's Index, and Nasdaq Index are the leading measures of return for the U.S. equity markets.) Lipper Analytical Services, now owned by Reuters, is the major provider of return comparison of managers versus other managers. Morningstar is another major provider of return information for mutual funds.

Because total return managers are generally compared to the return of other assets, they measure their risks based on how their portfolios differ from the index against which they are judged. They seek to find instruments that will outperform those in the index without taking excessive risk that the instruments that they purchase will underperform the index.

Many insurance company portfolios are evaluated on a total return basis, even though the insurance company as a whole must operate more like a spread investor. However, the broad range of liabilities and the uncertainty of insurance payouts make a strict spread analysis unwieldy. Because total return analysis includes both the income and price change effects of financial instruments, it is broadly used as a comprehensive analytical measure.

ANALYZING SECURITIES

There are many ways to analyze the securities that result from the securitization and structuring process. Each type of security and portfolio strategy demands a different method. In this book we utilize a framework that provides consistency across the different methods. The framework has four phases. Table 3.2 outlines the framework.

The four phases are **methodology, collateral, structure,** and **results.** In the methodology phase, the range of possible states of the world that affect the analysis are considered. In other words, various scenarios are created. In the collateral phase, the performance of the collateral, especially as it relates to prepayments, losses, or other features that will affect the cash flows, is determined. In the structure phase, the cash flows of the securities are calculated for each scenario using the prepayment, loss and other estimates, the structural features of the securities, and any other relevant factors. Finally, in the results phase, various calculations are performed to summarize the cash-flow results.

Different analyses reflect different choices for the four phases. A relatively simple analysis, yield calculation for MBS, is described in Chapter 8. OAS analysis for MBS, a more complex analysis, is presented in Chapter 13. In both cases, and in other analyses, the same four phases must be considered. Although the analysis is split into four phases for exposition, all phases are closely interrelated. For example, the choice of methodology will control

TABLE 3.2   The Analytical Framework

Phase of Analysis	Components
Methodology	Interest rates
	Economy
	Supply/demand
	Regulatory/tax/accounting
Collateral	Prepayments
	Defaults/losses
Structure	Collateral cash flows
	Security waterfall
	Portfolio
Results	Income
	Valuation
	Risk

the range of outcomes available for the results phase. The collateral phase requires output from the methodology phase and determines some of the key ingredients of the structure phase.

Methodology

The methodology phase sets the stage for the analysis. In this phase, the types of risk that will be considered are determined. The methodology phase is the most important phase and often the most overlooked. The goal of this phase is to specify the range of influences on the securities' performance that will be included in the analysis. The methodology phase is critical because it sets the boundaries of the analysis. Factors that are left out in this phase cannot be considered in the analysis.

Due to the complexity of securitization and structured securities, many factors need to be included when analyzing these types of securities. Too often, however, methods that work for other instruments are blindly applied, without due consideration of other factors. For example, the performance of an MBS might be related to activity in the housing market, the performance of a commercial mortgage deal may depend on the strength of retail sales, or the performance of a credit-card deal may depend on the level of personal bankruptcies. Failure to assess the impact of changing economic conditions might result in overlooking a potential risk of the investment.

The primary component of the economic environment that affects most fixed-income investments is interest rates. For noncallable, high-quality securities, the interest-rate environment determines the value and risk of the investment in a relatively straightforward manner. For callable securities, such as MBS and other structured products, interest rates affect these securities through the interaction of potential changes in interest rates with the potential changes in the securities cash flow. Determining value and risk is a more complex process.

A wide range of interest-rate assumptions are possible: Interest-rate assumptions can vary from the simple, where interest rates are expected to remain constant at their current levels; to dynamic, where, for example, interest rates change linearly over the next 12 months, each move having a probability given by the current volatility of interest rates; to the sophisticated, where interest rates are generated by a two-factor, log-normal, mean-reverting process, which satisfies a no-arbitrage condition and whose variances and covariance are consistent with historical observation.

Interest rates are not the only factors that affect performance of securities. As warm-blooded securities, the value and performance of these complex instruments are influenced by whatever factors affect the borrowers.

Changes in an individual's family (marriage, divorce, children, death) will affect the home ownership and creditworthiness of the borrower. As securitizations represent many different individual borrowers, the decisions of any one borrower will not have a significant impact on investors. Taken together, the behavior of individuals will determine the performance of the securities. For this reason, securities analysts look to economic data on employment and housing markets as well as other economic and demographic data.

One of the major complexities of this process is that these "soft" features of collateral and security performance must be viewed in the context of the interest-rate assumptions. It is not enough to determine that rising unemployment tends to slow prepayment levels. It is also necessary to determine how much unemployment will rise or fall as interest rates change.

The choice of methodology also requires choices about financial theory. Most analysis of fixed-income securities is relative-value analysis, which is a comparison of two or more securities. Some analytical tools are more suited to distinguishing between securities with different investment characteristics. There is a well-developed financial theory about interest rates and the valuation of contingent claims (options). Various methods have greater or less conformity to this theory. Even in cases where analysts may agree on the theory, they may choose implementation methods that differ in application and in results. The financial theory of interest rates is discussed in Chapters 7 and 12.

Collateral

Based on the choice of approach and the associated assumptions about the economic environment, investors can evaluate the characteristics and expected performance of the collateral. The goal of the analysis is to produce assumptions that can be used in determining the cash flows of the collateral and the securities. The assumptions are generally either in the form of a single number applied to a measure of performance, like an annual rate, or in the form of a model that relates inputs about the collateral and the economic environment to month-by-month forecasts of performance. The focus of this analysis is usually on prepayments and credit.

Prepayments represent the options of borrowers to prepay loans. Many products allow prepayment at any time; some have prepayment penalties or other contractual features that may limit prepayments. Unlike corporate bonds, prepayments on consumer assets are determined primarily based on analysis of historical data, rather than principles of optimal exercise because borrowers face unseen costs that are difficult to assess directly.

Credit evaluation is primarily an evaluation of the potential for delinquency and default and the associated severity of loss. Generally, loans that miss a payment are considered **delinquent**. Delinquency is measured in number of days payments are overdue. Delinquencies in excess of 60 days or 90 days are considered **seriously delinquent**. For some products, delinquencies of this magnitude are considered **defaults**. Default represents the beginning of the recovery process. A servicer may attempt to recover losses on nonpaying loans through renegotiations or **foreclosure**. The difference between the loan balance and any recoveries less expenses is the **severity** of the loss.

Prepayments and credit assumptions are usually created via analysis of historical data. The development and evaluation of these assumptions is a central part of developing structures for securitization and valuing the resulting securities. Each type of collateral requires an in-depth analysis of its performance characteristics.

Structure

The structure phase is the core of the analytical process. In this phase, the cash flows of the securities are calculated based on the environmental assumptions of the methodology phase, the assumptions generated in the performance phase, and the legal and contractual features of the collateral and the securitization. The results generated in the next phase generally are attempts to summarize the characteristics of the cash flows in useful ways. Calculation of the cash flow is theoretically the most straightforward phase, but for many applications it is the most time consuming.

The calculation procedure starts with the most basic component, the underlying collateral, and then derives the cash flows of the securities backed by those loans. Pass-through securities are calculated based on the loan cash flows. Structured securities cash flows are based on the pass-through cash flows. Portfolio cash flows are calculated based on the cash flows of the securities. The process of splitting the cash flows from the collateral into various securities is sometimes called the **waterfall**, as it describes how cash flows are divided among various instruments.

The greatest complexity in this phase is gathering the appropriate indicative data that describe the securities. Each loan has unique characteristics that determine its cash flows and each security may be governed by a complex set of rules that determine how the incoming cash is split between several different securities. Another important consideration in this phase is determining the appropriate level of detail for the analysis. In some cases, loan-by-loan information is not available, so the analysis must be based on weighted-average characteristics. In other cases, more information may be available. The analyst must then determine the tradeoff between additional accuracy and computational efficiency.

Results

The final phase of the analysis is the results phase. Based on the calculated cash flows, and the theoretical framework of the methodology, summary measures are produced in the results phase. The purpose of these measures is to aid in the investment process. These analytical results generally provide insight into income, valuation, and risk.

Income measures provide insight into the pattern of future cash flows and the levels of income. Valuation measures provide guidance in identifying rich and cheap securities. While better measures provide more reliable indicators of future performance, all existing measures have both strengths and weaknesses. Risk measures provide guidance in assessing the range of outcomes for an investment, as well as how a particular investment will perform relative to other securities (see Table 3.3).

For securities that can experience credit losses, there are measures that can address credit risk. Some of these risks are addressed in the structuring process, when a rating is assigned to each class, but additional analysis may be required to assess the credit risk from an investment standpoint.

The accuracy and effectiveness of these measures stem from the full analysis process. The results phase only captures those factors contemplated in the methodology phase, impounded in the collateral phase, transmitted in the structure phase, and summarized in the results phase.

The varying complexity of collateral types, securitization structures, and investment strategies creates the need for a variety of analytical tools. Different problems require different types and scopes of analysis. While analysis tools differ greatly in ease of computation, data requirements, and

TABLE 3.3 Types of Analytical Results

	Static	Scenario	Option-Based
Income	Yield	Total return	OA-yield (not commonly used)
Value	Yield spread	Return profile	OAS
Risk	Weighted-average life Cash-flow duration	Effective duration	OA-duration OA-convexity

technical complexity, most require the same four phases of analysis: methodology, collateral, structure, and results.

The choices made in each phase will determine the effectiveness of the tool for addressing a specific problem. Each phase is closely related to the others. A good tool maintains comparable levels of complexity across the four phases. Complex measures based on simple assumptions would provide unrealistic appearance of accuracy, while simplistic measures based on complex assumptions are a waste of effort. Good analysis requires matching the solution to the problem and designing the solution method effectively.

EXERCISES

Exercise 3.1a   For the three investor types; trading, spread, and total return, what are the short-term and long-term impacts of spread widening for an investment that they hold? Assume that spread widening means that the price of the security that they hold falls relative to the hedge instrument for the trader, the liability for the spread investor, and the index for the total return player.

Exercise 3.1b   If the firm has additional money to invest in that instrument, what are the short-term and long-term impacts of a spread widening?

Exercise 3.2   Given the differences between the investor types, what is the strength or weakness of mark-to-market accounting versus cost-based accounting for each one?

CHAPTER 4

Historical Performance of Asset-Backed Securities and Mortgage-Backed Securities

In order to develop a better understanding of asset-backed securities (ABS) and mortgage-backed securities (MBS) as described in Chapter 1, it is helpful to examine their historical performance relative to other fixed-income securities (FIS). In this chapter, we find that ABS and MBS have generated lower average returns than other FIS (such as Treasury bonds) since 1993, but have also had less risk. Furthermore, we find that ABS has actually outperformed the industry-standard benchmark Lehman Brothers Aggregate Bond Index over the same time period. In contrast, we find that MBS have not outperformed other FIS.

COMPARING RETURNS ON ALTERNATIVE ASSET-BACKED SECURITIES AND MORTGAGE-BACKED SECURITIES INVESTMENTS

Since 1993, the fixed-income market has experienced several cycles where returns to ABS and MBS have risen considerably and then fallen. Part of the reason for these cycles is the fluctuation in the equity markets. As equity markets experience a downturn, investors typically follow a "flight to quality" strategy where money is removed from the equity markets and placed in lower-risk (or lower-volatility) investments such as U.S. Treasury securities, ABS, and MBS. As the equity market recovers, investors shift a portion of their assets from the fixed-income market back to the equity markets.

As expected, the average return on the S&P 500 index has a higher average return than the typical FIS indexes. However, the higher average return on the S&P 500 index is tempered by the dramatically higher risk (or volatility) of the S&P 500 index. Table 4.1 shows the average return on the

TABLE 4.1   Average Returns and Risk of Competing Investments (Annualized Returns January 1993–March 2002)

Index	Average Return (%)	Standard Deviation (%)
30-day T-bills	4.4987	0.3327
Long-term government bonds	8.3718	8.3423
Long-term corporate bonds	7.6809	6.6136
S&P 500 index	13.4866	14.3970
Lehman Brothers Aggregate Bond	6.8746	3.7546
Lehman Brothers MBS	6.8584	3.0116
Merrill Lynch MBS	6.9275	3.0173
Salomon Brothers MBS	6.8914	2.9751
Merrill Lynch ABS	6.3470	1.9711
Salomon Brothers ABS	6.8134	2.8383
HFRI Fixed-Income Hedge Fund	9.2270	3.2850
HFRI MBS Hedge Fund	10.7254	4.6563

S&P 500 index from January 1993 through March 2002, which is 13.49 percent compared with an average return of 8.37 percent for long-term government bonds over the same period. However, the standard deviation of returns for the S&P 500 index is 14.40 percent compared to only 8.34 percent for long-term government bonds.

ABS and MBS have experienced slightly lower returns than long-term government bonds since 1993. For example, the Lehman Brothers MBS, Merrill Lynch MBS, and Salomon Brother MBS (representing investments in 15-year and 30-year Ginnie Mae, Fannie Mae, and Freddie Mac MBS) experienced annual returns averaging about 6.9 percent. The standard deviation of these MBS indexes is about 3.0 percent (which is less than half of the standard deviation of long-term government bonds and, in fact, is about one-third of the risk of long-term government bonds). Given the lower risk exposure of MBS compared with equities and long-term government bonds, it is not surprising that MBS thrive in markets where riskier securities are performing poorly.

ABS returns, as measured by the Merrill Lynch and Salomon Brothers ABS indexes, were slightly lower than MBS returns from January 1993 through March 2002. The standard deviation of ABS returns, particularly the Merrill Lynch ABS index, was lower as well. This result is somewhat puzzling given the greater credit risk associated with ABS (in that ABS con-

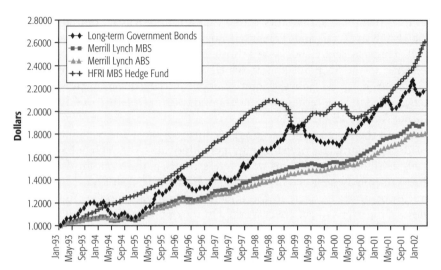

FIGURE 4.1 Return on $1 invested in various fixed-income indexes on December 31, 1992.

sists mostly of home equity loans, credit cards, and car loans). However, the increased credit risk of these loans must be weighed against the shorter maturity of ABS versus MBS. For example, car loans typically have a stated maturity of 3 to 5 years, whereas single-family home mortgages have a stated maturity of 15 to 30 years. For the ABS products used in the indexes by Merrill Lynch and Salomon Brothers, it is clear that the combined credit and interest-rate risk are smaller for ABS as a whole.

Figure 4.1 depicts the return on investment of $1 in different fixed-income products since 1992. Clearly, investing in the Hedge Fund Research, Inc. (HFRI) MBS hedge fund would have provided the greatest return on investment (although there was substantial volatility around 1998–2000). Long-term government bonds had the next highest return but higher volatility. MBS and ABS had steady returns with little volatility; hence, MBS and ABS are considered excellent investments for risk-averse investors.

A CASE STUDY OF MARKET TURBULENCE

Many investors remember the market turbulence of 1998. Toward the middle of 1998, international markets were struck by what is called "The Russian Credit Crisis." This event was caused by the threat of Russia defaulting on its foreign loans. Investors feared that not only Russia, but other countries (such as Brazil and Argentina) might default on their foreign debt as well. This fear sent a shockwave throughout the world. Investor fears were reflected in the S&P 500 index, which fell 14.46 percent in August 1998. The flight of capital from the equity markets into the government bond market resulted in long-term government bonds posting a return of 4.65 percent during August 1998.

With the lowering of interest rates during August and September 1998, residential mortgages prepaid at an incredible rate. Although MBS will typically exhibit positive returns when interest rates in the economy decline, the flurry of prepayment activity resulted in decreasing cash flows (since there are fewer mortgages left in the underlying mortgage pools). As a consequence, the prepayment effect worked in the opposite direction of the interest-rate effect, resulting in MBS returns of only 0.91 percent for the Lehman Brothers MBS Index and 0.90 percent for the Merrill Lynch MBS index. In summary, MBS had positive returns during August 1998, but they were far less than the returns on long-term government bonds.

Not surprisingly, MBS hedge funds performed poorly in August 1998 compared with the MBS indexes. The HFRI MBS Hedge-Fund Index fell by 1.17 percent during that month, as a result of mortgage derivatives (such as interest-only [IO] strips), which decline with interest-rate declines. The HFRI Fixed-Income Hedge-Fund Index fell by 3.13 percent during August 1998.

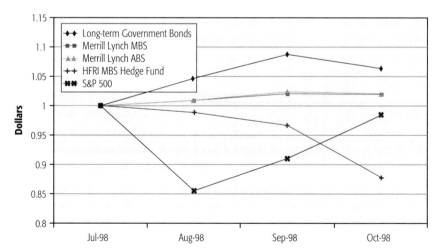

FIGURE 4.2   Return on $1 invested in various fixed-income indexes on July 31, 1998, for the Russian credit crisis.

This decline was undoubtedly upsetting to investors seeking a safe haven from the equity markets.

The stock market rebounded in September 1998 with a return on the S&P 500 index of 6.40 percent. Long-term government bonds rose as well, experiencing an increase of 3.95 percent. The MBS indexes rose approximately 1.20 percent. Once again, we can see that MBS returns increase when long-term government bond returns increase, but at a slower rate. Unlike MBS, ABS (as measured by the Salomon Brothers ABS index) rose by 2.27 percent. However, the HFRI MBS Hedge-Fund Index fell by 2.15 percent. MBS hedge funds can actually experience negative returns with a decline in interest rates, given their investments in mortgage derivatives such as IO strips.

October 1998 demonstrated a further strengthening of the equity markets. The S&P 500 index showed a return of 8.13 percent, while long-term government bonds suffered a negative return of 2.18 percent. Like the long-term government bonds, the MBS indexes declined as well, although only by 0.11 percent. The Salomon Brothers ABS Index declined by a greater amount: 0.63 percent. The HFRI MBS Hedge-Fund Index fell by 9.24 percent (compared to a 3.27 percent drop in the HFRI Fixed-Income Hedge-Fund Index). The large negative returns for the MBS hedge funds were due to the meltdown in the mortgage derivatives market. In addition, hedge funds use extensive financial leverage and can react quite negatively with a downturn in the MBS and Treasury markets.

By November 1998, the market had stabilized. But as a result of a downturn in the stock market and MBS hedge funds, which lasted several months, many hedge funds lost substantial amounts of investors' capital (e.g., Long-Term Capital, Laser Capital, and Ellington Capital).

PERFORMANCE OF MORTGAGE-BACKED SECURITIES AND ASSET-BACKED SECURITIES

While MBS and ABS generated similar returns over the January 1993 through March 2002 period, the standard deviations of returns were more profound. In order to measure the relative performance of ABS and MBS, we employ the Sharpe Ratio of investment performance. The Sharpe Ratio is defined as the excess return on a security (over the 30-day Treasury bill rate) divided by the excess risk of the security (over the standard deviation of the 30-day Treasury bill rate)

$$SR = \frac{\bar{r}_I - \bar{r}_{rf}}{SD_I - SD_{rf}} \qquad (4.1)$$

where r_I is the average return on the security (or index), r_{rf} is the average return on the 30-day Treasury bill, SD_I is the standard deviation of returns for the investment (or index) and SD_I is the standard deviation of returns for the 30-day Treasury bill.

The Sharpe Ratio measures which investment (or index) generates the most return for a given level of risk (or, in this case, standard deviation). The investments (or indexes) with the highest Sharpe Ratio have, in the past, performed the best on a risk-adjusted basis.

We begin with a comparison of Sharpe Ratios of the benchmark equity (S&P 500) and debt (Lehman Brothers Aggregate Bond) indexes shown in Table 4.2. The Sharpe Ratio for the S&P 500 index over the period of January 1993 through March 2002 was 0.9323, while the Sharpe Ratio for the Lehman Brothers Aggregate Bond Index was 0.6943. Based on the Sharpe Ratio, the S&P 500 index generated a superior return relative to its risk.

For MBS, the various indexes were all about 0.90, indicating that the relative performance of MBS was superior to that of the Lehman Brothers Aggregate Bond Index. For ABS, both the Salomon Brothers (0.90) and Merrill Lynch (1.13) indexes were superior to the Lehman Brothers Aggregate Bond Index. In summary, MBS and ABS have generated superior returns relative to the bond market as a whole once we account for the total risk of the security.

Despite their poor performance during the 1998 Russian Credit Crisis, fixed-income and MBS hedge funds have performed well according to the

TABLE 4.2 Sharpe Ratio for Competing Investments (January 1993–March 2002)

Index	Sharpe Index (%)
Long-term government bonds	0.4836
Long-term corporate bonds	0.5067
S&P 500 index	0.9323
Lehman Brothers Aggregate Bond	0.6943
Lehman Brothers MBS	0.8809
Merrill Lynch MBS	0.9047
Salomon Brothers MBS	0.9055
Merrill Lynch ABS	1.1281
Salomon Brothers ABS	0.9238
HFRI Fixed-Income Hedge Fund	1.6016
HFRI MBS Hedge Fund	1.4402

Sharpe Ratio. The HFRI Fixed-Income Hedge-Fund Index had a Sharpe Ratio of 1.60 while the HFRI MBS Hedge-Fund Index had a Sharpe Ratio of 1.44, signifying that these hedge funds had superior investment performance to MBS and ABS as well as the S&P 500 index. So, while hedge funds have received some bad publicity for their performance in extreme market conditions (such as the Russian Credit Crisis of 1998 and the St. Valentine's Day Massacre of 1994 when the Federal Reserve raised rates numerous times during February and March of 1994), overall they have performed well given their level of risk.

In this chapter, we examined the historical performance of Treasury bonds, MBS, and ABS. We found that MBS and ABS had lower risk (as measured by the standard deviation of returns) than the Long-term Government Bond Index and the Lehman Brothers Aggregate Bond Index. The reason for the lower risk of MBS and ABS is the shorter stated maturity of ABS and the lower effective maturity of MBS (since home owners can refinance their home loans prior to maturity); as a result, MBS and ABS have lower risk than long-term Treasuries, which, for the most part, cannot be refinanced.

MBS and ABS have generated superior returns (on a risk-adjusted basis) relative to the Long-term Government Bond Index and the Lehman Brothers Aggregate Bond Index. MBS hedge funds have outperformed Treasuries, MBS, and ABS since 1993 despite their poor performance during the Russian Credit Crisis.

EXERCISES

Exercise 4.1   Why do long-term government bonds have greater return volatility than MBS?

Exercise 4.2   The Russian Credit Crisis of 1998 saw a substantial decrease in the S&P 500 index during August 1998. What happened to the returns of long-term government bonds and MBS? Why did they behave this way?

Exercise 4.3   What is the Sharpe Ratio? Which MBS-related indexes have the best Sharpe Ratio?

Exercise 4.4   Why would ABS have a higher Sharpe Ratio than MBS?

Agency Mortgage-Backed Securities

Mortgage Loans: The Basis of Mortgage- Backed Securities

The residential mortgage segment is the largest product segment that has been securitized to date. Although the majority of mortgages that have been securitized are 30-year fixed-rate mortgages, there are a number of other alternative mortgage designs such as adjustable-rate mortgages, graduated-payment mortgages (GPMs), and shared-appreciation mortgages (SAMs). Even within a category such as fixed-rate mortgages, there are variations such as 30-year fixed-rate mortgages and 15-year fixed-rate mortgages.

WHAT IS A MORTGAGE?

A **mortgage** is an instrument in which the title to real estate is held as security against the repayment of a debt. A **lien** is a legal claim on the property that allows the lien holder to satisfy the debt through foreclosure and sale of the property, if necessary.

All mortgages are basically composed of two parts: (1) the mortgage deed or deed of trust, and (2) the promissory note. The **mortgage deed** describes the real estate to be used as collateral against the repayment of the note. A **deed of trust** is similar to a mortgage deed except that the borrower creates a trust and conveys the title of the property to a trustee who holds it as security for the benefit of the lender. The deed of trust is used in Alabama, Arkansas, California, Colorado, District of Columbia, Delaware, Illinois, Mississippi, Missouri, Nevada, New Mexico, Tennessee, Texas, Utah, Virginia, and West Virginia. In Georgia, a **security deed** secures the payment of the debt, grants power of attorney to sell the property on default (avoiding court delays), and cancels the deed on payment of the debt.

The **promissory note** is a personal promise to repay the note, and even in the absence of any real estate security, the borrower would still have an obligation to repay the note. The note spells out the financial terms of repayment as well as the rights and interest of the lender and borrower.

Two general approaches are used in most states to establish the legal relationship between a borrower and a lender. One is called **title theory**, where title is held by, or rests with, the mortgagee (lender). The other is called **lien theory**, where the mortgagor (borrower) retains title and the mortgagee merely has a lien against the property. Lien theory is more modern in origin and the most common approach in most states, although many states have a hybrid approach encompassing both theories in part.

The basic difference between lien-theory and title-theory states lies in the process of foreclosure and the rights of the borrower and lender during this process. In all states, on default of the borrower, the lender must initiate a foreclosure process in order to recoup the balance of the note owned. But in states that use title theory, the right of possession and control of the property during the foreclosure process belongs to the lender, who is the title holder. In a lien-theory state, such as Ohio, the borrower would have the right to remain in possession of the property until the foreclosure process is completed. One

TABLE 5.1   Mortgage Debt Outstanding by Mortgage Type and Holder, 1994–2002 (millions)

	1994 ($)	1995 ($)	1996 ($)
Total Outstanding	4,392,794	4,603,982	4,868,297
By Mortgage Type			
1–4 Family	3,355,485	3,510,319	3,718,683
Multifamily	271,748	277,002	288,837
Commercial	682,590	732,100	773,643
Farm	82,971	84,561	87,134
By Holder			
Commercial banks	1,012,711	1,090,189	1,145,389
Savings institutions	596,191	596,763	628,335
Life insurance companies	210,904	213,137	208,162
Federal agency	315,580	308,757	295,192
Mortgage pools/trusts	1,730,004	1,863,210	2,040,848
Individuals/others	527,404	531,926	550,372

Source: The Bond Market Association and *Federal Reserve Bulletin.*

must keep in mind that while lenders may have eviction power, they need not exercise it, and many lenders are patient in exercising their full rights.

HOW LARGE IS THE MORTGAGE MARKET?

The mortgage market in the United States is the largest in the world and exceeded $8.5 trillion as of 2002 in terms of mortgage debt outstanding (see Table 5.1). Mortgages can be categorized either by the type of underlying property or by the type of institution that holds or owns the mortgage loans. In terms of property type, Table 5.1 shows that the outstanding mortgage debt is dominated by residential property also commonly referred to in mortgage parlance as 1–4 Family. Commercial mortgages represent the second largest segment of outstanding mortgage debt with close to $1.4 trillion as of 2002. In terms of mortgage holders, Table 5.1 shows that mortgage pools/trusts and commercial banks are the dominant players. In 2002, mortgage pools/trusts, the vehicles for securitizing mortgages, held more than $3.2 trillion in mortgages. The next largest category of holders was commercial banks with over $2.0 trillion.

1997 ($)	1998 ($)	1999 ($)	2000 ($)	2001 ($)	2002 ($)
5,204,119	5,737,162	6,385,919	6,938,109	7,589,578	8,481,400
3,973,692	4,362,699	4,793,966	5,226,585	5,732,523	6,462,900
302,291	332,121	374,596	414,386	454,715	496,900
837,837	945,836	1,114,392	1,188,302	1,286,001	1,396,400
90,299	96,506	102,965	108,836	116,329	125,200
1,245,315	1,337,217	1,495,502	1,661,411	1,789,819	2,059,100
631,826	643,957	668,634	723,534	758,236	781,300
206,840	213,640	230,787	235,942	243,021	247,300
286,194	293,613	322,352	343,962	376,999	360,800
2,239,350	2,589,800	2,954,784	3,232,338	3,715,692	3,158,300
594,594	658,935	713,857	740,923	705,811	1,874,600

One of the most notable trends exhibited in Table 5.1 is the tremendous growth that occurred in the mortgage market since 1994. The total amount of outstanding mortgage debt nearly doubled during the period shown. In terms of collateral type, the commercial mortgage debt outstanding more than doubled in size over this period. The size of mortgage pools/trusts increased by 80 percent from $1.7 trillion in 1994 to more than $3.2 trillion in 2002. Commercial banks also increased their holdings dramatically during this period.

TYPES OF MORTGAGES

Mortgage types are generally categorized by interest-rate type (fixed versus adjustable) and loan size. A fixed-rate mortgage, as the term implies, has a fixed rate of interest for the term of the loan. Loan terms can vary from 15 years to 30 years, although other terms are available as well. Adjustable-rate mortgages (ARMs) have varying rates of interest, depending on the specific mortgage product. For example, a 3/1 ARM would have a fixed-rate of interest for the first 3 years and would then float relative to a predetermined index for the remaining term (25 years) of the loan. The next distinguishing feature of a mortgage is the absolute size of the loan. For example, a conforming loan refers to a loan of $300,700 or less, whereas a jumbo loan is any loan greater than $300,700.

Table 5.2 provides a list of various mortgage products that were available in the market in May 2002. Notice that the first two products are both 30-year fixed-rate mortgages. However, the contracted rates of interest differ (5.38 percent versus 6.25 percent). The reason for the difference is that the first 30-year mortgage requires that 3 "points" or 3.0 percentage points of the loan amount be paid up front by the borrower at the time of loan origination, while the second 30-year mortgage product requires no payment of points. **Points** (sometimes referred to as **discount points**) are paid to the lender to reduce the overall interest rate of the loan. Another important feature of these 30-year fixed-rate mortgage products is that they both allow a maximum loan-to-value ratio of 95 percent. Loan to value (LTV) is the value of the loan relative to the market value of the property being financed.

Further down the table, the interest rates of two fixed-rate jumbo mortgages (30 year and 15 year) can be compared to their conforming counterparts. Jumbo mortgages generally command higher interest rates because of greater loan amounts, and thus there is a higher degree of risk. The two ARM products (3/1 ARM and 5-year ARM) have lower interest rates than the fixed-rate mortgage products because these mortgages will adjust after the fixed period has expired. Table 5.2 also shows the annual percentage

TABLE 5.2   Mortgage Products and Rates Available on May 29, 2002

Program	Rate (%)	Points	APR (%)	LTV (%)	Lock
30-year fixed rate	5.38	3	5.56	95	30 days
30-year fixed rate	6.25	0	6.34	95	30 days
20-year fixed rate	6.13	0	6.19	95	30 days
15-year fixed rate	4.88	3	5.19	95	30 days
15-year fixed rate	5.63	0	5.78	95	30 days
30-year fixed rate jumbo	6.38	0	6.49	90	30 days
15-year fixed rate jumbo	5.88	0	6.03	90	30 days
30-year 100% purchase	7.25	0	7.45	100	30 days
30-year FHA	6.25	0	6.45	97	30 days
3/1 ARM	4.88	0	5.14	95	30 days
5-year ARM with 40-year AMT	5.50	0	5.76	95	30 days

rate (APR) for each of the mortgage products listed. The APR is generally higher than the original contracted interest rate because it accounts for all costs, including any origination fees, discount points, and private mortgage insurance that may be part of the loan agreement.

Fixed-Rate Mortgages

Perhaps the most important attribute of fixed-rate mortgages (and what differentiates them from U.S. Treasury securities) is that they are typically fully amortized over their life. This means that the principal is repaid gradually over time (and, of course, is prepayable by the borrower), compared to U.S. Treasury securities, which make periodic interest payments, but repay the principal in one lump sum at the stated maturity.

There are several variations of amortizing mortgages. The **constant-payment mortgage** (CPM), also referred to as a **level-payment mortgage**, is the most common type of amortizing mortgage. In a CPM, the monthly mortgage payment is constant over the life of the loan. While the monthly payment remains constant, the composition of interest and principal constantly changes as shown in Figure 5.1. The figure graphically depicts the relationship between interest and principal. In the early years of a mortgage, the interest component eclipses the principal component, but declines at an increasing rate over time. As the loan seasons, the principal component becomes an increasing proportion of the monthly payment until the principal is completely repaid.

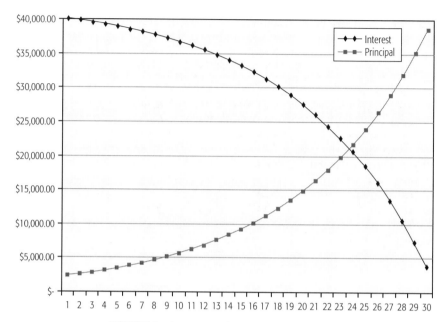

FIGURE 5.1   Interest and principal on a CPM.

Another type of amortizing mortgage is known as a **constant-amortizing mortgage** (CAM) in which the principal component remains constant throughout the life of the loan while the interest payment declines over time.

Calculating the Periodic Payment

In order to compute the periodic payment of a CPM that is fully amortized over 30 years, consider the following property with a current market value (V_0) of \$500,000, a loan-to-value ratio (m_0) of 0.80 or 80 percent, and a mortgage interest rate (i) of 10 percent. The beginning loan amount (\$400,000) is the product of the purchase price (\$500,000) and the loan-to-value ratio (0.80). The mortgage constant (f) is calculated according to the formula in equation (5.1), where i is the annual interest rate and n is the number of years in the example. (Note that in this particular example an annual mortgage constant is calculated, but a monthly mortgage constant can be calculated by substituting a monthly interest rate for i and the loan term in months for n.)

$$f = \frac{i\ (1 + i)^n}{(1 + i)^n - 1} = \frac{0.10\ (1.10)^{30}}{(1.10)^{30} - 1} = 0.106079 \qquad (5.1)$$

The product of the loan amount ($400,000) and the mortgage constant (0.106079) is equal to the annual mortgage payment or debt service of $42,431.70. The debt service includes both the principal and interest components.

The amortization table in Table 5.3 shows the amount of interest and principal paid in each period as well as the remaining loan balance at any point in time. Notice that the overall payment remains constant over the

TABLE 5.3 Amortization Table: Constant-Payment Mortgage (CPM)

Year	Amount ($)	Payment ($)	Interest ($)	Principal ($)	Ending Amount ($)
0					400,000.00
1	400,000.00	42,431.70	40,000.00	2,431.70	397,568.30
2	397,568.30	42,431.70	39,756.83	2,674.87	394,893.43
3	394,893.43	42,431.70	39,489.34	2,942.36	391,951.08
4	391,951.08	42,431.70	39,195.11	3,236.59	388,714.48
5	388,714.48	42,431.70	38,871.45	3,560.25	385,154.23
6	385,154.23	42,431.70	38,515.42	3,916.28	381,237.96
7	381,237.96	42,431.70	38,123.80	4,307.90	376,930.05
8	376,930.05	42,431.70	37,693.01	4,738.69	372,191.36
9	372,191.36	42,431.70	37,219.14	5,212.56	366,978.80
10	366,978.80	42,431.70	36,697.88	5,733.82	361,244.98
11	361,244.98	42,431.70	36,124.50	6,307.20	354,937.77
12	354,937.77	42,431.70	35,493.78	6,937.92	347,999.85
13	347,999.85	42,431.70	34,799.99	7,631.71	340,368.14
14	340,368.14	42,431.70	34,036.81	8,394.89	331,973.25
15	331,973.25	42,431.70	33,197.33	9,234.37	322,738.88
16	322,738.88	42,431.70	32,273.89	10,157.81	312,581.07
17	312,581.07	42,431.70	31,258.11	11,173.59	301,407.47
18	301,407.47	42,431.70	30,140.75	12,290.95	289,116.52
19	289,116.52	42,431.70	28,911.65	13,520.05	275,596.48
20	275,596.48	42,431.70	27,559.65	14,872.05	260,724.42
21	260,724.42	42,431.70	26,072.44	16,359.26	244,365.17
22	244,365.17	42,431.70	24,436.52	17,995.18	226,369.98
23	226,369.98	42,431.70	22,637.00	19,794.70	206,575.28
24	206,575.28	42,431.70	20,657.53	21,774.17	184,801.11
25	184,801.11	42,431.70	18,480.11	23,951.59	160,849.52
26	160,849.52	42,431.70	16,084.95	26,346.75	134,502.78
27	134,502.78	42,431.70	13,450.28	28,981.42	105,521.36
28	105,521.36	42,431.70	10,552.14	31,879.56	73,641.79
29	73,641.79	42,431.70	7,364.18	35,067.52	38,574.27
30	38,574.27	42,431.70	3,857.43	38,574.27	0.00

entire 30 years, while the interest portion declines and the principal portion increases over time.

Compare Table 5.3 with an amortization table of a **constant-interest mortgage** (CIM), for which the payments remain constant in each period but no amortization takes place. The CIM amortization schedule in Table 5.4 shows that the principal amount remains at $400,000 throughout the life of

TABLE 5.4 Amortization Table: Constant-Interest Mortgage (CIM)

Year	Amount ($)	Payment ($)	Interest ($)	Principal	End Amount ($)
0					400,000.00
1	400,000.00	40,000.00	40,000.00	–	400,000.00
2	400,000.00	40,000.00	40,000.00	–	400,000.00
3	400,000.00	40,000.00	40,000.00	–	400,000.00
4	400,000.00	40,000.00	40,000.00	–	400,000.00
5	400,000.00	40,000.00	40,000.00	–	400,000.00
6	400,000.00	40,000.00	40,000.00	–	400,000.00
7	400,000.00	40,000.00	40,000.00	–	400,000.00
8	400,000.00	40,000.00	40,000.00	–	400,000.00
9	400,000.00	40,000.00	40,000.00	–	400,000.00
10	400,000.00	40,000.00	40,000.00	–	400,000.00
11	400,000.00	40,000.00	40,000.00	–	400,000.00
12	400,000.00	40,000.00	40,000.00	–	400,000.00
13	400,000.00	40,000.00	40,000.00	–	400,000.00
14	400,000.00	40,000.00	40,000.00	–	400,000.00
15	400,000.00	40,000.00	40,000.00	–	400,000.00
16	400,000.00	40,000.00	40,000.00	–	400,000.00
17	400,000.00	40,000.00	40,000.00	–	400,000.00
18	400,000.00	40,000.00	40,000.00	–	400,000.00
19	400,000.00	40,000.00	40,000.00	–	400,000.00
20	400,000.00	40,000.00	40,000.00	–	400,000.00
21	400,000.00	40,000.00	40,000.00	–	400,000.00
22	400,000.00	40,000.00	40,000.00	–	400,000.00
23	400,000.00	40,000.00	40,000.00	–	400,000.00
24	400,000.00	40,000.00	40,000.00	–	400,000.00
25	400,000.00	40,000.00	40,000.00	–	400,000.00
26	400,000.00	40,000.00	40,000.00	–	400,000.00
27	400,000.00	40,000.00	40,000.00	–	400,000.00
28	400,000.00	40,000.00	40,000.00	–	400,000.00
29	400,000.00	40,000.00	40,000.00	–	400,000.00
30	400,000.00	40,000.00	40,000.00	400,000.00	0

the mortgage and the interest payment is also constant in each period. The principal is then repaid in one lump sum at maturity.

Table 5.5 shows the amortization schedule of a CAM in which the periodic amortization amount remains constant over the life of the loan. Notice the declining interest stream compared with the other amortization schedules presented.

TABLE 5.5 Amortization Table: Constant-Amortization Mortgage (CAM)

Year	Amount ($)	Payment ($)	Interest ($)	Principal ($)	End Amount ($)
0					400,000.00
1	400,000.00	53,333.33	40,000.00	13,333.33	386,666.67
2	386,666.67	52,000.00	38,666.67	13,333.33	373,333.33
3	373,333.33	50,666.67	37,333.33	13,333.33	360,000.00
4	360,000.00	49,333.33	36,000.00	13,333.33	346,666.67
5	346,666.67	48,000.00	34,666.67	13,333.33	333,333.33
6	333,333.33	46,666.67	33,333.33	13,333.33	320,000.00
7	320,000.00	45,333.33	32,000.00	13,333.33	306,666.67
8	306,666.67	44,000.00	30,666.67	13,333.33	293,333.33
9	293,333.33	42,666.67	29,333.33	13,333.33	280,000.00
10	280,000.00	41,333.33	28,000.00	13,333.33	266,666.67
11	266,666.67	40,000.00	26,666.67	13,333.33	253,333.33
12	253,333.33	38,666.67	25,333.33	13,333.33	240,000.00
13	240,000.00	37,333.33	24,000.00	13,333.33	226,666.67
14	226,666.67	36,000.00	22,666.67	13,333.33	213,333.33
15	213,333.33	34,666.67	21,333.33	13,333.33	200,000.00
16	200,000.00	33,333.33	20,000.00	13,333.33	186,666.67
17	186,666.67	32,000.00	18,666.67	13,333.33	173,333.33
18	173,333.33	30,666.67	17,333.33	13,333.33	160,000.00
19	160,000.00	29,333.33	16,000.00	13,333.33	146,666.67
20	146,666.67	28,000.00	14,666.67	13,333.33	133,333.33
21	133,333.33	26,666.67	13,333.33	13,333.33	120,000.00
22	120,000.00	25,333.33	12,000.00	13,333.33	106,666.67
23	106,666.67	24,000.00	10,666.67	13,333.33	93,333.33
24	93,333.33	22,666.67	9,333.33	13,333.33	80,000.00
25	80,000.00	21,333.33	8,000.00	13,333.33	66,666.67
26	66,666.67	20,000.00	6,666.67	13,333.33	53,333.33
27	53,333.33	18,666.67	5,333.33	13,333.33	40,000.00
28	40,000.00	17,333.33	4,000.00	13,333.33	26,666.67
29	26,666.67	16,000.00	2,666.67	13,333.33	13,333.33
30	13,333.33	14,666.67	1,333.33	13,333.33	0.00

Figure 5.2 depicts the trajectories of the remaining loan balances of the three types of amortizing mortgages presented—CIM, CAM, and CPM. What is clear from the tables and figure is that each of these mortgages have varying degrees of risk.

The CIM has the lowest annual payment among the three, but also does not amortize. Since it does not amortize, there are two important ramifications. First, its duration (or weighted-average life) will be longer than the others since the principal is not repaid until maturity or until the mortgage is refinanced. Second, the failure to amortize the loan means that a greater amount of the loan will still be outstanding in case of financial distress by the borrower; a greater amount of the loan outstanding in the case of financial distress increases the loss to the lender (holding everything else the same). Hence, the CIM is not a popular mortgage contract from the standpoint of duration and risk exposure for the lender.

The CAM is the opposite of the CIM in that it amortizes the fastest of the three mortgages but also has the highest annual mortgage payment (by far). Since it amortizes so quickly, it has the lowest duration (and the lowest sensitivity to interest-rate changes) and poses the least threat to lenders in the case of financial distress. However, households may balk from an afford-

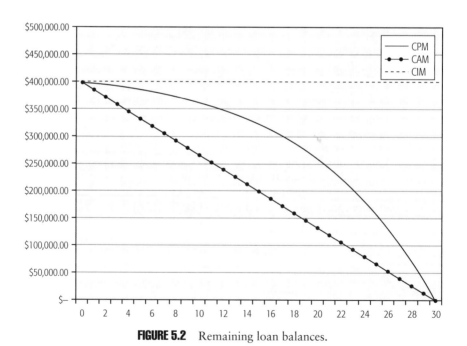

FIGURE 5.2   Remaining loan balances.

ability standpoint to the higher payment. So, what benefits the lender does not necessarily benefit the borrower.

The third mortgage type is the CPM, the most common form of mortgage in the United States. It is in the middle of both the CAM and CIM in terms of speed of amortization and annual mortgage payment. In other words, it is a loan type that both the lender and the borrower mutually agree on.

An interesting feature of the CPM relates to its breakdown on interest and principal over time. As can be seen in Figure 5.1, the interest on a CPM declines over time at an increasing rate. The principal stream, however, begins at a low level but increases at an increasing rate over time. This breakdown on a mortgage payment into interest and principal streams is the backbone of mortgage products that are discussed later in the book: interest-only (IO) and principal-only (PO) strips.

Within the realm of fixed-rate mortgages, there are a plethora of options. First, borrowers can select a 30-year or 15-year amortization period for the mortgage. Second, they can choose a number of different LTV combinations that require down payments from a large percentage all the way to 100 percent LTV loans (no money down) sponsored, for example, by Freddie Mac. It should be noted that loans with LTVs below 80 percent are not usually required to purchase private mortgage insurance (which insures against losses in the case of default on the top 20 percent of the loan). However, loans with LTVs between 80 percent and 100 percent are typically required to purchase private mortgage insurance (or PMI).

Fixed-Rate Mortgage Terms

As we saw in Table 5.2, fixed-rate mortgages come in a variety of maturities ranging from 5 years to 30 years. The primary distinction between the different maturities is that the shorter-term mortgages amortize much more quickly (and have higher mortgage payments, of course). Since the shorter-term mortgages amortize quickly, they have shorter durations (weighted-average life of the loan) and less risk to the holder. As a consequence, the shorter-maturity mortgages have lower rates. As mentioned previously, the shorter-maturity mortgages also reduce the likelihood of loss to the lender in case of default.

Each of the fixed-rate mortgages have different point options available. Points are a fee that is paid by the borrower stated in terms of a percentage of the loan amount; points are used by the borrower to lower the rate on the mortgage. Typically, borrowers who plan to stay in the dwelling for a greater length of time pay the points up front in order to lower the interest rate. Borrowers who plan to stay in the dwelling for a shorter term tend not to pay the points up front. Some researchers consider the choice of points by the borrower as a revelation of expected tenure (how long the borrower expects to stay in the dwelling); it is hoped that this aids researchers in predicting mortgage prepayments on mortgage pass-throughs and collateralized mortgage obligations (CMOs).

Finally, there is a distinction between conforming mortgages and jumbo mortgages. Essentially, conforming mortgages are those that can be sold by the lending institution to Fannie Mae and Freddie Mac; these loans are under $22,700 and represent about 85 percent of the mortgage market. Jumbo mortgages are those mortgages over $22,700. It should be noted that the coupon rate on jumbo mortgages is higher than that of conforming mortgages. There are a variety of explanations for why jumbos have higher rates than conforming. The first explanation is that the conforming market is far larger and has greater liquidity. The second explanation is the house that underlies the jumbo loan is less liquid than the house that underlies the conforming note. The correct answer is likely a combination of both these explanations.

ADJUSTABLE-RATE MORTGAGES

Many lenders in the United States offer ARMs as well as fixed-rate mortgages. In essence, ARMs differ from fixed-rate mortgages in that the rate on the mortgage varies every month or year (depending on the terms of the ARM). As a consequence, there are a number of variations on the ARMs (also known as variable-rate mortgages). ARMs are not as popular in the current low-interest-rate environment, but may return to popularity when interest rates begin to increase.

Adjustable-Rate-Mortgage Indexation

As the name implies, the contract rate of interest on an ARM varies and may go up or down at specific time intervals as spelled out in the mortgage note. The key to whether the contract rate moves up or down is an index to which the rate is tied. Typically, this index is tied to the yield on comparable term Treasury bills where the number of years between interest-rate adjustment dates determines the term of the index security. But, some ARMs are tied to other external indexes based on the market cost of funds or yields such as the London InterBank Offer Rate (LIBOR) or the Eleventh District Cost of Funds Index (COFI). The key to an acceptable index from the federal regulator's (and borrower's) point of view is that the index cannot be manipulated in any way by the lending institution, but is primarily affected by market conditions.

Prior to 1981, ARMs were restricted as to the minimum acceptable interval for payment adjustments, such as no more than once or twice a year. Another "old" regulation limited such adjustments to no more than 0.5 percent annually with a total minimum or maximum interest rate limit of plus or minus 5 percent. Today, all those regulations are gone and the way ARMs are being set up is much more flexible and negotiable.

Currently, there is no limit as to the minimum acceptable time interval for mortgage payment adjustments, and even monthly changes are permissible. Note that lenders must give a borrower notice between 30 and 45 days in advance of any interest adjustments. That is not to say all ARMs are set up on such a flexible basis. Most lenders select a combination of adjustments that are currently acceptable to consumers (and to the lenders as well). Thus, the market will restrain some of the lender's options. However, administrative costs may preclude lenders from using indexes that are too short term in nature (e.g., three-month Treasury bills) with typically rapid interest rate changes.

In theory, there does not have to be a limit on the minimum or maximum interest rate change from one interval to another or in total for the life of the mortgage. A typical cap structure on ARMs is 2 percent periodic interest rate change caps and 6 percent lifetime caps meaning that the contract rate can only increase by 2 percent in any one year and only up to a maximum above the original contract rate of 6 percent. The tighter the rate caps, the more the loan behaves like a standard fixed-rate mortgage.

One of the most daunting problems facing investors interested in the ARM market has been the extensive use of "teaser rates." Teasers are used to reduce the effective interest rate of the ARM below the fully indexed rate at the beginning of the loan term. This teaser makes the ARM more attractive to borrowers since payments are quite low initially as compared to the fixed-rate mortgage alternative. Then, usually at the first interest-rate-adjustment date, the mortgage becomes fully indexed, which means that the payments will likely increase, even when interest rates do not change. Unfortunately, the potential for dramatic increases in mortgage rates may lead borrowers to be placed in a position of having to default on the loan (if they are unable to sell their dwelling and pay off the loan without declaring default). As a consequence, there are prohibitions against ARMs with teasers in some mortgage pass-throughs.

Adjusting the Adjustable-Rate-Mortgage Payment

Assume that an individual borrows $100,000 at 7 percent for 25 years (300 months), so that the initial monthly payments are $706.78. Also assume initially that the appropriate index is at 5 percent, with a 2 percent margin. The fully indexed rate is 7 percent (5 + 2 percent). Also assume that the index adjusts annually. One year later, suppose the index moves to 5.5 percent. The new interest rate on the mortgage at that time is 7.5 percent. Subsequently, the new payments will be $738.14.

If the borrower decided to increase the term of the mortgage and hold payments nearly constant (if such an option was given), the remaining term would have to be increased from 288 months to 329 months, an increase of 41 months. This change shows one of the problems lenders have in extending the term of the mortgage to accommodate interest-rate changes. In this case, a slight change of 0.5 of 1 percent in interest rates, which would have required only a 4.4 percent increase in the size of the monthly payment, required a term increase of 41 months, or over 14 percent of the existing term, in order to accommodate the borrower's desire to hold payments constant. For extreme interest-rate increases, terms could be infinity with the entire mortgage payment only going toward interest if sufficient to cover that. In the previous case, if the index rate were increased beyond 7 percent or so, payments would have to be increased in order to pay off the mortgage. For this reason, most options on extending mortgage terms are constrained to 40 years (480 months) even though most initial loan terms are 30 years (360 months).

Adjustable-Rate Mortgage with Capped Payments

For all ARMs, the interest rate varies with an index at set intervals (e.g., annually, every 3 years, etc.). The payments are also adjusted up or down as a result of the interest rate change. However, for ARMs with capped payments, an upper limit that is predetermined in the mortgage note is placed on the potential increase per interval, thus limiting extremely high payment movements. For example, if a borrower begins with a $100,000 mortgage at 13.5 percent for a 30-year term, initial monthly payments would be $1,145.41. Assuming annual interval adjustments, 1 year later, the index to which the contract rate is tied requires an interest increase to 15.5 percent. Unless the payments were capped, this would mean new monthly payments of $1,303.27 based on the existing balance of $99,739 with 29 years remaining. But, if the payments were capped at a maximum of 1.0 percent increase per year, then the maximum new payment would be $1,259.95 for the second year. Since the interest due during the second year is based on 15.5 percent, the interest required, if not capped, would exceed the payment cap.

In the first month of the second year, the interest due is equal to the new interest rate multiplied by the mortgage balance (15.5 × 99,739 = $1,288.29). The payment of $1,259.95 leaves a deficit of $28.34, which would be added onto the balance, with similar additions for each following month during the year, including interest on the increased balance.

The previous example was rather extreme, but certainly not impossible, in that the interest-rate adjustment was a full 2 percent. Most interest rate adjustments of 1 or 1.5 percent would have been within the limit of the capped mortgage payments. The major advantage to the borrowers under such an arrangement is simply protection from payment increases that may exceed their capacity to pay. Lower payment-increase maximums would give even greater protection from erratic payment changes, but they also allow for the possibility of an increasing mortgage balance under extreme circumstances.

Adjustable-Rate Mortgage Terms

While ARMs have similar options to fixed-rate mortgages, such as 30-year and 15-year mortgages and a variety of LTV and point combinations, ARMs also have some unique features. In particular, these features refer to the resetting or recalibration of interest rates. Typically, the contract rate on ARMs reset once a year (subject to cap restrictions). Some ARMs convert to fixed-rate mortgages after a number of years, while other ARMs have a balloon payment after a number of years (requiring the borrower to refinance the mortgage at prevailing market rates); although the balloon may occur after the third year, the mortgage is still amortized over 30 years on origination. The plethora of options available on ARMs make them difficult to manage in a mortgage portfolio.

GRADUATED-PAYMENT MORTGAGES

Although not a popular mortgage alternative, there is a place for the graduated-payment mortgage (GPM). A problem facing the mortgage market is how to get first-time home buyers into a house. To facilitate borrowers who aspire to home ownership, but cannot afford the mortgage payments to match their desires, a beneficial variation of mortgage payment patterns is possible. Most GPM plans are designed for younger borrowers with expectations of increasing income. A GPM begins with a base mortgage payment that increases over time, even if interest rates do not change. In some cases, the initial payments may actually be lower than the interest due, thus increasing the mortgage balance owed in the early years by adding on the unpaid interest. GPMs may also be combined with variable-rate mortgages or variable-balance mortgages. Some of these variations are discussed after the common types of GPM plans are explored.

The GPM is an odd mortgage contract. The people who want a GPM really cannot afford the house with a standard fixed-rate mortgage. Since the borrower is more risky, the lender should demand a higher down payment or higher interest rate. Young people probably do not have the savings to make a higher down payment, nor can they afford a higher contract rate. These conditions would lead lenders to require a cosigner for the note (in many cases, parents). Consequently, the GPM is not for everyone. Indeed, because of these problems, many lenders are reluctant to offer GPMs.

While GPM plans may help facilitate borrowers to push up the price limits of what they can pay for a home, there is also the burden and risk of an increasing mortgage balance. If the price of the home does not increase as fast as the mortgage balance in the early years, sellers could face the possibility of having less cash equity in their home than when they bought it.

SHARED-APPRECIATION MORTGAGES

Even less popular than the GPM is the shared-appreciation mortgage (SAM). The SAM is a significant departure from the lender's traditional role of being interested in a return of his or her loan along with the required yield. With a SAM arrangement, the lender actually shares in the future appreciation of the property. The percentage of future appreciation, called a **contingent interest,** is agreed on when the loan is initially underwritten. SAM loans can be set up with the lender receiving as much as 40 percent of the net appreciation on the property up to 10 years from the time the loan is made. If the borrower sells the property before the agreed-on time limit, the contingent interest would have to be paid at that time. In exchange for a share of appreciation, the lender reduces the interest rate used in the determination of current mortgage payments. Note that the amortization term can still be 30 years, even though the balances are due in 10 years or at the time of sale, whichever comes first. If the borrower does not wish to sell the home when the contingent interest is due, the expected **net appreciated value** can be determined by a professional appraisal and the contingent interest paid directly to the lender from the borrower at that time.

Net appreciated value of the property is determined by subtracting from the market value (selling price or appraisal) of the property: (1) the original cost to the borrower, (2) the cost of any legitimate capital improvements made to the property by the borrower, (3) the cost of any appraisals needed to determine market value, and (4) any direct selling costs such as commissions, cost of title insurance, inspection fees, legal fees, and payments to clear title of prior liens.

There are several obvious problems with SAMs. One is that the lender now has a greater interest in your home and what you do to it, how you modify it, and how you live in it, since these actions typically affect value. The lender will want protection from activities that could negatively affect value. Some problems can be prevented by very clear and extensive legal documents spelling out the rights, interests, and responsibilities of the lender/borrower in a SAM arrangement; but, nevertheless, all problems and conflicts cannot be predicted.

From the lender's point of view, the uncertainty of the contingent-interest return requires that the total expected return via a SAM arrangement versus other noncontingent interest mortgages must be greater. The higher-risk position of the lender requires a higher expected return.

A recent innovation by Bank of Scotland is the Euro SAM. A Euro SAM is targeted toward those people who have paid off their mortgages (and therefore are likely to be in their 50s, 60s, and 70s). Since the mortgages are paid off and the home owners have 100 percent equity in their property, the Euro SAM lender writes a check to the homeowner (for, say, 300,000 pounds) and in return receives, say, 50 percent of appreciation in the property over a specified period of time. Of course, the repayment of the principal amount plus a percentage of appreciation occurs if the loan is repaid or the borrower passes away. The Euro SAM has been extremely popular with borrowers in the United Kingdom. However, the secondary market has been reluctant to embrace the Euro SAM concept.

REVERSE-ANNUITY MORTGAGE

The reverse-annuity mortgage (RAM) is more of a retirement annuity than it is a traditional mortgage. It allows a home owner to draw on the equity in his or her home as a source of income. RAMs have been generally designed to assist elderly home owners with significant home equities in their retirement plans. There are several variations of RAMs, with two of the more common plans discussed here.

Mortgage annuity payments are made directly from the lender to the borrower with each payment increasing the balance of the debt owed, along with compounded interest on the balance. This is the purest form of the **reverse annuity**, where payments go from the lender to the borrower. The payments are usually made for a fixed term or the life of the borrower, whichever ends first.

Assuming the borrower had sufficient home-equity value, the lender arranges to pay $434.71 per month for 10 years at a 12 percent interest-rate charge built in. At the end of 10 years, the borrower will owe $100,000, which must be paid through refinancing or the sale of the property. The primary risk for the borrower is that he or she may be forced to sell the house, although for elderly borrowers that may be consistent with their financial plans. Current regulations require the lender to renegotiate the loan with the home owner, should he or she still be alive, at the end of the loan term. If the borrower should die (the last living borrower in the case of a jointly financed RAM), the proceeds of the estate would be used to pay the mortgage balance owed.

A fixed-debt, interest-only loan is paid from the lender to the borrower, which is used to purchase a straight-life annuity or straight-plus-variable-life annuity combination. This situation is similar to borrowing an IO mortgage and using the proceeds to purchase a retirement annuity. Retirement annuities are purchased from life insurance companies. The straight portion of the annuity must be sufficient to cover the interest expense on the mortgage note. The difference above the interest is paid on a net basis to the borrower. Such annuities can be purchased on a fixed-term basis or for life. Fixed-term plans have similar risks as the previously discussed plan, where the borrower may be forced to sell the property or refinance if he or she has sufficient income to qualify.

In order to avoid the possibility of a forced sale, many borrowers, as well as lenders, will desire a term life insurance policy in the event of death of the borrower. The insurance proceeds would be used to pay off the mortgage balance with the lender established as a beneficiary.

MORTGAGE DEFAULT AND LEGAL ISSUES CONCERNING MORTGAGES

From the lender's perspective, the most important issue in underwriting a residential mortgage is trying to determine the likelihood of default. Defaults can result in curtailed revenues to the lender or to the ultimate holder of the note. Therefore, it is important to understand why default occurs and how financial institutions attempt to prevent it from occurring.

What Is Default?

Mortgage default is the failure to fulfill the terms and conditions of the mortgage contract. The most common failure is not making the mortgage payments. For example, a household that makes its mortgage payment based on the combined income of a husband and wife might default if one of the household wage earners were to lose his or her job. Mortgage default can also result from not paying property taxes or allowing other liens to form against the property.

Defaults are much more common than foreclosures. One must keep in mind that a lender is generally not interested in foreclosing on property since the lender becomes the owner. If possible, lenders will try to work out a plan with borrowers that will avoid foreclosure. Many lenders, if the borrower's problem is perceived to be temporary, will attempt to work out a temporary arrangement, such as IO mortgage payments or adding a few payments onto the mortgage balance. This modification to the mortgage is termed recasting the mortgage. In the preceding example, the lender might allow the household to make a nominal payment on the loan for 3 months (the difference between the promised payment and the new payment is added to the loan balance).

What Is Foreclosure?

Suppose that the unemployed wage earner in the preceding example has no employment prospects that are sufficient to generate additional income to cover the mortgage payment? This outcome may result in what is called foreclosure. **Foreclosure** is the process of collecting on a mortgage where the mortgagor has defaulted and there appears to be no other remedy than to sell the property. Technically, foreclosure is an elimination of the mortgagor's equity of redemption rights. **Equity of redemption** is the right of the mortgagor to redeem his or her property on meeting all obligations. The equity of redemption ceases at the time a property is sold, but up until then a mortgagor could pay all back interest, legal, and other expenses expended by the lender in the process of foreclosure, and again be on good terms with respect to the mortgage note. In a few states there is a similar right, which extends beyond the point of sale, called statutory redemption. In such a state, the new purchaser only has a tentative title while the foreclosed-on mortgagor tries to redeem himself or herself.

If a property is foreclosed on and the proceeds from the sale are not enough to cover all funds owed the mortgagee, a deficiency judgment can be obtained by the mortgagee against the mortgagor so that the balance owed can still be collected, even at a later date.

Why Most Mortgages Do Not Proceed to the Foreclosure Stage

Typically, a household that defaults will not go into foreclosure because it is not in the best interest of the household to do so. Consider a household that owns a house with a market value of $200,000. The household owes $170,000 to the lender. Now, suppose that the primary wage earner in the household loses his or her job. Depending on their other assets (e.g., savings account, common stock, mutual funds), the household may have to default. If the household sells the house, it can take the proceeds from the sale of $188,000 ($200,000 less realtor fees of 6 percent) and repay the loan of $170,000. The household has protected its credit record and walked away with $18,000. As long as the household has a significant equity position in the house, foreclosure is unlikely to occur.

However, suppose that the primary wage earner in the household becomes unemployed, but the house has a market value of $170,000. If the household sells the house, it can take the proceeds from the sale of $159,800 ($170,000 less realtor fees of 6 percent) and repay the loan of $170,000. The household has protected its credit record, but is $10,200 out of pocket to the lender. If the primary wage earner is unemployed, there is a good chance that the household will not desire to go $10,200 out of pocket to the lender. Instead, the household may let the loan go into foreclosure.

If foreclosure occurs, the bank will seize the house and sell it (usually at a discount in order to get it off of its books). For example, the lender may sell the house for $155,000. The legal and related fees can be as high as $10,000, resulting in a net sale price of $145,000 leading to a loss of $25,000 on the loan. The lender may wish to obtain a deficiency judgment against the household, but many courts are hesitant to rule against households where unemployment is the reason behind the foreclosure.

Important Clauses in Uniform Mortgages

Independent of the particular type of mortgage, most mortgages contain similar types of clauses. The purposes of these clauses is to clearly identify the property rights of both the borrower and lender so that there is as little ambiguity as possible.

Mortgage Covenants A mortgage covenant is an agreement from the borrower to keep the property in good repair, to insure it against loss (fire), to pay property taxes, and not to remove or damage any of the property in such a way as to negatively affect value.

Acceleration Clause An acceleration clause specifies that if the mortgagor fails to comply with the covenants or is otherwise in default, then the entire debt balance becomes due and collectible through the foreclosure process. This clause may also apply where there are provisions against assumption, lease, or sale. In such a case, the acceleration clause is referred to as due-on-sale clause, or nonassumption clause. Lenders today, in their attempts to prevent assumptions of mortgages that may be at below-market rates or may be otherwise assumed by a nonqualified borrower, are taking great care to insert nonassumption, due-on-sale, or due-on-lease clauses into current mortgage instruments.

Defeasance Clause   The defeasance clause voids the mortgage on repayment of the entire debt, and is sometimes called a release of mortgage clause.

Prepayment Clause   The prepayment clause, or prepayment privilege, generally describes the acceptable arrangements or conditions for early repayment of a substantial portion (or the entire balance) of the mortgage principal owed. Prepayment penalties, when they exist, are usually a small percentage of the mortgage balance (often as low as 1 percent), and are often eliminated as the mortgage ages. Generally, most lenders today have low or no prepayment penalties if the property is sold or refinanced. The borrower, however, should explicitly verify whether or not any prepayment restrictions exist before signing the mortgage contract.

Subordination Clause   The subordination clause asserts a lower lien position for a mortgage that may otherwise assert a higher or first-lien position. For example, if a seller acted as a lender and took part of the price of the sold property in the form of a mortgage, such a mortgage would normally have a first lien on the property. Most financial institutions, however, require first liens on the mortgage loans they hold. If the buyer were to arrange a new first mortgage, the new lender would insist on a subordination clause in the existing mortgage, forcing the seller to release his first-lien position to the lender.

The Estoppel Clause   The estoppel clause states that on request of the mortgagee, the mortgagor will furnish a written statement, or estoppel certificate, that will duly acknowledge the amount due on the mortgage and whether any offsets or defenses exist against the mortgage debt. This clause allows the mortgage to be sold to another investor without concern over the actual amount owed or having to execute a completely new mortgage agreement.

Mortgage Priority   The priorities for funds in case of default are fairly straightforward. The local government can file a lien against the property in the case of delinquent taxes and force foreclosure. As a consequence, the local government is the de facto first lienholder on your property. Once you have made the property taxes due the local taxing authority, you must then make payments on your first mortgage and second mortgage (if applicable).

First mortgage simply means a first lien and a second mortgage means a second lien. Second mortgages are also sometimes called **junior mortgages** and second mortgages provided by sellers are generally referred to as **purchase money mortgages**. When a junior lien exists, in the event of foreclosure, the proceeds of the sale would be allocated first to the first lien holders then to second lien holders and so forth.

A good example of mortgage priority is the following. Suppose that you apply for a mortgage loan with a lender in order to borrow $200,000 for a housing purchase of $225,000. They will ask if you have any outstanding loans that are secured by the dwelling. Why do they ask this question? If you went to a lender and borrowed $200,000 to purchase your house and then went to a different lender and borrowed another $200,000, the first lender would actually have the first mortgage and the second lender would have the second mortgage. If you defaulted on your mortgage loan (and the loan went into foreclosure), the proceeds from liquidation ($225,000 less legal and related fees) would first go to the first lender. Any other proceeds from liquidation (say $10,000) would go to the second lender. Since $10,000 represents a rather poor return on their $200,000 investment, the second lender will want to avoid being an accidental second in terms of mortgage priority.

The Due-on-Sale Clause   Mortgages can be originated without a due-on-sale clause. These mortgages are called assumable mortgages. Suppose that you borrow funds from a lender to purchase a home. The interest rate on the mortgage is 8 percent and the mortgage life is 30 years. After 5 years, you decide to sell the house and buy another house. Mortgage interest rates have climbed from 8 percent to 12 percent. If the mortgage had a due-on-sale clause, you would sell your house, repay the mortgage to the lender, and apply for a new mortgage at the new rate of 12 percent.

The assumable mortgage is different. The mortgage actually stays with the house. So, when you sell the house after 5 years, the sales price of the house will include the present value of the difference between 8 percent for 25 years (because the buyer assumes the payments on the mortgage) and 12 percent for 25 years (what the buyer would have to pay the lender if it received a mortgage). As a consequence, you would receive a windfall gain of this difference on sale of your house.

As you can imagine, the lender does not want you to have this windfall because it comes at the expense of the lender. If you have a due-on-sale clause, the lender can take the remaining balance of the loan from your house and lend it to someone else at 12 percent. If you have an assumable mortgage, the lender continues to receive only 8 percent interest (and you get the difference in terms of a higher selling price on your home). Most banks today will originate mortgages only if there is a due-on-sale clause.

While due-on-sale clauses are common in the United States, they are not as common in the international market. Furthermore, due-on-sale clauses are typically found on large-ticket assets such as residential mortgages, commercial mortgages, and auto loans; they are not found on loans in the form of credit cards or installment loans.

THE FEDERAL NATIONAL MORTGAGE ASSOCIATION/FEDERAL HOME LOAN MORTGAGE CORPORATION UNIFORM LOAN CONTRACT

The FNMA/FHLMC Uniform Loan Contracts mortgage documents can be found on the CD. Provision of these documents is important since the majority of mortgage loans originated in the United States use the FNMA/FHLMC Uniform Loan Contract. Why?

First, it makes sense from a cost standpoint to use a uniform loan contract. Can you imagine the legal fees involved in writing a mortgage loan from scratch each time a loan is originated? Suppose that an attorney charges $200 an hour for legal services and it takes 8 hours to write a "new" mortgage; that amounts to $1,600 in legal fees. With the uniform loan contract, the lender simply has to fill in the blanks.

Second, the uniform loan contract reduces the costs associated with selling mortgages into the secondary mortgage market. Suppose that you are Goldman Sachs in New York and you want to purchase 1,000 mortgages from the Midwest. If all mortgages had the same legal rights clearly assigned, it would reduce the cost of purchasing mortgages. Once again, can you imagine the costs associated with acquiring 1,000 mortgages with radically different mortgage covenants?

A mortgage is a highly developed financial instrument. The market has developed a variety of amortization and interest-rate rules for mortgages. The diversity of products allows lenders to provide borrowers with a range of mortgage instruments to better meet their individual needs. More importantly, mortgages exist within a legal framework that provides a clear set of rules as to how the borrower and lender are treated in the event of default. Due to the legal framework, lenders and investors have a greater degree of certainty of the outcome of borrower default. This legal framework is one of the main reasons why the securitization of mortgages has been so successful.

EXERCISES

⊚ **Exercise 5.1**   Using an Excel spreadsheet, generate a mortgage amortization schedule for a 15-year CPM.

⊚ **Exercise 5.2**   How does your answer in Exercise 5.1 differ from the mortgage amortization schedule for the CAM and CIM?

⊚ **Exercise 5.3**   Do you think that SAMs would be more popular in high-interest rate or low-interest rate environments? Explain.

⊚ **Exercise 5.4**   GPMs seem like the perfect mortgage for professionals graduating from college. If this statement is true, why are they not very popular as a mortgage contract?

⊚ **Exercise 5.5**   Shorter-maturity mortgages (such as 15 years) have certain advantages over the longer-term mortgages (such as 30 years). What are the advantages? What are the disadvantages?

CHAPTER 6

Agency Pass-Throughs

Agency pass-throughs are perhaps the simplest form of securitization. Essentially, agency pass-throughs allow investors to receive cash flows (principal and interest less servicing and guarantee fees) from a pool of single-family home mortgages accumulated by one of the mortgage-related agencies (or government-sponsored entities). The agency then provides a guarantee of payment to the investor.

THE ROLE OF GOVERNMENT AGENCIES AND GOVERNMENT-SPONSORED ENTERPRISES

In order to understand agency pass-throughs, it is necessary to understand the role of the government agencies and government-sponsored enterprises (GSEs) that are the backbone of this market. Three mortgage agencies are chartered by the U.S. government: the Government National Mortgage Association (GNMA or Ginnie Mae), Fannie Mae (formerly known as the Federal National Mortgage Association or FNMA), and Freddie Mac (formerly known as the Federal Home Loan Mortgage Corporation or FHLMC). While they are all engaged in helping to generate affordable loans to households and in sustaining an active secondary mortgage market, they vary in subtle (and not-so-subtle) ways. The agencies stimulate the availability of low-cost mortgage funds with their implicit (Fannie Mae and Freddie Mac) or explicit (Ginnie Mae) government guarantee. Fannie Mae and Freddie Mac, in particular, are quite active in the purchasing of conforming mortgage loans and the issuance of pass-throughs.

Ginnie Mae, an agency under the supervision of the U.S. Department of Housing and Urban Development (HUD), securitizes primarily Federal Housing Administration (FHA) insured or Veterans Administration (VA) guaranteed mortgage loans. Fannie Mae and Freddie Mac securitize conventional mortgage loans that conform to their loan size and underwriting standards.

Nonconforming conventional loans (those that do not meet the loan size or underwriting standards) are traded in the non-agency (or private label) market; the non-agency market does not carry an agency guarantee against credit losses. Thus, in order to qualify for a rating that would make investors comfortable investing in non-agency mortgage-backed securities (MBS), the securities backed by non-agency mortgages must carry some form of credit enhancement. Non-agency loans are discussed in more detail in Chapters 15 and 17.

Currently, about $8.5 trillion of mortgages are outstanding of which 55 percent, $4.7 trillion, is in the form of MBS. (See Table 5.1.)

BRIEF HISTORY OF THE AGENCY MARKET

Fannie Mae was established in the 1930s to provide a government-owned secondary market for FHA loans. Essentially, Fannie Mae has operated for much of its life as a national savings and loan in the sense that it gathered funds by issuing its own debt and buying mortgages that were held in portfolio. In 1968, Fannie Mae was moved off the government's budget and was recreated as a shareholder-owned, government-sponsored agency. In the 1970s, it switched its focus toward conventional mortgages rather than government-insured mortgages. As a consequence, Ginnie Mae was created in 1968 to provide a secondary market for the government-insured loans.

Ginnie Mae developed the first mortgage pass-through in 1970. Freddie Mac was created in 1970 to be a secondary market for the savings and loans industry. Freddie Mac was created as a GSE (like Fannie Mae). Its first mortgage pass-through program for conventional loans was created shortly thereafter, in 1971. It is important to note that since Ginnie Mae is on the federal budget (and is a part of HUD), its securities have a full faith and credit federal guarantee. Freddie Mac and Fannie Mae, however, are private corporations and neither has an explicit guarantee; however, both have an implicit guarantee. Studies by Sanders (2002) and Ambrose and Warga (2002) found that Fannie Mae and Freddie Mac have lower interest rates on bonds they issue in comparison to similarly rated commercial banks; as a consequence, the marketplace is inferring that the federal government will stand by the GSEs in case of financial insolvency. Both Fannie Mae and Freddie Mac are regulated by HUD for their public-purpose missions, and by the Office of Federal Housing Enterprise Oversight (OFHEO) for their risk exposure.

Currently, Fannie Mae and Freddie Mac are competitors in the conventional mortgage market. There are constraints on their activities in that they cannot buy loans above the **conforming loan limit,** which is currently approximately $322,700 for a single-family home mortgage (in the year 2003); this limit is adjusted each year by an index of house prices. Approximately 80 percent of mortgages in the United States fall under this conforming loan limit.

During the 1970s and early 1980s, the majority of mortgage-backed securities were issued in the form of a mortgage pass-through (such as the well-known Ginnie Mae pass-throughs). Mortgage pass-throughs allow investors to receive cash flows from underlying pools of individual home mortgages. In 1983, declines in interest rates and a growing housing market caused mortgage originations to double. Much of the new originations were sold in the capital markets as mortgage pass-throughs. As a consequence, mortgage pass-through issuance leaped from $54.2 billion in 1982 to $85.4 billion in 1983 as shown in Figure 6.1. Figure 6.2 also shows that, interestingly, Ginnie Mae issuance rose from $16.0 billion in 1982 to $50.7 billions in 1983, while Fannie Mae and Freddie Mac issuance actually fell over the same period.

Issuance of Ginnie Mae MBS actually fell after 1986 and remained fairly constant until 1993. Fannie Mae and Freddie Mac issuance rose steadily

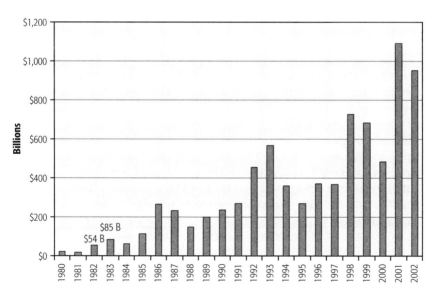

FIGURE 6.1 Issuance of agency MBS, 1980 through September 30, 2002.
Source: Ginnie Mae, Fannie Mae, and Freddie Mac.

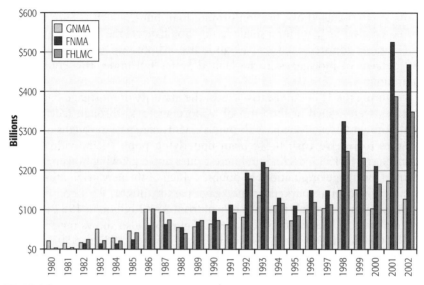

FIGURE 6.2 Issuance of agency MBS by issuer, 1980 through September 30, 2002.
Source: Ginnie Mae, Fannie Mae, and Freddie Mac.

from 1984 until 1993 (with the exception of a spike in issuance for Freddie Mac during 1986). After 1993, issuance of MBS by the agencies fell only to spike again in 1998 and 2001. Each of the spikes in agency issuance occurred in low interest-rate environments (and growing housing markets).

Figure 6.3 shows that the outstanding volume of agency MBS has been growing dramatically since 1987. In order to provide investors with additional choices (and hedging tools), Wall Street researchers created an alternative investment vehicle that would expand the number of MBS investors. In 1983, Freddie Mac issued the first collateralized-mortgage obligation (CMO). It was a simple, three-class structure offering short-, intermediate- and long-term securities from the cash flows of a pool of mortgages. The growth of CMOs has been enormous, particularly during 1991–1992, 1998, and 2001, as can be seen in Figure 6.4, which shows the outstanding volume of agency CMOs. These were periods when interest rates were declining and when fixed-income securities were gaining popularity with investors.

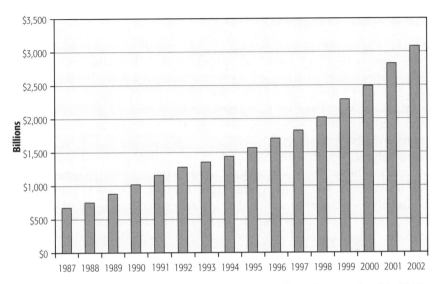

FIGURE 6.3 Outstanding volume of agency MBS, 1987 through September 30, 2002.
Source: Ginnie Mae, Fannie Mae, and Freddie Mac.

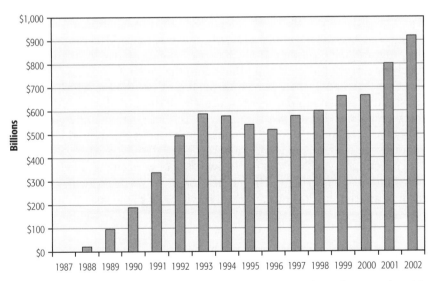

FIGURE 6.4 Outstanding volume of agency CMOs, 1987 through September 30, 2002.

How an Agency Pass-Through Works

Simply put, an agency pass-through is as simple as its name implies. Consider an example of a Ginnie Mae pass-through. A mortgage lender such as Wells Fargo makes a mortgage loan commitment to a home buyer to finance (or refinance) a mortgage loan. Wells Fargo would then obtain a guarantee from Ginnie Mae. Once the home buyer settles (or closes) and the mortgage loan is created, Wells Fargo would include the mortgage in a pool (of similar mortgages) and deliver the mortgage pool to a securities dealer. The securities dealer will then sell MBS, which are guaranteed by Ginnie Mae to investors (Ginnie Mae guarantees the timely payment of interest and principal to investors). The sales of the securities are then reported to Ginnie Mae. Wells Fargo continues to service the mortgage by collecting monthly principal and interest payments from the borrower and forwarding the payments to Ginnie Mae. Ginnie Mae in turn forwards or **passes through** the payments to investors. Thus, a mortgage-backed security is often called a **mortgage pass-through** or **mortgage pass-through certificate**.

In actuality, the agency MBS market relies on a network of lenders that includes not only commercial banks such as Wells Fargo, but savings and loan associations and mortgage bankers to originate the loans underlying the MBS. Lenders submit bundles of mortgage loans to the agencies for securitization; as mentioned in the previous paragraph, the loans are bundled so that they are similar. The agencies examine the loans so that they meet their credit-quality guidelines; once the loans pass the examination, they are then included in a mortgage pool and finally converted into MBS. Depending on the program, the resulting MBS will carry some combination of guaranteed timely payment of interest and principal to the investor.

Each MBS pool carries a pass-through rate, or coupon, which is the interest rate passed on to the investor, usually on the 25th day after the end of the accrual period. The pass-through rate is lower than the interest rate on the underlying mortgages in the pool. This interest differential covers the guaranty fee paid to Fannie Mae, and the fee paid to the servicing institution for collecting payments from home owners and performing other servicing functions. The lender that delivers the mortgages for securitization or sells them to another institution can retain servicing of the loans.

KEY TERMS FOR AGENCY PASS-THROUGHS

There are a number of important terms used when examining an agency pass-through (although many of the terms are used for CMOs and other products as well).

Weighted-Average Coupon

When analyzing an agency pass-through, it is important to examine the characteristics of the underlying pool of mortgages. Since each of 1,000 mortgages in a pool will have some variation in its mortgage rate, the weighted-average coupon (WAC), or rate, is calculated. Typically, the dispersion of coupons or rates in the pool is fairly small, particularly when compared to the WAC for some of the non-agency pools. WAC is important since it tells the investors not only the interest rates on the underlying mortgage pools, but it also gives an indication of how sensitive the pass-through value will be toward prepayment. When current mortgage rates fall beneath, say, 1.5 percent or 150 basis points of the underlying pool's WAC, we would anticipate that the pass-through will be sensitive to further interest rate declines and prepayment. If, however, current mortgage rates were above the WAC on the underlying pool, we would expect that the pass-through is not sensitive (at the moment) to prepayment risk.

It is important to note that the dispersion of WAC is important as well. The higher coupon mortgages in the underlying pool will, on average, prepay first. This prepayment possibility causes the WAC of the underlying pool to decline over time (making it progressively less sensitive to interest-rate declines and prepayments). The larger the dispersion in the coupons in the underlying pool, the greater is the effect.

Weighted-Average Maturity

Like WAC, the weighted-average maturity (WAM) is a weighted-average measure of the maturity of the mortgages in the underlying pool. As time goes on, the WAM naturally decreases. WAM is particularly important since it gives investors an idea of how many payments are left to be paid.

Servicing Fee

The investor's proceeds from a mortgage pass-through can be stated on a gross or a net basis. Gross WAC refers to the actual weighted-average coupon of the mortgages in the underlying pool. Net WAC refers to the mortgage rate less any servicing fee that is paid for servicing the loan and, as a consequence, the investor is not entitled to these fees. Servicing refers to a third party who processes the household's mortgage payment, makes payments to local governments for property taxes, pays the property insurance, and mortgage insurance premium, if necessary. Furthermore, the servicer interacts with the borrower to ensure that timely payments are made on the mortgage.

MECHANICS OF THE POOL PROGRAMS

To demonstrate how a pool program works, we use the case of Fannie Mae. When fixed-rate mortgages are pooled together, Fannie Mae allows the interest rates on the underlying mortgages to fall within a 250-basis-point range. The WAC of each security is the weighted average of the mortgage note rates and is provided to the investor to help evaluate the cash flows of the pool. Further, the WAM is available as an indicator of the remaining terms (in months) of the mortgages underlying the MBS as of the issue date. The **weighted-average loan age** (WALA) and the **weighted-average loan term at origination** (WALT) are also available to help analyze the potential cash flows of the pool.

Securities dealers sell Fannie Mae MBS to investors. Certificates issued in book-entry form initially will represent at least $1,000 of the unpaid principal amount of the mortgage loans in the pool. Fannie Mae MBS issued in book-entry form are paid by wire transfer, which is both convenient and safe. Fannie Mae's central paying agent, the Federal Reserve Bank of New York, wires monthly payments to depository institutions on behalf of registered security holders on the 25th of each month, or the first business day after that if the 25th of a month is not a business day. This central paying agent concept simplifies accounting procedures because investors can receive just one payment monthly for all their book-entry MBS.

AGENCY PROGRAMS

Although we focused on the example of Fannie Mae, there are numerous programs available for agency MBS. The major programs are listed in Table 6.1. Each of the major players in this market has multiple programs.

Ginnie Mae

Ginnie Mae offers several programs: Ginnie Mae I, Ginnie Mae II, and Ginnie Mae Platinum. Each of these programs offers full and timely payment of principal and interest, backed by the full faith and credit guarantee of the U.S. government. The latter part of the last sentence has particular importance in that the other agencies (Fannie Mae and Freddie Mac) are not backed by the full faith and credit guarantee of the U.S. government.

The Ginnie Mae I program consists of pass-through MBS where registered holders receive separate principal and interest payments on their certificates. The MBS are based on a single-issuer pool. The underlying

TABLE 6.1 Comparison of Pass-Through Mortgage Securities Characteristics

Security	Guarantee
GINNIE MAE I and II pass-throughs	Full and timely payment of principal and interest, backed by the full faith and credit guarantee of the U.S. government
GINNIE MAE PLATINUM pass-throughs	Full and timely payment of principal and interest, backed by the full faith and credit guarantee of the U.S. government
FANNIE MAE pass-throughs	Full and timely payment of principal and interest guaranteed by Fannie Mae.
FREDDIE MAC participation certificates	Full and timely payment of interest and ultimate payment of principal guaranteed by Freddie Mac
FREDDIE MAC GOLD participation certificates	Full and timely payment of interest and scheduled principal guaranteed by Freddie Mac

mortgages have roughly the same maturities and interest rates. The single-family home pools have a 50-basis-point guaranty and servicing fee. Payments are made to the holders on the 15th day of each month.

Introduced in 1983, the Ginnie Mae II program allows registered holders to receive an aggregate principal and interest payment from a central paying agent on all of their Ginnie Mae II MBS. There is greater flexibility with the Ginnie Mae II program; for example, the coupon rates on underlying mortgages can vary between 50 and 150 basis points above the interest rate on the pool. Multiple-issuers as well as single-issuers are allowed under the Ginnie Mae II program. Additional flexibility of the Ginnie Mae II program includes allowing small issuers (who do not meet the minimum dollar pool requirements of Ginnie Mae I) and the securitization of adjustable-rate mortgages (ARMs). Ginnie Mae II MBS pay on the 20th day of each month.

Ginnie Mae Platinum securities are issued under the Ginnie Mae Multiclass Securities Program. A Ginnie Mae Platinum security is created by combining Ginnie Mae MBS pools that have uniform coupons and original terms to maturity into a single certificate. An interesting feature of the Ginnie Mae Platinum program is that investors owning several MBS that have a relatively small remaining balance have the ability to aggregate the MBS; this aggregation provides critical liquidity to investors. Platinum pools can be used by investors as collateral for borrowings, such as repurchase agreements, and in structured financing.

Fannie Mae

Fannie Mae offers a pass-through program that offers full and timely payment of principal and interest. However, Fannie Mae, not the full faith and credit guarantee of the U.S. government, guarantees the full and timely payment. Fannie Mae MBS pay interest on the 25th day of each month (after the accrual period). The pass-through rate is lower than the interest rate on the underlying mortgages; this interest differential covers the guaranty fee paid to Fannie Mae (as well as the servicing fee paid to the servicer). When the underlying loans are pooled together, Fannie Mae permits the interest rates on the loans to fall within a 250-basis-point range.

Freddie Mac

Freddie Mac's pass-through program offers full and timely payment of interest and ultimate payment of principal guaranteed by Freddie Mac, not the full faith and credit guarantee of the U.S. government. The Freddie Mac Gold program offers full and timely payment of interest and scheduled principal guaranteed by Freddie Mac. The Gold program is very competitive with the Fannie Mae MBS program; hence, it is Freddie Mac's most popular MBS program. The Gold program pays interest on the 15th of every month. Freddie Mac also offers a Giant program that is similar in nature to the Ginnie Mae Platinum program as described earlier.

TRADING OF AGENCY MORTGAGE-BACKED SECURITIES

The trading of agency mortgage-backed securities involves certain conventions that are not found in the trading of other securities. It is important to understand these conventions in order to correctly determine the value of a mortgage-backed security.

Settlement and To-Be-Announced Markets

Like most other financial transactions, settlement for MBS is the process by which the buyers and sellers exchange cash and securities. For our purposes, we examine key issues related to settling MBS trades: timing and determining the amount of cash to change hands.

Typically, pass-through MBS trade on a forward basis, where settlement occurs once per month. Each type of mortgage is assigned a particular day during the month for trade settlement. During any particular calendar month, the active month for which most trades will settle will be the next monthly settlement for that security. For example, during the month of June the active trading month will be for July settlement. By the middle of July, traders will generally shift the active settlement month to August. Secondary CMO securities trade primarily on a corporate (five business days) settlement basis.

Active trading in the one-month-forward market stems from the settlement procedures for MBS coupled with the increased importance of the CMO market. Among most Wall Street dealers, the biggest trading counter party of the MBS pass-through trader is the dealer's primary CMO desk. The pass-through trader will be responsible for purchasing the CMO collateral needed for any deal. As most CMO deals settle one (or more) calendar month from the pricing date, trading for collateral is most active in the one-month-forward market. This does not preclude other settlement possibilities for investors. Up until 2 days before the settlement within any particular month, it is still possible for investors to purchase bonds for current-month settlement. Dealers will still make markets for current-month settlement, but not always with the same liquidity as the most actively traded month.

However, there are times when attractive opportunities arise for investors as current settlement approaches. In cases when a dealer still needs collateral to settle a CMO, he or she may have an aggressive bid for current settlement collateral or be willing to create an attractive drop in the role market.

There are also times when buyers and sellers arrange for immediate settlement. These trades occur more in unusual situations, subject to arrangements made between dealers and institutional investors.

Settlement Cash Flows and Security Delivery

At the time of the trade, the two counter parties agree to the date, price, and quantity of securities. At the time of settlement, the purchaser will pay the price times the quantity of securities, plus any accrued interest. The interest-accrual period will cover the time from the first of the month until the settlement date.

Most trades occur on a **to-be-announced** (TBA) basis. Mortgage lenders are allowed by the agencies to sell mortgages forward by securitizing the mortgages for purchase in the secondary market. In order to allow lenders to hedge (or fund) their origination pipelines, settlement dates are set

between 1 and 9 months from the date on which the transaction is negotiated. This arrangement permits lenders to lock in a price for the mortgages
they are in the process of originating. An interesting feature of the TBA
market is that the purchaser does not know the actual pools being delivered
until just prior to settlement. Since the number of pools that will be delivered
(and the characteristics of the pools) are unknown, TBAs are analyzed using
the *average characteristics* of the MBS that are likely to be delivered.

Trades also occur on a specified pool basis. These trades may reflect special inventory that a dealer holds or that a client needs. Trades on specific
pools usually occur at prices above the current TBA quotes. In addition to
specific pools, buyers and sellers may negotiate other types of characteristics
such as year of origination or number of pools to be delivered.

Specified pool trading occurs frequently for seasoned or WAM bonds.
These are mortgage pools that have older or seasoned loans. Due to their
prepayment characteristics relative to the average pools (faster for lower-
coupon mortgages and slower for high-coupon mortgages), WAM bonds
tend to have greater value than the generic pool and, therefore, sell at higher
prices than the TBA price. Wall Street traders also use specified pool trading
to obtain pools for structured transactions or to reduce back office costs by
restricting the number of pools to be delivered.

Trading and settlement of MBS generally follow rules established by the
Bond Market Association (www.bondmarkets.com).

Delay of Cash Flows

Nearly all borrowers make their mortgage payments in arrears on a monthly
basis. Likewise, investors receive their cash just once a month. The time between the expected cash payment from the borrower and the ultimate cash
flow received by the investor is called **the delay**. The effect of this delay must
be treated by the yield calculations performed on MBS because it represents
a true loss of economic opportunity. The delay varies slightly among the
agencies and GSEs.

While the delay factor is meant to cover many of the exigencies that
occur when borrowers are late with their payments and the mechanical complications of processing the cash flows, it also provides an important source
of income to the financial intermediaries. Both Fannie Mae and Freddie
Mac derive significant income from the float earned between the time they
collect cash flows and the time they disperse them to investors.

Accrued Interest

MBS begin to accrue interest on the first calendar day of the month, which
corresponds to the same accrual period of the borrower. At the time of set-

tlement, the investor must pay the previous holder the interest through the settlement date. After settlement, the investor is entitled to the entire month's interest.

MBS accrue interest on a 30/360-day basis. That is, accrued interest calculations assume that each month has 30 days and that each year has 360 days. Practically speaking, this means that each month the investor receives 1/12 of the annual coupon. Also for calculating accrued interest, the investor receives 1/30 of the monthly interest payment for each day up until settlement. No additional interest is paid for settlement on the 31st of the month. Typically most settlement occurs in the middle of the month, so the extra day is not an issue.

EXERCISES

Exercise 6.1 Each of the agencies has a Web site that contains valuable information about their growth prospects. In particular, Fannie Mae (www.fanniemae.com) offers detailed financial information about its business (hint: look under investor relations). Your assignment is to determine the magnitude of the mortgage purchases over the past several years by Fannie Mae as well as the MBS issues acquired by others. Place your information in an Excel spreadsheet and graph the growth of Fannie Mae's mortgage purchases and MBS issues acquired by others. Discuss what you have learned about Fannie Mae's growth.

Exercise 6.2 Fannie Mae purchased $270,584 million of mortgage during 2001. Suppose that each mortgage was in the amount of $100,000. This implies that Fannie Mae purchased approximately 2,705,840 loans during 2001. Suppose that Fannie Mae saves borrowers approximately 25 basis points per loan. How much savings did Fannie Mae generate for borrowers in 2001. Suppose that the savings is only five basis points; what would be the savings to borrowers during 2001?

Exercise 6.3 What would be the impact of privatizing Fannie Mae and Freddie Mac? Bear in mind that Fannie Mae and Freddie Mac would no longer have their implicit guarantee from the U.S. government. However, it would allow them to enter other mortgage markets that they currently have little or no presence in (such as international mortgage markets and subprime lending). Would privatization be a good thing or a bad thing?

CHAPTER 7

Fundamentals of the Interest-Rate Market

The entire fixed-income universe revolves around the concept of interest rates. Interest rates are central to the valuation of thousands of traded financial instruments ranging in complexity from Treasuries and swaps to mortgages and their derivatives. Based on observable interest rates, the values for option-free, default-free bonds and other instruments can be computed via a set of simple, almost definitional, formulas.

But the application of simple formulas for valuing options or embedded-option securities (such as are found in the mortgage-backed securities (MBS) and asset-backed securities (ABS) market) is not feasible. Their cash flows (payoffs) depend on the interest rates themselves. Valuing instruments with embedded options is a real challenge, since it requires an educated guess, if not a rigorous model, for the future behavior of interest rates. Sound like a job for a fortuneteller? Surprisingly enough, Wall Street does not hire prophets for their financial engineering spots. As we show in Chapter 12, the future evolution of interest rates, though unknown, can be modeled in a way that is consistent with today's market. Before delving into the world of the unknown, however, let us review some fundamental definitions and relationships.

Some portions of these chapters require knowledge of calculus or facility with more complex formulas. These portions are shaded. Readers may skim or skip these sections, while still gathering the major themes of the chapter.

BOND PRICES AND INTEREST RATES

In the following sections, we first review quantitative basics of fixed income: present valuing, discounting, and rates. We then immediately illustrate these concepts with most common fixed-income instruments: bonds and swaps.

Economic Rationale of Present Valuing and Discounting

Suppose we deposit $100 with a bank for 1 year. The bank guarantees to add 10 percent at the end of the term, which means we will have $110 on the deposit after 1 year. This simple example provides the setting for some basic concepts and definitions. The 10 percent is called the **interest rate**, applicable for a 1-year period (denote it r). The $110 on deposit that we are assured of after 1 year is called **future value**. The $100 we deposited initially is known as **present value**. The length of the contract is often called **maturity**. For this rudimentary, one-period setting, we have

$$\text{Present Value} = \frac{\text{Future Value}}{1 + r} \qquad (7.1a)$$

The fraction $1/(1 + r)$ that brings future value to the current moment is called the **discount factor**. The application of equation (7.1a) is known as **discounting**, and r, in this context, is called the **discount rate**.

Suppose now we decided to leave $100 for n years in hope of receiving 10 percent interest rate per annum. At the end of the first year we will have, of course, $110. The account will continue to accrue 10 percent, but on the already grown value. If this were not true, we could close the account and reopen another one, thus depositing $110 for the second year. At the end of the second year, we will have $100 \times (1 + 0.1)^2$, or simply $121. At the end of the nth period, our original (present) investment will grow in $(1 + r)^n$ times. Therefore,

$$\text{Present Value} = \frac{\text{Future Value}}{(1 + r)^n} \qquad (7.1b)$$

Raising $(1 + r)$ to a power is a direct consequence of **compounding** (i.e., crediting interest on the accrued, rather than the original, value). In our deposit example, the compounding was performed annually. The cumulative result of our investment depends on the original amount, the interest rate, maturity, and the compounding frequency.

---

1. Compute the future value of a $100 deposit made for a 5-year term compounding 10 percent per annum.
2. Recompute the result assuming that the bank credits half of the annual interest (e.g., 5 percent) twice a year.
3. Compare the two results.

Can we really ask the bank to split the interest rate in parts and compound it more often? Since, as the previous example shows, we would be better off if they did, they may not agree to do it. Nevertheless, it is possible to change the rate so that it would produce the same result as changing the compounding frequency. In order to find a breakeven semiannual rate (let us denote it x for a moment) for the 10 percent annual rate, we need to compare $1 + 0.1$ with $(1 + x/2)^2$. A simple arithmetic exercise leads to $x = 9.76$ percent. The instrument's maturity does not enter in this conversion: It is enough to ensure that these two compounding patterns yield the same results after 1 year.

Investors in different sectors of the fixed-income market are accustomed to differing compounding conventions. Most banks credit interest on a monthly basis. The same convention applies also to the mortgage market. The monthly compounded rate is usually abbreviated MEY, standing for **monthly equivalent yield** or **mortgage equivalent yield**. The bond market typically uses semi-annual compounding; the rates under this convention are **bond equivalent yield** (BEY). All types of rules, including quarterly and annual compounding conventions, are met in the borrowing markets. In addition, most banks publicly state their rates in both MEY and **annual percentage yield** (APY) to allow customers to assess the annual result.

In general, the rate conversion from an m period per annum compounding to an l period per annum compounding should yield the same annual result, therefore:

$$(1 + \frac{r^{(m)}}{m})^m = (1 + \frac{r^{(l)}}{l})^l \tag{7.2}$$

where r^m is the m period per annum rate.

In particular, two most important rate conversions are

$$\frac{BEY}{2} = \left(1 + \frac{MEY}{12}\right)^6 - 1 \text{ and } \frac{MEY}{12} = \left(1 + \frac{BEY}{2}\right)^{1/6} - 1$$

One additional case we might add to the list is continuous compounding. While it may not be practical to implement, it is a convenient model that, as shown later, allows financial engineers to communicate their concepts concisely. (There have been times that banks offered continuously compounded rates, but that reflected the need to offer higher rates in a period of rate regulation. In practice the banks still paid interest on a monthly basis.) Let us consider relationship (7.2) again, and imagine what will happen if we replace m with a very large ("infinite") number. This will mean an instrument that credits an infinitesimal fraction of interest an infinite number of times per annum. As known from calculus, $(1 + r/l)^l \rightarrow e^r$ as l approaches infinity. Therefore, any m-period rate (MEY, BEY, etc.) can be converted into the continuously compounded one by taking the logarithm of the annual growth: $r = m\ln(1 + r^{(m)}/m)$. The n-year discount factor becomes just e^{-rn}.

The previous equations assumed that the same interest rate could be used for every period, but do the interest rates used during different time periods have to be the same? The reader has likely already figured out that the discount factor can be comprised of annual constituents. If a deposit accrues 10 percent for the first year, 5 percent for the second, and 20 percent for the third, then the cumulative growth will be $(1 + 0.1)$ times $(1 + 0.05)$ times $(1 + 0.2)$. In general,

$$\text{Present Value} = \frac{\text{Future Value}}{\prod_{k=1}^{n} (1 + r_k)} \qquad (7.1c)$$

where r_k is the periodic rate for the k-th investment period. The symbol $\prod$ means take the product, just as Σ means take the sum. Formula (7.1c) is the same as:

$$\text{Present Value} = \frac{\text{Future Value}}{(1 + r_1)(1 + r_2) \ldots (1 + r_n)}$$

Compounding continuously, we will have yet another version of this formula:

$$(\text{Present Value}) = (\text{Future Value}) \ \exp[-\int_0^n r(t)dt] \qquad (7.1d)$$

In the last expression, rate $r(t)$ is often called *the short rate*. Because it is an instantaneous rate measuring the speed of deposit growth at time t, it does not really make sense to wonder "how short" this rate is. However, if it is difficult to conceptualize, you may want to think of it as the overnight rate.

Bonds and Their Rates

A **zero-coupon** bond ("zero") is a financial instrument that is almost identical to a bank certificate of deposit (CD). The bond issuer promises to pay, say, $100 (known as **face value**) at maturity. No other payments are to be made until then. If the market rate for this bond is known, the present value can be computed using equation (7.1b). This present value is also referred to as **bond price**. Keeping in mind a bank CD as an alternative investment, it is very easy to understand why the price paid for the bond should be identical to the theoretical present value. We can simply calculate what it would take to open a deposit that will grow to $100 for the same term. The constant rate r used in formula (7.1b) is called the **yield to maturity** or just the **yield**. It can be expressed in BEY (most often), MEY, or any other form. The terms *rates* and *yields* are used interchangeably in the bond market. Rate is a more general term, however, because yield to maturity is, by definition, the one constant rate applied through the life of financial instruments.

Although it may sound like a tautology, yield to maturity depends on . . . maturity. This is shown in Table 7.1.

Note the standard percentage quotations for price. For example, a quote of 87.63 means that the bond costs 87.63 percent of its face amount. All the prices are below 100 percent, because the zero does not pay anything before maturity. Zero-coupon bonds are often called pure discount bonds.

Since rates generally do depend on maturity, investors refer to the entire collection of interest rates as the **yield curve** or the **interest-rate term structure**. The reader will encounter these important notions many times in this book. Later in this chapter, we discuss the main forces contributing to this phenomenon and the financial consequences. Without an understanding of

TABLE 7.1 Yield to Maturity

Maturity (years)	Yield (%)	Price (%)
1	3.00	97.09
2	4.00	92.46
3	4.50	87.63
5	5.00	78.35
10	6.00	55.84

the economic consequences, the reader might wonder why a profit-seeking investor would ever invest in a 1-year, 2-year, 3-year, or even 5-year zero, once there is a 10-year bond "generously" paying a 6 percent rate. However, this naive question is a smart one. Yet, like materialist philosophers, financial engineers do not judge the yield curve; they simply employ it as an objective reality.

The zeros are building blocks of financial modeling. Any combination of payments made at the end of Year 1, Year 2, and so forth will be valued using the prices for constituent zeros as the weights.

A **coupon bond** is an obligation to make periodic interest payments (coupons) and to return the **principal** amount at maturity. Let us denote c to be periodic coupon rate, n to be the number of periods (maturity), and assume that the par is \$100. The value of this bond is just the sum of present values of all n payments. The first $n-1$ payments are even and equal to $100c$. The last payment includes the face amount, that is, it is $100 + 100c$. Therefore, the price of the bond is computed as:

$$P = \sum_{k=1}^{n} \frac{100c}{(1+r)^k} + \frac{100}{(1+r)^n} \qquad (7.3a)$$

In this formula, as elsewhere, r is the bond's yield to maturity, that is, a single interest rate employed for the entire discounting job. It is, of course, not the same rate as the one for an n-maturity zero. By summing the geometric progression in (7.3a), we can transform it to:

$$P = 100 \frac{c}{r} \left[1 - \frac{1}{(1+r)^n} \right] + \frac{100}{(1+r)^n} \qquad (7.3b)$$

Let us analyze the last result. If $c = r$, then the bond is worth par (\$100). This is a typical case for a newly issued bond. In other terms, the bond's market rate and its coupon are often born as identical twins. As market conditions change, so will the rate r, but not the coupon c. Note that the right-hand side of (7.3b) is **linear in** c (linear in c means that the change in price is directly proportional to the change in coupon for a given yield) and the price of the bond equals par for $c = r$. Therefore, if market rate rises so that $c < r$, then the bond's price falls below par ($P < 100$). It is said the bond is traded at a **discount**. If $c > r$, then $P > 100$, and the bond will be priced at a **premium**.

Formula (7.3b) shows that bond prices are linear in coupons and inverse in market rates. Most market participants are very well versed in potential gains and losses caused by the market-rate dynamics; falling rates produce higher bond prices.

How is the coupon rate determined? Suppose we know the zero-coupon rates for all maturities that correspond to the bond coupon payments. It is possible to find the coupon rate that relates to the zero-coupon rates. Denote the zero coupon rates as r_k for the k-th coupon anniversary. Then we can re-express the bond pricing as:

$$P = \sum_{k=1}^{n} \frac{100c}{(1 + r_k)^k} + \frac{100}{(1 + r_n)^n}$$

In order to find the coupon rate, let us equate this value to par and solve for c:

$$c = \frac{1 - \dfrac{1}{(1 + r_n)^n}}{\displaystyle\sum_{k=1}^{n} \dfrac{1}{(1 + r_k)^k}} \qquad (7.4)$$

The denominator can be interpreted as an annuity paying \$1 per annum, periodically.

Table 7.2 illustrates calculations performed sequentially for all 10 maturity points. The coupon rates seem to "chase" the zero rates, but cannot quite reach them. Since the zero-rate curve grows steeply with maturity in our example, coupon rates lag the race.

TABLE 7.2 Zero Rates and Coupon Rates

Maturity	Zero Rate (%)	Discount Factor (%)	Annuity	Coupon Rate (%)
1	3.00	97.09	0.971	3.000
2	4.00	92.46	1.895	3.980
3	4.50	87.63	2.772	4.463
4	4.75	83.06	3.602	4.703
5	5.00	78.35	4.386	4.936
6	5.25	73.56	5.121	5.162
7	5.50	68.74	5.809	5.381
8	5.75	63.94	6.448	5.593
9	5.90	59.69	7.045	5.721
10	6.00	55.84	7.604	5.808

Swaps and Their Rates

A **swap** is a contract between two parties to exchange interest payments that are computed off the same **notional** amount. While the notional amount plays a similar role as the principal of a bond for computing the periodic interest payments, there is no exchange of principal; hence the transaction is denominated in a notional rather than real principal. One party (fixed payer) will pay a preset fixed rate, whereas another party (fixed receiver) will pay a floating rate indexed to a variable market rate. This market rate is most often determined as **LIBOR** (London InterBank Offered Rate). The two parties of a swap transaction are often referred to as "fixed leg" and "floating leg," respectively. A standard market swap has the fixed leg paying semiannually and the floating leg resetting and paying quarterly. Namely, a period-beginning 3-month LIBOR rate is measured and applied for the floating-leg payment made at the end of that period.

Standard swap transactions are normally structured such as to ensure no cost for entering either side. Any particular (nonstandard) swap can be customized so that the above rules may not apply. For example, the floating leg can reset monthly instead of quarterly, there may be an initial cost for the transaction, margin to the index, and so forth. For the purpose of our introduction, understanding the standard swap is all we need.

Since any swap has two legs, it may be a bit confusing at first glance. In fact, a swap and a coupon bond are close relatives. The reason for this seemingly paradoxical statement is that we could add two identical fictitious payments equal to the notional amount of the swap that each party virtually pays to one another at maturity. Since the two identical payments would cancel out, there is no need to actually swap $100 bills. The fixed leg of a swap plus a terminal par payment is a coupon bond. The floating leg plus the par payment is known as a **perfect floater**. Although we are not quite ready yet to formally value this instrument, we can understand its value using basic financial principles. Suppose that a bank pays us the 3-month interest accrued on a deposit every 3 months instead of adding it to the balance. On every pay date, we would be left with the initial balance. Therefore, the value of a floater, which has the identical cash flows, would be par on any reset date. Based on this analysis we can conclude that

$$\text{Swap} = \text{Coupon Bond} - \text{Par} \qquad (7.5)$$

provided that the swap's fixed rate and the bond's coupon rate are the same. Thus, if a bond paying a 7 percent coupon rate is worth 102, then a swap with a 7 percent fixed rate is worth 2 percentage points for the receiver of its fixed leg. This consideration lets us think of swaps as regular coupon bonds. In practice, there is no real bond market that operates with the same level of rates as the swap market. Yet for now, it is enough to assume that

TABLE 7.3 Yield Curves

Maturity (months)	Treasury	LIBOR/Swap	AA Corporate
3	1.82	2.01	2.27
6	2.07	2.29	2.54
12	2.52	2.92	3.16
24	3.53	3.98	3.93
60	4.67	5.27	5.46
120	5.28	5.95	6.13
360	5.73	6.31	6.71

the swap rates are equivalent to some coupon bond rates. Table 7.3 depicts several actual coupon curves for different markets as of March 19, 2002.

We can even consider (at least, mathematically) a curve of the zero-coupon swap rates, which are linked to the regular swap curve via relationship (7.4). We should not even care if zero-coupon swaps actually exist on financial markets. All we know for sure now is that each of the swap's payments should have a theoretical present value, and each value can be converted into a zero-coupon rate.

A **bond** generically refers to a financial instrument given by its sequence of promised cash flows, or by a set of legal rules that unambiguously determine them. The principal amount may change over the life of such an instrument as a result of **amortization** (principal reductions) or growth (principal increases that are sometimes called **negative amortization**). Coupon rates may be fixed or may vary according to a formula—much like the swap's floating leg that we met before. The rules can be stated in a form **contingent** (dependent) on prevailing market rates. For example, a constant-maturity Treasury adjustable-rate mortgage may pay the rate of 1-year U.S. Treasury bill plus 2.75 percent, resetting once a year. Some rules may not even be mathematically formalized. For example, a mortgage investor is obliged to accept the notional amount prepaid by the pool of home owners or a stated share of it. This is easier said than done, especially for the investor who is not aware of the home owners' intentions. As we see throughout this book, in the MBS/ABS market we find a great variety and complexity of bonds. No matter how complex the bond, however, if the cash-flow sequence is known and certain (denote it CF_k for the k-the period), and we know suitable zero-coupon (discount) rates to employ, then the present value can always be found as

$$\text{Present Value} = \sum_{k=1}^{n} \frac{CF_k}{(1 + r_k)^k} \qquad (7.6)$$

FORWARD RATES AND RISK NEUTRALITY

We have explained how to compute the present value of a bank deposit, a bond, or a swap. This value becomes the fair market price for immediate delivery of the financial instrument, in exchange for cash. The immediate delivery transactions constitute the **spot market**; the market for delivery at some future time is known as **forward market**. These two must agree with one another to preclude **arbitrage**. Quotes for the forward market (rates and prices) are known today. They drive the key aspect of valuation, **risk neutrality**.

Forward Rates

Suppose we would like to buy a 1-year zero-coupon bond to be delivered in 10 years. How much would we need to pay on delivery? Suppose the answer is F; to compute F let us consider two investment alternatives:

1. We invest some cash today in a 10-year zero in order to have exactly F in 10 years. As formula (7.1b) suggests, the amount of initial investment must be $F/(1 + r_{10})^{10}$ where r_{10} is the zero-coupon 10-year rate today (assuming annual compounding). Concurrently, we buy the 1-year zero-coupon bond to be delivered in 10 years. This combination will bring us $100 in 11 years.
2. We use the same initial cash, $F/(1 + r_{10})^{10}$, to buy an 11-year zero today having a rate of r_{11}. It will pay $[F/(1 + r_{10})^{10}](1 + r_{11})^{11}$ in 11 years.

Since the initial investments are assumed to be identical and there exist no uncertainties in the terminal payoffs, we expect them to coincide as well, that is, $[F/(1 + r_{10})^{10}](1 + r_{11})^{11} = 100$, leading to $F = (1 + r_{10})^{10}/(1 + r_{11})^{11}$. Let us denote $f_1(10)$ to be the rate on this 1-year zero. According to the one-period discount formula (7.1), $F = 1/[1 + f_1(10)]$, thereby the forward rate is determined as

$$f_1(10) = \frac{(1 + r_{11})^{11}}{(1 + r_{10})^{10}} - 1 \tag{7.7}$$

Rate $f_1(10)$ in this example is known as the **forward rate** and price F is called **forward price**, both quoted for a 1-year zero-coupon bond, for delivery in 10 years. Forward prices may exist or be theoretically computed for virtually any stock, bond, or commodity.

Let us try to generalize the concept of forward rates: Suppose the bond to be delivered in t years is an n-year maturity zero. Then, the forward rate, $f_n(t)$, and the forward price, F, are related to the spot-market rates as

$$\frac{1}{F} = [1 + f_n(t)]^n = \frac{(1 + r_{t+n})^{t+n}}{(1 + r_t)^t} \tag{7.8}$$

We can also reconstruct the forward coupon rates using the same formula (7.4) that was proven valid for the spot market. The only thing we have to change is to replace spot-market rates r_k with forward rates $f_k(t)$.

Consider the following problem:

On the spot market, the 5-year zero-coupon rate is 5 percent, and the 10-year rate is 6 percent. What is the 5-year zero-coupon rate, 5 years forward?

Since the full 10-year maturity term is comprised of two 5-year terms, it is intuitively clear that the 10-year spot rate should be close to the average of two other rates, the 5-year spot rate, and the 5-year forward rate. The average of 5 percent and 7 percent is 6 percent, so those who completed this exercise can verify that the naively grabbed 7 percent is rather a decent guess for the forward rate in question. The exact relationship (7.8) does not suggest taking the simple average. For a very steep curve and longer terms, the rule of simple average may be inaccurate for trading.

The forward rates are market rates today, not in the future. Though applied for future delivery, these rates remain unchanged—once negotiated. Many markets trade forward as well as spot. Swap forward market is very active, for a wide variety of delivery terms. Treasuries and MBS are often traded forward, but with shorter delivery than seen in the swap market. Interestingly enough, forward trading for new mortgage pools is the rule rather than the exception, with active markets for delivery 1 to 3 months forward.

The relationships between the spot market rates and the forward market rates can be made clear if we consider continuously compounded rates introduced in the beginning of this chapter. Let us suppose that r_t denotes the t-maturity zero-coupon rate, $f(t)$ denotes the short rate t-years forward, both compounded continuously. Let us replace the power functions in formula (7.8) by the exponents and assume that maturity n is infinitesimally small:

$$f(t) = \lim_{n \to 0} \frac{(t + n)r_{t+n} - tr_t}{n} = t \lim_{n \to 0} \frac{r_{t+n} - r_t}{n} + \lim_{n \to 0} r_{t+n} = t\frac{dr_t}{dt} + r_t \quad (7.9)$$

The short forward rate curve considered against the spot rate curve appears to contain its first derivative component. Therefore, any inaccuracies in computing the spot rates will be magnified when moving to the forward rates.

Three particular practical rules are worth mentioning here:

1. If the spot curve experiences a sudden slope change, the short forward curve jumps (becomes discontinuous).
2. The "double slope" rule: any slope found in the spot curve is doubled in the short forward curve. Indeed, assuming that $r_t = \alpha + \beta t$ we find from (7.9) that $f(t) = \alpha + 2\beta t$.
3. If the spot curve has a flat part, the short forward curve will have one too.

Figure 7.1 (see page 106) illustrates these rules.

As we have already learned, the forward curve can be constructed for any maturity, not only for the short rate. Let us use $f_n(t)$ to denote the forward rate on the n-year maturity, then, in the continuously compounded form,

$$nf_n(t) = r_{n+t}(n + t) - r_t t \quad (7.10)$$

Reviewing the way we have introduced the forward rates, one could notice that discount factors can be expressed through forward rates as well as through the zero-coupon rates. The expression $(1 + r_n)^n$ is identical to the result of cumulative accrual of one-period rates, $f_1(t)$, applied for n forward times, $t = 0, 1, \ldots, n-1$. That is, the value of \$1 paid in n periods from now equals:

$$\text{Present Value} = \frac{1}{(1 + r_n)^n} \equiv \prod_{t=0}^{n-1} \frac{1}{1 + f_1(t)} \qquad (7.11)$$

This identity follows right from the definition of forward rates.

The Real Economy: What Makes the Curve?

When introducing the forward rate concept, we considered two investment alternatives, marked (1) and (2). Let us slightly change the (1) alternative:

(1A) We invest some cash today in a 10-year zero so as to have exactly F in 10 years. In 10 years, we use these guaranteed proceeds (i.e., F) to buy a 1-year zero available *then* on the spot market.

There is a seemingly small difference between strategy (1) and strategy (1A). When following investment path (1) we secure the $100 in 11 years. We do not know the result of investment path (1A) because the spot market in 10 years for a 1-year zero (and for anything else) is simply unknown. It is one of the attractive features found in the forward markets that one can lock in a desirable transaction not being exposed to the uncertainty of the spot markets in the future.

Although we cannot know the final investment result for strategy (1A), we can assume that the market perception about expected future rates (if any) are generally built into today's forward market. For instance, if some event triggers future hyperinflation, the zero-rate curve should get much steeper. Rare inversions of the yield curve (long rates are smaller than the short rate) often indicate that the market anticipates the rates to drop. Therefore, **market expectation** is the first apparent factor affecting the term structure of interest rates.

Risk premium is the second important factor affecting the curve's shape. Longer-maturity bonds are more volatile as their prices are sensitive to the market rates. A majority of investors are risk averse; they demand compensation (a price cut) for investing in long bonds. This typical risk aversion causes the long rates to be statistically upward biased.

Liquidity premium is the third contributor to the curve; it is often mentioned in reference to the **segmentation theory**. It is perceived that some categories of the fixed-income investors have systematic preferences in the maturity sectors. For example, insurance companies prefer investing in long maturities since this strategy matches their liability structure (pension plans, life insurance products). Banks like borrowing at shorter rates and quicker rollovers. Market segmentation is relatively stable but can be affected by structural changes.

Credit spread is often found in any yield curve except for the Treasuries. The U.S. government is perceived as a perfect (benchmark) debtor

who guarantees returning the promised cash flow. Other markets will in-
evitably have lower credit quality. For example, swap and LIBOR rates are
commercial rates, not guaranteed by the government, at which banks and
other financial institutions lend money to each other (often with collateral).
Corporate bonds are traded at a spread, over Treasuries and even over
swaps because these types of debt are not collateralized and expose investors
to potential default contingent on the company's financial health. Credit
spreads are typically wider for longer bonds. Investors perceive events such
as credit downgrading as a prelude to bankruptcy, and this unfortunate
combination of events is less likely to occur within a short horizon.

Therefore, we could express the real economy's term structure of interest rates as

$$\text{Yield Curve} = \text{Expectation} + \text{Risk Premium} \\ + \text{Liquidity Premium} + \text{Credit Spread} \quad (7.12)$$

Any changes of the components listed on the right-hand side affect the curve
in an additive fashion. In real life, however, it is virtually impossible to
quantify each contributor—only the resultant yield curve is observed.

The Arbitrage-Free Economy

How would we approach valuation of a generic instrument, the cash flows
of which are not certain and contingent on rates themselves? MBS and ABS
certainly fall into this category, along with callable corporates, floaters, and
interest-rate options. Chapter 12 deals with these issues in more detail. At
this stage, it is enough to understand that we might need to know how to
forecast future rates. Suppose that we somehow determined the market expectation for future rates. How would we add pricing components for risk,
liquidity, and credit? We would need to include them too.

Fortunately, there is no need to solve one equation for four unknowns.
The transformation of the valuation problem used by financial engineers
leads to another construct called the **arbitrage-free economy**. In this model,
the risk, liquidity, and credit components are discarded altogether. The entire
term structure of interest rates is explained solely by the rate expectation:

$$\text{Yield Curve} = \text{Arbitrage-Free Expectation} \quad (7.13)$$

The arbitrage-free expectation is, of course, different than the expectation in the real economy. We simply say that the market expects rates to rise
if the curve is steep, or fall if it is inversed. Since most of the time the curve
is steep, the rates are likely to rise in the arbitrage-free world. In the real

world, however, rises and falls are anticipated in an alternating order; they cancel each other over the long run. After all, the level of rates at the beginning of the 21st century is not much different from that of the 1900s.

Why is arbitrage-free economy a legitimate model? The proof is simple: prices of instruments will come up the same as those actually observed, including the forward prices. Let us pretend that the market is certain in the future. Then, the previously mentioned investment strategy (1) that uses the forward market, and (1A) that relies on the spot market in the future, should yield identical results. The price of a 1-year zero-coupon bond will be equal to $100/[1+r_1(10)]$ in 10 years where $r_1(10)$ is the certain spot rate then. However, the same bond is worth $100/[1+f_1(10)]$ on today's forward market. Equating these two prices to preclude an arbitrage between two markets, we must have $r_1(10) = f_1(10)$. In short, if the economy is arbitrage-free and certain, future rates are equal to the currently observed forward rates.

This universal statement holds true for any maturity, any forward delivery time, for zero-coupon or coupon rates. It also reveals a great importance of the forward rates: They can be used in lieu of future rates for an arbitrage-free mathematical pricing model. This model, remember, is not for the real economy. The model does not make an assertion about how the real rates will evolve—even in a completely certain world. It is only a convenient and legitimate pricing construct. It is therefore foolish to argue whether the forward curve predicts actual rates or not. People consciously betting on or against the curve are often equally blind. Many people have remarked that they do not "believe" in forward rates. To this one can only say that forward rates do not require any measure of belief. They simply present the way the current market values forward transactions.

Many investors make (and lose) a lot of money by betting on or against forward rates. The best example of this scenario occurred in 1992—the year of the inverse floater. Based on the steepness of the yield curve, the implied forward rates gave a naive indication that short-term rates were expected to rise sharply. Some investors, however, reasoned that outside influences from parties such as the Federal Reserve would want to keep short-term rates down in order to stimulate the economy out of a recession. This strategy turned out to be profitable. However, in the spring of 1994, after the economy recovered, this strategy turned into a losing one. Arguably, the forward curve could be a directional predictor of future rates in extreme situations, when the curve is inverted or excessively steep. As seen from equation (7.12), in the absence of *structural* events that would drastically alter risk, liquidity, or credit components, expectation may be the cause of the shape of the curve. In general, however, investors should not infer much about rates in the future, since the curve has been upward sloped 90 percent of the time. Other factors (as discussed earlier) contributing to the curve need to be investigated before making an investment decision using the shape or slope of the yield curve as a forecast of future rates

COMPLETING THE CURVE

Awareness of the forward curve is a must for fixed-income analysts. But, how can one find this forward curve? A mortgage analytical system, for example, typically requires the knowledge of at least a 360-month vector of forward rates. Using the definitional formulas from the previous section would do the job—provided we know 360 zero-coupon rates. This is a rather impractical demand. Most markets used as pricing benchmarks (swaps, Treasuries, agencies) are given by their several coupon rate points. The example presented in Table 7.3 is a typical input to the pricing system. As seen, there exists a long way between taking this input and delivering a rich set of forward rates. In the final section of this chapter, we review some of the common techniques aimed at solving the problem.

Bootstrapping

Suppose we have a monthly array of zero-coupon rates. Equation (7.4) explicitly maps this set into the matching monthly array of coupon rates. What if we knew the coupon rates? The inverse operation is called **bootstrapping**. Mathematically, we still employ equation (7.4) but sequentially solve for the longest zero-coupon rate, r_n.

Suppose that the coupons are paid periodically. Obviously, r_1 will be equal to the coupon rates on a one-period bond. In order to find r_n for $n = 2, 3, \ldots$, we resolve equation (7.4):

$$(1 + r_n)^n = \frac{1 + c_n}{1 - c_n \sum_{k=1}^{n-1} \frac{1}{(1 + r_k)^k}} \tag{7.14}$$

Note that zero-coupon rates $r_1, \ldots, r_{n-1}$, used in the right-hand side, are assumed to be already found. Coupon rates c_n are the input coupon rates. Table 7.2 can be used to illustrate this process, assuming that the coupon rates are given. The running sum standing in the denominator of the bootstrapping formula (7.14) is the annuity of the previous period.

Let us practice with this calculation the mechanics of reconstructing the zero-coupon curve out of a set of coupon rates. We compute sequentially the third and fourth columns in Table 7.4.

TABLE 7.4 Bootstrapping Table

Maturity	Given Coupon Rate (%)	Computed Annuity (previous period)	Computed Zero Rate (%)
1	3.00	*0*	*3.00*
2	4.00	*0.9709*	*4.0202*
3	5.00	*1.8951*	*5.0689*
4	5.50	?	?

The first line ($n = 1$) seems apparent because the one-period zero- and coupon-rates are identical to each other. The previous period annuity has zero maturity, therefore, is worth zero. To bootstrap the two-period coupon bond ($n = 2$), we find the one-period annuity first. Since it pays $1 at the end of its only period, the value is $1/(1 + 0.03) = 0.9709$; then, the right-hand side of formula (7.14) is computed as $(1 + 0.04)/(1 - 0.04 \times 0.9709) = 1.08202$, which becomes the value for $(1 + r_2)^2$. Taking the square root, we find $r_2 = 4.0202$ percent. We immediately update the table placing just computed annuity and the zero-coupon rate in the second row (italic).

Continuing the bootstrapping job, we move to the third row ($n = 3$). The two-period annuity consists of the one-period annuity (already valued at 0.9709) and $1 paid at the end of the second period. We have found the two-period zero rate (4.0202%); therefore, the two-period annuity is worth $0.9709 + 1/(1 + 0.040202)^2 = 1.8951$. Employing formula (7.14) again, we compute the value for $(1 + r_3)^3$ as $1.05/(1 - 0.05 \times 1.8951) = 1.1600$, or $r_3 = 5.0689$ percent.

This exercise teaches us that the bootstrapping procedure can be easily automated. All it takes to renovate the annuity's value is to add one new term to the previous period annuity. Once we have reconstructed the zero-curve, we can proceed with computing the forward curve, either zero or coupon. We will no longer need to know the spot coupon rates (second column).

Interpolation

Note that, if any of the coupon rates c_n are missing, one will not be able to figure either the zero-coupon rate, r_n, or any longer rates. One simple technique that assumes very few input rates is interpolation. There are a number of interpolation methods that suit different goals and guarantee different degrees of smoothness. Typical results of the simplest approach, **linear interpolation**, are shown in Figure 7.1. We simply draw a straight line connecting two known maturity points, the short rate and the three-year rate, the

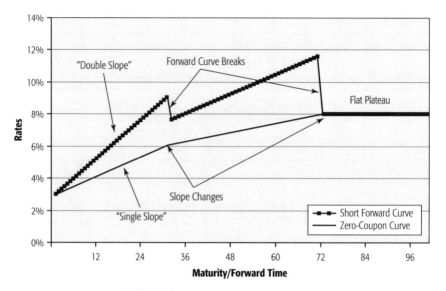

FIGURE 7.1   Spot and forward curves.

three-year rate and the six-year rate, and so forth. Recall that the short forward rate depends on the first derivative of the zero-coupon curve. A piecewise linear zero-coupon curve leads to a discontinuous short forward curve. It may be undesirable for financial engineers.

Another technique, **spline extrapolation**, provides a much smoother curve. For example, cubic splines maintain continuous second derivatives, throughout the entire interpolation range. Therefore, the short forward rate will be continuous, along with its first derivative (slope). It will be by two orders of magnitude smoother than the line in Figure 7.1. Figure 7.2 depicts the result for May 13, 2002, with a bar drawn for the discrete inputs (only the first 120 months are shown).

We have introduced fundamental notions of the fixed-income market: the zero-coupon rate curve, the coupon rate curve, and the forward curve. These curves are mathematically related to each other; they describe the same financial market in different terms. A key modeling idea—the arbitrage-free economy—should not be confused with rate forecasting. The prices will not change if we compute them in an arbitrage-free economy where the rates in the future are the forward rates today. With a firm foundation in the static (certain) market, we are now ready to explore the world of randomness, options, and term-structure models.

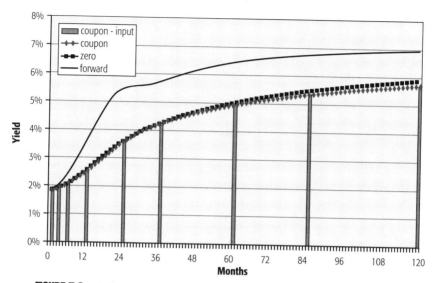

FIGURE 7.2 Spline-interpolated coupon, spot, and short forward curves.

EXERCISES

Exercise 7.1a Convert a 10 percent BEY into MEY and continuously compounded rate.

Exercise 7.1b Assess the difference between MEY and the continuously compounded rate.

Exercise 7.2 Using formula (7.4), check theoretically that the coupon curve would be flat if the zero-coupon curve were flat (i.e., assume that all r_k's are the same).

Exercise 7.3 Using formula (7.10), prove that rules 2 and 3 (on page 100) hold for any maturity n.

Exercise 7.4 Fill in the fourth row of Table 7.4.

CHAPTER 8

Static Analysis for Mortgage Pass-Through Securities

Assets are at the heart of every securitization. They breathe life into the transaction. They form the basis for the investment characteristics of the securities, ranging from credit risk to interest-rate risk and legal structuring. In mortgage-backed securities (MBS), understanding the cash-flow characteristics of the underlying mortgages is the key to creating and evaluating the securities.

Cash flows represent the interplay between the contractual features of the underlying loans and the behavior of the borrowers. In this chapter, we demonstrate how to calculate the cash flows of mortgages and MBS in the context of static analysis. These same cash-flow tools are generalized in other chapters in two different ways. First, cash flows can be calculated for a range of possible economic scenarios. The resulting analysis for a few scenarios is called scenario analysis. When many scenarios are constructed following a particular set of rules, the result is **option-adjusted analysis**. Second, cash flows can also be segmented into a variety of investment instruments, creating structured products such as collateralized-mortgage obligations (CMOs).

Even in the static environment, we must focus on the four phases of analysis: **methodology, collateral, structure,** and **results**.

METHODOLOGY

The static environment is a fantasy used by traders and investors to deal with the uncertainty of the real world. In the static environment, the future is seen with certainty; our crystal ball foresees the correct path of interest rates, prepayment rates, and mortgage cash flows. The static environment holds all factors constant when analyzing value between securities. This method may not be the most advanced way to look at the securities, but it proves to be a useful starting point. The danger of starting with such a tool is that investors often have also used static analysis as an ending point. With complex securities in a dynamic economy, that can be a serious miscalculation.

COLLATERAL

Features of Mortgage Loans

Mortgage **payments** made by fixed-rate borrowers have two interesting features: level payments and payment in arrears. A standard mortgage loan allows the borrower to make the same payment each month during the life of the loan. A portion of the payment is allocated to interest and the remainder is used to reduce the amount of principal. Initially, the amount of interest greatly exceeds the amount allocated to principal. Over time, this relationship changes and the allocation to principal increases greatly. The amount of the monthly cash flow is determined by using an annuity formula.

Payment in arrears means that the borrower makes the first payment one month after the loan is taken out. That is, for a borrower who receives his loan on the first day of September, the first payment is due on October 1. The interest amount will be based on the balance as of September 1.

To determine the monthly payment, we use equation (8.1).

$$\text{Payment} = \frac{\text{Balance} \times \text{Coupon}/1200}{1 - (1 + \text{Coupon}/1200)^{-\text{Remaining Term}}} \tag{8.1}$$

Balance and payment are expressed in dollars, remaining term is in months, and coupon is expressed in annual terms; use 8 for an 8 percent annual rate.

Determining the Monthly Payment

Table 8.1 shows an example of the monthly payment for a 9 percent mortgage with a balance of $200,000.

TABLE 8.1   Mortgage Characteristics

Balance	$200,000.00
Coupon	9.00%
Term	360
Payment	1,609.25

Allocating Monthly Cash Flow Between Principal and Interest

Using the calculations for monthly payment and balance, we can calculate the cash flows for a mortgage loan. Using these cash flows, we can split the monthly payment into a payment for interest and a payment for principal.

For equation (8.2), we can solve for the monthly loan payment. This payment consists of two pieces as shown in equation (8.2).

$$\text{Monthly Payment} = \text{Interest Payment} + \text{Scheduled Principal Payment} \quad (8.2)$$

where,

$$\text{Interest Payment} = \frac{\text{Coupon}}{1200} \times \text{Starting Principal}$$

To solve for the scheduled principal we can use either of two methods. First, we could calculate scheduled principal as the difference between the monthly payment and the interest payment. Alternatively, we could project the scheduled balances using equation (8.3). The differences between consecutive monthly scheduled balances equal the scheduled principal payment.

$$\% \text{ Balance}_t = 1 - \frac{(1 + \text{Coupon}/1200)^{\text{Age}} - 1}{(1 + \text{Coupon}/1200)^{\text{Original Term}} - 1} \quad (8.3)$$

Using the cash flow in Table 8.1, we can allocate the first month's payment between interest and principal, as shown in Table 8.2.

TABLE 8.2 Allocation of Monthly Payment Between Interest and Principal

Balance	$200,000.00
Coupon	9.00%
Term	360
Payment	1,609.25
Interest	1,500.00
Principal	109.25

Prepayments and Curtailments

Borrowers generally have the right to prepay their loans at any time without penalty. (As an exception, many subprime loans, discussed in Chapter 17, do have prepayment penalties.) Borrowers may pay off their loans in full or in part. Borrower motivation for prepayments are discussed in Chapter 9. For a full prepayment, the borrower pays the remaining outstanding balance on the loan. Partial prepayments can be of any amount. While partial prepayments reduce the balance of the loan, they do not alter the scheduled monthly payment. Since the payment remains constant while the balance is reduced, the number of remaining payments declines. Because partial prepayments have the effect of shortening the life of the loan, they are also called **curtailments**.

To this point, we have described mortgage math as it applies to a single loan. A pool of loans works in a similar manner. Generally, only loans with similar characteristics are combined together in a pool; therefore, one can intuitively think of a pool as one huge loan. While this analogy works fairly well, it breaks down with the inclusion of prepayments.

For individual loans, a partial prepayment shortens the life of the loan. However, for a pool, a full prepayment by one borrower does not have the same effect as a partial prepayment of the huge pool. Consider what happens to a pool of loans when borrowers make full prepayments—the average maturity will not be affected. To see this, think of the average of the set {30, 30, 30}. If one of the loans is fully prepaid, the average of {30, 30} is still 30. What will change is the combined monthly scheduled payment. While partial prepayments would alter the maturity of the pool, generally, partial prepayments in aggregate reflect a small portion of the total amounts prepaid and are frequently not included in analysis of MBS.

Prepayment Conventions

While prepayments for an individual borrower are usually an all-or-nothing proposition, for a mortgage pool usually only a portion of the pool prepays in any one month. Prepayments are defined as the difference between the actual balance of the MBS pool compared with the balance expected due to normal amortization. To describe this activity, the market has developed several approaches to describing the amount of prepayments for a pool of loans. Because MBS pools contain different dollar balances, simply reporting prepayments as dollars, would make comparisons across pools difficult. Therefore, all three of these methods reflect a concept of a prepayment percentage or prepayment rate. The market conventions are summarized in Table 8.3.

TABLE 8.3 Prepayment Conventions

Single monthly mortality (SMM)	The SMM measures the percentage of dollars prepaid in any month, expressed as a percentage of the expected mortgage balance.
Conditional prepayment rate (CPR)	CPR reflects the percentage prepayment rate resulting from converting the SMM to an annual rate. The CPR is best understood as the percentage of nonamortized balance prepaid on an annual basis.
Public Securities Association (PSA) model	An industry convention adopted by the Public Securities Association in which prepayment rates, expressed in CPR, are assumed to follow a standard path over time. This path assumes that the prepayment rate for a pool of loans increases gradually over the first 30 months and then levels out at a constant rate. Along the 100 percent PSA curve, the prepayment rate starts at 0.2 percent CPR in the first month and then rises 0.2 percent CPR per month until month 30 when the prepayment rate levels out at 6 percent CPR.

Note: The Public Securities Association is now the Bond Market Association, but the name PSA for the prepayment convention has not changed.

In order to develop a familiarity with the conventions, we present a few equations and then work through some numerical examples.* Equation (8.4) is the calculation for single monthly mortality (SMM). It is the building block for all prepayment calculations.

$$\text{SMM} = 100 \times \frac{(\text{Scheduled Balance} - \text{Actual Balance})}{\text{Scheduled Balance}} \qquad (8.4)$$

In equation (8.4), the scheduled balance represents the expected based on normal amortization.

$$\text{CPR} = 100 \times \left(1 - \left(1 - \frac{\text{SMM}}{100}\right)^{12}\right) \qquad (8.5)$$

---

*Formulas for calculating SMM, CPR, and PSA can be found in The Bond Market Association's *Standard Formulas* manual (2000). Many of the other formulas in this chapter can also be found there.

TABLE 8.4 Sample Prepayment Rate Calculations

Scheduled balance	154,000.00
Actual balance	153,000.00
Age (months)	25
SMM	0.65%
CPR	7.53%
PSA	150.54%

$$PSA = 100 \times \frac{CPR}{\text{Minimum (age, 30)} \times 0.2} \qquad (8.6)$$

Using information about the scheduled balance, actual balance, and age, we can calculate the prepayment rates in SMM, CPR, and PSA formats as seen in Table 8.4.*

STRUCTURE

Pools of Loans

A mortgage pool represents a collection of loans made to individual borrowers. The basic characteristics of these loans generally have been standardized, depending on the agency and program. For example, 30-year loans are grouped together in pools, 15-year loans are grouped together in other pools, and so on. While the loans may share broad similarities, differences do exist: not all the borrowers may be paying the same coupon. The loans may not be the same age when grouped. In recognition of these differences, aggregate pool indicatives are calculated. The values of these indicatives are important inputs to the cash-flow calculations. Fixed-rate MBS generally have the indicatives summarized in Table 8.5.

The indicatives in Table 8.5 have a direct bearing on the determination of the cash flows for an MBS. The WAC and WAM are used to amortize the pool. This information plus the loan age is used to estimate prepayment assumptions.

---

*SMM, CPR, and PSA all represent percentages. It is common, however, for the percent sign to be dropped and to refer, for example, to 200 percent PSA simply as 200 PSA.

TABLE 8.5 Indicatives for Fixed-Rate MBS

Weighted-average remaining maturity (WAM, sometimes called WART or WARM)	The average remaining term of the loans in the pool, averaged based on current balances.
Weighed-average mortgage coupon (WAC)	The WAC represents the gross coupon (the coupon paid by the borrower) weighted by current balance. For GNMA fixed-rate loans, the WAC will be 50 basis points above the net coupon paid to the investor. FHLMC and FNMA will permit a range for the gross coupons in their fixed-rate pools.
Loan age	The number of months since the origination date of the mortgage note. For FHLMC and GNMA fixed-rate MBS, this term is actually computed each month and goes by the name Weighted-Average Loan Age (WALA). In the case of FNMA securities, the age is inferred based on the original loan terms and the number of months since the creation of the pool. FNMA calls this term Calculated Age (CAGE).
Net coupon	The coupon paid to the investor. All loans in a FNMA and FHLMC fixed-rate pool have a gross coupon higher than the net coupon.
Servicing and guarantee fee	The difference between the gross coupon and the net coupon equals the servicing and guarantee fee paid to the agency. Servicing is the fee paid to the party who collects the monthly cash flows from borrowers and passes them along to the investors. The guarantee fee reflects the "insurance" premium paid to the agency. In the event of borrower delinquency or default, cash is paid to the investor from the guarantee fund.

Mortgage-Backed Securities Cash Flows

The cash flows for pass-through MBS can be calculated using the information and equations described earlier. There are several possible approaches that will lead to the same results. The two main alternatives are to calculate the cash flows month by month, applying prepayments each month, or to calculate the cash flows for all months and then scale for prepayments. The month-by-month method is described first.

There are nine steps as follows:

1. Start with the current balance of the pool and the indicative WAC, net coupon, WAM, and age as described in Table 8.5.
2. Compute the scheduled payment for the loan based on the balance, WAC, and WAM at the start of the period.
3. Compute the interest and principal payments.
4. Compute the net interest and servicing cash flows.
5. Compute the scheduled principal balance.
6. Compute the prepayment amount.
7. Deduct the scheduled principal and prepayment amount to determine the beginning principal balance for the next period.
8. Compute the MBS cash flows as the sum of the scheduled principal, prepaid principal, and net interest cash flows.
9. Update the WAM and age and repeat for each period until the pool balance is reduced to zero.

Let us start with the analysis of Table 8.2 and extend from a $200,000 loan to a $20,000,000 pool. We need to use weighted-average coupon, maturity, and age, and we need to separately compute the net interest payment to the investor and the payment to the servicer (see Table 8.6). Normally prepayment rates are specified as either a PSA or CPR equivalent. When calculating cash flows, a translation will have to be made to turn assumed PSA or CPR into an SMM.

Recall from equation (8.4) that SMM is defined by examining the difference between the scheduled balance and the actual balance. We can modify the formula to solve for the actual balance at the end of the first month,

TABLE 8.6   From a $200,000 Loan to a $20,000,000 Pool

Loan		Pool	
Balance	$200,000.00	Pool balance	$20,000,000.00
Coupon	9.00%	WAC	9.00%
Term	360	WAM	360
Payment	1,609.25	Payment	160,925
Interest	1,500.00	Gross interest	150,000
Principal	109.25	Principal	10,925
		Net interest	141,667
		Servicing	8,333

given a scheduled balance and an SMM. Restating equation (8.4) in these terms would provide the following:

$$\text{Actual Balance}_1 = \text{Scheduled Balance}_1 \times \left(1 - \frac{SMM_1}{100}\right) \quad (8.4A)$$

Including prepayments, assuming a 1 percent SMM, we can extend Table 8.6 to Table 8.7.

The first five months of the cash flows are shown in Table 8.8. These results and the graphs that follow can be calculated using the spreadsheet entitled "MBS Price Yield Calculator" on the CD.

Note that using this approach necessitated recomputing the mortgage payment each period based on the new balance and the new remaining term. In the second approach, the mortgage payment is only calculated once. We can generalize equation (8.4A) as:

$$\text{Actual Balance} = \text{Scheduled Balance}_t \times \left[1 - \frac{SMM_t}{100}\right]^t \quad (8.4B)$$

Thus, for any constant prepayment rate we can determine the actual balance by only knowing the scheduled balance and the age of the loan (represented by the subscript t). The scheduled principal payment and the interest payment can be computed in the same way. Equation (8.4B) can be taken one step further, generalizing for the case when the SMM is not constant each month, as shown in equation (8.4C).

$$\text{Actual Balance} = \text{Scheduled Balance}_t \times \prod_{t=1}^{Age} \left(1 - \frac{SMM_t}{100}\right) \quad (8.4C)$$

The mathematical symbol $\prod$ means we take the product of the terms starting from $t = 1$ and proceeding until the actual age of the mortgage in order to find the cumulative prepayment amount.

TABLE 8.7 Including Prepayments, Assuming a 1 Percent SMM

Scheduled balance	19,989,075
Prepaid principal	199,890
Ending balance	19,789,185

TABLE 8.8   Mortgage Cash Flows

Month	Ending Balance	Prepayment Rate (SMM) (%)	Payment
0	20,000,000.00		
1	19,789,184.72	1.00	160,924.52
2	19,580,505.45	1.00	159,315.28
3	19,373,940.74	1.00	157,722.13
4	19,169,469.39	1.00	156,144.90
5	18,967,070.38	1.00	154,583.46

Since prepayment assumptions are usually given in CPR or PSA, it is necessary to convert to SMM to compute the mortgage cash flows. Restating equations (8.5) and (8.6) are exercises at the end of the chapter.

With these tools in hand we can explore the cash flows of MBS under a variety of prepayment assumptions. Figure 8.1 shows the cash flows assuming no prepayments. This example shows how a level-payment loan works.

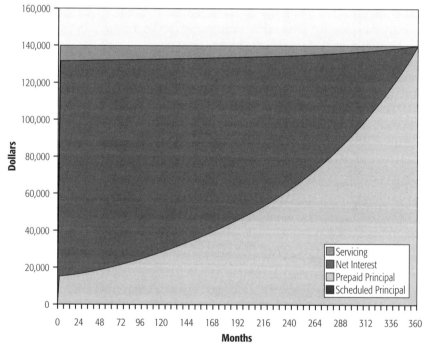

FIGURE 8.1   Zero CPR.

Servicing	Net Interest	Scheduled Principal	Amortized Balance	Prepaid Principal
8,333.33	141,666.67	10,924.52	19,989,075.48	199,890.75
8,245.49	140,173.39	10,896.39	19,778,288.33	197,782.88
8,158.54	138,695.25	10,868.33	19,569,637.11	195,696.37
8,072.48	137,232.08	10,840.35	19,363,100.39	193,631.00
7,987.28	135,783.74	10,812.43	19,158,656.95	191,586.57

The total payment is constant over the 360 months of the loan. The interest portion declines and the principal portion rises each period. The balance tracks the interest payment, since the interest payment represents a fixed percentage of the outstanding balance.

It is extremely unlikely that there would be no prepayments at all. Figure 8.2 represents a relatively low level of prepayments. Loans with no

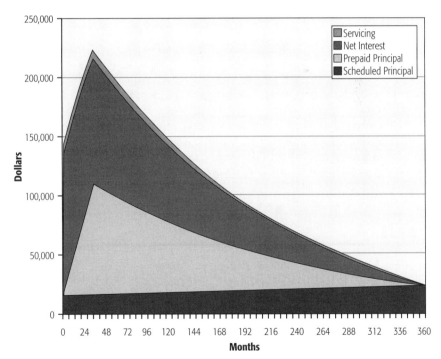

FIGURE 8.2   100 percent PSA.

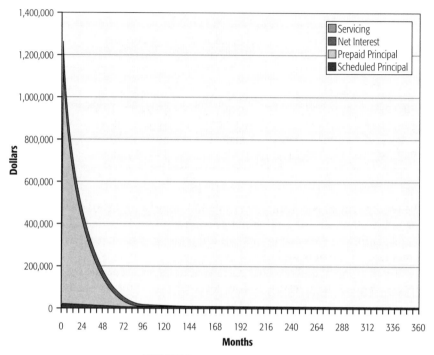

FIGURE 8.3 50 percent CPR.

incentive to refinance may prepay at similar prepayment speeds. Note that even at these relatively slow speeds, prepayment income is about equal to interest income.

In the presence of low interest rates, very fast prepayments are possible. At a 50 percent CPR, as shown in Figure 8.3, the mortgages are substantially paid off in a very few years. The range of possible cash-flow profiles from Figure 8.2 to Figure 8.3 for the same instrument is one of the primary challenges of MBS.

RESULTS

Once we have computed the security cash flows, we are ready to calculate the results for the static methodology (see Table 8.9).

Income

The basic measure of the income associated with an investment is its yield. Yield represents the internal rate of return of the security cash flows as an in-

TABLE 8.9 Results

	Static
Income	Yield
Value	Yield spread
Risk	Weighted-average life Cash-flow duration

vestment, assuming that the purchase of the security is the initial outflow. The purchase price of the security is stated as a percentage of the face amount. For example, at a price of 105, the purchase price of a $1,000,000 MBS pool would be $1,050,000 plus accrued interest. Fractions of 1 percent are expressed in thirty-seconds (1/32). A price of 102–16, equals 102.5 where the –16 represents 16 thirty-seconds (16/32) or one-half (1/2). Sixty-fourths (1/64) are expressed by adding a plus (+) to the price. In this way, a price of 97–5+ would represent 97.171875 percent of face value.

If a security is priced at par and has no delay days, the yield is calculated in such a way so that the yield is equal to the coupon. Delay days reduce the yield because they extend the time until you get your money back. Accrued interest generally serves to offset the impact of the settlement day not being the first day of interest accrual. The combined effect on yield of settlement day and accrued interest together is generally fairly small, but cannot be ignored.

The mathematical definition of yield is shown in equation (8.6).

$$\text{Price} = \frac{\text{Cash Flow}_1}{(1 + \text{Yield}/1200)^{T_1}} + \ldots + \frac{\text{Cash Flow}_{\text{WAM}}}{(1 + \text{Yield}/1200)^{T_{\text{WAM}}}}$$

$$= \sum_{i=1}^{\text{WAM}} \frac{\text{Cash Flow}_i}{(1 + \text{Yield}/1200)^{T_i}}$$

(8.6)

where yield is stated as a percentage, cash flow$_i$ is the cash flow of the security in period i and T_i is the time of the cash flow$_i$ in months. Note that in computing the price the yield is divided by 12. This is because mortgage cash flows occur monthly. Yield calculated in this way is called a mortgage-equivalent yield or MEY.

To account for delay, T in equation (8.6) needs to take into account the time from settlement day to the payment day for the cash flows. To account for accrued interest, the price computed in equation (8.6) is called the full price. The quoted price is the full price minus any accrued interest. Accrued interest is calculated as the interest at the coupon rate on a 30/360 basis. Accrued interest will be calculated as:

$$\text{Balance} \times \text{Coupon}/1200 \times (\text{Settlement Day} -1)$$

For example, if the settlement day is August 20th, there will be 19 days of accrued interest.

Most other fixed-income securities such as government bonds and corporate bonds have semiannual cash flows; that is, interest payments are made twice a year. When calculating yields on these securities, the period of analysis is 6 months. Because of the traditional predominance of these securities and because Treasuries, which pay interest semiannually were typically the benchmark securities, mortgage yields are also most always converted to bond-equivalent basis to ease comparison. To convert MEY to bond-equivalent yield (BEY) it is necessary to determine what coupon would give the same annual return.

$$(1 + \text{MEY})^{12} = (1 + \text{BEY})^2 = 1 + \text{AEY} \qquad (8.7)$$

where AEY is annual-equivalent yield. Since mortgage yields assume more frequent reinvestment, converting MEY to BEY increases the yield. For example, an 8.0 percent MEY is equivalent to an 8.13 percent BEY.

The use of pricing in thirty-seconds (1/32), conventions for accrued interest, and the use of BEYs are all arbitrary market conventions. It is important that market participants learn these conventions in order to better understand results presented by others. Such market conventions, even if they create obstacles to evaluating transactions, tend to have tremendous staying power and are not readily replaced with more easy-to-use measures. (Note: Stock markets have recently moved to decimal pricing.)

Value

Virtually all measures of value are relative value measures. We do not generally seek to say that A or B is a good or bad investment. We generally seek merely to say that A is a better investment than B given some set of objectives. Yield spread, the difference between two yields, can be used as a measure of value if two bonds have similar characteristics, but differ in price and coupon. Typically, yield spreads are calculated by subtracting the yield of an "on-the-run" (actively traded) Treasury from the yield of the MBS. Yield spreads are quoted in basis points. A basis point is one-hundredth of a percent.

TABLE 8.10 Fannie Mae 30-Year MBS Static Analysis

Cpn	Price	WAC	WAM	PSA	Yield	WAL	Bmk	T Yield	Spread
5.5	94–08	6.18	356	139	6.44	9.4	10	5.29	115
6.0	97–11	6.64	356	178	6.49	8.1	10	5.29	120
6.5	99–25	7.03	357	282	6.54	5.9	5	4.79	191
7	101–28	7.59	346	404	6.34	3.8	5	4.79	171
7.5	103–13	8.13	352	553	6.13	3.1	2	3.52	264
8	104–30	8.59	339	604	5.47	2.4	2	3.52	198

Source: Bloomberg L.P., March 13, 2002.

Notes: **Cpn** stands for the net coupon of the pass-through. **Price** is the price in 32nds. **WAC** is the weighted-average coupon. **WAM** is the weighted-average maturity. **PSA** is the projected prepayment speed using the PSA model based on the Bloomberg Median of dealer forecasts. **Yield** is expressed in bond-equivalent format. **WAL** is weighted-average life. **Bmk** is the benchmark Treasury for the yield spread. **T yield** is the yield of the benchmark Treasury. **Spread** represents the difference in yield of the MBS and the benchmark Treasuries.

Table 8.10 shows the calculation of yields and spread for Fannie Mae 30-year mortgage pass-throughs as of March 13, 2002. In the table, the Fannie Mae 6 percent pass-through has a yield of 6.49 percent, while a 10-year Treasury has a yield of 5.29 percent. The yield spread is 1.20 percent or 120 basis points. In this case, the 10-year Treasury is used as the benchmark because the mortgage has a weighted-average life (WAL) of 8.1 years, which is close to 10 years. The WAL is one possible measure of risk. More risk measures are discussed in the next section. It is clear from Table 8.10 that the various pass-throughs do not all have the same yield or spread. The spread rises as the mortgages increase in coupon until 7.5 percent. The 8 percent coupon mortgage then has a lower spread. This variation in spread is one reason why static analysis needs to be supplemented with other tools to assess the value of MBS.

The use of Treasury securities as the benchmark for MBS has been declining over the past few years, as the volume of Treasuries has declined and Treasuries are issued at fewer points along the yield curve. Instead, many investors now compare mortgages to rates in the swap market.

Risk

The standard measure of risk for MBS under static analysis is WAL. For most other fixed-income securities, maturity is the basic measure of risk. Securities with longer maturities tend to fluctuate in price more than securities with shorter maturities as interest rates change. Maturity is not a useful measure of risk for MBS. All newly issued 30-year MBS have 30-year maturities; however, most of the cash flow will be received substantially earlier.

Moreover, the risk characteristics of the security will change as prepayment rates change, but the maturity will remain constant. WAL provides a better measure of the cash-flow timing for MBS because it is calculated by weighting the principal cash flows (scheduled and prepayments) by the time of receipt. Interest cash flows are not included in the calculation.

Figure 8.4 shows an example of the average-life calculation. The graph shows the annual principal cash flows of the security. Note that the last cash flow occurs in year five, so the maturity of the security is 5 years. However, more than half of the cash flow occurs in the first 2 years. In this case, the WAL is 2.33 years. MBS are typically compared to the Treasury with a maturity near the average life of the mortgage. As in the previous example, the Fannie Mae 6 with an average life of 9.4 is spread off of the 10-year Treasury, while the Fannie Mae 8 with an average life of 2.4 is spread off of the 2-year Treasury.

Table 8.11 shows the effect of changing the prepayment assumption on the yield and average life of two MBS. In order to calculate the yield, it is necessary to know also the WAC and WAM of the MBS. Those numbers are taken from Table 8.10. Based on that information, a yield can be calculated

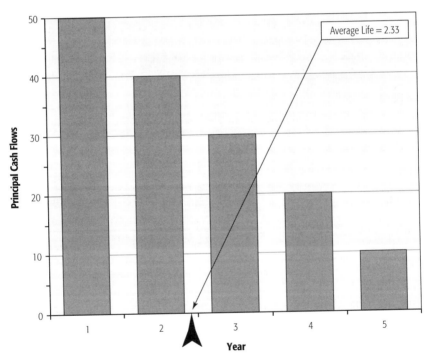

FIGURE 8.4 Average-life calculation.

TABLE 8.11 Prepayment Sensitivity of Yield and WAL

Coupon	Price				
6.0	97-11	CPR	6	9	12
		Yield	6.42	6.49	6.56
		WAL	10.7	8.4	6.7
7.5	103-13	CPR	20	30	40
		Yield	6.44	5.95	5.4
		WAL	4.3	2.8	2.0

given a price and a prepayment speed. Without a prepayment speed, it is impossible to calculate a yield and an average life. Note how higher prepayment speeds result in shorter average lives. Higher prepayment speeds result in higher yields for the discount securities (with price below 100), and lower yields for the premium securities.

Cash-Flow Duration

Duration is a difficult issue for MBS. Normally, we think of duration as providing some measure for the time-value weighting of cash flows. Duration can alternatively be used as a risk measure. In this case, duration would represent the price sensitivity to a change in interest rates. MBS market participants should be aware that duration comes in three basic varieties: Macaulay, modified, and effective.

Macaulay Duration The Macaulay duration represents a time-weighted value of cash flows. For a security whose cash flows do not change with interest rates, the Macaulay duration can be shown to equal the percentage change in price for a percentage change in yield.

$$\text{Duration} = \frac{1}{\text{Price}} \times \left(\sum_{i=1}^{WAM} \frac{T_i \times \text{Cash Flow}_i}{(1 + \text{Yield}/200)^{2T_i}} \right) \quad (8.8)$$

where T is the time elapsed from settlement until receipt of cash flows and yield is the BEY.

Table 8.12 computes the Macaulay duration for a 2-year, semiannual 6 percent coupon-bearing security, currently priced at $100, having a yield of 6 percent. The third column in the table represents the term that is summed in equation (8.8). This term has been labeled the time-weighted discounted cash flow.

TABLE 8.12 Sample Macaulay Duration Calculation

Time	Cash Flow	Time-Weighted Discounted Cash Flow
0.5	3.00	1.4563
1.0	3.00	2.8278
1.5	3.00	4.1181
2.0	103.00	183.0283
Yield	6.00	
Price	100.00	
Duration	1.91	

Modified Duration The modified duration makes a slight change in the Macaulay duration formula. It represents the percentage change in price for a basis-point change in yield, rather than a percentage change in yield.

$$\text{Modified Duration} = \frac{\text{Duration}}{1 + \dfrac{\text{Yield}}{200}} \qquad (8.9)$$

Effective Modified Duration For securities like MBS, measures of modified and Macaulay duration have little meaning when it comes to interest-rate risk management. Both modified and Macaulay durations do not take into account the effect changes in interest rates have on MBS cash flows through prepayments. This cash-flow sensitivity of MBS leads us to use an empirical calculation for duration, shown in equation (8.10).

The prices in the shifted scenarios will reflect changing prepayments and pricing assumptions. These prices can be estimated either by using a valuation model such as option-adjusted spread (OAS), or by determining an approximate change in the prepayment rates and spread of an MBS to an appropriate Treasury benchmark based on the shift in the yield curve.

$$\text{Effective Modified Duration} = \frac{-100}{\text{Price}_{\text{Base}}} \qquad (8.10)$$

$$\times \frac{\text{Price}_{+\Delta\text{Yield Scenario}} - \text{Price}_{-\Delta\text{Yield Scenario}}}{2 \times \Delta\text{Yield}}$$

EXERCISES

Exercise 8.1 Assume a 30-year loan with an 8.5 percent coupon and starting balance of $200,000. Break down the monthly payment between interest and principal and fill in the missing cells of the table. In the exercise, you can solve for the balance in two different ways. You can decrease the balance by subtracting out the scheduled principal, or you can use the scheduled-balance formula. Try using both methods. The first month has already been filled in.

Month	Ending Balance	Principal	Interest
0	200,000		
1	199,878.84	121.16	1,416.67
2			
3			
4			
5			
6			

Exercise 8.2 The impact of a partial prepayment on the life of the loan can be calculated using equation (8.1) and solving for the remaining term. Compute the remaining term of a mortgage with characteristics as in Exercise 8.1: Assume that the borrower makes an extra $2,000 payment in the first month, what is the new remaining term? Assume an extra $100,000 payment in the first month, what is the new remaining term?

Exercise 8.3 Given an MBS with an age of three and a CPR of 1 percent, what is the equivalent PSA rate?

Exercise 8.4 Restate equations (8.6) and (8.5) to solve for CPR given PSA, and SMM given CPR.

Exercise 8.5 Now repeat Exercise 8.4 for the following pairs of ages and CPRs. The first month has already been calculated.

CPR	Age	PSA
1	1	500
1	2	
1	3	
1	4	
1	5	
6	30	
12	60	

Exercise 8.6 Convert PSA rates to CPR.

PSA	Age	CPR
100	1	
500	1	
1000	1	
1666	30	
200	2	

Exercise 8.7 Convert SMM to CPR and PSA equivalents.

Age	SMM	CPR	PSA
5	0.6		
6	1.0		
7	2.0		

⊚ **Exercise 8.8**   Convert the Macaulay duration from Table 8.12 to a modified duration.

⊚ **Exercise 8.9**   Build a price/yield calculator for fixed-rate MBS using the equations in Chapter 8. Compare the calculator to the spreadsheet on the CD or to Bloomberg or another source.

CHAPTER **9**

Mortgage-Backed Securities Prepayments

Prepayments are the primary distinguishing feature of mortgage-backed securities (MBS). Understanding and forecasting prepayments is essential to successful evaluation of MBS as investments. Without prepayments, mortgages would be easy to analyze. However, if MBS were so simple, the number and scope of investment opportunities would be severely limited. Prepayments are the double-edged sword of the MBS market. They create opportunity, but they also create risk.

The individual mortgages underlying MBS are the collateral for the securities. The performance of the collateral drives the performance of the securities. In this chapter, we take a closer look at an important aspect of the collateral, its prepayment behavior. The complexities of prepayment behavior are the source of much of the complexity of the securities created from mortgages. Thus, sophisticated valuation tools are required to evaluate MBS and collateralized-mortgage obligations (CMOs) created from mortgage collateral. Prepayments represent the actions of individuals; therefore, forecasting prepayments requires forecasting the aggregate impact of these individual decisions. In this chapter, we look at actual prepayment data. Before we even begin the modeling process, thorough analysis of the data is required. We need to understand the limitations of the data while we are identifying the key factors that drive prepayments.

Changing prepayment patterns can drastically alter the cash flows of MBS. The figures in Chapter 8 show a comparison of the cash flows of a security with no prepayments at a 100 percent Public Securities Association (PSA) assumption and at a 50 percent conditional prepayment rate (CPR). The cash flow pattern of the security is determined almost entirely by the prepayment rate. Even at the relatively slow prepayment rate of 100 percent PSA, the prepaid principal cash flow is a large portion of the monthly cash flow.

To value MBS, it is crucial to forecast prepayment rates properly. Proper forecasting requires understanding the causes of prepayments historically, and then uses judgment to determine whether those same forces or new factors will produce prepayments in the future. Because prepayments represent the combined actions of millions of individual borrowers, statistical techniques are used to measure and forecast prepayments.

SOURCES OF PREPAYMENTS

Prepayments arise from **moving, refinancing,** and **default**. Prepayments from moving establish a base prepayment rate for most securities. This base rate of prepayments is referred to as **turnover**. Most conventional (nongovernment) mortgages contain a **due-on-sale** clause. When the house is sold, the mortgage must be paid in full. Government mortgages (those insured by the FHA and VA) are generally assumable. Assumable loans can be passed to the next home owner, provided that the home owner meets certain requirements. Factors that increase household relocation such as job changes, marriage, divorce, and children will increase turnover.

Technically, defaults are not prepayments. However, for security holders, the effects are the same as a prepayment. When a loan defaults, the principal balance of the loan is paid to the investor. In this way, the investor is protected from the credit risk of the borrowers and need only look to the guarantor, generally Ginnie Mae, Fannie Mae, or Freddie Mac, for assurance that the principal is secure. Prepayments due to default for agency MBS represent only a small fraction of the monthly prepayments and do not need to be forecast separately. (For non-agency pass-throughs, lower quality mortgages, and other types of collateral, defaults may represent a significant component of security performance. For those securities, it is important to forecast defaults to determine if the credit support is sufficient and to assess the impact of defaults on security cash flows (see Chapter 15).

Refinancing represents the largest and most variable component of prepayments. Refinancing reflects the borrower's right to prepay the loan at any time without penalty. In periods of falling rates, borrowers may seek to reduce their mortgage costs by paying off their higher-coupon loans and taking out new lower-coupon loans. Borrowers may take advantage of lower interest rates or improving home values to borrow more money when refinancing by means of what is called a **cash-out refinance**. In addition, some borrowers may seek to accelerate their loan payments. Additional principal payments reduce the principal outstanding but do not reduce the required monthly payment. Loans with additional prepayments will be paid off prior to their original terms, therefore, the additional payments are called **curtailments**, since they curtail or shorten the term of the loan.

A borrower's decision to refinance is driven by a wide range of factors. Each borrower faces a unique set of conditions, so borrowers tend to exercise their options differently. In this respect, we say the borrowers are **heterogeneous**. Some borrowers require only a slight economic incentive to prepay, while others require a greater incentive. Forecasting prepayments involves estimating how these various borrowers will react to changing economic conditions.

PREPAYMENT DATA

The key to understanding prepayments is prepayment data. Since each borrower faces a different prepayment decision, and since borrowers exercise their options differently, it is impossible to predict prepayments on purely economic grounds without understanding the borrowers' characteristics. Early attempts to value MBS relied on economic models to value the borrower's option. These models tended to overstate payments severely. The modelers then concluded that borrowers exercised their options inefficiently and tried to measure the degree of inefficiency for different types of loans. Rather than assume that the model is right and people are wrong, we feel it is more appropriate to attempt to find a model that describes people's actions. In real life, people face costs and life situations that reduce their incentives to refinance. We must examine actual prepayment patterns to assess the impact of these factors on borrower behavior.

Prepayment data is perhaps the most extensive source of information on individual's financial decision making. Most prepayment data is available at the pool level, but more and more loan-level data is becoming available. Prepayment data are available for a variety of loan types and across a variety of interest-rate environments. While the amount of prepayment data available is extensive, there are still limitations. Figure 9.1 shows the amount of GNMA 30-year mortgages outstanding as of May of 2002 based on year and quarter of origination (starting in 1996) and at varying coupon levels. This is the raw material we have to work with.

Figure 9.1 is a contour graph. It is like looking at a mountain range from above. The various shades reflect the height of the mountains. From the graph, we can see that there are only a limited range of coupons produced each year. The ridge of the mountain reflects where the prevailing mortgage rates were each quarter. Low interest rates at the end of 1998 sparked a strong round of mortgage issuance. Over the time period, most of the mortgages were created

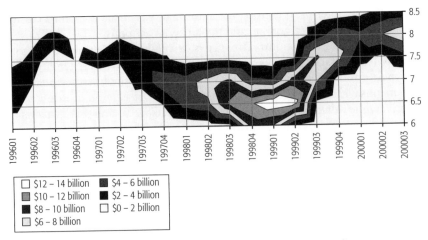

FIGURE 9.1   GNMA 30-year: Current amount outstanding.

with net coupons of 6.5 percent to 8 percent. Thus, while we might be interested to know how GNMA 6.5s that originated in the fourth quarter of 1996 have prepaid in 1999, there are little or no data available.

When forecasting prepayments, we attempt to understand how similarly situated loans prepaid in the past. Two of the most important determinants of prepayments are the age of the loan and the coupon of the loan relative to current refinancing opportunities. Many mortgage modelers use the difference between the mortgage rate and the current coupon yield (the yield on the MBS trading closest to par) as a measure of the refinancing incentive.

Figure 9.2 shows a different view of the loans in Figure 9.1. This figure shows the range of loan age and coupon difference that has occurred for the

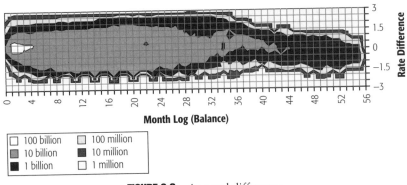

FIGURE 9.2   Age and difference.

loans originated since 1996. Outside these ranges, it is necessary to extrapolate to forecast prepayment rates. For example, over the past few years, few loans have experienced a coupon difference in excess of 2.5 percent or less than –2.0 percent. Therefore, it is difficult to know how these loans would have performed under more extreme interest-rate scenarios. Therefore, estimates of prepayments outside the range of recent experience must be developed using older loans and different time periods. However, as economic conditions change, past prepayment data become less valuable for forecasting future prepayments.

For example, prior to the early 1980s, there were no adjustable-rate mortgages (ARMs), so prepayments that result from borrowers switching to ARMs cannot be forecast from earlier data. Likewise, in the middle of the 1990s, a variety of new loan types with various balloon periods, ARMs with long first resets, and loans to borrowers with a variety of credit impairments, became more widespread. These product innovations alter the prepayment behavior of borrowers.

The strength of the economy and the shape of the yield curve can also have a significant impact on prepayments. When current economic conditions and yield curve shapes differ markedly from recent experience, historical prepayment data become a less reliable source for predicting future prepayments. Therefore, all prepayment forecasts must be tempered with some degree of judgment.

The primary source of prepayment data for agency loans is factor tapes. These data are not produced to support prepayment analysis, but are a by-product of trading information. To buy or sell MBS, it is necessary to know the current balance of the pools in the transaction. The balance is expressed by the pool factor. These pool factors are produced monthly and can be used to calculate prepayments. Analysis of prepayments involves linking prepayments to pool characteristics.

While it might be helpful to link prepayments to a variety of details about the borrower, such as income or number of children, that information generally is not available at the pool level. The data that are available include: type of loans, average maturity, average loan age, and average loan coupon. In some cases information about loan size, the geographic distribution of the pool, and some additional information about the distribution of loan coupons are available. Prepayments must be forecast using only the features that are available.

In addition to the information provided by the agencies in conjunction with factor tapes, other market participants have sought out more detailed loan and pool data to facilitate prepayment forecasts and to identify groups of loans that may have superior investment characteristics. Financial institutions, including Fannie Mae and Freddie Mac, which originate, service, or guarantee the loans they hold on their books frequently have substantially more information about the borrowers and their homes. They can capitalize on these data to refine their understanding of prepayments within their portfolios.

ANALYZING PREPAYMENTS

Prepayments change based on a variety of factors. One way to understand prepayments is through graphical analysis. Prepayment patterns can be viewed by slicing the prepayment data into various cuts, which expose different aspects of prepayment behavior.

Figure 9.3 is an example of some prepayment data. This chart represents the prepayments on a variety of GNMA loans originated in 1996 with a range of coupons. Each line is the prepayment rate of a different cohort of loans over the period from 1996 to 2000. The prepayment rates are expressed as conditional prepayment rates (CPRs). The chart also shows the

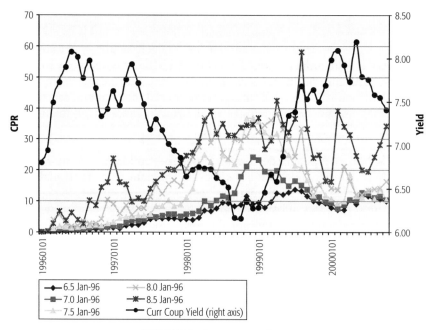

FIGURE 9.3 Prepayment data.

interest rate for the current coupon GNMA MBS. This chart shows the dynamic nature of prepayments. (The data for this chart are included on the CD (see "GNMA Prepayment Data") and can be used for the exercises at the end of the chapter.) Several of the important factors that affect prepayments can be seen in this graph. We discuss several of them in the following paragraphs.

Interest-rate levels are the most important influence on prepayment rates. As interest rates fall, borrowers refinance their loans, leading to higher prepayment rates. Figure 9.4 demonstrates this effect. Differences greater than zero indicate that the coupon on the loan is higher than the current interest-rate levels. Differences less than one indicate that the coupon on the loan is below market-rate levels. As the difference increases, prepayment rates accelerate. Prepayments on loans with differences below zero are relatively constant.

The interest-rate effect reflects the fact that borrowers will exercise their prepayment option when they can **refinance** on more favorable terms. Whether borrowers are focused on changes in rates, changes in monthly payments, or a more complex economic formula is an area of much discussion. The relatively constant prepayments for the loans with differences less than zero represent prepayments that are not motivated by the opportunity

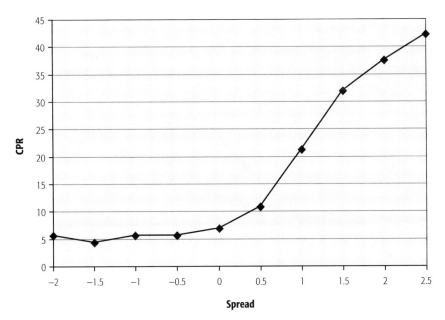

FIGURE 9.4 Interest-rate effect GNSF (Ginnie Mae Single Family) CPR.

to refinance. Instead, these prepayments reflect the fundamental **turnover** in the housing market. These loans are generally discount loans, because they would have prices less than par or 100. Loans with a positive difference are called premium loans. This chart clearly shows the significance of refinancing on prepayments.

Borrowers do not prepay their mortgages immediately when rates fall. There is a time lag between changes in interest rates and changes in prepayment rates. This lag is generally about 2 months, which reflects the amount of time for borrowers to apply, qualify, and close a new loan to prepay the old loan. It also reflects the time from when the borrower prepays the loan until the time that the principal payment is received by the MBS investor. A close look at Figure 9.3 shows this effect. Find the lows and highs of mortgage rates during a variety of periods. You will see that the highs and lows of prepayments trail by a few months.

MBS from different loan programs may face differing refinance incentives. Figure 9.5 shows the prepayment rates on GNMA and FNMA 30-year mortgages and 15-year maturity GNMA mortgages all originated in the year 2000 as of April 2001. The graph shows the prepayment speed for various net coupon mortgages. During this time period, the FNMA current coupon yield was around 6.5 percent. The FNMA MBS show the greatest refinancing effect. The FNMA prepayments rise more rapidly than the GNMA MBS prepayments as you move from discount coupons to premium

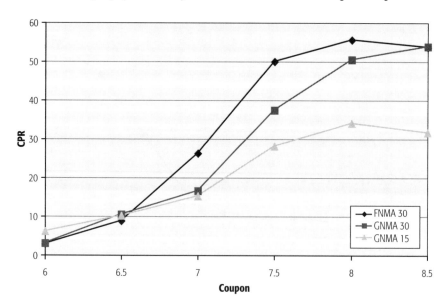

FIGURE 9.5 Comparison of rate effects.

coupons. The 15-year mortgages have less of a refinancing effect. The reduced interest-rate effect for 15-year loans may reflect the shorter time horizon to recover any interest savings when refinancing, or the reduced savings from lowering the mortgage coupon.

Aging is the second major influence on prepayments. Aging reflects that new loans prepay more slowly. Aging is the reason for the development of the Public Securities Association (PSA) curve described in Chapter 8. Figure 9.6 shows the aging pattern of GNMA loans, divided between premium and discount coupons. The premium loans have a positive incentive to refinance since their coupons are greater than the prevailing market rate, whereas discount loans do not since their coupons are less than current market rates. The graph clearly shows that newer loans tend to prepay more slowly. For discount loans, prepayments rise at a steady rate and then level off at a peak CPR. However, not all loans age at the same rate. The premium loans shown in the graph reach their peak speeds sooner than the discount loans. In recent years, many new loans have exhibited very short ramping periods in falling interest-rate environments. Different types of loans may also have different aging periods. Because of the variation in the time period for aging, the PSA curve should be used with caution, since it assumes the same aging period for all types of loans and all coupons.

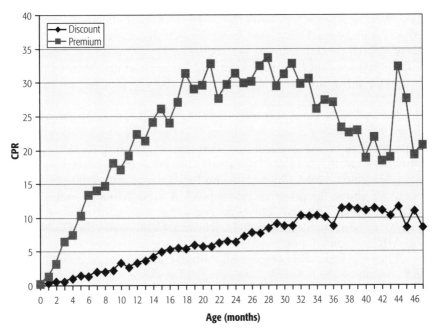

FIGURE 9.6   Prepayments by loan age.

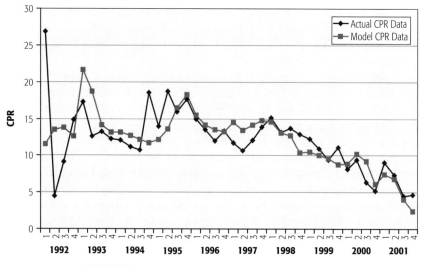

FIGURE 9.7   Prepayments by quarter of origination.

Looking at loans originated at different time periods provides another view of aging. Figure 9.7 shows the prepayments for FNMA 6.0s originated in different quarters. Note how the new loans, issued in the more recent quarters, exhibit slower prepayments. The loans do not reach their peak speeds until they are 3 to 4 years old. The chart also shows the forecast prepayment rate from the Andrew Davidson & Co., Inc. prepayment model.

Burnout is the next most important effect on prepayments, and probably the most difficult to measure. Burnout reflects that as interest rates fall, prepayment rates increase and then decrease, even if interest rates remain constant. Even if rates then fall further, the prepayment rates may never reach their initial peaks. Once again graphical analysis can demonstrate this. Figure 9.8 shows the prepayments on GNMA 9.5s originated in the fourth quarter of 1989. The chart shows the prepayment speeds from the time the loans were originated through 2001. The chart also shows the GNMA 30-year MBS current coupon yield.

When the loans were originated, mortgage rates were near the 9.5 percent coupon on the loans. As interest rates fell at the end of 1993, prepayment speeds increased rapidly reaching a peak of 58 percent CPR. As interest rates rose in 1994, the prepayment speeds declined. However, in 1998 when interest rates fell back to around 6 percent, the prepayment speeds for the most part stayed below 40 percent CPR. Burnout depends on

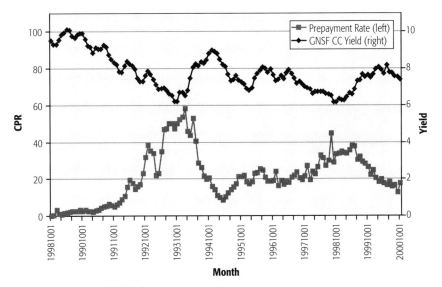

FIGURE 9.8 Burnout effect for GNMA 30 9.5.

past levels of interest rates and prepayment rates, therefore making prepayment modeling and forecasting more difficult.

Another view of burnout can be seen by looking at loans with the same coupon originated at different time periods. Figure 9.9 shows the prepayments on FNMA 7.5s originated in different time periods. The newest loans are prepaying at 40 percent CPR, while the slightly older loans have prepayments of about 70 percent. These loans are reaching their peak speeds after about 12 months. Older loans are exhibiting much slower prepayment speeds than the new loans.

The burnout effect can best be understood by viewing an MBS pool as the loans of a collection of heterogeneous borrowers. Each borrower faces unique conditions. Some have large families, others are single. They live in different parts of the country and have different educational and economic backgrounds. Given the diversity of the borrowers, it is not surprising that they require different incentives to refinance. As rates fall, first the borrowers with the greatest propensity to refinance do so. The borrowers left in the pool face higher refinancing costs (economic and noneconomic). These borrowers tend to prepay at a slower rate than the first group of borrowers. Eventually, the only borrowers left in the pool are those who have a very high refinancing threshold. At this point we say that the pool is burnt out. It will continue to show some prepayments, but those prepayment rates will be lower than for new pools.

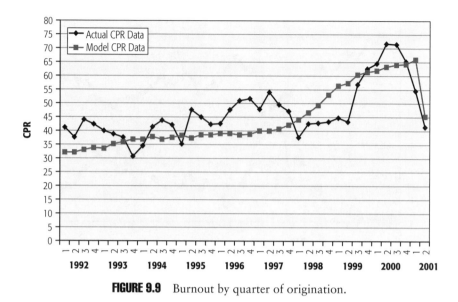

FIGURE 9.9   Burnout by quarter of origination.

Figure 9.10 shows a simple example of burnout. Suppose a pool of 100 loans is made of 80 fast prepaying borrowers who prepay at 75 percent per year and 20 slow prepayers who prepay at 10 percent per year. During the first period, you would expect prepayments of 62 percent $(0.80 \times 75\% + .20 \times 10\%)$. After one year, three-quarters of the fast prepaying borrowers are

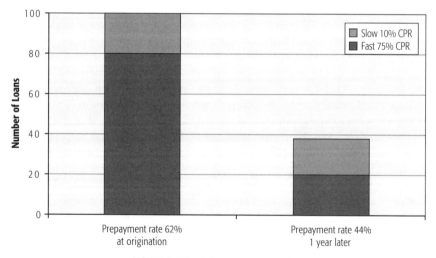

FIGURE 9.10   A burnout example.

gone. Only 10 percent of the slow prepaying borrowers have prepaid. The remaining composition is 20 fast and 18 slow. The new expected prepayment rate is about 44 percent.

Seasonality is another major influence on prepayment rates. Seasonality reflects the close interaction of prepayments with housing market activity. As shown in Figure 9.11, prepayments tend to be faster during the summer months and slower during the winter months, reflecting increased home turnover during the summer months. Seasonality is more pronounced on discount loans where the refinancing effects do not swap the turnover component of prepayments. Refinancing does not seem to have as large a seasonal component. While this information is based on a limited data sample, it reflects some commonly observed features. Prepayments tend to be highest in May and July and there is usually a slight uptick in December, perhaps reflecting year-end tax strategies and moving during the holidays. Seasonality tends to have little effect on the valuation of most MBS. However, seasonality is important when evaluating reported prepayments. Faster prepayments in the summer may not reflect any shift in longer-term prepayment patterns and will probably be followed by slower prepayments in the fall and winter.

Housing markets and **yield-curve shape** also influence prepayments. Weaker economic activity, declining house prices, and unemployment all

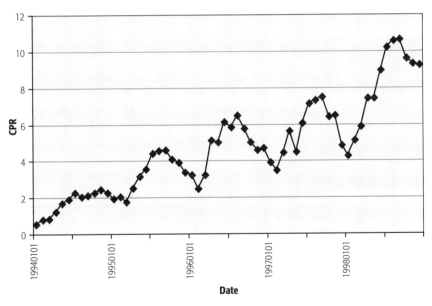

FIGURE 9.11   Seasonality.

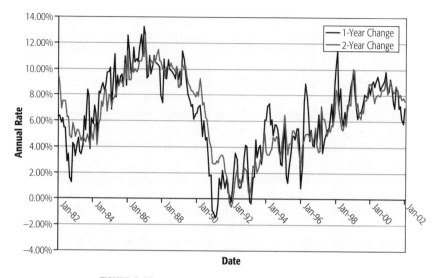

FIGURE 9.12   One-year home price appreciation.

tend to depress prepayments. These factors are sometimes regional in nature and can lead to large differences in prepayments across the United States. During the 1990s home price appreciation varied greatly from almost no growth during the first part of the decade to rapid growth during the last few years of the 1990s. Home price appreciation affects prepayments because rising home prices increase the financial opportunities available to borrowers (see Figure 9.12).

The shape of the yield curve can also impact prepayments. With the development of a variety of mortgage products, such as ARMs and balloon loans, borrowers can choose products that price off of different parts of the yield curve. When the curve is steep, borrowers may refinance into shorter maturity loans to reduce their borrowing costs.

PREPAYMENT MODELS

Evaluation of the investment characteristics of MBS requires estimates of prepayment rates. These estimates can take various forms, from a single assumption chosen based on experience to complex models, which take into account loan level details.

These forecasts, regardless of their source, are used to understand the performance characteristics of MBS and to determine appropriate valuation of different investments. Prepayment forecasters face a fundamental problem. They seek to estimate future events in a changing world. For example, new loan types are constantly being created and the loan origination process is continually evolving. Still, the primary guide to future prepayments is past prepayments. Thus, forecasters develop models that seek to explain prior prepayments. They hope that this information will provide valuable insights into future prepayments. Since the economic and social environments are constantly changing and prepayments are affected by a host of factors, it is unlikely that any historically based analysis will completely reflect future prepayments.

Investing based on prepayment models is a little like driving while looking through the rearview mirror. It may be hard to stay on the road, but it is better than driving with your eyes closed.

Good models are robust and parsimonious. Robust models provide good forecasts under a variety of conditions; that is, they do not need to be adjusted continually in order to reflect changing environments. If the models need to be changed frequently, then they probably will not provide accurate forecasts of future prepayments. Parsimonious means that the models are as simple as possible. Parsimonious models capture the major variables that affect prepayments using the fewest number of parameters and have the advantage that they do not "over fit" the data like a model with too many factors. The use of complex models with many parameters may result in an excellent fit to historical data, but will not provide accurate projections. The added variables may reflect a spurious one-time correlation rather than real long-term relationships. Parsimonious models are also easier to incorporate into valuation tools.

Many approaches have been used to transform the economic features observed in the data into mathematical equations. These approaches may differ in econometric sophistication and in their requirements for data. Some models may be easy to implement in a variety of analytical tools. Some may be restricted to only certain types of analysis.

By far the simplest technique is to develop a table that says what the average prepayment speed would be for shifting interest rates. Such a table could use the difference between the weighted-average coupon (WAC) and the current coupon yield as the driving variable. The entries in the table could reflect some historical average experience. Such a table might look something like Table 9.1.

TABLE 9.1 Rate Effect

Difference	−2	−1	0	1	2	3
CPR	6	8	10	15	45	50

Graphically, Table 9.1 would look like Figure 9.13. This graph has an S-like shape that starts off at a low level and then rises to a peak level. Early prepayment analysts (in the 1980s) noticed that this shape was similar to the arctangent function shown in Figure 9.14. A transformation of the arctangent function to roughly match the shape of Figure 9.13 would provide a simple model of prepayments. While the arctangent function could roughly capture the interest-rate effect, it was not capable of incorporating the other observed features of prepayments. Moreover, arctangent is not particularly tractable in a statistical framework.

Another form of prepayment modeling is using ordinary least squares (OLS) regression. The prepayment speed is the dependent variable and the various driving factors are the independent variables. In this form

$$CPR = \alpha + \beta_1 x_1 + \beta_2 x_2 + \beta_3 x_3 + \varepsilon \qquad (9.1)$$

Exercise 9.3 shows how to build a model in this form. OLS presents several problems for prepayment modeling. The first problem is that it is possible for the output to be negative. There are two potential solutions to this problem. One is to constrain the inputs, outputs, or regression so that the results are always positive. Another is to transform the equation so the output is always positive.

There are many possible transformations of prepayment rates for analysis. The first transformation is choosing the form of prepayment to be modeled. Prepayments can be expressed in dollar amounts, single monthly mortality (SMM), CPR, PSA, or even a number of loans. Generally, we believe that it is best to forecast SMMs, since that is the number most likely to be used in further analysis. SMM has the additional advantage that it is analogous to the monthly probability of prepayment for loan level models (discussed in Chapter 16).

The logit transformation has the form:

$$SMM = 1/[1 + \exp(-x)] \qquad (9.2)$$

$$x = -\ln((1/SMM) - 1) \qquad (9.3)$$

After the transformation using equation (9.3) it is possible to perform OLS or a variety of other techniques. The results of the regression equation are transformed using equation (9.3) to produce the prepayment forecast as an SMM.

Using linear-regression techniques poses another problem for prepayment modeling. Many of the factors affecting prepayments are nonlinear and may interact with other factors. Using linear techniques requires the

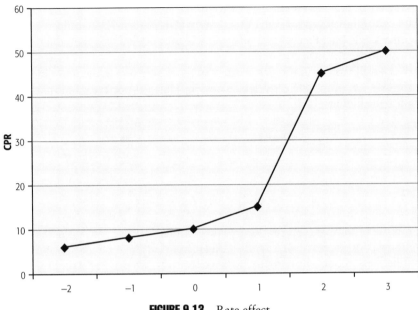

FIGURE 9.13   Rate effect.

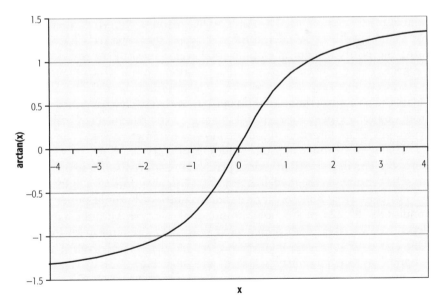

FIGURE 9.14   Arctangent function.

modeler to reformulate the input variables to reflect these nonlinear features. For example, the refinancing curve shown in Figure 9.13 could not be fit with a single line. Piecewise, linear models can be used, but then the modeler must choose the inflection points.

To address the nonlinear features of mortgage prepayments, some modelers use nonparametric models. These models do not require a particular function such as

$$y = a + bx, \quad \text{or} \quad y = a + bx^2 \quad\quad (9.4)$$

or even

$$y = a + b \times \arctan(c + d \times x) \quad\quad (9.5)$$

to fit the nonlinear features. Rather the data itself is used to derive the shape of the various factors such as the aging effect and the interest-rate incentive. While these models have many positive features, we generally find that nonparametric models do not always provide the best forecasts and are generally cumbersome to implement because of the general nature of the relationships between variables.

With pool-level models, fast computers allow for the use of a variety of other solution techniques. These may involve various optimization techniques and hybrid approaches that allow for the use of linear, nonlinear, and nonparametric functions. The Andrew Davidson & Co., Inc., model used for a comparison of actual and forecast prepayment speeds was developed using the NLIN (nonlinear optimization techniques) of the SAS statistical package. The approach is to develop a functional form, which the modelers believe describes prepayment patterns. The optimization is then used to calculate the parameter values. For loan types with less data, parameter values from one loan type are used to fill in some of the parameters for the other type and the optimization fills in the missing parameter values.

Prepayment modeling techniques also vary in how they address burnout. The degree of burnout depends on past events. These past events must be captured in the modeling process. Moreover, forecasts of future prepayments must be able to capture the dynamics of burnout under varying conditions. Simple models of burnout may capture burnout as a time-dependent variable, with prepayment sensitivity declining with loan age. This approach may appear attractive due to its simplicity, but it will not properly capture the prepayment dynamics since burnout is driven by interest changes, not time.

A good burnout measure must dynamically measure the refinancing opportunity faced by the borrowers. One good candidate for a measure of burnout is the pool factor. Since past prepayments reduce the pool balance, the pool factor may be a good proxy for the degree of burnout in a pool. Other models may use various constructed variables to reflect the degree of burnout. One such variable would be similar to pool factor, but would exclude the impact of amortization and turnover. Another potential variable used as a proxy for burnout could be based on the history of past interest rates. Modeling prepayments in this fashion makes evaluation of MBS more difficult. These types of prepayment functions are path-dependent, in that for any period, the prepayment forecast does not only depend on the state of the input variables today, but also on the state of certain variables in the past. Path-dependent prepayment models cannot be used with some of the valuation techniques described in Chapter 12, instead, they require the use of simulation techniques as described in Chapter 13.

Rather than modeling burnout indirectly through a proxy variable, burnout can be modeled directly by dividing the mortgage pool into component parts that have different prepayment rates. A simple, but powerful method is **active/passive decomposition.***

In active/passive decomposition the active portion of the pool is assumed to be sensitive to interest rates, while the passive portion is insensitive to rates. The passive portion experiences turnover. In falling interest-rate environments the proportion of fast-paying active borrowers declines, reducing the overall prepayment speed on the pool. The active and passive components can be valued separately using standard valuation techniques, thereby avoiding the need for the more time-consuming simulation techniques commonly used for MBS.

Evaluating Prepayment Models

Prepayment models represent a fit of an equation to past data. One of the best ways to evaluate the model is to examine the fit for various mortgage coupons. Traditional econometric and statistical analysis may not provide sufficient insight into the strength and weakness of various approaches, especially for the more complex models. Figures 9.15 and 9.16 show the fit of the Andrew Davidson & Co., Inc., Version 4.3 model against actual historical prepayment patterns.

Figure 9.15 shows the results of the Andrew Davidson & Co., Inc., prepayment model for October 2002. The graph shows the actual prepayment speeds versus the forecast prepayment speeds across coupons of Fannie Mae

---

*A. Levin. "Deriving Closed-Form Solutions for Gaussian Pricing Models: A Systematic Time-Domain Approach," *International Journal of Theoretical and Applied Finance* 1, no. 3 (1988): 349–376.

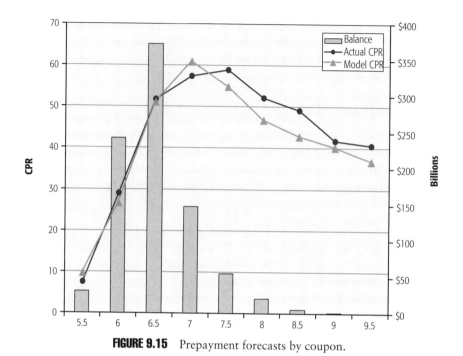

FIGURE 9.15 Prepayment forecasts by coupon.

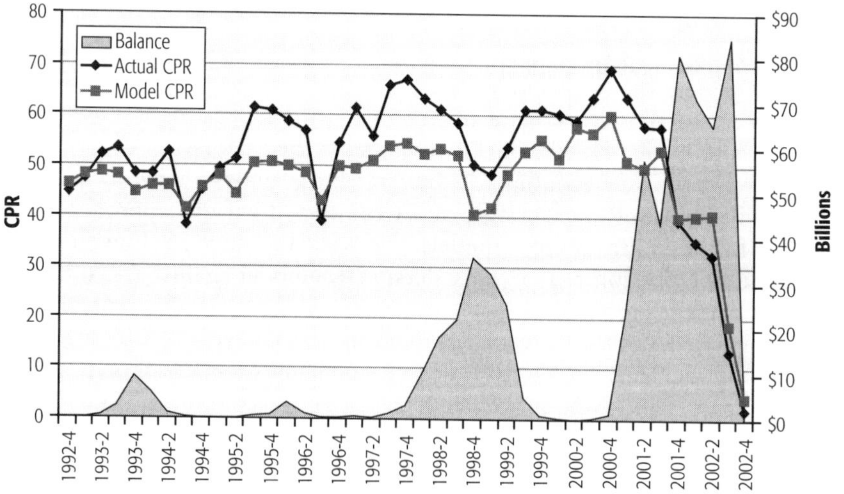

FIGURE 9.16 Prepayment forecasts by year of origination.

30-year mortgages. The bars show the amount of loans outstanding for each coupon. At this time the 6.5 mortgages had the greatest amount outstanding. Note also how prepayment speeds increase and then decline. At the time this graph was constructed, current coupon mortgages had a yield of about 5.3 percent. The prepayment speeds decline for the higher-coupon mortgages, reflecting the impact of burnout offsetting the increased incentive to prepay.

Figure 9.16 also shows prepayment forecasts versus actual prepayment speeds for October 2002. This chart shows the prepayments as a function of the date of origination of the loans for 6 and 6.5 percent coupon loans. Older loans are on the left of the chart. Prepayments are low for recently originated loans and then rise. Older loans tend to have slower prepayment speeds.

The major Wall Street firms have similar prepayment models. Bloomberg L.P. computes the median prepayment speeds for the dealers. A sample of the median results is shown in Figure 9.17.

Although the prepayment model does a good job of capturing the major movements in prepayments, there is still some variability that the model does not explain. Many modelers seek to get an extremely good fit to the historical data. However, a good fit does not necessarily produce a good model. Developing a model that captures the essential economics of prepayments

Page   DG65 Govt   **VMED**

B.Median   Mortgage Default Table   Mortgage Ticker: FNCL   Age:TBA
12/13/02
LAST UPDATE   **Bloomberg**   Page 2 of 2
            PAGE   for   Graph   MEDIAN PREPAYMENTS

		WAM			TRSRY								
							DIRECTED		VALUES				
CPN	PSA	YR	MO	WAC	SPRD	-300	-200	-100	-50	+50	+100	+200	+300
5.000	166	29	8	5.770	10	1522	1625	525	248	134	123	121	121
5.500	281	29	10	6.150	5	1910	1980	1249	555	164	139	122	108
6.000	466	29	8	6.560	5	1976	1908	1686	1118	259	177	142	124
6.500	782	29	1	7.015	2	1623	1622	1604	1321	377	245	164	139
7.000	911	28	6	7.550	2	1241	1235	1230	1121	623	363	193	161
7.500	805	29	5	8.130	2	1011	1000	952	898	686	517	249	175
8.000	730	27	8	8.590	2	879	855	832	820	642	542	301	186
8.500	681	27	7	9.115	2	816	797	770	735	623	570	390	231
9.000	696	27	7	9.720	2	735	736	734	729	663	621	531	305
9.500	546	22	7	9.960	2	626	622	599	580	501	466	372	261
10.000	506	18	1	10.540	2	888	691	551	541	452	415	340	242
10.500	441	17	7	11.050	2	477	468	459	455	405	357	296	255

FIGURE 9.17   Median prepayment speeds.

Source: Copyright 2002 Bloomberg LP. Reprinted with permission. All rights reserved.

will produce a more reliable forecasting and cash-flow-generation tool than will a model that has many additional parameters that improve historical fit without providing any additional insight into prepayment behavior.

The prepayment models described so far deal with aggregate data. The models are driven primarily by pool-level characteristics such as the weighted-average coupon, the age of the loans, and perhaps the state of origination. With increasing access to mortgage data and increasing computational power to handle that data, it is possible to develop models that address prepayments at the most fundamental level—the individual borrower. Using underwriting information and zip code-level home price indexes, the models may be able to predict prepayment more precisely. These types of models are also used to assess the credit risk of mortgage pools. Loan-level modeling is discussed in Chapter 16 in conjunction with non-agency mortgages.

EXERCISES

Exercise 9.1 Compute the change in payment for a 100-basis-point drop in rates for a 15-year mortgage and a 30-year mortgage. Compute the present value (PV) savings.

Term (yrs)	Balance ($)	Rate (%)	Payment ($)	New Rate (%)	Payment ($)	PV at New Rate ($)
15	X	8				
30	X	8				
30	100,000	8				
30	100,000	12				
30	100,000	5				
30	50,000	8				
30	200,000	8				

Exercise 9.2 In order to use the arctangent function for prepayment analysis, it is necessary to transform the function to match the prepayment curve. The arctangent function can be transformed by using a function of the form: $CPR = a + b \times (\arctan(c + d \times (diff)))$, where a, b, c, and d are constants and

diff is the difference between the coupon on the loan and the current coupon yield expressed in basis points. The constants a, b, c, and d need to be chosen in order to match the arctangent curve to the prepayment data. The equation has four constants (a, b, c, and d), therefore we need four points on the prepayment curve to solve for these values.

Solve for a, b, c, and d in the formula. (Note: In MS Excel, the arctangent function is atan(x).) Assume:

■ The maximum CPR is 50 percent.
■ The minimum CPR is 6 percent.
■ The midpoint 28 percent CPR occurs at diff = 200 basis points.
■ At midpoint, max slope is 6 percent CPR for a 10-basis-point rate shift.

Using a little algebra and calculus, the equation in this exercise gives the following relationships:

$$
\begin{aligned}
a &= (\text{max CPR} + \text{min CPR})/2 \\
b &= (\text{max CPR} - a)/(\text{pi}/2) \\
d &= \text{max slope}/b \\
c &= -d \times \text{midpoint diff}
\end{aligned}
$$

Based on these equations, solve for a, b, c, and d. Note that this is not an actual prepayment function. While these numbers are similar to GNMA prepayment estimates the results are only intended as an example of how to fit the arctangent curve to prepayment data. Note: More advanced readers can derive these equations.

Exercise 9.3   Use the data from Figure 9.3 to create a simple prepayment model using linear regression.

Step 1. Create a graph showing the prepayment rate by age for all four pools. At what age do the prepayment rates appear to level off for the lower coupon loans? Call this age *M*.

Step 2. Create a new variable *A* for each month for each pool that is equal to age if age < = *M* and equal to *M* if age > *M*.

Step 3. Create a new variable *D* for each month for each pool that is equal to the difference between the coupon on the pool and the GNMA current coupon rate for the period 2 months prior. (Assume that interest rates were constant at the first month's rate for 2 months prior to the start of the data.)

Step 4. Graph the prepayment rates versus the new variable *D*. (A scatter plot in Excel will work well.) Remember that every month each pool will have a different D, and D will be different across the pools, requiring that you rearrange the data.

Step 5. Find the value of D at which the prepayment rates appear to increase. Call this value T. Find the value of D at which the prepayments reach their maximum. Call this value P. Compute a new variable $I = \min (\max (D - T, 0), P)$

Step 6. Calculate the regression:

$$CPR = \alpha + \beta_1 A + \beta_2 I + \varepsilon$$

If you set $\alpha = 0$, then CPR will always be positive, provided that the β's are positive.

Step 7. Compare the predicted values to the actual values.

Exercise 9.4 Compute the pool factor and modified factor where modified factor excluded amortization and turnover. Assume a prepayment speed of 40 percent and a turnover rate of 9 percent on a 30-year mortgage for a mortgage that is 36 months old and has a coupon of 8 percent.

Exercise 9.5 What happens to the usefulness of the pool factor in forecasting burnout if the pool consists of loans that were seasoned before they were pooled? Hint: the pool factor is 1 when the pool is created, regardless of the age of the loans.

Exercise 9.6 Active/passive exercise (no amortization).

- 15 percent passive prepay at 8 CPR percent.
- 90 percent active prepay at 8 CPR percent if rates are up; 60 CPR percent if rates are down.

Compute average prepayment speed if rates are down in the first month and after 3 years (36 months) if 60 percent of the loans have prepaid.

CHAPTER 10

Total-Return
Scenario Analysis

The Frenchman Alphonse Karr said: *"Plus ça change, plus c'est la même chose."* The more things change, the more they stay the same. One cannot say the same for mortgage-backed securities (MBS). Changes in economic conditions, especially interest rates, can significantly alter the investment characteristics of MBS and other securitized assets. While the analytical framework described in Chapter 8 may provide a good basis for beginning to evaluate securities, a dynamic evaluation is required to address the range of potential outcomes in MBS investment. Scenario analysis is one form of dynamic analysis; it utilizes several specially designed input conditions to extract information about a security's performance. While scenario analysis does not describe all possible outcomes, it produces a limited number of outputs that can be carefully analyzed.

Total-return analysis over multiple scenarios serves as a critical tool in understanding the dynamics or the performance of fixed-income securities, especially those with cash flows that depend on interest rates. Unlike static measures of yield and spread, total-return analysis produces some measures that describe the expected benefits from holding a security for some period less than the stated maturity. These measures of expected performance let us know about the expected price volatility as interest rates and prepayment rates change.

Table 10.1 outlines the steps taken and the results produced using the scenario-analysis method. The first phase establishes the methodology and sets key assumptions. In the second phase, the performance of the collateral is calculated based on the input assumptions. In the third phase, the cash flows and values of the securities are calculated. Finally, in the fourth phase, critical results are produced, including income and value measures of total return and expected total return. Important measures of risk, effective duration, and convexity can be calculated using scenario analysis. These measures are critical to understanding the risk characteristics of securitized

TABLE 10.1 Scenario Analysis Method

Phase of Analysis	Components
Methodology	Total-return calculation horizon Interest-rate scenarios Reinvestment
Collateral	Prepayments Static Vector Model
Structure	Security cash flows Horizon pricing

Results	Income—total rate of return
	Valuation—total rate of return
	comparisons
	Risk
	  effective duration
	  effective convexity

investments. Total-return scenario analysis is such a powerful tool that if an investor does not like the scenario profile of an investment, it would probably be a good idea not to purchase that security even if the yield or some other measure of value seems irresistible.

METHODOLOGY

Total-return scenario analysis is not a formal valuation method. It relies on numerous assumptions regarding how the problem will be framed. Furthermore, once the major assumptions have been selected, there are numerous subjective decisions required to implement the method. Poor or ill-informed determinations could undermine the integrity of the results. Used improperly, total-return scenario analysis could produce results that mislead rather than inform.

In short, total-return scenario analysis compares the amount of cash on hand at the end of some holding period with the amount of cash on hand at the start of the period for a handful of carefully chosen interest-rate environments. The cash at the end of the period is derived from cash flow received during the period as well as the value of the security at the end of the period. The growth rate by which the starting cash becomes the ending cash is the **total return**. The total return can be calculated using equation (10.1).

$$\text{Total Return} = \frac{\text{Ending Cash}}{\text{Starting Cash}} - 1 \tag{10.1}$$

$$
\begin{aligned}
\text{Ending Cash} = {} & \text{Interest} + \text{Principal (amortized and prepaid)} \\
& + \text{Market Value of Remaining Principal} \\
& + \text{Reinvestment Income} \tag{10.2}
\end{aligned}
$$

The starting cash equals the market price of the security plus any accrued interest. The interim cash flows will equal all cash flows received by the investor up until and including the horizon date. This includes the market price of the security on the horizon date plus any accrued interest, as well as any reinvestment income earned on the cash flow received between the starting and ending dates. There are three critical parameters for the analysis; each will have a significant bearing on the results.

Horizon is the first critical assumption. The horizon determines the length of the holding period for the security. At the end of this period, the security will be repriced and the overall performance will be measured. In most cases, a 12-month horizon will be used. Choice of horizon will depend on the need. Some investors may choose other holding periods, such as a holding period that is tied to the end of the year.

Choosing the right holding period is somewhat of a balancing act, as shown in Figure 10.1. When the horizon is short, the price component of total return outweighs all the other components. As the holding period extends, less weight is placed on the price performance of the security and the return is determined more based on the reinvestment rate for the interim cash flows. Placing too much weight on the reinvestment rate may not be a good idea, because it tends to make the returns of disparate securities resemble each other.

Scenarios generally consist of a starting yield curve and ending yield curve, and a path between them. While the method generally involves several different interest-rate scenarios, there is usually a central scenario called

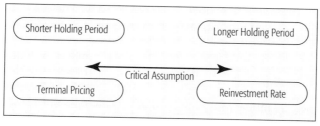

FIGURE 10.1   Holding-period effect.

the **base case**. Frequently, the current yield curve, or the yield curve at the start of the period, is used as the base case. The scenarios must cover the entire time period from the start to the horizon, which means that all interest rates are assumed to remain constant over the entire period.

As discussed in Chapter 7, holding all rates constant would not be consistent with no-arbitrage conditions. However, since several different scenarios will be calculated, holding the yield curve constant may be an acceptable solution, assuming that you understand the limitations of this approach.

Basing horizon pricing and intermediate cash flows on the forward curve is a more rigorous analytical approach that will reduce the bias of the calculations. Using the forward curve would mean that the yield curve at the horizon would be the yield curve that is implied by the yield curve at the start of the period. Use of the forward curve for the base-case scenario assumes that all investors would receive the same return from the bonds used to derive the initial yield curve.

When using the current yield curve as the base case, the user is implicitly assuming that the forward rates will not materialize. In essence, a yield-curve bet is built into the analysis. In an upward-sloping yield-curve environment, longer-duration securities would consistently outperform shorter-duration securities. If multiple scenarios are created with the current yield curve as the base case, it will be difficult to assign probabilities to the various scenarios. It would generally be more appropriate to use only the current yield curve method to compare the return profiles of relatively similar securities.

The method requires that several different yield curves be created at the horizon. These yield curves can be created in any way the user chooses, but they are generally split into **parallel shifts** and **nonparallel shifts**. Parallel shifts are the most common assumption. A parallel shift involves moving all of the interest rates in the yield curve by the same amount. Frequently, the sizes of the shifts are in even increments such as 50 or 100 basis points. A commonly used set of scenarios are the seven scenarios from up 300 basis points to down 300 basis points in 100-basis-point increments. The up and down 50-basis-point scenarios are also frequently included in an analysis, as it is not necessary that all of the scenarios be equally spaced. It makes sense to use shifts approximately equal to one standard deviation in rates over the time horizon, allowing the calculation of probabilities that can be assigned to each of the scenarios. Suppose that the standard deviation of rates over a 1-year time period is 100 basis points. If shifts for an annual analysis are set at much lower levels, say 10 basis points, then three up shifts and three down shifts, a typical number of shifts, will only span 60 basis points, and there will be a significant probability that rates will be outside the range of interest rates used in the analysis. However, if shifts of 100 basis points were used for a 1-month analysis, then most of the analysis would be for outcomes that are beyond the reasonable range of expectation as the 1-month standard deviation would be

$$100\text{bp} \times \frac{1}{\sqrt{12}} \cong 29\text{bp} \qquad (10.3)$$

and the smallest shift would already exceed three standard deviations.

Parallel shifts are not really as straightforward as one might think. Chapter 7 described several types of yield curves: par, zero, and forward. Unless the yield curve is flat, a parallel shift in one yield curve is not a parallel shift in the other.

Any other horizon yield curve that is not a parallel shift is a nonparallel shift. Generally, investors look at specific changes in the yield curve that interest them. These could reflect steepening or flattening patterns that had been observed in the past, or other changes in the shape of the yield curve that might create risk for the bonds or portfolio being examined.

The next step is to link the starting yield curve to the horizon yield curve. There are many possible **interest-rate paths** that would link the starting yield curve to the horizon yield curve. Yogi Berra is reputed to have said: "You got to be very careful if you don't know where you're going, because you might not get there." In scenario analysis, we know where we are starting and we know where we are going. Nevertheless, we still need to be careful about how we get there. The importance of the choice of path will depend on the length of the horizon and the amount of cash flow received during the holding period. For zero-coupon bonds, or other bonds with no cash flows during the holding period, the path of interest rates during the period will not affect the results. The choice of path has two effects on the total return for that scenario. First, as we saw in Chapter 9, prepayments on MBS depend on interest rates. Generally, lower interest rates will lead to faster prepayment speeds. The faster interest rates fall, the sooner prepayment rates will increase. We discuss how to formulate prepayment assumptions for scenario analysis in the section on Collateral. Second, the path of interest rates will affect the reinvestment rate for cash flows received during the holding period.

The usual assumptions are either that interest rates shift immediately to the horizon yield curve or that there is a linear change over time. The first is easier to implement. Unfortunately, the approach deviates significantly from reality. Still, this approach is more conservative because it accentuates the impact of the changes in rates.

Alternatively, we can have the interest rates move gradually. This approach adds a more realistic dimension to the manner in which interest rates move. One well-accepted fashion is to allow the rates to move linearly over the

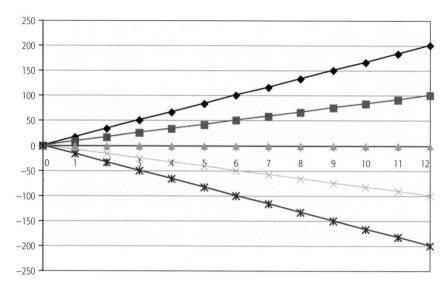

FIGURE 10.2 Gradual shifts.

entire holding period. For a 12-month holding period, we would assume that one-twelfth of the shift would occur each month. For a 100-basis-point shift, the monthly shift would be 8.33 basis points. For a 200-basis-point shift, the monthly shift would be 16.67 basis points. This is shown in Figure 10.2.

A variation on the gradual rate-shift movement would be to let the rate shifts occur on different time scales. Suppose we are looking at a 5-year horizon analysis. We could assume that interest rates have a general movement of 100 basis points per year. A gradual shift in the +200-basis-point scenario would take 2 years, the +300-basis-point shift would take 3 years, and so on. This approach stretches out the length of rate shifts. Overall, this method would register the least impact on MBS as the slower gradual shifts reduce the changes in prepayments rates. Shifts that are too gradual may severely understate the risk of the security being analyzed. Even when the standard deviation of interest rates is 100 basis points a year, shifts of 200 basis points or more during a 1-year horizon are not impossible, and have occurred. Figure 12.2 shows the volatility of interest rates.

A third way to create interest-rate scenarios is to allow multiple paths between the beginning and yield curve. This method can be very useful for MBS, because of the dependency of cash flows on the path of interest rates. Sometimes this approach is called whipsaw analysis. Figure 10.3 shows several paths of interest rates between two endpoints. In mathematical terms, there are actually an infinite number of possible paths between the two

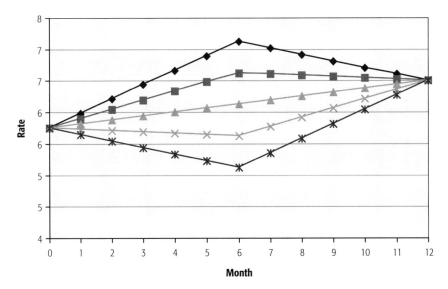

FIGURE 10.3 Whipsaw analysis.

points. These possible paths are mathematically described by a concept called the **Brownian Bridge.** Under probability theory, these paths, as well as the gradual paths in Figure 10.2, would more likely change with the square root of time rather than linearly with time. Figure 10.4 shows paths that change with the square root of time. Utilizing a horizon yield curve based on forward rates, paths with multiple paths to each endpoint, and a Brownian Bridge-based connection between the endpoints begin to provide a complete picture of security performance. However, with so many complex paths, it becomes difficult to assess the results of each path. In that case, it is necessary to rely on summary measures of value and risk. The option-adjusted-spread (OAS) method described in Chapter 13 is a formal way of performing that analysis.

While most total-return scenario analysis is performed with gradual parallel shifts, a method pioneered by Andrew Davidson for the National Association of Insurance Commissioners (NAIC) called FLUX (FLow Uncertainty IndeX) does utilize multiple paths using different adjustment time periods and multiple paths to an ending yield curve. FLUX uses seven scenarios as shown in Figure 10.5.

The **reinvestment rate** is the second critical assumption. It is frequently overlooked. Improper choice of reinvestment rate can turn a carefully conceived analysis into a misleading morass. During the holding period, the security will be throwing off cash flow. For an MBS, this will represent the interest and principal payments. Total-return analysis assumes that this cash

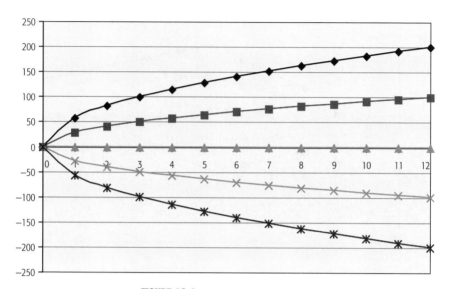

FIGURE 10.4   Square root of time.

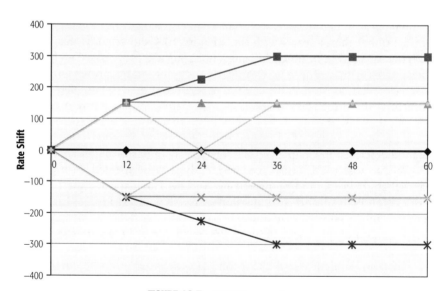

FIGURE 10.5   FLUX scenarios.

will be reinvested at some rate until the end of the holding period at the horizon date. The choice of rate will be important as the length of the holding period increases and as the interim cash flow increases.

There are a wide range of assumptions used for the reinvestment rate, however, *the only truly reliable analyses are those where the reinvestment rate is based on a short-term low-risk investment.* The reinvestment rate is then generally constructed as a spread to the short-term Treasury or LIBOR rate on the yield curve for the scenario. These rates should vary along with the scenario.

There are two frequently used forms of reinvestment rate that can lead to misleading results. The first is to assume a reinvestment rate that is too high. The second is to assume a reinvestment rate that does not vary with the yield-curve scenario. Figure 10.6 shows the importance of reinvestment rate in a relatively simple example. The results in Figure 10.6 are based on a bond that matures in 2 years with a 6 percent coupon. Depending on the rate scenario, a portion of the bond prepays at the end of the first year. The short-term rate in the base case is 6 percent. Table 10.2 describes the analysis. The table shows the prepayment rate of the bond at the end of the first year and the reinvestment assumptions for the three cases.

In this example, it is clear how the choice of reinvestment rate dramatically alters the analysis of the bonds. In the short-rate case, the bond clearly

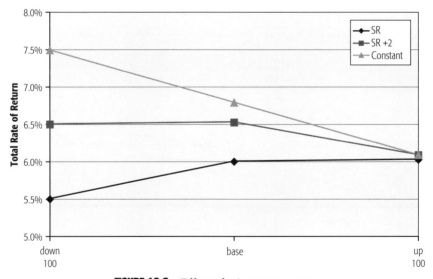

FIGURE 10.6 Effect of reinvestment rate.

TABLE 10.2   Reinvestment Rates

Scenario	Down (%)	Base (%)	Up (%)
Prepayment	100	50	0
Reinvestment rates			
Short-rate case	5	6	7
Short-rate + 2 case	7	8	9
Constant-rate case	9	9	9

suffers when interest rates fall. In the other two cases, the impact of falling rates on the performance of the bond is diminished, or even reversed.

COLLATERAL

Building prepayments into scenario analysis provides a measure of the risk of options exposure. Changing prepayment rates will affect both the interim cash flows and the valuation of the MBS and the end of the holding period. The impact of prepayments on scenario returns can be seen in Figure 10.7.

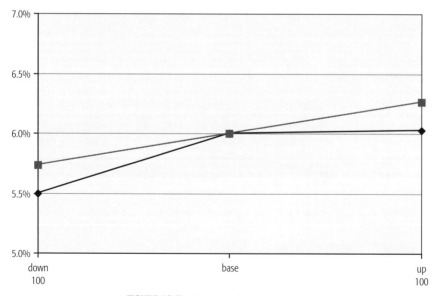

FIGURE 10.7   Impact of prepayments.

One bond is the same as the bond in Figure 10.6, the other bond has a 50 percent paydown in year one in all three scenarios. In other words, it is insensitive to interest rate changes. Note that while both bonds have the same return in the base-case scenario (since they have identical cash flows), the bond with the variable prepayments underperforms in both the rising and falling interest-rate scenarios.

Prepayment assumptions for scenario analysis can be provided using static forecasts, vectors forecasts, or a prepayment model. Each scenario will require its own prepayment assumption. Most scenario analyses use static prepayment rates. For a static forecast we could assume, for example, that if interest rates remained constant, an MBS would prepay at 150 percent Public Securities Association (PSA), and if rates were to drop, the MBS would prepay at 250 percent PSA. This static forecast would be used for the entire life of the security in that particular scenario. Table 10.3 shows the median dealer forecasts on Bloomberg for a Fannie Mae 30-year MBS in November 2002. Bloomberg shows the forecasts for immediate shifts in rates. The static forecast method can be adapted to the gradual-shift scenario approach. Like the interest rates, the prepayment rates would also move gradually. During the period of the shift, prepayment rates would change linearly from the unchanged scenario forecast to the specific scenario forecast.

The static measure ignores the time-series characteristics of prepayments, such as aging and burnout. In a period of high prepayment rates, we would expect prepayments to decline due to burnout. In this case, a vector approach might be valuable—we could have prepayment rates start at one level and then decline over time.

A more precise way to build prepayment assumptions into the scenario-analysis method is to use a prepayment model to produce the prepayment rates. This method fully builds in the dynamics of interest-rate effect, aging, burnout, and seasonality. It also adds flexibility for considering the macro-economic data affecting prepayments. For example, we may wish to change estimates of home price appreciation for various scenarios. The disadvantage of using a prepayment model for the scenario analysis is that the

TABLE 10.3 Bloomberg Median Forecasts (11/25/02)

	−300	−200	−100	Base	100	200	300
FNCL 5	1522	1625	525	166	123	121	121
FNCL 6	1971	1886	1639	563	172	135	125
FNCL 7	1269	1262	1290	1010	414	200	169

Source: Bloomberg L.P.

method becomes something of a black box. An investor may feel uncomfortable about not seeing the prepayment forecast as a single value. One way to get some understanding about the prepayment rates used in a particular scenario would be to come up with a measure to summarize the vector of prepayment forecasts from the model. The single PSA (or CPR) that gives the same weighted-average life (WAL) as the model for that scenario can be used. This is called the **equivalent PSA** (or CPR), or average-life-equivalent PSA (or CPR), and is frequently used as the static prepayment forecast in scenario analysis. The dealer prepayment forecasts used to compute the Bloomberg Dealer Median, were most likely calculated using such a method.

STRUCTURE

The structure of the MBS or other securitized asset enters the analysis when we need to compute the cash flows for the total rate of return (TRR) calculations. The calculations require the cash flows during the holding period. The cash flows are calculated in the same manner as described in the static-yield analysis in Chapter 8. For more complicated securities such as collaterized-mortgage obligations (CMOs), it is necessary to have a model that will generate the month-by-month cash flows of the security.

The analysis also requires a **terminal value**. The terminal value is the market value of the remaining principal at the horizon date. Total-return calculations will be very dependent on this value because it is usually the largest component of the total ending cash. There are several methods that can be used. The most common method is based on the static-yield method of Chapter 8.

For each scenario it is possible to compute the value of the MBS at the horizon using the scenario prepayment rate at a yield. The question then is what is the appropriate yield to use. In each scenario we have a shifted yield curve. One simple solution would be to shift the yield of the security by the amount of the shift of the scenario.

This method—called the **yield method**—can be summarized as:

- Based on the price and base-case prepayment speed, compute a yield.
- Adjust the horizon yield by the scenario shift.
- Compute the horizon price using the characteristics of the MBS at the horizon date, the horizon yield, and the scenario prepayment speed.

While this method may be appropriate in some cases, for MBS there are better assumptions that could be used. We know that in each scenario the characteristics of the MBS may change. Lower rates will lead to faster pre-payments and shorter securities. Since we have a yield curve at the horizon date, we can adjust the yield by reflecting the changing average life of the se-curity. One way to do this is to modify the yield method and use a **spread method.**

- Based on the price, base-case prepayment speed, and yield curve com-pute a yield spread.
- Compute a new average life and add the spread to the appropriate point on the horizon yield curve to produce a horizon yield.
- Compute the horizon price using the characteristics of the MBS at the horizon date, the horizon yield, and the scenario prepayment speed.

A third variation on this theme would be to adjust the horizon spread based on the spread of other similar instruments for scenario shifts.

Table 10.4 shows the static analysis of the GNMA market on July 5, 2002. The LIBOR/Swap rates for that day were: for monthly maturities of 3, 6, 12, 24, 60, 120, and 360; 1.86, 1.96, 2.3, 3.22, 4.54, 5.35, and 5.98, respectively. The GNMA current coupon yield was 6.09.

PSA is the Andrew Davidson & Co., Inc., average-life equivalent pre-payment forecast. Yield is stated as a bond equivalent. WAL is weighted-average life using the prepayment forecast. Spreads are calculated to LIBOR. For each coupon Figure 10.8 shows the resulting spreads graphed against the left axis and the WAL against the right axis. Moving from discount coupons to premium coupons, average life falls as prepayment speeds rise. Yield spreads rise, peaking at the 7.0 coupon, and then decline.

For a scenario analysis, the spread could be adjusted to reflect the per-formance of the relative coupon. For example, with a GNMA 6.5, the spread in the base case would be 148 basis points. It would decrease to 100

TABLE 10.4   Static Analysis of GNMA Market (7/5/02)

Coupon	Price	PSA	WAL	Yield	Spread
5.5	96.63	145	8.58	6.12	100
6.0	99.53	178	7.76	6.13	114
6.5	101.69	283	5.58	6.13	148
7.0	103.5	420	3.68	5.86	182
7.5	105.06	494	2.94	5.47	173
8.0	106.28	507	2.73	5.31	167

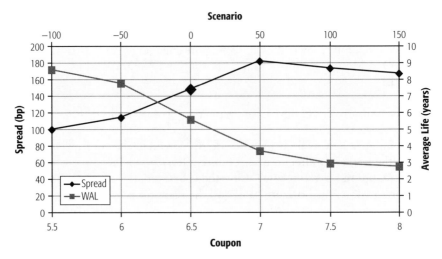

FIGURE 10.8   Relative spread method.

basis points in the up-100-basis-point scenario and would increase to 173 in the down-100-basis-point scenario.

The horizon pricing method can be refined as the **relative spread method:**

- Based on the price of several MBS, base-case prepayment speeds, and yield curve, compute the yield spreads for each coupon.
- Compute a new average life and add the spread determined on a relative-scenario basis to the appropriate point on the horizon yield curve to produce a horizon yield.
- Compute the horizon price using the characteristics of the MBS at the horizon date, the horizon yield, and the scenario prepayment speed.

The relative spread method is a reasonable way to determine the terminal prices for investors who do not have more sophisticated option models at their disposal, as it approximates how the market currently prices option risk. However, the method relies on the assumption that the characteristics of the relative coupon securities are somewhat similar. In the previous example, the remaining term on the GNMA 8s might be significantly shorter than the GNMA 6.5s. In an interest-rate scenario where rates fall 150 basis points, it may not be appropriate to use the spread on seasoned GNMA 8s for the pricing of unseasoned GNMA 6.5s. The relative spread method is also a good way to keep the scenario analysis from relying on "black box" results. The method can be applied to other structured securities as well, but it becomes difficult to justify the relative spread pricing.

An alternative to using a static spread-based method for horizon pricing, one could employ an option-based pricing model. Typically an OAS model (described in Chapter 13) would be used to determine the value of the MBS in the different interest-rate scenarios. The **constant OAS method** would have the following steps.

- Based on the price, prepayment model, yield curve, and volatility assumptions, compute an OAS.
- Compute the horizon price using the base-case OAS and the characteristics of the MBS at the horizon date, the prepayment model, and the horizon yield and volatility assumptions.

The constant OAS method presents a general solution to the problem of computing horizon values. As discussed in Chapter 13, the OAS method incorporates the option features in valuation method, reducing the need for ad hoc adjustments in spread. For various complicated products (see Chapter 11 on structuring CMOs), it may be the only reasonable way to determine the price. A variant of this method would be a **relative OAS method**, which uses changing OAS in much the same way as relative spreads are used in the static method. This relative OAS method is especially useful for interest-only and principal-only securities that are also described in Chapter 11.

Despite its apparent strengths, the OAS method does have drawbacks. First, the OAS method once again makes the scenario-analysis results look like a black box to the trader. If some results seem unrealistic, it is difficult to determine the appropriate adjustments. Second, OAS calculations are time-consuming. For individual securities this may not be a problem. However, when applied to an entire portfolio, the required computer time may be too great compared with the benefit of the analysis.

RESULTS

Total rate of return scenario analysis is a very flexible tool that can provide a variety of insights into the income, value, risk, and risk characteristics of a security. The basic TRR provides measures of absolute and relative return, with a number of methods to compare performance. In addition we show two special cases of this analysis, one where the reinvestment rate is varied in a particular fashion, and one where the horizon is set equal to the starting date.

Value

The basic single scenario total return provides a realistic assessment of the performance of a bond over the specified holding period. The analysis includes the effect of the purchase price, interim cash flows including interest, scheduled and prepaid principal, reinvestment income, and proceeds from the sale at the horizon date. With reasonable assumptions, TRR provides a reasonable result.

The choice of horizon yield curve will affect the interpretation of the results. Consider the yield curve and the 1-year forward yield curve shown in Figure 10.9. The base yield curve is upward sloping; therefore, the forward yield curve is higher than the base yield curve. As described in Chapter 7, in a no-arbitrage, certain world, we would expect the same 1-year return across all default-free bonds. The rate would be equal to the 1-year rate. For a 5-year security, we would expect that the initial yield and higher coupon than the 1-year instrument would be offset by a decline in price. That price decline is reflected in the higher forward yield. However, if we were to assume that the yield curve remained unchanged, then the 5-year security would have a higher return than the 1-year security. Not only would it have a higher yield and coupon, but it would also benefit from "rolling down" the curve. That is, at the horizon, our 5-year instrument would have a 4-year maturity and would be priced using a lower yield.

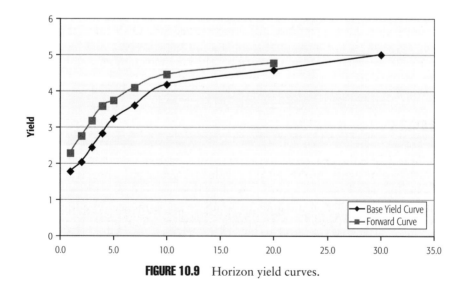

FIGURE 10.9 Horizon yield curves.

TABLE 10.5 Forward TRR Analysis

	Base TRR (%)	Forward TRR (%)
1 year	1.78	1.78
5 years	3.22	1.78
10 years	4.17	1.78

In addition to higher discount rates, the forward-rate case generally produces slower prepayment assumptions, since the rates that drive prepayment rates would also be higher in the forward-rate case than in the stable-rate case. Table 10.5 shows the TRR of Treasury instruments assuming the stable yield curve at the horizon and the forward yield curve at the horizon.

The case where the horizon yield curve is equal to the base yield curve consistently shows higher returns, which is primarily due to the impact on horizon prices. Instruments of different maturities also have different returns, so it is difficult to make comparisons. Nevertheless, the stable-rate approach can be used to compare similar instruments.

As a measure of relative value, we can compare the return on the MBS to the return on another, usually similar security. In addition to taking the difference between the total return of the two securities, we can calculate how much the spread on the MBS would have to increase before the return on the MBS would equal the return on the other security, say, a Treasury. Knowledge of this **breakeven spread** would provide some subjective understanding of the likelihood that the MBS would underperform the other security under the chosen scenario. For example, in Table 10.6 the break-even spread increase for the FNMA 6 to underperform the 5-year Treasury is 39 basis points.

Value measures can be extended to multiple scenarios by computing an **expected return**. The expected return represents a probability-weighted

TABLE 10.6 Total-Return Profiles

	−200	−100	0	100	200
FNCL 5	13.31	15.39	5.3	−8.84	−19.84
FNCL 6	5.1	4.35	5.06	−5.45	−17.38
FNCL 7	3.31	1.95	5.07	8.42	5.66
5-year Treasury	20.37	11.58	3.2	−4.79	−12.41

return across multiple scenarios. It is necessary to make some assumptions about the distribution of interest-rate changes. Standard approaches assume that rates are either normally or lognormally distributed around the horizon yield curve.

As described in Chapter 12, under the normal distribution interest-rate movements of the same magnitude (in basis points) are assumed to be equally likely. That is, we would expect the probability of a downward shift of 100 basis points to equal the probability of an upward shift of 100 basis points. For the lognormal distribution, proportional changes are considered equally likely. That is, we would have the same probability of a 10 percent increase or a 10 percent decrease in rates. In order to compute the probabilities, an assumption of volatility is required. Figure 10.10 shows the probability distribution for a 1-year horizon using an annual standard deviation of 90 basis points for the normal distribution and 15 percent for the lognormal distribution with a base rate of 6 percent.

Regardless of the choice of normal or lognormal probabilities, use of forward rates for the horizon scenario will produce results that are more consistent with the financial theory described in Chapters 7 and 12. Unfortunately, even with the horizon centered on forward rates, and OAS-based pricing, expected returns from TRR analysis are not likely to fully meet all of the rigorous requirements of an option-valuation model.

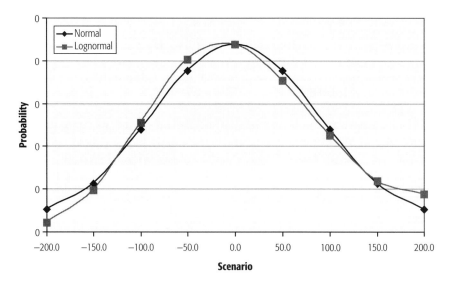

FIGURE 10.10 Probability distribution for a 1-year horizon.

Risk

The total rate of return scenario analysis method provides a wealth of information about the overall risk characteristics of an MBS. The method can provide information relating both to the price variability and the cash-flow variability of the bond. The key measure from the analysis is the total-return profile (Table 10.6), as shown in Figure 10.11.

Figure 10.11 shows the total-return profiles of three MBS, the Fannie Mae 30-year 5 percent, 6 percent, and 7 percent coupons and a 5-year Treasury. The instruments show a wide range of investment results. The 5-year Treasury has a linear profile, improving in return as rates rise. The Fannie Mae 5 percent has a higher return than the 5-year Treasury in the stable and down 100 scenario, but underperforms in the other scenarios. The return on the Fannie Mae 6 percent does not increase as rates fall, but it does decline at about the same rate as the 5-year Treasury when rates increase. The Fannie Mae 7 percent has a relatively stable return across the interest-rate scenarios. Each of these instruments provides very different investment characteristics and risk return trade-offs.

Total rate of return scenario analysis is a flexible tool that can be used in a variety of circumstances. The typical use is in the form of Table 10.6, where one instrument is compared to another. Total return is useful in that setting because it simultaneously provides a measure of value and risk. An

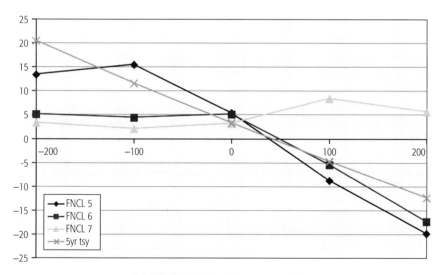

FIGURE 10.11   Total-return profiles.

investor can determine the range of scenarios in which the instrument being evaluated will outperform or underperform the alternatives. The analysis can also be used in more general portfolio contexts. For example, TRR analysis can be used to determine the effect of a swap, selling one security and purchasing another on the overall return profile of a portfolio. The return profile of the portfolio can also be compared to the return profile of a target portfolio, such as an index. Total return managers whose performance is generally measured relative to an index can compute the return profile of the index and compare their portfolios to that index. The TRR profile will help them to understand the risks being taken relative to the portfolio.

Yield Profiles

A variant on TRR analysis is another form of scenario analysis: **yield profiles**. Although yield profiles are used frequently, they have more potential to confuse than inform. Yield profiles can be thought of as TRR analysis where the reinvestment rate is equal to the yield of the security. For each scenario, a prepayment rate is chosen much like for TRR analysis. The static yield is calculated for each scenario.

In conjunction with the yield for each scenario, yield profiles are usually accompanied by other information, including the prepayment rate for the scenario, the average life of the security, and the cash flow duration (described in Chapter 8). Table 10.7 shows the yield profile of a Fannie Mae 6 percent mortgage. The total return of the same mortgage is shown in Table 10.6.

A comparison of the total-return profile and the yield profile reveals the benefit of the TRR analysis. The yield analysis masks the decline in value associated with a rising yield, but a longer average life in the rising rate scenario.

Risk Measures

Rather than the reinvestment-driven results of the yield profile, another form of analysis eliminates the effect of reinvestment. A scenario analysis can be performed with an instantaneous horizon. This analysis can be used to pro-

TABLE 10.7 Yield Profile of a Fannie Mae 6 Percent

	−200	−100	0	100	200
Yield	3.619	3.901	5.124	5.619	5.667
WAL	1.13	1.28	3.22	8.24	9.57
Duration	6.47	5.81	2.78	1.22	1.08

duce a price profile. Two measures of risk, **effective duration** and **effective convexity**, can be calculated from the price profile.

From an MBS investor's perspective, duration and convexity reflect the relationship between parallel change in the yield curve and price, recognizing that cash flows change with interest rates. The terminology in this area can be somewhat confusing; before laying out the mechanics of MBS duration, we look at convexity, which measures the change in duration.

Macaulay Duration   This measure comes in two units: years and percentage price changes. When expressed in years, the Macaulay duration equals the time-weighted present value of all cash flows. Macaulay duration can also be shown to be equal to the percentage change in price for a percentage change in yield. For a security with unchanging cash flows, the two measurements will be equal. Because of this assumption, Macaulay duration has little relevance to MBS.

Modified Duration   This measure is the percentage change in price for a basis-point change in yield. Modified duration can be calculated with a simple adjustment to the Macaulay duration calculation. This measurement also assumes that the cash flows for a security do not change with interest rates.

Effective Duration   This measure is the percentage change in price for a basis-point change in yield. This measure sounds like modified duration; however, cash flows are allowed to change with interest rates. Sometimes this measure is called effective modified duration. Calling the duration effective implies the option component has been recognized. The **dP/dY** measure is very similar to the duration, only it examines the actual change in price for a basis-point change in yield.

Using this perspective, effective duration will be the standard tool for MBS risk analysis. Calculating an effective duration requires some of the tools of scenario analysis. We have to determine how the MBS price changes in differing interest-rate scenarios. This concept of interest-rate scenarios can be seen from the effective-duration formula:

$$\text{Effective Duration} = \frac{\text{Price}_{-\Delta\text{Yield}} - \text{Price}_{+\Delta\text{Yield}}}{2 \times (\Delta\text{Yield}) \times \text{Price}_{\text{Base}}} \qquad (10.4)$$

In the formula, we start from a base-case price and then we look at an interest-rate shift up and down. The size of the shift is called ΔYield and should be large enough to cause some change in the prepayment rates. Generally, we consider changes of 25 basis points or greater.

For each of the scenarios, we allow prepayments to change and will reprice the securities at the new yield levels. The calculation of scenario prices can be made depending on the tools available. If you have access to an OAS model, then the MBS could be analyzed by shifting the yield curve and then repricing the security using the OAS from the base case.

For those without access to an OAS model, a simple bond calculator can be used to get a value for effective duration. For each scenario, a revised prepayment forecast and static-pricing spread should be used to calculate the price. Approaches to pricing spreads could use some of the methods we have described earlier for terminal scenario prices.

To illustrate the calculation of effective duration we can use information from the price-profile graph. Looking at the 7.5 percent MBS in the up and down 100-basis-point scenarios, we would calculate effective duration as follows:

Given

$$\Delta \text{Yield} = .01$$

$$\text{Price}_{-\Delta \text{Yield}} = 105.58$$

$$\text{Price}_{+\Delta \text{Yield}} = 98.21$$

$$\text{Price}_{\text{Base}} = 102.44$$

$$\text{Effective Duration} = \frac{105.58 - 98.21}{2 \times (.01) \times 102.44}$$

$$= 3.597$$

The effective duration implies that we would expect prices to change by 3.597 percent for a 100-basis-point change in interest rates. This interpretation assumes that duration does not change, that is, convexity equals zero. However, for MBS, the interest-rate sensitivity does change and so to fully understand the interest-rate sensitivity, we must also consider convexity.

Convexity measures the change in duration, making it equal to the change in the change in price. This is known as second-order term, reflecting the curvature of the price-profile graph. Unlike duration, it is a bit harder to get an intuitive feel for convexity, still we can draw some conclusions based on the sign of the convexity term.

From a formal perspective, convexity can be measured as follows:

$$\frac{\text{Price}_{-\Delta \text{Yield}} + \text{Price}_{+\Delta \text{Yield}} - 2 \times \text{Price}_{\text{Base}}}{100 \times (\Delta \text{Yield}^2 \times \text{Price}_{\text{Base}})}$$

$$\text{Effective Convexity} = \frac{105.58 + 98.21 - 2 \times 102.44}{100 \times 0.0001 \times 102.44}$$

$$= -1.064$$

Most MBS are negatively convex, which would imply that as yields decline, so does the duration. When yields rise, duration extends. These undesirable results present both an opportunity and a risk to investors. The opportunity stems from the yield premium the investor demands for holding a security with these attributes. The risk stems from the difficulty in measuring the duration drift and in determining the proper yield premium.

We can use the duration and convexity measures when calculating the approximate change in price for a change in yield. For a given change in yield (ΔYield), the price change would be given by the following formula:

$$\text{Percentage Change in Price} = (\text{Duration} \times \Delta\text{Yield}) \tag{10.5}$$
$$+ \left[0.5 \times (\text{Convexity} \times \Delta\text{Yield}^2) \right] \times 100$$

When applying the formula, we usually use the negative of the duration. Yield and price have inverse relations to one another for nearly all MBS but by convention we report durations as positive numbers. The formula indicates that for a negative convex security, price increases will be limited in falling-rate scenarios, whereas price declines will be exacerbated in rising-rate cases.

Returning to the 7.5 percent MBS, the approximate change in price for a 200-basis-point decline in rates (ΔYield = 0.02) would equal:

$$\text{Percentage Change in Price} = \left[3.597 \times 0.02 + 0.5 \times -1.064 \times 0.02^2 \right] \times 100$$
$$= \left[0.05066 \right] \times 100$$
$$= 5.066$$

From our price profile, we had a base price of $102.44 and a down-200 scenario price of $108.51. The calculated price equals $102.44 \times 1.05066 = $107.629. Using the duration and convexity, we were able to fit the price to within 88 cents of the actual price. Our ability to fit the price depends on the degree by which duration and convexity describe the function between price and yield.

EXERCISES

Exercise 10.1   Assume the following base par yield curve with annual coupons.

Maturity	1	2	3	4
Yield	5.0	5.5	6.0	6.3

Step 1. Calculate the zero curve and forward curve.
Step 2. Shift the base curve up by 100 basis points.
Step 3. Recalculate the zero curve and forward curve.

Exercise 10.2   **Computation of Total Return.** Assume we purchase a semi-annual coupon-bearing bond with a 5.9126 percent coupon at a price of par. At the end of 6 months, we receive a semiannual coupon and we sell the bond at par. The total return computation is shown in equation (10.6).

$$\text{6MM TRR} = \frac{\text{Coupon + Terminal Value}}{\text{Starting Value}} - 1$$

$$= \frac{\$2.9563 + \$100}{\$100} - 1 \qquad (10.6)$$

$$= 2.9563\%$$

Now, this is the total return assuming a 6-month holding period. Normally, we should put this into an annual equivalent. In our case, we would assume that the investor is able to put the money to work at the same rate for another 6 months. The annualized return is shown in equation (10.7).

$$\text{Annual TRR} = \left(1 + \frac{\text{6-Month Return}^2}{100}\right) - 1$$

$$= \left(1 + \frac{2.9563}{100}\right)^2 - 1 \qquad (10.7)$$

$$= \left(1.0296\right)^2 - 1$$

$$= 0.06 \text{ or } 6\%$$

Using the previous security, assume that the security is sold at the end of 6 months for a price of $101. Compute total return over the 6-month period, then convert the 6-month holding-period return to an annual equivalent. Convert the 6-month return to a bond-equivalent return.

(◎) **Exercise 10.3** Compute the returns underlying Figure 10.6. The figure assumes that the bond matures in 2 years with a 6 percent coupon. Use the information in Table 10.2.

(◎) **Exercise 10.4** Using the cash flows from Table 10.8 and assuming a starting balance of $1,000, compute the missing numbers in the following table. Use the first column (which assumes a terminal price of $95) as an example.

TABLE 10.8 Cash Flows for 8.5 Percent MBS at 15 Percent CPR

Month	Balance	Amortized Principal	Prepaid Principal	Interest	Servicing	Investor Cash Flow	CPR (%)
0	1,000.00						
1	985.99	0.57	13.44	7.08	0.42	21.10	15
2	972.17	0.57	13.26	6.98	0.41	20.81	15
3	958.53	0.56	13.07	6.89	0.41	20.52	15
4	945.09	0.56	12.89	6.79	0.40	20.23	15
5	931.83	0.55	12.71	6.69	0.39	19.96	15
6	918.75	0.55	12.53	6.60	0.39	19.98	15

	Base Case	Case 1	Case 2
Starting price	100.00	100.00	100.00
Terminal price	95.00	100.00	110.00
Terminal balance	918.75	918.75	918.75
Terminal value	872.81		
Coupon income	41.04	41.04	41.04
Principal returned	81.25	81.25	81.25
Ending cash	995.10		
Total return	−0.49%		
Total return	−0.98%		

Exercise 10.5 Compute the effective duration for the securities in the following table.

	Bond 1	Bond 2	Bond 3
−50 bp	55.83	105.19	23.03
Base	45.00	104.22	26.75
+50bp	36.38	103.03	29.92
Effective Duration			

Exercise 10.6 Using the prices from the previous exercise, compute the convexity of the three securities.

	Bond 1	Bond 2	Bond 3
−50 bp	55.83	105.19	23.03
Base	45.00	104.22	26.75
+50bp	36.38	103.03	29.92
Convexity			

Exercise 10.7 Percentage Price Change = Duration $\times \Delta$Yield + 0.5 $\times$ Convexity $\times \Delta$Yield^2. Using the calculated durations and convexities, compute the percentage price changes and resulting prices for 25- and 100-basis-point shifts in the yield curve for the three bonds in Exercises 10.6 and 10.7.

Price Change	Bond 1	Bond 2	Bond 3
25 bp			
100 bp			

Prices	Bond 1	Bond 2	Bond 3
25 bp			
100 bp			

Exercise 10.8 Show that the total return to any horizon equals the yield when the yield is used as the reinvestment rate.

Advanced Mortgage-Backed Securities and Analysis

CHAPTER 11

Structuring CMOs, IOs, and POs

With the size of the securitized mortgage market exceeding the corporate bond market and approaching the size of the Treasury market, it is not surprising that the mortgage market has found a way to restructure mortgage cash flows to meet the needs and views of a variety of investors. The basic mortgage pass-throughs all have very similar cash-flow structures and performance characteristics. Discounts and premiums differ to some extent, but the overall investment patterns are quite similar. While the investment characteristics of these loans are similar, the needs of the investors vary significantly. The collateralized-mortgage obligation (CMO) has become the vehicle to transform mortgage cash flow into a variety of investment instruments.

The driving force behind the creation of CMOs is arbitrage. CMOs will be created when the underwriter sees the ability to buy mortgage collateral, structure a CMO, and sell the CMO bonds for more than the price of the underlying collateral plus expenses. Because of the dynamic nature of the arbitrage opportunities, the types of CMOs created will reflect current market conditions and can change significantly. If all the CMO did was rearrange cash flows, it would be difficult to create added value. CMOs are successful, nevertheless, for two main reasons. First, investors have varying needs and are willing to pay extra for a bond that meets their specific needs. Second, investors misanalyze bonds. Many investors rely on tools such as yield spread and average-life analysis. These tools are insufficient to analyze mortgage-backed securities and CMO bonds.

A CMO can be defined as a bond secured by mortgage cash flows. The mortgage cash flows are distributed to the bond based on a set of prespecified rules. The rules determine the order of principal allocation and the coupon level. The specific choice of which CMOs and other structured mortgage products are created stems from the interaction of market demand, with credit, legal, tax, and accounting requirements. The primary

185

ingredient in CMO creation is the availability of mortgage cash flows. The cash flows provide the raw material for the CMOs. Every CMO must address the amount and availability of cash flow.

The focus here is on the cash-flow aspects of CMOs; however, a brief discussion of the other aspects of CMO creation is warranted. An important component of the CMO is the assurance that the investor will get the promised cash flows. The market has developed several methods for achieving this goal. Generally, the mortgages or the agency-backed mortgage pools are placed in a trust and the CMO bonds are issued out of that trust. Various legal structures can be used to create a bankruptcy-remote entity to hold the mortgages and issue the bonds. The investor looks to the trust and cash flows of the mortgages to provide the bond's principal and interest payments. These payments are assured through either a rating agency assurance (that is, a triple A rating) or through the guarantee of a government-sponsored enterprise (GSE), either Fannie Mae or Freddie Mac. In recent years, the GSE-guaranteed CMOs have dominated the issuance of CMOs. Some mortgages cannot be used in CMOs guaranteed by the GSEs. CMOs backed by these loans are generally issued by Wall Street firms, large mortgage originators, or mortgage conduits and are rated by the rating agencies.

The tax treatment of CMOs is generally covered under the provisions of the Real Estate Mortgage Investment Conduit (REMIC) rules. Sometimes CMOs are referred to as REMICs. In order to be a REMIC, the bonds must have a certain structure and must elect REMIC status. REMIC election drives the tax treatment of the bonds. The regular interests of the REMIC are generally taxed as ordinary bonds, whereas the residual interest bears the tax consequences of the CMO structure. While the original intention was that the residual interest would receive any cash flow not distributed to the regular interests, most residuals now have little cash flow attached to them and are distributed primarily based on their tax consequences.

The accounting treatment for most CMOs is straightforward. However, CMO bonds sold at a premium or discount must be evaluated on a level yield basis. That is, income is determined by the yield of the bond, rather than its coupon. When prepayments change, the expected cash flows of the security changes. So, the income stream must be adjusted accordingly. This is a complex area, especially for some CMO residuals, interest-only (IO) and principal-only (PO) securities. The rules for treatment of these bonds are subject to change. Please consult with your tax and accounting advisors before purchasing CMOs.

Once the legal, tax, and accounting issues are resolved, the investment characteristics of a CMO will be driven by the cash flows of the underlying collateral and the structure of the CMO deal. In order to understand CMOs, it is necessary to understand the rules by which the mortgage cash flows are distributed to the bonds.

COLLATERALIZED-MORTGAGE OBLIGATIONS AS RULES

The CMO can be thought of as a set of rules. The rules tell the trustee how to divide the payments that it receives on the mortgages. The rules tell the trustee in what order to pay the bondholders and how much to pay them. The rules generally can be split between principal-payment rules and interest-payment rules. Market participants have developed standard definitions for CMO types; these types specify the nature of the rules used to distribute cash flows. These standard types include principal-pay types and interest-pay types. Each bond has both a principal-pay type and interest-pay type. Table 11.1 shows the standard CMO definitions.

Each CMO represents a combination of these bond types and, hence, of the mortgage rules. In the following examples, we show how these rules are applied and how complex CMO structures can grow out of these simple rules. In our analysis, we concentrate on several of the most common principal and interest rules.

The starting point for the creation of the CMO is the mortgage collateral. For the following examples, we use newly originated agency collateral with a net coupon of 8 percent and a gross coupon of 8.6 percent. Assume a 30-year maturity and an age of 5 months. CMOs are generally priced as structured using the Public Securities Association (PSA) model. We use 175 PSA as our base speed and look at the effects on the structure of prepayments at 100 PSA and at 400 PSA. Figures 11.1a and 11.1b show the principal balance outstanding and the cash flows of the mortgages. Note that the cash flows consist of principal and interest payments. The principal payments represent both the scheduled principal payments and the unscheduled payments (prepayments). The interest cash flows consist of the net interest payment to the investor and the payment to the servicer and guarantor. The change in balances and cash flows for speeds of 100 PSA and 400 PSA are shown in Figures 11.2 and 11.3. The cash flows of mortgages are the raw material for the CMO. The cash flows of the CMO bonds must come from the mortgage cash flows. As the cash flows of the underlying pass-through change, the cash flows of the CMO bonds must also change.

TABLE 11.1   Standard Definitions for REMIC and CMO Bonds

Agency Acronym	Category of Class	Principal-Pay Types
AD	Accretion Directed	Pays principal from specified accretions of accrual bonds. ADs may, in addition, receive principal from the collateral paydowns.
AFC	Available Funds	May receive as principal, in addition to other amounts, interest paid on the underlying assets of the series trust to the extent that the interest exceeds certain required interest distributions on this class (*or related class—Freddie Mac*).
CALL	Call	*Freddie Mac* only: Holders have the right to direct the issuer to redeem the related callable class or classes.
CALLABLE/ CC	Callable	Receive payments based on distributions on underlying callable securities (*directly or indirectly, at the direction of the holder of the related Call class—Freddie Mac*).
GMC	Guaranteed Maturity Class	*Freddie Mac* only: Final payment date is earlier than the latest date by which those classes could be retired by payments on their underlying assets. Typically, holders of a guaranteed maturity class receive payments up to their final payment date from payments made on a related underlying REMIC Class. On its final payment date, however, the holders of an outstanding GMC will be entitled to receive the entire outstanding principal balance of their certificates, plus interest at the applicable class coupon accrued during the related Accrual Period, even if the related underlying REMIC class has not retired.
NPR	No Payment Residual	Receives no payments of principal.
NSJ	Nonsticky Jump	Principal paydown is changed by the occurrence of one or more triggering events. The first time the trigger condition is met, the bond changes to its new priority for receiving principal and remains in its new priority for the life of the bond.
NTL	Notional	No principal balance and bears interest on its notional principal balance. The notional principal balance is used to determine interest distributions on an Interest Only Class that is not entitled to principal.

TABLE 11.1 (*Continued*)

Agency Acronym	Category of Class	Principal-Pay Types
PAC	Planned Amortization Class	Pays principal based on a predetermined schedule established for a group of PAC bonds. The principal redemption schedule of the PAC group is derived by amortizing the collateral based on two collateral prepayment speeds. These two speeds are endpoints for the "structuring PAC range." A PAC group is therefore defined as PAC bonds having the same structuring range. A group can be a single bond class.
PT	Pass-Through	Receives principal payments in direct relation to actual or scheduled payments on the underlying securities, but is not a Strip class.
SC	Structured Collateral	Receives principal payments based on the actual distributions on underlying securities representing regular interests in a REMIC trust.
SCH	Scheduled	Pays principal to a set redemption schedule(s), but does not fit the definition of a PAC or TAC.
SEG	Segment	Combined, in whole or part, with one or more classes (or portion of classes) to form a segment group or aggregate group for purposes of allocating certain principal distribution amounts.
SEQ	Sequential Pay	Starts to pay principal when classes with an earlier priority have paid to a zero balance. SEQ bonds enjoy uninterrupted payment of principal until paid to a zero balance. SEQ bonds may share principal paydown on a pro rata basis with another class.
SJ	Sticky Jump	Principal paydown is changed by the occurrence of one or more triggering events. The first time the trigger condition is met, the bond changes to its new priority for receiving principal and remains in its new priority for the life of the bond.
SPP	Shifting-Payment Percentage	*Freddie Mac only*: Receives principal attributable to prepayments on the underlying mortgages in a different manner than principal attributable to scheduled payments or shifting proportions over time.
STP	Strip	Receives a constant proportion, or strip, of the principal payments on the underlying securities or other assets of the series trust.

TABLE 11.1 (*Continued*)

Agency Acronym	Category of Class	Principal-Pay Types
SUP	Support (or Companion)	Receives principal payments after scheduled payments have been paid to some or all PAC, TAC, or SCH bonds for each payment date.
TAC	Target (or Targeted Amortization Class)	Pay principal based on a predetermined schedule, derived by amortizing the collateral based on a single prepayment speed
XAC	Index Allocation	Principal payment allocation is based on the value of an index.

Agency Acronym	Category of Class	Interest-Pay Types
AFC	Available Funds	Receives as interest certain interest or principal payments on the underlying assets of the related trust. These payments may be insufficient on any distribution date to cover fully the accrued and unpaid interest of this class at its specified interest rate for the related interest accrual period. In this case, the unpaid interest amount may be carried over to subsequent distribution dates (and any unpaid interest amount may itself accrue interest) until payments are sufficient to cover all unpaid interest amounts. It is possible that these insufficiencies will remain unpaid and, if so, they will not be covered by issuer's guaranty.
ARB	Ascending-Rate Bonds	Have predetermined coupon rates that take effect one or more times on dates set forth at issuance.
DLY	Delay	A floating rate, inverse-floating rate, or weighted-average coupon class for which there is a delay of 15 or more days from the end of its accrual period to the related payment date.
DRB	Descending-Rate Bond	Have predetermined class coupons that decrease one or more times on dates determined before issuance.
EXE	Excess	Entitled to collateral principal and interest paid that exceeds the amount of principal and interest obligated to all bonds in the deal.
FIX	Fixed	Coupons are fixed throughout the life of the bond.

TABLE 11.1 (*Continued*)

Agency Acronym	Category of Class	Interest-Pay Types
FLT	Floater (or Floating Rate)	Coupons reset periodically based on an index and may have a cap or floor. The coupon varies directly with changes in the index.
IDC/DIF	Index Differential	Has an interest rate that reset periodically computed in part on the basis of the difference (*or other specified relationship—Freddie Mac, Fannie Mae*) between two designated indexes (e.g., LIBOR and the 10-year Treasury index).
INV	Inverse Floater	Coupons reset periodically (like floaters) based on an index and may have a cap or floor. The coupon varies inversely with changes in the index.
IO	Interest only	Receive some or all of the interest portion of the underlying collateral and little or no principal. A notional amount is the amount of principal used as a reference to calculate the amount of interest due. A nominal amount is actual principal that will be paid to the bond. It is referred to as "nominal" since it is extremely small compared to other classes.
NPR (also above)	No payment residual	Receives no payment of interest.
PEC	Payment Exchange Certificates	*Freddie Mac only*: Class coupons vary, in whole or in part, based on payments of interest made to or from one or more related classes.
PO	Principal only	Receives no interest.
PZ	Partial accrual	Accretes interest (which is added to the outstanding principal balance) and receives interest distributions in the same period. These bonds have a stated coupon, which is equal to the sum of the accretion coupon and interest distribution coupon.
W/WAC	Weighted-Average Coupon	Represent a blended interest rate (*effective weighted-average interest rate—Fannie Mae*), which may change in any period. Bonds may be comprised of nondetachable components, some of which have different coupons.

TABLE 11.1   (*Continued*)

Agency Acronym	Category of Class	Interest-Pay Types
Z	Accrual	Accrete interest that is added to the outstanding principal balance. This accretion may continue until the bond begins paying principal or until some other event has occurred.

Agency Acronym		Other Types
CPT	Component	Comprised of nondetachable components. The principal pay type or sequence of principal pay of each component may vary.
IMD	Increased Minimum Denomination	*Ginnie Mae only:* To be offered and sold in higher minimum denominations than those of other classes.
LIQ	Liquidity	Intended to qualify as a liquid asset for savings institutions. LIQ bonds are any agency-issued bonds that have a stated maturity of 5 years (or less), or any non-agency issued bonds that have a stated maturity of 3 years (or less), in each case from issue date.
RTL	Retail	Designated to be sold to retail investors.
R, RS, RL	Residual	Designated for tax purposes as the residual interest in a REMIC.
RDM	Redeemable	*Fannie Mae only:* Certificate that is redeemable directly or indirectly as specified in the prospectus.
SP	Special	*Ginnie Mae only:* Having characteristics other than those identified above.
TBD	To Be Defined	Does not fit into any of the current definitions

Sources: Fannie Mae, Freddie Mac, and Ginnie Mae.

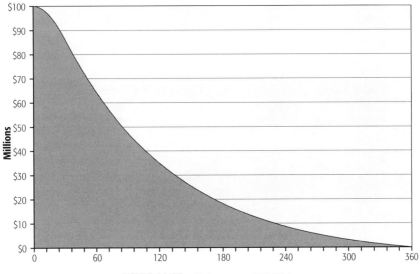

FIGURE 11.1A   Balance at 175 PSA.

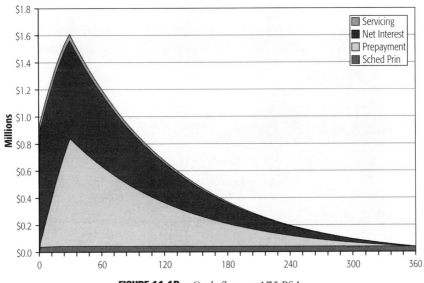

FIGURE 11.1B   Cash flow at 175 PSA.

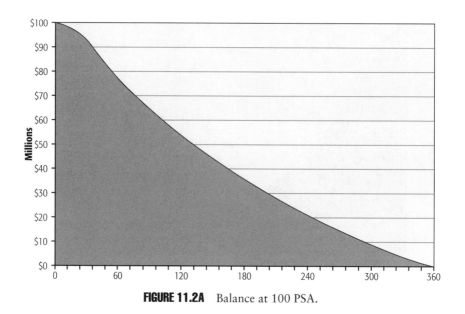

FIGURE 11.2A   Balance at 100 PSA.

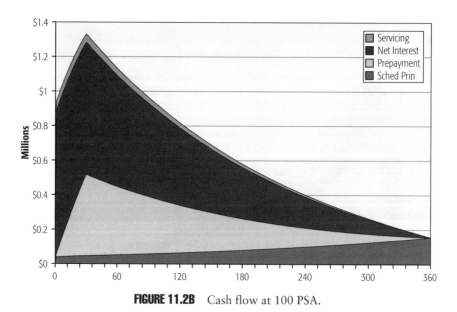

FIGURE 11.2B   Cash flow at 100 PSA.

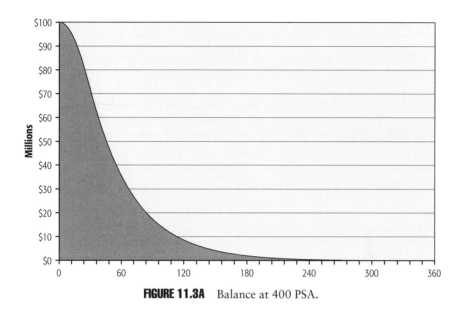

FIGURE 11.3A   Balance at 400 PSA.

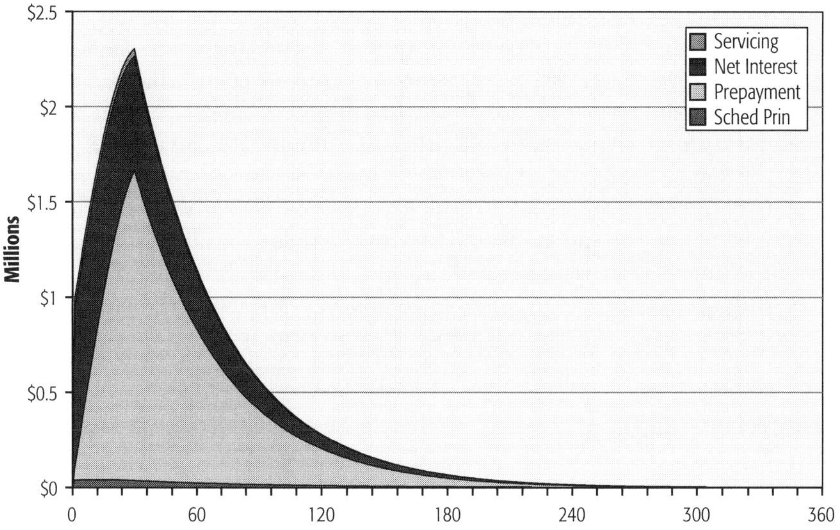

FIGURE 11.3B   Cash flow at 400 PSA.

PRINCIPAL-PAY TYPES

Principal-pay rules determine how principal payments are split between the
CMO tranches. These rules can be applied alone or in combination with one
another. For **sequential** bonds, one bond is completely paid down before
principal payment begins on the next. **Pro rata** bonds pay down simultaneously according to a fixed allocation. **Planned amortization classes** (PACs)
are part of a group of bonds classified as scheduled bonds. These bonds receive priority within the structure for certain principal payments. **Support**
bonds are created in conjunction with the scheduled bond and absorb the remaining principal payments.

INTEREST-PAY TYPES

Interest-pay rules determine the amount of interest received by the CMO
bondholders each period. Interest-payment rules are linked with principal-
pay rules to produce a wide variety of bond types. One rule of CMO creation is that the combined interest on the CMO bonds must be less than the
available interest from the collateral. **Fixed** interest payments are the most
common type. The bondholder receives an interest amount, which is a constant percentage of the outstanding balance. In an **accrual** bond (or Z bond),
the bondholder does not receive interest payments for some time period.
During this time, the interest payments are converted to principal and the
balance of the investment increases. A **floating**-rate bond's coupon changes
based on an underlying index. Floating-rate bonds typically pay a margin
above an index (frequently LIBOR) and have an interest-rate cap. **Inverse-
floating**-rate bonds are usually produced in conjunction with floating-rate
bonds. Their coupon moves inversely with the index, usually at some multiple of the index. They typically have a cap and a floor. **Principal-only** and **interest-only** payment types provide for bonds with principal payments and no
interest payment or interest payments with no principal.

SEQUENTIAL BONDS

The first CMO bonds were sequential CMOs. They were created to turn
mortgage-backed securities into more corporate bondlike investments. Sequential bonds tend to narrow the time over which principal payments are
received, creating a more bulletlike structure. Figure 11.4 shows the cash
flow of a typical sequential CMO. In this example, classes A, B, C, and Z are
sequential bonds. Class A receives all of the principal payments first. Once

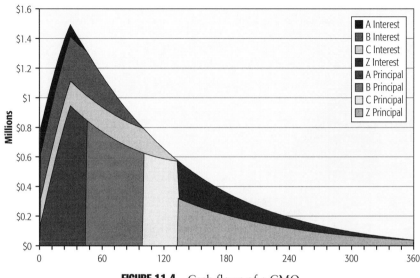

FIGURE 11.4 Cash flows of a CMO.

class A is completely paid off, then class B begins to receive principal payments. Once class B is paid off, then C begins principal payments, and so on until class Z is paid off. Note that each bond receives principal payments over a relatively narrow time period.

The interest payment on each of these tranches is fixed and equal to the net coupon of the underlying mortgage-backed securities (MBS). Each bond receives a monthly interest payment equal to the coupon divided by twelve times the outstanding balance of that tranche. Thus, tranches A, B, and C all receive interest payments beginning in month one. Class Z is an accrual bond. Rather than receiving its share of interest, its interest payment is converted to principal and is used to increase the balance of the Z tranche. The interest payment that should have gone to Z is used to make principal payments to tranches A, B, and C. This can also be seen in Figure 11.4. Figure 11.5 shows the balance outstanding of each tranche over time. Note that the balance of tranche A begins to decline immediately. The balance of tranches B and C are constant until the prior tranches are paid off. Tranche Z shows an increasing balance until all of the earlier tranches are paid off. The net effect is to shorten the average life of tranches A, B, and C. Typically, shorter tranches are priced at lower yields. By increasing the amount of principal received by the shorter tranches, CMO structures are able to increase the value of the CMO arbitrage.

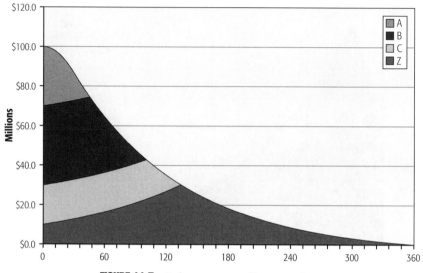

FIGURE 11.5   Balance outstanding over time.

As prepayments increase, the payments on the bonds will be received earlier. While some analysts have argued that sequential bonds offer protection from prepayment risk, it is difficult to make general statements about the amount of risk in a sequential bond. Rather than rely on a general prescription of which bonds are safe and which are risky, it is better to perform an analysis of the specific tranche you are considering. Chapters 8, 10, and 13 describe some of these methods in more detail.

PRO RATA BONDS

Much of the complexity of CMO structures arises from layering different types of principal-payment rules. Pro rata bonds provide one means to effect this layering. Pro rata bonds are two or more bonds that receive cash flows according to exactly the same rules. Cash flows available to these bonds are divided proportionally. Figure 11.6 shows an example of pro rata bonds. The figure shows only the principal payments of the bonds. Tranches B1 and B2 receive a pro rata share of the cash flows that went to class B in the earlier example. Here B1 receives 40 percent of the principal while B2 receives 60 percent of the principal.

Pro rata bonds are created to allow for different interest-payment rules for the same principal-payment pattern. Different interest-payment rules

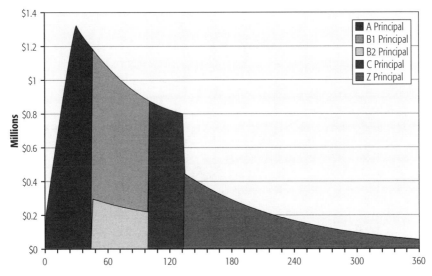

FIGURE 11.6   Principal payments of a pro rata bond.

will change the risk characteristics of the bonds and make them attractive to different investors. Given this pro rata structure, there are several choices of interest-pay rules possible for B1 and B2. One possibility is that they will both be fixed-rate bonds, but with different coupons. Say B1 has a coupon of 6 percent. The coupon of B2 cannot exceed 9.33 percent, since the weighted-average coupon cannot exceed 8 percent. Through this mechanism it is possible to create bonds that have coupons that are higher and lower than the collateral coupon.

Another example of a pro rata bond is an IO strip. It is possible to create an IO off of any bond. For some time, REMIC rules required that all regular interests have a principal component. At that time, IOs were created with a tiny piece of principal and generally had coupons of 1,200 percent due to federal wire requirements. The limitation on principal has now been removed so that a pure interest strip can be created off of any bond. Some people call IOs that are created off of CMO bonds IOettes to distinguish them from IO strips created using all the interest payments of an MBS. In a CMO, IO strips are used to lower the coupon of the CMO tranche. Due to prepayment risk, investors prefer to buy bonds at a slight discount, so their yield will be less affected by changing prepayments.

Other forms of pro rata bonds are floaters and inverse floaters. Just as it is possible to create two fixed-rate bonds, where the combined coupon equals the coupon of the collateral, it is possible to create a floating-rate

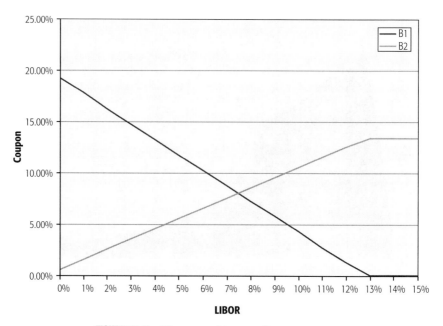

FIGURE 11.7   Floater and inverse floater coupons.

bond and an inverse floating-rate bond whose coupon equals the collateral coupon. Suppose bond B2 is a floating-rate bond with a coupon equal to LIBOR + 50 basis points: If LIBOR is currently 4 percent, then the coupon on B2 is 4.5 percent. The coupon on B1 would then be 13.25 percent. If LIBOR rises to 5 percent, the coupon on B2 becomes 5.5 percent, while the coupon on B1 must fall to 11.75 percent. As LIBOR rises, the coupon on B2 floats with LIBOR, while the coupon on B1 moves inversely to LIBOR. The coupon on B1 changes by 1.5 times the amount of the change in LIBOR. This inverse floater is said to have a slope of 1.5. Because the interest must come from the fixed-interest payment of the collateral, the coupon on these floaters must be capped. The floating-rate bond cannot exceed 13.33 percent, while the inverse floater cannot exceed 19.25 percent. Figure 11.7 is a graph of the possible coupon combinations of B1 and B2. The coupon on the inverse floater is usually described by a formula. In this case, the formula would be 19.25 percent − 1.5 × LIBOR.

SCHEDULED BONDS

While sequential bonds may offer some allocation of prepayment risk, investors seeking more protection from prepayment risk have turned to scheduled bonds for greater certainty of cash flow. Several types of scheduled bonds exist. Here we concentrate on planned-amortization classes (PACs). PACs are designed to produce constant cash flows within a range of prepayment rates. Unlike sequential bonds, PAC bonds provide a true allocation of risk. PAC bonds clearly have more stable cash flows than comparable non-PAC bonds. The additional stability of the PAC bonds comes at a cost. In order to create a more stable PAC bond, it is necessary to create a less stable support bond. Support bonds bear the risk of cash-flow changes. Although PAC bonds are somewhat protected from prepayment risk, they are not completely risk free. If prepayments are fast enough or slow enough, the cash flows of the PAC bonds will change. Furthermore, there can be great differences in the performance of PAC bonds. As with all CMO bonds, it is better to evaluate the cash-flow characteristics of the bond you are considering as an investment, than to rely on the type of the bond to indicate its riskiness. Some PAC bonds can be variable and some support bonds can be very stable.

PACs are created by calculating the cash flow available from the collateral using two different prepayment speeds: a fast speed, 300 PSA, for example, and a slow speed, such as 100 PSA.

Figure 11.8 shows the principal cash flows of our collateral using 100 PSA and 300 PSA. The cash flow available each period under each scenario is the cash flow that can be used to construct the PAC bond. Under the 100 PSA assumption, there is less available in the early years of the CMO and

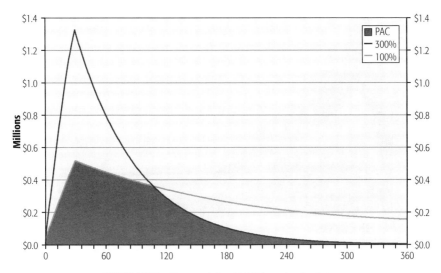

FIGURE 11.8 Determining PAC bond schedule.

more available in the later years. Under the 300 PSA assumption, there is more cash flow available during the early years of the CMO, and less available in the later years.

Figure 11.9 shows the cash flows of a CMO consisting of two classes, a PAC bond and a support bond, assuming a prepayment speed of 175 PSA. The PAC bond was constructed with a PAC bond of 100 PSA to 300 PSA. The principal payment pattern of the PAC bond is exactly equal to the schedule created using the two PAC band speeds. The cash flows are neither sequential nor pro rata. The support bond pays down simultaneously with the PAC bond, but the ratio of payments is determined by the PAC schedule and varies depending on prepayment rates. Figure 11.10 shows the paydown of the balance of the two classes at 175 PSA.

As prepayment rates change, the cash-flow characteristics shift. At a speed of 100 PSA, far less cash flow is available in the early years of the CMO. Figure 11.11 shows the cash flows are 100 PSA. In the early years, all the principal cash flows go to the PAC bond. Principal payments on the support bond are deferred. Under this scenario, the cash flows of the support bond extend. The support bond does, however, receive more interest payments. Since 100 PSA is within the PAC bonds, the PAC bond still receives cash flow according to the original PAC schedule.

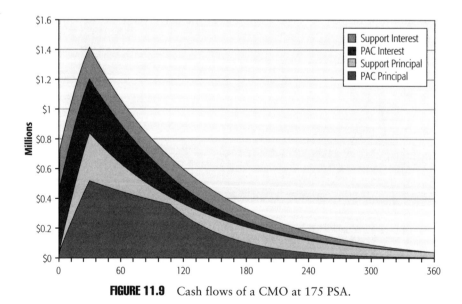

FIGURE 11.9   Cash flows of a CMO at 175 PSA.

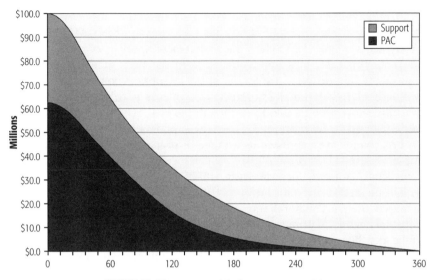

FIGURE 11.10 Principal balance at 175 PSA.

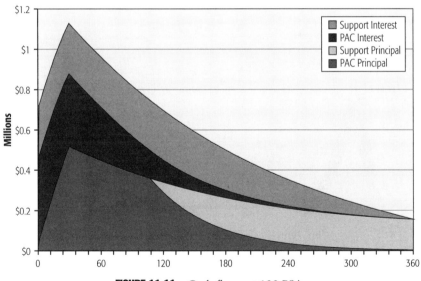

FIGURE 11.11 Cash flows at 100 PSA.

If prepayments are outside of the PAC bands, then the PAC schedule cannot be met. Figure 11.12 shows the cash flows of the CMO assuming prepayments at 400 PSA. Here the prepayment speed is outside the PAC bands. In this case, it is impossible to keep the PAC schedule. The cash flows to the support bond are accelerated. The support bond is fully paid off by month 91 and all remaining principal payments go to the PAC bond, significantly shortening its life. Even though the PAC schedule cannot be met, the PAC bond is still more stable than the support bond.

PAC bands are expressed as a range of prepayment speeds. In our example, we use 100 PSA to 300 PSA, which means that if prepayments occur at any single constant speed between 100 PSA and 300 PSA, the PAC schedule will be met. It does not mean that the PAC schedule will be met if prepayments on the collateral stay between 100 PSA and 300 PSA. Even if prepayments vary within the PAC bands, it is possible that the schedule will not be met. For example, if prepayments stay near 300 PSA for several years and then fall to near 100 PSA, the PAC bond will probably extend outside the PAC band. During the years at 300 PSA, the support bond will be nearly paid off. Then when prepayments slow, there is no way to cushion the extension of the PAC bond. Once again, analysis of the bond's cash flows are a more useful measure of the value of the bond than can be determined from its name alone.

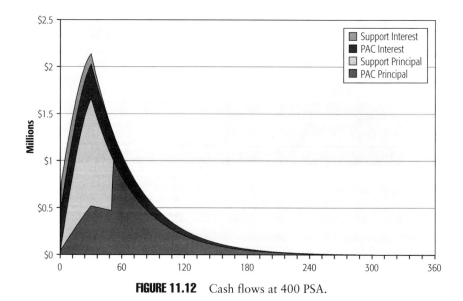

FIGURE 11.12   Cash flows at 400 PSA.

SEQUENTIAL PACs AND OTHER COMBINATIONS

Just as sequential bonds were created to allow investors to specify a maturity range for their investments, PACs can be divided sequentially to provide more narrow paydown structures. Figure 11.13 shows the cash flows of a CMO where the PAC has been split into several different bonds. These sequential PACs narrow the range of years over which principal payments occur. Investors with short horizons choose the earlier PACs, whereas investors with longer horizons choose the longer PACs. While these bonds were all structured using the 100 PSA to 300 PSA PAC band, the actual range of speeds over which their schedules will be met may differ. In particular, the early bonds can withstand faster speeds than the top of the PAC band, without varying from their scheduled payments.

Sequential PACs are another example of how the CMO structuring rules can be combined to create more complex structures to meet a wider variety of investor requirements. It is possible to take any bond and further structure it. For example, the sequential PACs could be split using a pro rata structure to create high- and low-coupon PACs.

One common structure takes mortgage collateral and strips off an IO piece to lower the coupon of all the CMO classes and splits the collateral into a PAC and a support. Then, a PAC class within the PAC class is created.

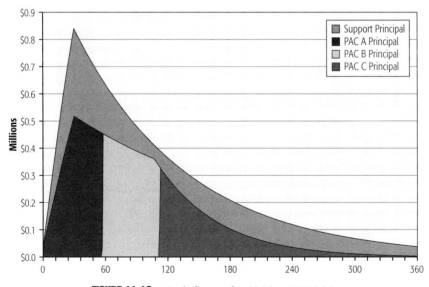

FIGURE 11.13 Cash flows of a CMO at 175 PSA.

The more stable PACs are called PAC Is and the less stable ones are called PAC IIs. These bonds are divided sequentially into PACs with various average lives. These sequential PACs are divided pro rata in order to strip down their coupons so that the bonds trade at or below par. The remaining IO strips are sold individually or together as IOettes. The structuring continues with the support piece, which is divided sequentially. The sequential support pieces are split pro rata to create a variety of fixed-rate, floating-rate, and inverse-floating-rate bonds. Using the few simple structures we saw previously, structures with 50 or more classes can be created.

INTEREST ONLY AND PRINCIPAL ONLY

IO and PO bonds can be created within CMO structures as a type of pro rata bond as described earlier. They can also be created independently by stripping MBS. Both FNMA and FHLMC offer programs under which MBS can be split into IOs and POs. IOs and POs tend to be very volatile. By splitting principal and interest, the effects of prepayments on value are amplified.

PO bonds receive all of the principal payments. Therefore, the total amount of cash flow to be received by the PO investor is known from the start. On our $100 million of collateral, the PO investor will receive $100 million of cash flow. The uncertainty is over the timing of the cash flows. At faster prepayment speeds, the cash flow is received over a relatively short period. The cash-flow pattern can vary greatly. Figure 11.14 shows the cash flows of the PO at various prepayment speeds.

Since POs receive no interest, they are priced at a discount. Due to discounting effects, the value of the PO increases as the cash flow is received sooner. That is, other things being equal, you would rather receive your money sooner than later. The value of a PO will then be affected by the discount rate and the timing of prepayments. As interest rates fall, the discount rates fall and prepayment rates increase. Both factors serve to increase the value of the PO. POs thus become very bullish instruments, strongly benefiting from falling rates. The performance characteristics of POs, however, are very dependent on the characteristics of the underlying collateral. POs from premium collateral have very different performance characteristics than POs from discount collateral due to their very different prepayment characteristics. Furthermore, POs are very volatile instruments because slight changes in prepayment rates can have a significant impact on value.

IO securities have no assured cash flows. The amount of interest received depends on the balance outstanding. As prepayments increase, the amount of cash flow received by the IO decreases. As prepayments decrease, the amount of cash flow increases. The change in cash flow can be significant. Figure 11.15 shows the cash flow of the IO under several prepayment

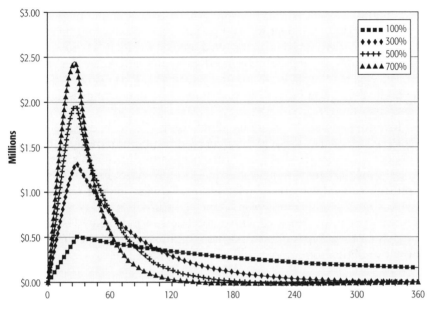

FIGURE 11.14 Cash flows of a PO at various prepayment speeds.

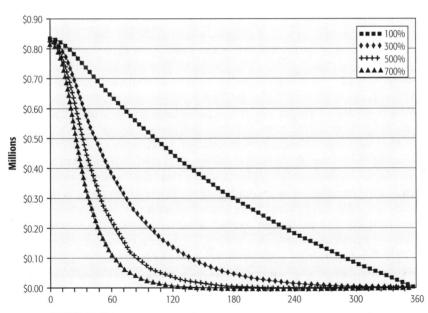

FIGURE 11.15 Cash flows of an IO at various prepayment speeds.

assumptions. Cash flow under the 700 percent PSA assumption is just a fraction of the cash flow under the 100 percent PSA assumption. IO securities have a feature that is unique in the fixed-income world. IOs tend to increase in value as rates rise and decrease in value as rates fall, because as rates rise, prepayments tend to slow. Slower prepayments lead to greater cash flows to the IO investor. The increase in cash flow more than compensates for the higher discount rate.

Investors should be cautious about using IOs to hedge other fixed-income instruments. Although the general direction of movement of an IO is opposite to other fixed-income instruments, it is difficult to assess precise hedge ratios. IOs are extremely sensitive to prepayment expectations and it is difficult to establish precise relationships between interest rates and prepayment rates. Highly sensitive instruments such as IOs and POs require sophisticated analysis tempered with a good deal of judgment. The difficulty in assessing these types of instruments is an indication of the limitation of current valuation tools.

SENIOR/SUBORDINATED STRUCTURES

So far we have concentrated on CMO structures where the underlying collateral or the CMO itself is guaranteed by the agencies (GNMA, FNMA, FHLMC). For collateral that does not meet the agency standards, a different type of structure is required. With agency collateral, the investor bears no default risk. In the case of a default, the investor receives a prepayment equal to the full principal amount of the loan. If the loan is not guaranteed by the agencies, other forms of credit enhancement are required to attract investors. Credit enhancement can be either external or internal. External credit enhancement is provided by a mortgage insurance company. The insurance operates at the pool level and provides investors with the assurance that they will not suffer from mortgage delinquencies and defaults.

Internal credit enhancement operates by relying on the overall credit quality of the mortgages to produce different classes of bonds with different exposure to credit loss. Generally, a senior class is produced, which is protected from credit losses, along with a junior piece, which absorbs the losses. Senior/subordinated structures are somewhat akin to PAC bonds. However, instead of offering protection against prepayment risk, the senior class is protected from default risk.

The construction of senior/subordinated deals can become quite complex. New structures are continually being developed to make the execution more efficient. In some structures, a junior class is set up so that it is large enough to absorb worst-case losses. The guidelines for the size of the subordinated structures are set by the rating agencies (Standard & Poor's, Moody's, or Fitch). Underwriters and issuers generally seek at least a double A rating on the senior class. The junior piece generally stays outstanding until the balance of the senior piece has declined sufficiently so that the risk of loss is minimal. Additional credit protection may come from a reserve account funded with cash or with excess interest that is not going to either the senior or junior class.

The senior/subordinated structures may be further structured using any of the tools described earlier. These CMOs tend to have fewer classes than the agency-backed CMOs. Credit risk and senior/subordinate structures are discussed in more detail in Chapters 15 and 16.

CMOs allow mortgage cash flows to be restructured to create securities with a wide variety of investment performance characteristics. Complex CMOs are generally the result of application of relatively simple cash-flow-allocation rules. While the rules may be simple, the resulting securities may be quite complex. Knowing the structure of a CMO may provide some insight into the risks of the bond. However, analysis of the actual cash flows under a variety of interest-rate and prepayment scenarios will produce more reliable results. Very often, the performance characteristics of two same-type bonds can differ dramatically.

EXERCISES

Constructing a CMO. In these exercises, we construct CMOs using principal and interest pay types described earlier. The following exercises should be done on a spreadsheet, using these assumptions:

- Monthly cash flows
- Monthly interest payments
- PSA model for prepayments
- 30-year level pay mortgages
- Net coupon and gross coupon

Exercise 11.1 Create the cash flows of the underlying securities. The structure of any CMO is dependent on the cash flows of the underlying mortgage pool. The cash flows in the first exercises form the basis for all the CMOs that we create in these exercises.

■ Use the cash-flow model from Chapter 8.
■ Assume an initial balance of $100 million.
■ Assume a new coupon of 10 percent and a gross coupon of 10.65 percent.
■ Assume a maturity of 30 years.

Calculate the cash flows of the mortgages assuming 100 percent PSA, 175 percent PSA, and 400 percent PSA. Graph the cash flows and balances.

Exercise 11.2   Compute the average life of the mortgages for 100 percent PSA, 175 percent PSA, and 400 percent PSA.

Exercise 11.3   Create a fixed-rate sequential CMO. Sequential bonds are formed using a principal payment rule. All principal payments go to the first bond until it is retired, then principal cash flows go to the next bond.

Fixed rate is an interest prepayment rule. Each bond receives an interest payment each period equal to its beginning of period times its coupon. Even if the bond is not receiving a principal payment, it still receives interest payments. In the following exercises, there will be interest payments from the collateral that are not distributed to any bond.

Start with the assumptions of Exercise 11.1. Assume the following bond characteristics:

Bond	Balance ($)	Coupon
A	30mm	7
B	40mm	9
C	30mm	10

Calculate and graph the cash flows of bonds A, B, and C, assuming 175 percent PSA.

Exercise 11.4 Calculate the average life of bonds A, B, and C, assuming 175 percent PSA.

Exercise 11.5 Create a sequential CMO with a Z-bond. A Z-bond or accrual bond is a principal-pay rule. The Z-bond receives no cash flow until the prior bonds are completely paid down. The interest due to the Z-bond, while the prior bonds are outstanding, is added (accrues) to the principal amount due to the Z-bond. That cash flow is then added to the principal available to pay down the prior bonds. In other words, the accrual structure converts the interest accruing to the Z-bond into principal for payment to other bonds. Once the other bonds are retired, the Z-bond pays interest and principal concurrently.

Replace Bond C in Exercise 11.3 with a Z-bond. Calculate and graph the cash flows of bonds A, B, and Z assuming 175 percent PSA.

Exercise 11.6 Calculate the average life of bonds A and B assuming 175 percent PSA. Compare these to the average lives calculated in Exercise 11.4.

	Average Life	
Bond	Balance	Coupon
A	30 mm	7
B	40 mm	9

Exercise 11.7   Calculate the average life of the Z-bond in Exercise 11.5. Accruals create negative principal cash flows. How does this impact the calculation of average life?

Exercise 11.8   Create a pro rata CMO. Pro rata is a principal-pay rule. It is primarily used to assign different coupons to bonds with the same principal-payment characteristics. Pro rata bonds receive principal payments in fixed proportion to each other. Splitting cash flows of a bond can create them. As created in Exercise 11.8, Figure 11.6 shows a pro rata bond created from Bond B of Figure 11.4.

Create pro rata bonds using Class B created in Exercise 11.3 (without the Z-bond). Assume Class B1 receives 75 percent of the principal payments of Bond B. Assume Class B2 receives 25 percent of the principal payments of Bond B. Compute and graph the cash flows of bonds B1 and B2 assuming 175 percent PSA.

Exercise 11.9   Create a PAC/support CMO. PAC is a principal-pay rule. A support bond is always created in conjunction with the PAC. A PAC is created so that its principal cash flows are fixed for a certain range of prepayment rates, called the PAC band.

The support bond absorbs the principal cash flows that exceed those scheduled to be paid to the PAC. The PAC structure provides for a reallocation of prepayment risk. For this exercise we return to the unstructured cash flows of Exercise 11.1. PAC cash flows are shown in Figure 11.9.

Use 100 percent PSA and 300 percent PSA for the bonds. Evaluate cash flows and average life at 75 percent PSA, 100 percent PSA, 175 percent PSA, 300 percent PSA, and 400 percent PSA.

PSA (%)	Average Life	
	PAC	Support
75		
100		
175		
300		
400		

CHAPTER 12

Interest-Rate Volatility, Options, and Models

The concepts of interest rates, forward curve, and discounting, introduced in Chapter 7, are the basis for *static* valuation. In reality, not only are future interest rates uncertain, but the future cash flows of many securitized investments are also uncertain, as they depend (are contingent) on interest rates. The need for sophisticated models for mortgage-backed securities (MBS) and asset-backed securities (ABS) is due to the embedded options found in most MBS and ABS products in the form of the borrowers option to prepay. But first, without any specific reference to the mortgage market, we introduce the concepts of market volatility and optionality. We reformulate the pricing concept to reflect a world of uncertainty and revisit the concept of arbitrage-free. **Term structure models**, discussed at the end of this chapter, may facilitate a well-defined quantitative valuation methodology.

THE CONCEPT AND MEASURES OF VOLATILITY

We cannot tell in advance what interest rates will be. Investors may be either enriched or bankrupted from sudden changes in interest rates. Financial institutions devote considerable resources to risk management and hedging. Yet, if future interest rates were deterministic, there would be no need to hedge. Coping with uncertainty is a central feature of investment markets.

Basic Definitions and First Findings

The pricing of options and embedded-options instruments uses a statistical concept to describe the magnitude of potential interest-rate changes. The key notion is the **volatility of interest rates**. While this term conjures up images of instability, flares of activity, and unpredictability, it is actually a very specific description of the range of possible outcomes. More precisely, volatility can be defined as the annualized standard deviation of a rate's daily increments. Table 12.1 shows a calculation example for yields on the 10-year Treasury measured over the first half of June 2002 (10 business days). As part of the measurement, we take a daily time series and then transform it into *absolute changes* and *relative changes*, much as if we were measuring portfolio performance.

The absolute rate changes are computed by taking the difference between the interest rates on successive days. The relative changes are computed by dividing the absolute change by the starting rate (see Table 12.1). For example, for the first day the absolute change is 5.00343 − 5.03234 = −0.0289. The relative increment is −0.0289/5.03234 = −.0057. In order to calculate the daily volatility, we just take the standard deviation of the daily absolute and relative change series. In this example, the standard deviations are 0.048 (for absolute increments) and 0.00966 (for relative increments). To compute **volatility**, we place these daily measures on an annual basis, scaling by the number of trading days in the year (approximately 260):

$$\text{Relative Volatility} = \text{Daily Standard Relative Deviation} \times \sqrt{260}$$
$$= 0.00966 \times \sqrt{260} = 0.1557$$

$$\text{Absolute Volatility} = \text{Daily Standard Absolute Deviation} \times \sqrt{260}$$
$$= 0.0480 \times \sqrt{260} = 0.7730$$

Thus, in our example of the 10-day yield series, we would calculate the annual volatility as 77.3 basis points (absolute) or 15.57 percent (relative). The relative volatility times the average yield for the period $0.1557 \times 4.983 = 0.776$ is close to the absolute yield volatility of 0.773, as one would expect.

TABLE 12.1 Computing Rate Changes

Date	Rate	Absolute Increments	Relative Increments
03-Jun-02	5.03234		
04-Jun-02	5.00343	−0.0289	−0.0057
05-Jun-02	5.049	0.0456	0.0091
06-Jun-02	5.01176	−0.0372	−0.0074
07-Jun-02	5.06165	0.0499	0.0100
10-Jun-02	5.03885	−0.0228	−0.0045
11-Jun-02	4.975	−0.0639	−0.0127
12-Jun-02	4.95004	−0.0250	−0.0050
13-Jun-02	4.9028	−0.0472	−0.0095
14-Jun-02	4.80276	−0.1000	−0.0204

There are a couple of questions an attentive reader may ask here. First of all, why the square root? The explanation lies in stochastic calculus: When adding up independent numbers, the means are additive, as are the variances. The total annual period is comprised of 260 daily increments. Assuming for a moment that these daily components are independent of one another (i.e., the rate change from June 3 to June 4 has no relation to the one from June 13 to June 14), the annual variance should be 260 times greater than the daily variance. Taking the square root leads to the relationship for standard deviations.

The second relevant clarification may damage a naive understanding of volatility as the annual standard deviation. Volatility measures only the **rate of uncertainty;** this concept does not assume that the daily-measured volatility remains constant over time. Just as when driving in traffic with starts and stops there is a difference between instantaneous speed and the average velocity. Third, an important, assumption for annualizing the daily volatilities is that the daily increments are **serially independent.** If there is a relationship between rate changes on one day and another day, then we say there is **serial correlation.** The square-root rule will not produce an accurate measure of the annual standard deviation if there is serial correlation in the random process. Figures 12.1 and 12.2 illustrate that volatility has been volatile.

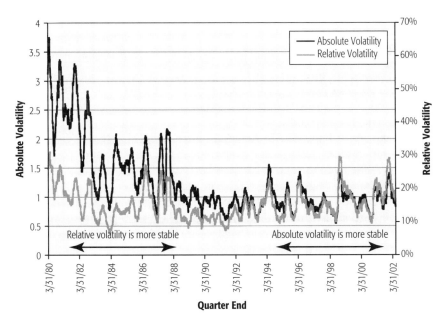

FIGURE 12.1   History of volatility for the 10-year Treasury yield.

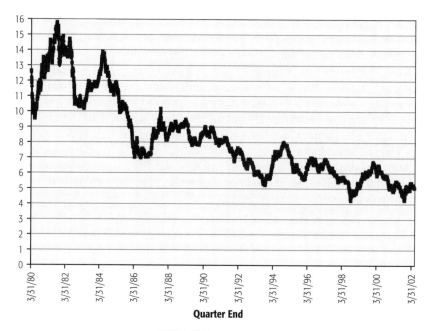

FIGURE 12.2   Rate level.

In the 1980s, both volatility measures exhibited instability, although the relative one appeared to be much more stable. However, since the 1990s, the absolute volatility measure has become more stable, oscillating around 1 percent (100 basis points). Based on these observations, it is not difficult to understand why during different time periods, the relative volatility was moving inversely, and the absolute volatility directly, with respect to the rate level as shown in Figure 12.2. As we see later in the chapter, pricing in the interest-rate market and associated options market reflects these important findings. Aside from the explicit level-related effect, both volatility measures seemingly synchronously react to economic disturbances.

Different points of the yield curve have differing volatility, too. This observation suggests that not only do the rates have a **term structure**, but their volatility has a term structure as well. A hump shape of such a volatility curve is often observed (Figure 12.3).

It can be attributed to the following two characteristics:

1. Absence of change in the short rates unless regulators take actions.
2. The dampening force of the mean reversion, which is explained further.

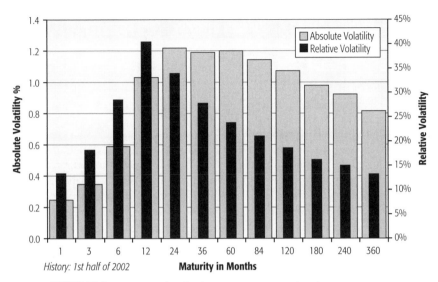

FIGURE 12.3 Historical volatility term structure for the swap rates.

A Model for Randomness

Can we describe the randomness mathematically? It is perhaps simpler than it sounds. In fact, having become acquainted with volatility, we did most of the task. A general model for an interest-rate process that describes how interest rates will vary over time, $r(t)$, will have the following form:

$$dr = (Drift)\, dt + (Volatility)\, dz \qquad (12.1)$$

What does this mean? Notations dr and dt refer to small increments measured over an infinitesimally short time period. Variable dz represents small changes in $z(t)$, which is called **Brownian motion** (also known as the **Wiener process**). It is the source of randomness. We cannot control the exact value of this variable. *Drift* and *Volatility* describe how the changes in rates are related to changes in time and the random variable dz. The mathematical model (12.1) can be thought of in the following way: The change in interest rate over a small time period is the result of a number representing systematic drift times the amount of time change plus a random shock scaled by the amount of volatility.

$$\Delta r = (Drift)(passage\ of\ time) + (Volatility)(random\ shock)$$

A BRIEF EXCURSION TO BROWNIAN MOTION

Brownian motion is

- Normally distributed.
- Has a zero mean ("centered").
- Its time increments are serially independent.
- Its own volatility is scaled to 1.

Therefore, $z(t)$ has a standard deviation of $\sqrt{t}$ (for the same reason that a square root appears in the annualization of daily volatility). Any particular function $z(t)$ is said to be a "realization" or a "sample path" of the Brownian motion. The Brownian motion, therefore, can be thought of as a container of random paths subject to the conditions described above. Figure 12.4 depicts a sample path and the single and double standard-deviation zones.

With the use of *Volatility* multiples, we can scale the rate process to any volatility level. The *Drift* variable simulates a systematic, non-random tendency. For example, it can model a central tendency function known as **mean reversion** (described later). Equation (12.1) is called the **stochastic differential equation**.

Both multiples, *Drift* and *Volatility*, do not have to be constants. They can be functions of time t and rate r. Any particular specification

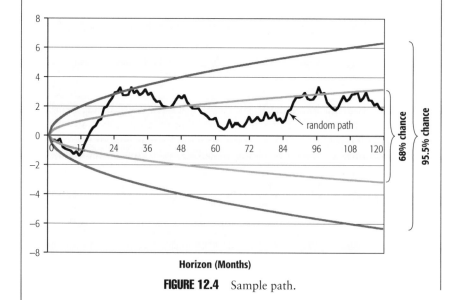

FIGURE 12.4 Sample path.

of *Drift* (*t*,*r*) and *Volatility* (*t*,*r*) leads to a specific rate model, but not necessarily a good one. At this stage, it is enough to understand that a good model can be a strong quantitative pricing tool. Although we cannot know what the random variable $z(t)$ is going to do, we, at least, can simulate its behavior with a large number of random scenarios. The **Monte-Carlo method**, explained in Chapter 13, draws on this idea. We may also be able to do some intelligent analytical work, making the brute-force simulations unnecessary. We could even make sure that the random process $r(t)$ is consistent with ("calibrated to") prices of widely traded interest-rate instruments; then we will feel more confident applying it to the MBS/ABS market.

Mean Reversion and Market Stability

Consider the following special form of equation (12.1): $dr = 5rdt + \sigma dz$. Can this equation model an actual interest rate? Using calculus, we note that the solution to this equation will not only grow with time, but will grow exponentially as it will contain an e^{5t} term. Since interest rates cannot increase exponentially forever (at least, they never have), we need to dismiss this formula as inappropriate for the job.

How about $dr = \sigma dz$? Since the drift is zero, and the initial value $r(0)$ is known, the process will randomly evolve around this value, on average. Whether the initial rate is high or low, the model will stay centered around it. The standard deviation, as we already know, will grow as $\sqrt{t}$. This may not be a very good thing either. A century from now, the magnitude of the standard deviation will be huge, at 10 times annual volatility σ. Figures 12.1 and 12.2 demonstrate that interest rates tend to stay within a range. Their uncertainty is limited.

Both of these models briefly described above suffer the same disease; they are unstable. Observable objects in economics, finance, engineering, or physics tend to be stable; otherwise, they would not be able to exist long enough to be observed. **Mean reversion** is the feature that makes financial markets stable. It is simply a properly chosen specification of the drift term that would ensure the dampening effect (also known as **central tendency**). If the rate has randomly grown too high or fallen too low, the drift term will help "return" it back. Here is an example:

$$dr = a(r_\infty - r)dt + \sigma dz \qquad (12.2)$$

where mean reversion $a > 0$. This time, the solution will contain e^{-at}, a decaying component that indicates stability. The mean converges to parameter,

r_∞, the long-term equilibrium (now we see the point for this strange notation). The standard deviation will grow with time as

$$\sigma\sqrt{(1 - e^{-2at})/2a}$$

and converges to

$$\sigma/\sqrt{2a}$$

as horizon extends. Figure 12.5 compares the standard deviation (lines launching from the origin) and equivalent (average) volatility, for different levels of mean reversion, including the zero one ($\sigma = 1\%$ was assumed).

Mean reversion, therefore, stabilizes the market. It also explains why volatility is typically measured on a daily basis: in the presence of mean reversion, the average volatility measured over a time horizon generally depends on this horizon. For example, if $a = 10$ percent, only 95 percent of actual volatility is seen in annual increments.

If the $r(t)$ in equation (12.2) is the short rate we introduced in Chapter 7, then every other rate (the 5-year, the 10-year, etc.) can be derived as a function of the short one, using generalizations of the equations of Chapter 7, for the world of uncertainty.

Does it seem that equation model (12.2) makes sense? Well, O. Vasicek noticed it in 1977 as one of the first interest-rate models. It has been popular and important since then and was a basis for many of the models that are used today.

The Rate Distribution

Equation (12.2) is a linear differential equation disturbed by a Brownian motion. The math tells us that the output of this equation, rate $r(t)$, is going to be normally distributed. Although it makes the model tractable, the negative rates are not precluded. Arguably, the actual rates should stay positive—at least, they always have been.

Consider the following exercise: Suppose a random rate is normally distributed, having the average of 5 percent for any future moment of time, and absolute volatility of 1 percent. What is the probability that the rate becomes negative in 4 years? 9 years? 16 years?

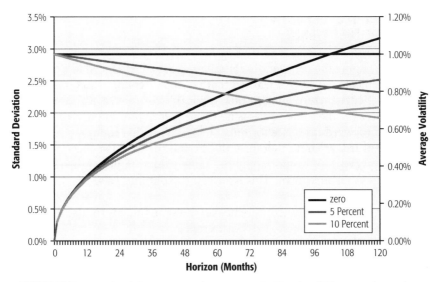

FIGURE 12.5   Standard deviation and average volatility for different values of *a*.

Negative rates may or may not be a problem. This event's odds grow with future time, (complete the above exercise) as the present value falls. In addition, mortgages and related securities are amortizing and may have small balances and cash flows years from now. Later in the chapter, we consider an example that provides a solid quantitative support for this conjecture.

The fact that a Brownian motion is normally distributed does not require that rate process be such. For example, considering exponential transformation $R = exp(r)$ and using R as the rate, rather than r, we ensure that the rate remains positive. Such a process is said to have *lognormal* distribution. Another popular example is the $R = r^2$ transformation that also guarantees that rate R stays positive; the distribution of such defined rate is known as *non-central χ^2-squared*. The mean and standard deviation for these known distributions are explicitly stated through the mean and the standard deviation of the original variable, $r(t)$. For example, for the lognormal case,

$$E(R) = \exp(\mu + \frac{1}{2}\sigma^2); \quad std(R) = \exp(\mu + \frac{1}{2}\sigma^2)\sqrt{\exp(\sigma^2) - 1} \quad (12.3)$$

where μ and σ are the mean and the standard deviation for r.

VALUATION IN STOCHASTIC ARBITRAGE-FREE WORLD

Let us now apply the concept of arbitrage-freeness, introduced in Chapter 7, to the stochastic world. We learned that we can discount any certain future cash by the current zero-coupon rate applicable for the term. Alternatively, we can arrive at the same value using the sequence of currently known single-period forward rates (see formula (7.11)). Note that today's rates, either spot or forward, are not random at all—even if the world is uncertain in the future. However, we cannot apply the same valuation principle directly, if the future cash is unknown. This issue can be split into two:

1. What is the well-defined "stochastic" present-value formula?
2. What should be done to avoid arbitrage?

Economic Value

Suppose we consider an investment made at some future time. Suppose further, that there will be only two future states of the financial world at that time, State 1 occurring with probability $P^{(1)}$, and State 2 occurring with probability $P^{(2)}$; of course, $P^{(1)} + P^{(2)} = 1$. The rate applicable for the investment period can be either $R^{(1)}$ for State 1 or $R^{(2)}$ for State 2, the cash paid at the end of the period is either $CF^{(1)}$ or $CF^{(2)}$. How much is this investment worth at the beginning of the period?

In bringing a financial rationale to this simple problem, let us consider borrowing alternatives. As we reach the beginning of the period, we will know the state of the world. If the world has evolved to State 1, we will need to borrow $CF^{(1)}/(1+ R^{(1)})$ at the beginning of the investment period to be able to return the lender $CF^{(1)}$ at the end. We can change the superscript from 1 to 2 to make a trivial extension for State 2. If we were given the opportunity to make this investment over and over again, we could play this "borrow and invest game" many, many times and compute the average amount that we borrowed. The result of that measurement will be:

$$P^{(1)} \frac{CF^{(1)}}{1 + R^{(1)}} + P^{(2)} \frac{CF^{(2)}}{1 + R^{(2)}} \tag{12.4}$$

If, instead of waiting to see what happens in the future, we decide to borrow this exact amount every play (no matter what!), then we will end up with a break-even investment. This tells us that (12.4) determines the fair value for the investment, at the beginning of the investment period. This value averages the borrowing needs weighted by probability-of-event occurrence, that is, recognized as mathematical expectation (denoted E) of $CF/(1+ R)$.

The terms *mathematical expectation, expectation,* and *expected value* are used interchangeably. They mean the same as the average value computed for the set of random outcomes and weighted by the probability their occurrence. If a casino gains $1 with probability of 80 percent and loses $2 with probability of 20 percent, it will have the expected gain of $0.8 \times \$1 + 0.2 \times (-\$2) = \$0.4$ per game. This gain is an average only; it will be firmly realized in a perpetual play (i.e., the casino may expect to pocket $40,000 after 100,000 games played). If we have a random outcome, X, then $E(X)$ mathematically denotes "average" or "expected" value of X.

This example can be extended to the complex financial world. We have numerous states (not just two) and can invest in a multiperiod horizon. Suppose that we have an n-period horizon and get paid an uncertain amount of cash, CF_n, at the end. The central valuation formula can be written as:

$$P_n = E\left[CF_n \left(\frac{1}{1 + r_1(0)} \right)\left(\frac{1}{1 + r_1(1)} \right) \cdots \left(\frac{1}{1 + r_1(n-1)} \right) \right] \quad (12.5)$$

or, with the shorter product (Π) notation,

$$P_n \equiv E\left[CF_n \prod_{t=0}^{n-1} \frac{1}{1 + r_1(t)} \right]$$

where $r_1(t)$ is the random periodic rate for the t-th discount period. Pricing formula (12.5) delivers the fair value for cash flow at a single future time (n). If the instrument pays cash every period, we can just add up P_n's for each pay period, $P = P_1 + \ldots + P_n$, to obtain the total fair price P.

If we prefer to use the instantaneous short rate $r(t)$ instead of periodic rate r_1, then the pricing formula (12.5) gets modified as

$$P_n = E\left[CF_n \exp[-\int_0^n r(t)dt] \right]$$

This transformation is no different than the one previously illustrated in formulas (7.1c) and (7.1d).

It seems that, with the stochastic-pricing formula (12.5) in hand, we are ready to price just about anything. Indeed, the stochastic differential equation (12.1) determines the rate evolution in the future and, eventually, allows for computing the expectation in (12.5) or (12.5a). The cash flow should, of course, be linked to the instantaneous short rate $r(t)$. But we should not rush with placing the model in business: The arbitrage-free constraint needs to be recalled and added before we produce a meaningful pricing result.

Arbitrage Freeness Revisited

Do we really know the expectation in the previous stochastic-pricing formula? We certainly would if the process (12.1) was specified. It appears, however, that we have less freedom in modeling the rates than one might think. Once the pricing formula (12.5) is established, it can be applied to value any contingent cash flow—including . . . the certain one. If the cash flow equals \$1 under any circumstances, then two pricing formulas, one for the certain world, and one for the stochastic world, correspondingly, should produce the same result:

$$E\left[\prod_{t=0}^{n-1} \frac{1}{1 + r_1(t)}\right] \equiv \prod_{t=0}^{n-1} \frac{1}{1 + f_1(t)} \tag{12.6}$$

in periodic compounding terms, or

$$E\left[\exp[-\int_0^n r(t)dt]\right] \equiv \exp[-\int_0^n f(t)dt] \tag{12.6a}$$

in continuous compounding.

The forward rates are perfectly known today; they unambiguously determine the right-hand sides. It is, therefore, up to the rate process to ensure that discount factors are as they need to be. Condition (12.6), above, is an important **arbitrage-free condition** for a stochastic-rate model.

The fair-pricing formulas (12.5) and the arbitrage-free condition (12.6) are valid for any valuation day, not only today. The interest-rate process (12.1) can be defined using only the information known today (i.e., current rates). Consider a modification of equation (12.5), in which the discounting starts from the next investment period:

$$P_{n-1}(1) = E\left[CF_n \prod_{t=1}^{n-1} \frac{1}{1 + r_1(t)}\right] \tag{12.7}$$

The financial meaning of this expression is the expected value of our zero-coupon bond, one period in the future. Compare now the current value (12.5) and the next-period expected value (12.7). The current one-period rate, $r_1(0)$, is known with certainty today. Therefore, when using formula (12.5), the first-period discount factor, $1/[1 + r_1(0)]$ can be factored out of the expectation operator, E. It can then be shown algebraically that,

$$\frac{P_{n-1}(1)}{P_n} = 1 + r_1(0) \tag{12.8}$$

This means that the investment's expected return is equal to the one-period current interest rate. Since this is the same relationship that defines the forward price, we conclude that the expected future value is equal to the observed forward value for a one-period horizon.

While equation (12.8) holds for any single period, it is not necessarily true for multiple periods; therefore one cannot conclude that the expected (or average) of possible future prices is equal to the forward price beyond the one-period horizon. Arbitrage-free conditions only require that the *present values* of guaranteed cash flows computed in the certain world (as in Chapter 7) and the random world (as in this chapter) are equal. It is possible to construct various arbitrage-free views of the same economy, differing in the probability distribution of market outcomes, but retaining the same prices today for cash and forward instruments.

One possible probability distribution for future market outcomes is called the **foward measure**. We construct the forward measure by applying the *deterministic* discount factor (known from today's market) between today and a future investment date. In this case, the average expected future values will equal the forward prices. This concept is convenient when dealing with a single payoff. It will rise again in this chapter in the discussion of the Black–Scholes option formula.

Another possible probability distribution is the **standard money-market measure**. We construct this measure by discounting using the single period *random* rates. In this case, the expected values of a bond are somewhat below forward prices. Even in this case, it is not possible to expect profit from buying in the random futures market and selling in today's forward market, as the present values of these positions are equal. (For further discussion of alternative measures see Hull, 2002.)

As we saw in Chapter 7, the future rates are the forward rates, in the certain arbitrage-free economy. In the uncertain arbitrage-free economy, future rates are stochastic and linked to the forward rates via the arbitrage-free conditions, established above. However, the forward rates are not the average values of the future stochastic rates. Although it may sound counterintuitive, the average rates are always greater than the current forward rates;

the difference between them is often called **convexity adjustment**. The paradox is explained by the positive convexity of the price-yield function.

Indeed, the forward value of a one-period zero-coupon bond is linked to its forward rate as $P = 1/[1 + f_1(t)]$. However, the same bond is going to be worth $1/[1 + r_1(t)]$ on the spot market, at the same delivery time t. Under the forward measures, these two values must agree with each other: $E\{1/[1 + r_1(t)]\} = 1/[1 + f_1(t)]$. We can now employ Jensen's inequality,

$$E\left(\frac{1}{X}\right) > \frac{1}{E(X)}$$

which is valid for any random positive variable X. Let X be $1/[1+ r_1(t)]$. Then, substituting into Jensen's inequality, one gets $E[1 + r_1(t)] > 1+ f_1(t)$, therefore, $E[r_1(t)] > f_1(t)$. This convexity-adjustment rule remains valid for any multiperiod rate (see Exercise 12.1 and 12.2), and the adjustment is even higher in the arbitrage-free economy based on the money market measure.

Much as in the certain case, the arbitrage-free approach does not tell us about the true expected returns, expected prices, nor expected rates, in the real economy. Since the real-world expectation is only one of four contributors to the yield curve (see Chapter 7), the true expectation cannot be determined from the yield curve. However, as we already know, for arbitrage-free valuation the true expectation is not necessary anyway.

VALUATION OF OPTIONS AND EMBEDDED-OPTION BONDS

An option is a financial instrument giving its holder a right to buy (**call option**) or to sell (**put option**) some other security (called the **underlying**) at a predetermined price (**strike price**). While legally, the decision to exercise this right belongs to the option holder, in practice, the decision depends primarily on the value of the underlying. A call option, once exercised, ceases to be an option and pays its owner the amount at which the current price exceeds the strike. It makes no sense to exercise a call option if the underlying is currently cheaper than the strike. Put options should be exercised only when the value of the underlying is less than the strike price. Options exercisable on a certain day are called European. If they are exercisable any day within a time window, they are called American; if only on some selected days, Bermudan. This terminology is a convention used to describe the option exercise style; no geography or politics is involved. While at one time, stocks were predominantly used as the underlying, the financial markets have grown and expanded; today, one can find options traded on just about everything that may have a value or be even linked to a value. Options are usually used either for *speculation* (betting on value), or *hedging* (financial insurance offsetting the risk of the underlying).

Interest Rate Options: A Brief Overview

Interest rate option is an option with a fixed-income underlying instrument (such as bonds and swaps). Interestingly enough, some option contracts may state an explicit contingency on interest rates, without bonds or swaps being mentioned.

Options on bonds, as follows from the name, give the right to buy (call) or sell (put) a certain bond. The exercise strategy is contingent on the bond's value, which, in turn, can be viewed as a function of prevailing interest rates. For example, if the rates drop, bonds rally, thereby making call options advantageous. Often bond options are *embedded* ones. For example, corporate bonds are often issued with an embedded call provision protecting the corporation from paying a too-high borrowing rate. Should the rate fall, the company could borrow at a lower rate and pay the outstanding debt off. An important option found in mortgages and all related securities is the **prepayment** option. It represents the option of the borrower to pay off the loan. (Prepayments are discussed in more detail in Chapter 9.)

Options on swaps (**swaptions**) are similar to those on bonds. It gives a right to enter into an interest-rate swap transaction, taking either the fixed-leg receiver (call) or the fixed-leg payer (put) position. Since we already know from Chapter 7 that a swap is seen on every reset day as a bond less its par, the analogy with bond options is apparent. A standard swaption can be viewed as an option on the same-rate bond struck at par. Much like in bonds, options can also be embedded in swaps making them either **cancelable** (callable) or **extendible** (putable). However, unlike options on bonds, a swaption's strike is a rate, not a price. For example, a swaption struck at 7 percent allows the purchaser to enter a swap transaction in which the fixed leg pays 7 percent. Different valuation approaches can view the rate or the price as the swaption underlying.

Calls and puts found in the interest rate market usually employ bonds or swaps as underlying assets. Sometimes, however, the rates themselves can be viewed as assets—if the financial contract uses them in determining the payoff rule. An example of an interest-rate option that explicitly interprets rates as assets is **LIBOR cap.** At the end of each time period, this option pays its holder the difference between the current LIBOR rate and the strike, or nothing. This rule applies to each period independently. Therefore, cap is a sequence ("portfolio") of European call options known as **caplets.** A standard cap resets quarterly and its payoff depends on the 3-month LIBOR rate, but particular over-the-counter contracts can be freely customized. A similar sequence of put options is called *floor*; it pays off if the rate falls below the strike. Caps and floors triggered by swap rates (Constant Maturity-Swap, CMS) or Treasury rates (Constant Maturity Treasury, CMT) have lately become widely popular in managing risk. In these cases, options can reset, say, quarterly, to the 10-year swap rate that will be compared with the strike. Generally a cap protects its holder from rising rates, and a floor protects its holder from falling rates.

Black–Scholes Formula for European Options

Since any option is a chance to get paid, it must have a positive fair market value. Once the holder pays the initial cost of the option, she cannot lose any more; in the worst case, she will forfeit her right. The theory and practice of option pricing has attracted many of the best mathematical minds to Wall Street during the last two decades. There was no widely accepted approach to option valuation until Fisher Black and Myron Scholes published their famous formula in 1973. Although their approach greatly simplifies the real world, it has remained one of the most influential ideas in modern finance. Although the Black–Scholes formula was originally derived for stock options, it has been modified and extended for many other problems, including all European interest-rate options. We present the results and derivations for the case most suitable for our purposes; a variant of Black's formula for options on stock futures.

Suppose that we have a European option on the "Forward Value" X (stock, bond, rate, commodity) exercisable at time T and struck at K. The "Forward Value" is a random process; it starts today from F and evolves in the future. Black–Scholes assumed that the value is lognormally distributed; its proportional volatility is σ.

The call option will pay $X\text{-}K$ at expiration if $X > K$ or nothing otherwise; this payoff function is often denoted $(X\text{-}K)^+$. If we are firm in the fundamental understanding of economic value formula (12.5a), we can put it to work immediately:

$$Call = E\left[(X - K)^+ \exp[-\int_0^T r(t)dt] \right]$$

The formula involves the short-rate process, which we have not even specified yet. Nor had Black and Scholes. After all, they thought of the stock options and factored the discount factor out of the expectation operator. We address this issue a bit later. Therefore,

$$Call = \exp(-r_T T)E\left[(X - K)^+\right]$$

where, as before, r_T stands for today's discount rate applicable for maturity T.

Because forward value X is lognormal, it can be represented as $X = Fe^x$ where x is a normally distributed random process, initialized at zero:

$$dx = -\frac{1}{2}\sigma^2 dt + \sigma dz \text{ and } x(0) = 0 \qquad (12.9)$$

What makes us sure in this equation? First, it is seen that σ is the absolute volatility for auxiliary variable x, therefore, it is the required relative volatility for X. Stochastic process (12.9) suggests that the expectation of $x(t)$ is $E(x) = -\frac{1}{2}\sigma^2 t$ and the variance is $var(x) = \sigma^2 t$ for any time instance t. Therefore, the expectation for X can be computed using the lognormal property (12.3):

$$E[X(t)] = F \exp\left[-\frac{1}{2}\sigma^2 t + \frac{1}{2}\sigma^2 t\right] \equiv F$$

In other terms, the expected forward value remains unchanged with the passage of time. This fact precludes arbitrage, in the Black–Scholes setting, and explains why we have selected the process (12.9) for normal variable $x(t)$. Since $X = Fe^x$ with x being normally distributed with known mean and standard deviation we can write the value for the call as:

$$Call = \exp(-r_T T) \frac{1}{\sqrt{2\pi t}\,\sigma} \int\limits_{\ln(K/F)}^{\infty} (Fe^x - K) \exp\left[-\frac{\left(x + \frac{1}{2}\sigma^2 t\right)^2}{2\sigma^2 t}\right] dx$$

One can compute the expectation explicitly; the value of the call was found as:

$$Call = \exp(-r_T T)[FN(d_1) - KN(d_2)] \qquad (12.10a)$$

where $N(d)$ is the standard cumulative normal distribution computed for

$$d_1 = \frac{\ln(K/F) + \frac{1}{2}\sigma^2 T}{\sigma\sqrt{T}}$$

and $d_2 = d_1 - \sigma\sqrt{T}$.

Similarly, the put option can be evaluated as:

$$Put = \exp(-r_T T)E[(K - X)^+] = \exp(-r_T T)[KN(-d_2) - FN(-d_1)] \quad (12.10b)$$

This result depends on a number of parameters; all of them but one are either option-specific (T, K) or easily obtainable from market values (r_T, F). The critical choice is the level of volatility, σ. Figure 12.6 illustrates this im-

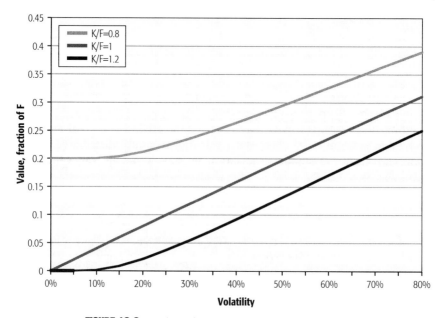

FIGURE 12.6 Value of a call as a function of volatility.

portance (option value is stated as a fraction of F; assumed horizon is 1 year, discount rates are disregarded).

Thus, it appears that the concept of market volatility that we started this chapter with is an important component of option pricing. Market participants maintain differing opinions on volatility and some engage in *volatility arbitrage*, for example, betting against the observed option prices. (See Exercise 12.3.)

The answer to Exercise 12.3 may seem counterintuitive: option prices are bound! Does not a higher volatility always increase the exercise chance and the potential pay off? It does, but at a reduced pace, according to Black–Scholes. The exponential transformation and a frozen (arbitrage-free) expectation for the forward value, $E(X) = F$, have jointly forced a negative, volatility-related drift in the stochastic equation (12.9).

The Black–Scholes formulas allow for direct differentiating with respect to each input parameter: first and second derivatives to current forward value (*Delta, Gamma*), first derivatives to volatility (*Vega*), expiration (*Theta*), and discount rate (*Rho*). These so-called **Greeks** are traditionally used to assess risk factors and are used for hedging. They describe how much the option price will change for a change in the associated parameter. Delta and Gamma are closely related to duration and convexity measures for bonds.

How should one apply the Black–Scholes model to European interest-rate options? Suppose we have a cap, that is, a portfolio of Δ-long caplets. Each caplet is struck at K and pays $\Delta(R - K)^+$ where R is the LIBOR rate at the beginning of the period. The caplet pays off at the end of the period, but we can "virtually move" this payment to the beginning of the same period using a one-period discounting: $\Delta(R - K)^+/(1 + R\Delta)$. Let us now assume that the denominator $1 + R\Delta$ entering this formula is a constant and taken from today's market. The numerator is considered random being linked to the forward LIBOR rate $X = R$. This is a Fisher Black's set up for cap pricing. Assuming that R is lognormally distributed, we can now apply the Black–Scholes pricing formulas simply scaling them to $\Delta/(1+ R\Delta)$.

Consider now a European "receive-fixed" swaption struck at K. It gives the option's holder the right to enter a swap that receives a fixed rate of K. First, let us express the random value of any swap (not the swap in question) as a function of its fixed-leg rate C:

$$swap(C) = bond(C) - 100 = \sum_{k=1}^{n} \frac{100C}{(1 + r_k)^k} + \frac{100}{(1 + r_n)^n} - 100$$

where r_k's are zero-coupon rates at expiration. Therefore, the swaption value at expiry is going to be the positive difference between the value of the swap having $C = K$ (i.e., the swap we are entitled to get) and random value of the market swap shown above:

$$swaption(C) = [swap(K) - swap(C)]^+ = \sum_{k=1}^{n} \frac{100}{(1 + r_k)^k} [K - C]^+$$

Let us take the discount rates r's as today's zero-coupon forward rates applicable for the option expiry date. We are going to treat them as constants. Interpreting the lognormal Forward Value X in the Black–Scholes model as the swap's forward rate C we arrive at an already familiar setup. Now the Black–Scholes prices should be scaled to the annuity value,

$$\sum_{k=1}^{n} \frac{100}{(1 + r_k)^k}$$

Note that, when using Black–Scholes, a receive-fixed swaption can be viewed as a put on swap's rate, whereas a pay-fixed swaption can be valued as a call on that rate.

Thus, there is a simple way to price caps and European swaptions— provided we agree on the underlying Black–Scholes assumptions. Let us briefly review them.

1. Lognormality.   Although lognormality is the traditionally accepted form for analyzing interest-rate market, we saw in Figure 12.1 that it was the absolute, not relative, volatility that appears to describe recent rate changes. This finding suggests normality of rates rather than lognormality. As an alternative to the standard (lognormal) Black–Scholes model we can assume that the random forward value X follows linear stochastic differential equation:

$$dX = \sigma dt \text{ subject to initial condition } X(0) = F \qquad (12.11)$$

Modification of the Black–Scholes model to the normal case is as simple as the original result:

$$\text{Call} = \exp(-r_T T)[(F - K)N(-d_1) + \sigma\sqrt{T}n(d_1)] \qquad (12.12a)$$

$$\text{Put} = \exp(-r_T T)[(K - F)N(d_1) + \sigma\sqrt{T}n(d_1)] \qquad (12.12b)$$

where $n(d)$ is the density function for standard normal distribution, $d_1 = (K - F)/\sigma\sqrt{T}$ and σ denotes absolute (not relative) volatility. As in the lognormal case, volatility is the key input. Unlike in the lognormal case, the option prices are now unbound if $\sigma \to \infty$. It holds true because the normal model (12.11) for the forward value now has a zero, volatility-independent, drift. Therefore, any increase in volatility boosts potential pay off, without limits.

2. Constant Volatility.   Although volatility does not appear to be constant, this problem can be solved in the valuation models by substituting its "average value" in the valuation equations. If volatility σ is time-dependent, we simply replace $\sigma^2 T$ each time we see it in the pricing formula with

$$\int_0^T \sigma^2(t)\,dt$$

3. Constant Discount Rates.   This assumption made by Black and Scholes for the stock options seems, at first glance, totally wrong for the interest-rate options. Indeed, we treat LIBOR rates or swap rates as random variables that trigger the exercise decision, but "freeze" them for the purpose of discounting. While market participants had been viewing these assumptions as apparent shortcomings, in the 1990s the notion **forward measure** was introduced and used to prove that the discount factors can indeed be deemed deterministic—provided that expectation operator agrees with observed forward prices. This mathematical understanding enforced the validity and applicability of Black–Scholes to the interest-rate option market.

Values of caps and swaptions are widely quoted in the form of volatility used by the Black–Scholes model (*Black volatility*). For example, if a swaption is said to trade at a $\sigma = 15$ percent volatility, it means that this σ delivers that currently observed market price when substituted into the Black–Scholes model. No belief in the assumptions underlying this theory is required; it is just another form of quoting a price using the Black–Scholes as the conversion tool.

Binomial-Tree Approach

The Black–Scholes closed-form method is applicable only to simple European options. Another popular method, called binomial-tree model, proposes a discrete approach to simulating the future rates and extracting fair values. It can be used for American or Bermudan options. The structure of a binomial tree is shown in Figure 12.7.

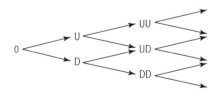

FIGURE 12.7   Structure of a binomial tree.

Each node represents a state of economy, that is, the entire set of the yield-curve points. The zero node is called *the root*; it contains today's rates. At each attained stage, there can be two possible paths the economy can evolve to, the up path, and the down path. The tree is said to *recombine* in the sense that the result of an up step followed by a down step is the same as the result of a down step followed by an up step. Therefore, there will be n nodes at the n-th time step, and $n(n + 1)/2$ nodes in an entire n-step tree. The rate evolution on the tree attempts to mirror that of a generic stochastic model, just in the discrete fashion. The displacement between the up moves and the down moves agrees with the selected model's volatility. The valuation technique used for the investment strategy that led us to pricing formula (12.4) exactly is needed for working on a tree. The prices are found backwards (*backward induction*), starting from the instrument's maturity when the value is surely known.

Let us illustrate this approach assuming a lognormal model for the one period rate $r_1(t) = R(t) \exp[x(t)]$. In this transformation, $x(t)$ is the normally distributed random variable, $R(t)$ is often known as the *calibrating function*. If we preferred to have a normal model, we would employ a rate $r_1(t) = R(t) + x(t)$ rate transformation. The evolution of the auxiliary variable x can follow some linear stochastic equation. For simplicity, assume that $dx = \sigma dt$, with volatility σ being 20 percent per period, zero initial value, $x(0) = 0$, and zero drift. We can implement this process on the binomial tree setting each move to be either 0.2 up or 0.2 down with 50/50 probability. This setup indeed results in a zero mean and 20 percent deviation, for each one-period horizon. The distribution of $x(t)$ on binomial tree is not going to be normal: a discrete set of outcomes is not identical to the continuous normal distribution. However, for a small time step, and a large number of steps, this binomial scheme may be considered a good approximation. After implementing all the up and down steps, we will have the tree for $x(t)$ as seen in Figure 12.8.

If we knew the calibrating function $R(t)$, we could easily compute the discount rates for every node of the tree. We could, therefore, employ the fair-value formula (12.4) and proceed to calculating values when stepping

$t=0$	$t=1$	$t=2$	$t=3$
			0.6
		0.4	
	0.2		0.2
0		0	
	−0.2		−0.2
		−0.4	
			−0.6

FIGURE 12.8   Tree for the auxiliary variable x.

	t=0	t=1	t=2	
Coupon		6	6	
R(t)	4.00	8.026 ←		Found
Price				
Rate				
			100	
		96.536		
	100.000	9.803	100	
	4.000	99.464		
		6.571	100	

FIGURE 12.9 Pricing the two-period 6 percent coupon bond.

backwards. Instead of cash flows $CF^{(1)}$ and $CF^{(2)}$, we would use the previous-step values plus any cash received. Instead of different discount rates, $R^{(1)}$ and $R^{(2)}$, we use the one-period rate found for that particular node (same for both paths). Suppose that the interest-rate market is given by the coupon rates of 4 percent (one period), 6 percent (two periods), and 7 percent (three periods). Hence, $R(0) = r_1(0) = 4$ percent since the current one-period rate is not random. Considering the two-period coupon bond priced at par ($100), we know that it pays $100 + $6 = $106 at time $t = 2$, and $6 at time $t = 1$. Iterating for $R(1)$, we find its value, $R(1) = 8.026$ percent. Figure 12.9 shows all values (light gray) and discount rates (dark gray) used to prove that the two-period coupon bond is indeed worth $100 today.

Note that we did not need to know the rates in period three. We will have to extend the tree to fit the par price for a given 7 percent three-period bond. Having already calibrated for the first two periods, we iterate to obtain $R(2) = 9.000$ percent; the implied rates and values are shown in Figure 12.10.

This completes the three-period calibration. We can use the tree shown in Figure 12.11 to price other financial instruments.

	t=0	t=1	t=2	t=3	
Coupon		7	7	7	
R(t)	4.00	8.026	9.000 ←		Found
Price					
Rate					
				100	
			94.334		
		94.031	13.427	100	
	100	9.803	98.165		
	4.000	99.969	9.000	100	
		6.571	100.912		
			6.033	100	

FIGURE 12.10 Pricing the three-period 7 percent coupon bond.

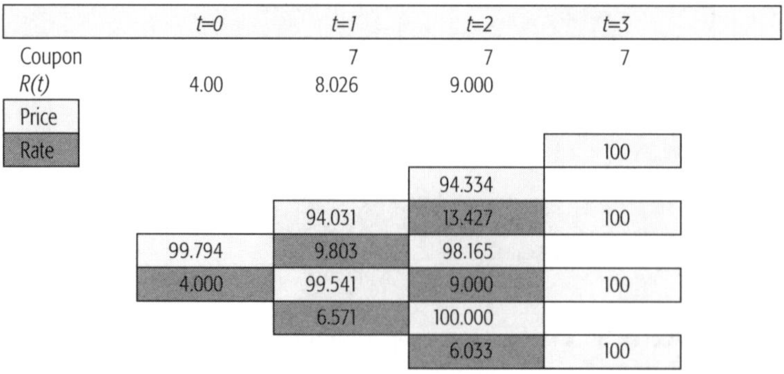

	t=0	t=1	t=2	t=3
Coupon		7	7	7
R(t)	4.00	8.026	9.000	
Price				
Rate				100
			94.334	
		94.031	13.427	100
	99.794	9.803	98.165	
	4.000	99.541	9.000	100
		6.571	100.000	
			6.033	100

FIGURE 12.11   Pricing the three-period 7 percent coupon bond callable at par.

Finding Long Rates on Each Node   Some instruments require explicit knowledge of multiperiod rates at each node. Finding a long zero-coupon rate for future nodes calls for a backward pricing of the matching-maturity zero. Finding a long coupon-bond rate requires computing values for two instruments: the same-term zero (let us denote it Z), and the same-term annuity paying $1 per period (denote it A). Since a coupon bond is the zero-coupon bond plus the annuity paying the bond's coupon rate c (rather than $1), then this unknown rate is recovered as $c = (100 - Z)/A$.

Pricing Embedded-Option Bonds

The backward valuation on a binomial tree can be generalized to include any explicit call or put (or call and put) provision. For example, such an option may have American exercise that cannot be valued by the Black–Scholes. Suppose that the three-period 7 percent coupon bond shown in Figure 12.10 is actually callable at par, at any moment. Therefore, the value of this instrument cannot exceed 100 at any node. Thus, theoretical value 100.912 found in node DD would make no financial significance for the investor as long as she knows the issuer can call the bond at only $100. Only a minor change in the backward induction algorithm accommodates for embedded call option: capping all computed prices by the call strikes if the call can be exercised at that time.

Only one node, DD, was subject to the explicit price capping, but the prices for preceding nodes, node D and the root, were subsequently affected in the course of backward induction. With this simple tree, we have achieved many goals. First, we have priced the bond. Second, we can state the value of embedded call option: *call* = 100 − 99.794 = 0.206 (recall the same bond was worth par, without the call). Third, we can perhaps charge the bond's issuer (a corporation) a fat consulting fee for informing it on the optimal call exercise strategy. The tree instructs us to exercise the call option only if the rates fall by two volatility steps in two periods from now.

If the bond is putable, the investor can sell it at the strike. This sets a floor on potential price drop. For example, a bond putable at 97 cannot be cheaper than 97, at any node where put is available. (See Exercise 12.6.)

This pricing method can be extended to a call (or put) schedule when the strike changes with time. Many corporate bonds are issued with a declining call schedule, which starts after a certain "no-call" period.

Pricing Bonds with Variable Amortization

Suppose that a borrower pays off the debt gradually, in a fashion that depends on the level of interest rates. No explicit call schedule is stated, but, rather, an experimental relationship between amortization speed (denote it λ) and the rates is established. For example, $\lambda = a + b \arctan [\, c(r - d)]$ where parameters a, b, c, and d are properly selected. The arctangent function will simulate the gradual call exercise. This model can prototype the prepayment modeling, at least, in a very simple way.

Let us now show how the backward induction method can be adapted. We know that, for nonamortizing assets, the beginning-period value should be chosen such as to ensure the total return being equal the same-period market rate. Consider now an asset changing its notional balance, B, from one period to another; the notional decrements are paid to the investors. Denoting P to be the price and c the coupon, we could compute the total return for any investment period as

$$\text{Total Return} = \frac{P_k B_k / 100 - P_{k-1} B_{k-1} / 100 + B_{k-1} - B_k + c B_{k-1} / 100}{P_{k-1} B_{k-1} / 100}$$

In this formula, the cash paid includes the paid off notional, $B_{k-1} - B_k$, and interest, $c B_{k-1}/100$. Amortization speed λ is defined as $1 - B_k/B_{k-1}$; excluding B_k we obtain:

$$\text{Total Return} = \frac{c + P_k - P_{k-1} + \lambda(100 - P_k)}{P_{k-1}}$$

Note that the balance variables have disappeared altogether; they do not enter the total return formula. Only the amortization speed and its dependence on market rate matters. We also see that the amortization speed influences return only for non-par-priced bonds, $P_k \neq 100$; this agrees with financial intuition. Equating the total return to the effective market rate r we get:

$$P_{k-1} = \frac{c + P_k + \lambda(100 - P_k)}{1 + r} \qquad (12.13)$$

This is the amortizing-asset pricing formula for one investment period, for which ending value, P_k, is known. For $\lambda = 0$, we will have the usual rule that combines the end-period cash and value to find the beginning-period value.

Here is how it works on a tree. First, we assign some values for our amortization model's parameters (say, a = 30 percent, b = 25 percent, c = 40 percent, and d = 7 percent). Second, we have to calculate amortization speed (arctangent) at each node. Third, we will work through the tree backwards, each time applying formula (12.13) for every branch; the result at each node is probability-weighted, as it is in the regular case. In short, we have just generalized the pricing formula, without altering the rates and probabilities of the binomial tree (Figure 12.12).

Why have we not shown the notional balance along with the amortization speed? It is simply impossible. The balance depends not only on the node, but also on the path to that node as well. We essentially have proven that the knowledge of the balance remained at each pricing node is redundant for deriving the fair value. One strong assumption that has been made, however, is the ability to compute amortization speed in every node.

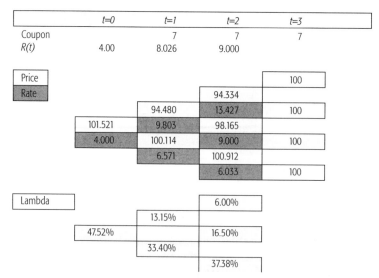

FIGURE 12.12 Pricing a randomly amortizing three-period 7 percent coupon bond.

TERM-STRUCTURE MODELS

We conclude this chapter with a brief consideration of some interest-rate models widely used by market participants. As we have seen, both closed-end formulas (Black–Scholes) and numerical pricing (trees) rely on some type of model that describes mathematical behavior of interest rates. Why do we call these models term-structure models? Are there not too many rates for one model? The binomial-tree example shows us that we can reconstruct the entire term structure using only dynamics of a one-period rate.

This observation does not mean that any term-structure model is a one-factor model or depends only on the short rate. It would be correct to state that *any maturity rate can be recovered using only factors that determine the evolution of the short rate (continuous setting) or one-period rate (discrete setting)*.

In particular, if only one Brownian motion drives the short-rate dynamics, it will define the entire yield curve as well. We restrict our coverage here to single-factor models that employ the short rate as the only factor and give some evidence on the relative performance of the models. All these models are special cases of our general stochastic equation (12.1). For each of the models considered, we emphasize three key aspects: the model's formulation, its arbitrage-free calibration, and the inter-rate relationship that recovers the entire term structure contingent on the short rate.

The Hull–White Model

The Hull–White (HW) model describes the dynamics of the short rate $r(t)$ in the form similar to the Vasicek process (12.2):

$$dr = a(t)(\theta(t) - r)dt + \sigma(t)dz \qquad (12.14)$$

Once again, $a(t)$ denotes mean reversion, $\sigma(t)$ stands for absolute volatility; both can be time-dependent. Function $\theta(t)$ *is* sometimes referred to as arbitrage-free drift. This terminology is caused by the fact that, by selecting proper $\theta(t)$, we can match any observed yield curve.

Since equation (12.14) is a linear equation disturbed by the Brownian motion (a normally distributed variable), the short rate is normally distributed as well. Therefore, its integral is normally distributed. Recalling the arbitrage-free condition (12.6a),

$$E\left[\exp\left[-\int_0^n r(t)dt\right]\right] \equiv \exp\left[-\int_0^n f(t)dt\right]$$

we now realize that the expectation in the left-hand side can be computed in a closed form (using lognormal expectation (12.3)). Without going through the math, we provide here the analytical calibration results to the observed short-forward curve $f(t)$ for the constant-volatility case:

$$\theta(t) = f(t) + \frac{1}{a}\frac{df(t)}{dt} + \frac{\sigma^2}{2a^2}(1 - e^{-2at}) \tag{12.15}$$

The short rate's expectation is found as

$$E[r(t)] = f(t) + \frac{\sigma^2}{2a^2}(1 - e^{-at})^2 \tag{12.16}$$

The last term in formula (12.16) is the convexity adjustment we first mentioned earlier in the chapter. This adjustment is proportional to volatility squared; for zero mean reversion, it is simply equal to $\frac{1}{2}\sigma^2 t$. It is therefore up to financial engineers to make sure the convexity adjustment is properly found in a pricing system; it is very volatility-sensitive.

Expected value for any long, T-maturity, zero-coupon rate is proven to be in the same form: forward rate + convexity adjustment. This time, the exact formula for this relation is

$$E[r_T(t)] = f_T(t) + \frac{\sigma^2}{4a^3 T}(1 - e^{-aT})[2(1 - e^{-at})^2 \\ +(1 - e^{-2at})(1 - e^{-aT})] \tag{12.17}$$

Any long zero-coupon rate is normally distributed and proven to be linear in the short rate; deviations from their respective mean levels are related as

$$\frac{\Delta r_T}{\Delta r} = \frac{1 - e^{-aT}}{aT} \equiv B_T \tag{12.18}$$

Function B_T of maturity T plays an important role in the HW model. It allows, for example, linking the short-rate volatility to the long-rate one and explicitly calibrating it to the market. If $a = 0$, then this function becomes identical to 1, regardless of the maturity, T. This important special case allows for a pure parallel change in the entire curve (every point moves by the same amount). This particular setup can be suitable for standardized risk measurement tests.

The HW model is a very tractable arbitrage-free model, which allows for the use of analytical solutions as well as Monte Carlo simulation or binomial tree pricing. Its most feared drawback is that it produces negative interest rates; however, with mean reversion the effect of negative rates is reduced. Recent rate history supports this type of formulation of a term-structure model.

The Cox–Ingersoll–Ross Model

The Cox–Ingersoll–Ross (CIR) model is a unique example of a model supported by econometric arguments. The authors argued that fixed-income investment opportunities should not be dominated by either expected return (the rate) or the risk. The latter was associated with the return variance, thus suggesting that volatility-squared should be of the same magnitude as the rate:

$$dr = a(t)(\theta(t) - r)dt + \sigma(t)\sqrt{r}dz \qquad (12.19)$$

Model (12.19) is actually a no-arbitrage extension to the original CIR that allows fitting the rates and volatilities. Since the volatility term is proportional to the square root of the short rate, the latter is meant to remain positive. The extended CIR model is analytically tractable, but to a lesser extent than the HW model. Perhaps, the most important result of CIR is that the long zero-coupon rates were also proven linear in the short rate—in line with relationship (12.18). However, the ratio has now a quite different form; it depends on both maturity T and time t and found as $B_T(t) = -b(t, t + T)/T$. Function $b(t,T)$ used in this expression solves a Ricatti-type differential equation, considered for any fixed maturity T:

$$\frac{db(t, T)}{dt} = a(t)b(t, T) - \frac{1}{2}\sigma^2(t)b^2(t, T) + 1 \qquad (12.20)$$

subject to terminal condition $b(T,T) = 0$.

If the mean reversion a and CIR volatility σ are constant (the original CIR), equation (12.20) allows for an explicit solution. In this case, $b(t,T)$ is a function of $T - t$ only, and B_T appears to be time-independent:

$$B_T = \frac{2(e^{\gamma T} - 1)}{(\gamma T + aT)(e^{\gamma T} - 1) + 2\gamma T} \quad \text{where } \gamma = \sqrt{a^2 + 2\sigma^2} \quad (12.21)$$

Without a mean reversion, this formula reduces to a more concise

$$B_T = \frac{\tanh(\gamma T / 2)}{(\gamma T / 2)}$$

Note that this ratio is always less than 1, which means that the long rates are less volatile than the short ones, even without a mean reversion. This finding is in contrast to the HW model where, with $a = 0$, the yield curve would experience a strictly parallel reaction to a short rate shock. Although the inter-rate relationship in the extended CIR model can generally be time-dependent, it never depends on the rate level always remaining linear.

Generally speaking, calibration to the currently observed short forward curve $f(T)$ cannot be done as elegantly and explicitly as in the HW model. Once the $b(t,T)$ function is found, the calibrating function $\theta(t)$ satisfies an integral equation:

$$-f(T) = \int_0^T \frac{db(t,T)}{dT} \theta(t)a(t)dt + \frac{db(0,T)}{dT} r_0 \qquad (12.22)$$

Numerical methods, well developed for the integral equations, should be employed.

It is known that all rates, under the CIR model, have noncentral χ-squared distributions. Economic rationale, non-negative rates, and analytic tractability have made the CIR model deservedly popular; it is one of the most attractive and useful interest-rate models. It is also consistent with recent rate history.

The Black–Karasinski Model

Once very popular, the Black–Karasinski (BK) model expresses the short rate as $r(t) = R(t)\exp[x(t)]$, where random process $x(t)$ is normally distributed, and follows the linear stochastic differential equation:

$$dx = -a(t)xdt + \sigma(t)dz$$

The short rate is, therefore, lognormally distributed. We employed this model for our binomial tree in the previous section. Assuming the same process for $x(t)$, we can write the stochastic differential equation for the short rate as

$$dr = r\left(\frac{R'}{R} + \frac{1}{2}\sigma^2 - a\ln\frac{r}{R}\right)dc + r\sigma dz \qquad (12.23)$$

The rate's absolute volatility is therefore proportional to the rate level. Although the entire short-rate distribution is known (including the mean and variance), no closed-form pricing solution is available, because the cumulative discount rate, the integral of r, has an unknown distribution. Traditionally, the BK model is implemented on a tree. Calibration to the yield curve and volatility curve can be done using purely numeric procedures. For example, one could iterate to find $R(t)$ period by period until all the coupon bonds or zero-coupon bonds (used as input) are priced exactly. Alternatively, one could find approximate formulas and build a faster, but not exact scheme.

Despite its popularity, the BK model's main assumption, rate lognormality, is not supported by recent rate history. The volatility parameter σ entering the BK model is not the same as the Black volatility for swaptions. For example, $\sigma = 0.15$ does not ensure 15 percent volatility for the long rates. Hence, calibration of the model to volatilities found in the swaption market is not an easy task.

Which Model Is Better?   The HW model, the CIR model, and the BK model are special cases of a more general class of models that Mark Rubenstein introduced in the 1980s:

$$dr = (Drift)dt + \sigma r^\gamma dz \qquad (12.24)$$

Parameter γ is called constant elasticity of variance (CEV). For $\gamma = 0$ we have the HW model, for $\gamma = 0.5$, the CIR model; for $\gamma = 1$ the BK model. There are no specific economic arguments supporting this r^γ functional form for volatility. Typically, the CEV constant is between 0 and 1, but not necessarily.

Blyth and Uglum (1999) linked the CEV constant to the *volatility skew* found in the swaption market. They argue that market participants should track the Black volatility according to the following simple formula:

$$\frac{\sigma_K}{\sigma_F} \approx \left(\frac{F}{K}\right)^{\frac{1-\gamma}{2}} \qquad (12.25)$$

Formula (12.25) describes the skew; σ_K is the Black volatility for the option struck at K, σ_F is the Black volatility for the "at-the-money" option struck at today's forward rate, F. Importantly, one can recover the best CEV constant to use in the model just by measuring the observed skew.

The skew measured for options on the 10-year swap quoted for the last 4 to 5 years suggests $\gamma = 0.23$ on average, which means that the most suitable model lies between the HW and the CIR (Figure 12.13). The most recent tendency has been toward $\gamma = 0$, that is, normality (Figure 12.14), making the HW the best choice currently. Note that neither the rate history of the last 15 years nor the available volatility skew data support lognormality, although earlier rate history did appear to support $\gamma = 1$.

Market randomness makes the fair value of a financial instrument an expectation. It also requires a rigorous quantification of the dynamics of interest rates, that is, a well-defined interest-rate model. Prices of interest-rate options, caps, floors, swaptions, and options embedded in bonds such as MBS and ABS will firmly depend on this modeling work, in particular, on the volatility specification.

In some cases, prices can be found as explicitly computed expectations. Models can and should use available information about currently observed forward rates or prices and be calibrated to them. This is the case for the Black–Scholes formula, which, despite its simplistic setup, has revolutionized the option market. Some more rigorous models, such as the HW model and the CIR model, also allow computing pricing expectations explicitly. Valuation of American options and some simple mortgage prototypes can be done on a binomial tree, using the backward-induction technique. The same technique can be employed for nonanalytical models such as the BK model.

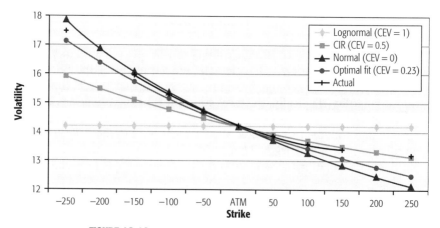

FIGURE 12.13   Determining the most suitable model.

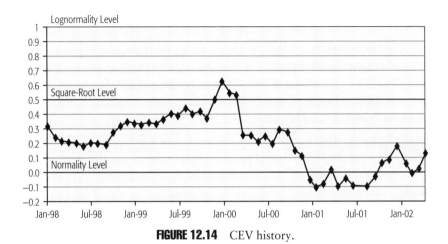

FIGURE 12.14 CEV history.

Selecting the best term-structure model is becoming more a conscientious task and less a matter of taste. Measuring volatility skew for widely traded swaptions is a simple technique that yields rich results. Recent trading history indicates that the market currently values options as though future interest-rate changes are drawn from a normal distribution, rather than from a lognormal distribution. Thus, the HW model and the CIR model are more attractive than the widely used lognormal models, such as the BK model.

EXERCISES

Exercise 12.1 Consider the two-state borrow-and-invest game described on page 224; the investment asset will now be a 10-year zero-coupon bond. Suppose that the future two states of economy are equally likely and the 10-year zero rate is going to be either 5 percent or 10 percent. Find the bond's fair value and its forward rate. Compare the computed forward rate with the average rate.

Exercise 12.2 Assume that the short rate, $r(t)$, is normally distributed. Using arbitrage-free condition (equation (12.6a)) and the expectation formula for the lognormal distribution (equation (12.3)) prove that $E[r(t)] \geq f(t)$.

Exercise 12.3 What will happen with Black–Scholes prices (equation (12.10)) if $\sigma \to \infty$? Is there a pricing limit?

Exercise 12.4   The following entertaining exercise objectively quantifies the role of negative rates that can occur in the normal model. Review exercise on page 222. Assuming the forward-rate curve is flat at $r_T = F = 5$ percent, and absolute volatility $\sigma = 1$ percent, assess the value of a floor struck at a zero rate ($K = 0$), under the normal model. Use equation (12.12b) when considering the same set of horizons: $T = 4$ years, 9 years, 16 years. Compare results with the actual value of the floor (do not call brokers for quotes!).

Exercise 12.5   Find the two-period zero-coupon rate and the coupon rate at the U node. Show your work on the binomial tree.

Exercise 12.6   Find the value of the three-period 7 percent coupon bond putable at 97. Show your work on the binomial tree. What is the optimal put exercise strategy?

CHAPTER 13

Option-Adjusted Spread

To compare bonds, investors require a metric that will equate dissimilar alternatives. For mortgage-backed securities (MBS), that tool is option-adjusted spread (OAS). Although OAS has limitations, it is one tool that can be used to compare a wide variety of fixed-income instruments with varying characteristics.

OAS models extend the scenario-analysis approach. Instead of confining the analysis to consider only a limited number of interest-rate scenarios, the OAS approach aims to understand the relative value and risk of a security by considering its average performance over a large number of future scenarios. The number of scenarios needed depends on the degree of accuracy required by the analysis.

The strength of OAS in combining a large number of potential outcomes also leads to its greatest weakness. While OAS combines a tremendous amount of information about a security into a single number, that process also hides the details from the user. Therefore, it is extremely important that users of OAS understand the process by which the results are generated.

In our investigation of OAS technology, we continue to apply the general framework of methodology, collateral, structure, and results established earlier in the book (see Table 13.1).

METHODOLOGY

OAS, as the name implies, is an extension of the concept of spread described in Chapter 8. Spread measures the difference between the yield of one instrument and the yield of another instrument. Yields have the same unfortunate feature of internal rates of return, that is, direct comparisons of yields may not lead to correct choices. Yields suffer from two main shortcomings. First, it is difficult to compare yields of instruments with different cash-flow

TABLE 13.1   OAS Methodology

Phase of Analysis	Components	Process

Methodology	Spreads
	Backward induction versus
	   forward simulation
	Monte Carlo simulation
		Generate arbitrage-free
		   interest-rate paths

Collateral	Prepayments
	Link to interest rates
		Generate collateral cash
		   flows using prepay-
		   ment model

Structure	Collateral cash flows	Generate security cash
		   flows using collateral
		   cash flows and deal
		   structure

	Collateralized-mortgage obligation cash flows	

Results	Valuation—OAS
	Risk—Effective duration,
	   convexity
		Compute OAS and other
		   value and risk
		   measures.

patterns. For example, it is difficult to determine which is a better investment, a 2-year bullet, or a 30-year amortizing security. Second, it is difficult to compare yields of instruments whose cash flows are dynamic with the yields of instruments that are static. OAS is a tool to help overcome these shortcomings.

OAS can be understood by extending the concept of spread one step at a time. The first step is the static spread of Chapter 8. The next step is a zero spread, then comes the forward spread, and finally the OAS. Let us look at these one at a time.

As described earlier, static spread is the difference between the yield of the MBS and the yield of a benchmark security. The concept of yield spread can be expanded by evaluating each cash flow of the MBS as a separate bond, and then computing the spread that equates the portfolio of MBS cash flows to a portfolio of zero-coupon bonds.

For this analysis we use interest-rate data from May 13, 2002 as in Figure 7.2. Figure 13.1 shows the cash flows of a Fannie Mae 7 percent MBS using a 417 percent PSA prepayment assumption. Using a price of 101.69, the yield on the bond is 6.53 percent with an average life of 3.68 years. If we interpolate the yields between Treasuries with maturities of 36 months and

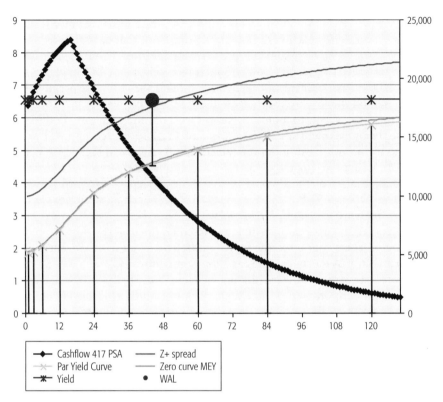

FIGURE 13.1 Cash flows of a Fannie Mae 7 percent MBS using 417 PSA.

60 months, we can determine that a Treasury with a maturity of 3.68 years would have a yield of 4.53 percent. Therefore the static yield spread would be 199 basis points.

Zero spread is calculated by discounting each cash flow at the zero rate plus a spread using the formula:

$$P = \sum_{k=1}^{n} \frac{cf(k)}{(1 + r_k + s)^k} \qquad (13.1)$$

Using this formula, the spread that produces a price equal to 101.69 is 170 basis points. Figure 13.1 shows the cash flows of the bonds and then shows the yield of the bond versus the zero-coupon discount rates. Note that the zero-coupon discount rates including the spread are lower than the yield for shorter time horizons and then higher for longer time horizons. It is clear that the zero-coupon spread is a more accurate measure since it links the discount rate for each cash flow to the timing of that cash flow.

In Figure 13.1, we assumed a prepayment speed of 417 PSA. But what is the right speed to use, and how should it be determined? In Chapter 9, we described the development of prepayment models that forecast prepayment rates based on the level of mortgage rates. Clearly, one way of developing a prepayment forecast is to input the current level of mortgage rates and to determine the prepayment speeds. The speed of 417 PSA was computed by calculating the month-by-month prepayment speeds shown in Figure 13.3, and then computing the single PSA that would produce the same average life.

An alternative method would be to use the concept of forward rates described in Chapter 7. For every maturity of the benchmark curve, we can compute forward rates. In particular, we compute the path of forward rates for the 2-year and 10-year instruments. Based on the past relationship of the mortgage current coupon to the 2-year and 10-year rates, we can forecast a forward vector of mortgage rates as shown in Figure 13.2.

Note that with an upward-sloping yield curve the path of forward mortgage current coupon rates will be higher than the current level. The impact will be to produce slower prepayment speeds, as seen in Figure 13.3.

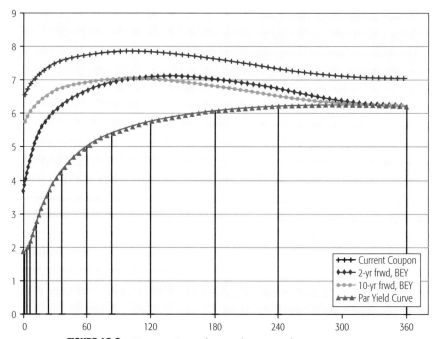

FIGURE 13.2 Forecasting a forward vector of mortgage rates.

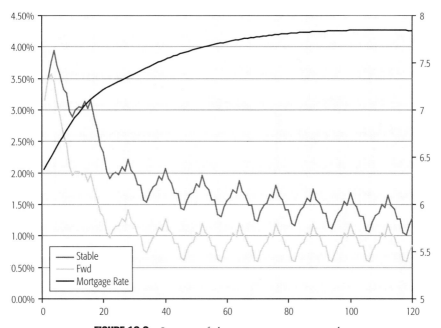

FIGURE 13.3   Impact of slower prepayment speeds.

Slower prepayment speeds will produce a longer average life. The average life using stable mortgage rates is 3.68 years, whereas the average life using forward rates is 5.7 years.

With the cash flows generated using these prepayment speeds, it is now possible to compute two new Z-spreads. First, using model prepayment speeds based on stable mortgage rates, the zero spread is 151 basis points. Second, using model prepayment speeds based on forward mortgage rates, the zero spread is 126 basis points. Figure 13.4 shows the cash flows and interest rates associated with these values.

The spread to the zero rates using the forward curve to generate prepayments has a special economic meaning. It is the arbitrage-free, no-volatility valuation. Thus, the zero-coupon spread is also the zero-volatility spread.

OAS is the extension of spread to the curve to the world of volatility. OAS for MBS can be distinguished from pure option valuation (as in Chapter 12) in two ways. First, generally it is not possible to value MBS using backward-induction methods. Second, to equate the value of an MBS to the modeled option-adjusted value, it is generally necessary to add a spread to the discount rates. OAS is the spread that is used to adjust model values to market values. As such, it represents the average additional return that the

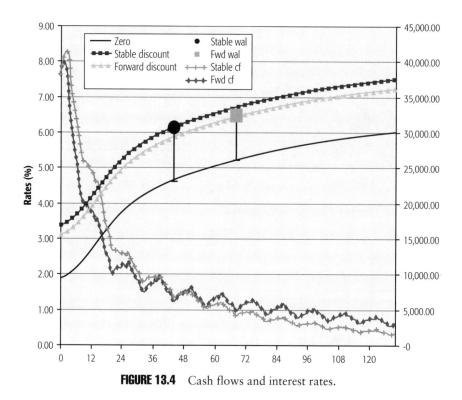

FIGURE 13.4   Cash flows and interest rates.

MBS provides relative to the base yield curve. Each of these topics is discussed in more depth.

In Chapter 12, we demonstrated the valuation of fixed-income securities with embedded options using backward induction on a binomial lattice. For reasons that we describe later, MBS are not easily evaluated using backward induction. Instead MBS valuation is usually conducted in a **pathwise** manner. Pathwise means that an entire interest-rate path is generated starting now and continuing to the maturity of the security. This path may be a single interest rate or a set of rates representing the full yield curve. Each path represents just one possible path for interest rates to take. A large number of paths are used to simulate the entire range of possible outcomes. This methodology is generally called the **Monte Carlo** method.

Figure 13.5 demonstrates the connection between pathwise valuation and lattice-based backward induction. The example shows that there is a direct link between the two approaches and that pathwise valuation and backward induction can produce the same results. We use the binomial trees shown in Chapter 12.

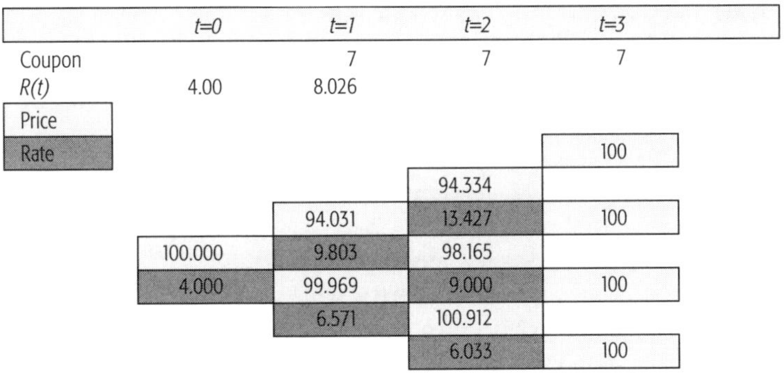

	t=0	t=1	t=2	t=3
Coupon		7	7	7
R(t)	4.00	8.026		
Price				
Rate				
				100
			94.334	
		94.031	13.427	100
	100.000	9.803	98.165	
	4.000	99.969	9.000	100
		6.571	100.912	
			6.033	100

FIGURE 13.5 Pricing the three-period 7 percent coupon bond.

Creating a Pathwise Analysis

Step 1. The binomial tree specifies all of the possible interest-rate states over time. We need to establish a list of all possible interest-rate paths through the tree. All of the paths start at the 4 percent rate. From there, the path can go either up to 9.8 percent or down to 6.6 percent. Note that the down rate is actually higher than the initial rate. This situation is still called the down path. From either of these points, the rate path can go either up or down. Thus, there are two times two or four possible paths. Generally, there are 2^n possible paths, where n is the number of steps. For a mortgage valuation with 360 months of cash flows there could be 2^{360} or over 1×10^{100} possible paths! The fastest computers could not process that many paths in a reasonable time. Even if each path took 1/100th of a second, we could only calculate about 1×10^{11} paths before the mortgage matured. Table 13.2 lists the four possible paths and the interest rates for each path.

Step 2. Determine the cash flows of the bond for each path. Assume the bond matures at the end of year three and has an annual coupon of 7 percent. Since the bond is option-free, the cash flows are the same for each path. The bond receives a coupon of 7 in years one and two and receives principal of 100 and coupon of 7 in year three.

Step 3. Value a fixed-rate bond using pathwise valuation. For path one, start at the last period. The cash flow at the end of period three is 107. That cash flow is discounted back one period at 13.427 percent, resulting in a value of 94.334. That value plus the 7 percent coupon received in period 2 is discounted at 9.803 percent to produce a value of 92.287. That value plus the 7 percent coupon received in period 1 is discounted at 4 percent to produce a value of 95.468. That value, 95.468, represents the value of the

TABLE 13.2 Possible Interest Rate Paths

Path	Year		
	1	2	3
1		up	up
2		up	down
3		down	up
4		down	down
1	4.000%	9.803%	13.427%
2	4.000%	9.803%	9.000%
3	4.000%	6.571%	9.000%
4	4.000%	6.571%	6.033%

security for the first path. It is the value of the security if you were certain that rates would follow path 1 (up, up; 4.0 percent, 9.8 percent, 13.4 percent). The same calculation can be repeated for each of the other three paths as shown in Table 13.3.

Step 4. The results of the valuation for each path are then averaged to produce an expected value for the bond. The average value is 100.000. Note that this is the exact same value as achieved in Figure 13.5 using the binomial tree.

Evaluating Embedded Options

The evaluation of embedded options using pathwise valuation requires a different type of decision rule than lattice-based valuation. In lattice-based models, the decision to exercise is based on a comparison of the value of pursuing the strategy of exercise versus the strategy of differing exercise. The

TABLE 13.3 Discounted Cash Flows All Paths

Path	Year		
	1	2	3
Cash flow	7	7	107
1	95.468	92.287	94.334
2	98.823	95.776	98.165
3	101.616	98.681	98.165
4	104.095	101.258	100.912
Average	100.000		

TABLE 13.4 Callable Bond Cash Flow

Path	Year 1	Year 2	Year 3
1	7	7	107
2	7	7	107
3	7	7	107
4	7	107	

strategy with the lowest cost is selected. In a pathwise valuation, it is not possible to fully evaluate both strategies, since only a single possible rate path is analyzed at a time. Therefore, it is necessary to develop a decision rule that relies on information about coupon and current interest-rate levels rather than prices.

The bond from Figure 12.11 can also be evaluated using pathwise valuation. That bond has a coupon of 7 percent, a maturity of 3 years, and is callable at par after 1 year. Here, additional work is required. It is necessary to determine when the call option will be exercised.

Step 1. The same as the previous Step 1.

Step 2. Working forward through time, determine when the bond will be called. To do this we need a decision rule. Assume that the bond will be called when the discount rate is less than 6.5 percent after the first year. Therefore the bond is called at the end of year two in path four. Table 13.4 shows the cash flows of the bond.

Step 3. Value the bond as previously, calculating the present value for each path. See Table 13.5.

Step 4. Calculate the average value as previously. Note that the average value is 99.794, which is the same value as in Figure 12.11.

TABLE 13.5 Callable Bond Valuation

Path	Year 1	Year 2	Year 3
1	95.468	92.287	94.334
2	98.823	95.776	98.165
3	101.616	98.681	98.165
4	103.272	100.403	0.000
Average	99.794		

This analysis has shown that backward induction and pathwise valuation can give the same results for callable and noncallable bonds. It is important to note that the callable bond valuation required an ad-hoc call rule that may not be economically optimal. Therefore it is generally better to value callable bonds using backward induction.

Path Dependence

Since pathwise valuation produces the same result as backward induction and backward induction is substantially faster than pathwise analysis, what is the motivation for using pathwise analysis?

The need for pathwise analysis arises from the feature of MBS that the cash flow today depends on prior interest rate and prepayment level. The critical question is what is needed to compute the amortization of the security (scheduled principal plus prepayments) at each node of the binomial tree.

Case 1: $\lambda(r^t,t) = f(r^t,t)$, amortization is a function only of time, t, and the rate at time t. As shown in Chapter 12, backward induction can be used.

Case 2: $\lambda(r_T,T) = f(r_T,T, s_T)$, where s_T is a function of r_t for $t < T$, then λ is path dependent. Amortization is a function not only of time t and the rate at time t, but also is a function of the "state" of the security, which depends on prior rates. In this case, backward solution will not work.

To understand this, take a look at Figure 13.6, showing valuation using backward induction. To calculate the value at point B, take the price at points D and E. Discount the price at point D back to point B, using rate and probability for path 3 and discount the price at point E back to point B using rate and probability for path 4. Value at point E equals price for outstanding balance, coupon cash flow at point E, and prepayments at point E; likewise for point D.

With a path-dependent prepayment model, prepayments at path E depend on whether you arrive at E from A via B (paths 1 and 4) or via C (paths

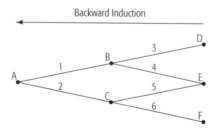

FIGURE 13.6   Backward induction.

2 and 5). Since the prepayment amount is unknown, you cannot use a backward solution method.

With forward simulation as shown in Figure 13.7, the prepayments for point D are calculated separately for the paths 1 and 4 and paths 2 and 5. Therefore, it is possible to take into account the prior history of interest rates when determining the prepayment speed as point D.

The path-dependent nature of MBS arises from prepayment characteristics and structural characteristics. Burnout is the prepayment characteristic that plays the largest role in creating path-dependent cash flows. Borrowers who did not prepay at the first opportunity to do so, may face different costs of refinancing than other borrowers. Thus, past prepayments (and therefore past interest-rate levels) affect our forecasts of future prepayments. Some OAS models are able to overcome this path-dependent aspect of mortgage valuation by splitting the mortgage pool into discrete segments with varying refinancing thresholds. Each segment can then be evaluated in a non-path-dependent fashion. This approach requires that the prepayment estimates be constructed in a particular fashion.

The second source of path dependency is not as easily overcome. This is the path dependence that arises from collateralized mortgage obligation (CMO) structures. For many structures, future cash flows depend on past performance, particularly structures with scheduled and support classes. The past history of prepayments will affect future distribution of cash flow. For these structures it is extremely difficult to segment the CMO into pieces that are independent of each other and thus avoid path dependence.

Monte Carlo Analysis and Sampling

As shown above, pathwise valuation is more readily adaptable for path-dependent securities such as mortgages. However, pathwise analysis has the disadvantage that it is much more time consuming. In a lattice-based model, the number of calculations grows roughly proportionally to the square of the number of periods. This result can be seen by counting the nodes. For a

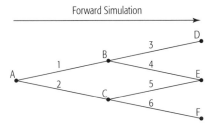

FIGURE 13.7 Forward simulation.

one-period binomial there are three nodes. For a two-period binomial there are six nodes. The number of nodes equals $(n + 1) \times (n + 2)/2$. The number of calculations is roughly proportional to the number of nodes. For a pathwise analysis the number of calculations is roughly proportional to the number of paths. For a one-period binomial there are two paths (one up, one down) For a two-period model there are four paths, and for a three-period model there are eight paths. However, the number of paths begins to grow quickly as the number of paths equals 2^n. Thus for a 10-period model the number of nodes in a binomial model is 66, the number of paths is 1,024. For a greater number of periods, the number of paths soon becomes unmanageable.

In order to use the advantages of path-based modeling without bearing the computational cost of calculating billions of paths, analysts have developed a method of randomly sampling from all available paths. These methods are called Monte Carlo evaluation. A Monte Carlo method, involves randomly selecting paths in order to approximate the results of a full pathwise evaluation.

One way of generating interest-rate levels is to use a precalculated binomial tree to determine the rate levels at each time period. The Monte Carlo process involves selecting whether to go up or down from the previous node. The interest-rate level is then read off of the precalculated tree. Another method is to create a random interest-rate path based on an equation that describes how interest rates change over time. If the second method is used, one must adjust these interest-rate paths to insure proper pricing of the Treasury curve.

Regardless of which method is chosen, analysts seek to find ways of choosing paths so that the paths are representative, while at the same time require the fewest number of paths. These methods are generally referred to as variance-reduction methods. A commonly used method is the use of antithetical paths. In this method, for each path that is generated, an additional path is created that moves in exactly the opposite fashion. For example, if one path began with the sequence "up, up down," the antithetical path would begin "down, down, up." This technique serves to produce more accurate results with fewer paths. Many other techniques are possible.

Computing the Spread

By combining the spread to the curve concepts and the pathwise valuation concepts, we can define option adjusted spread:

$$P = \frac{1}{N} \sum_{i=1}^{N} \sum_{j=1}^{n} \frac{cf(i,j)}{\prod_{k=1}^{j} (1 + r_{i,k} + s)} \tag{13.2}$$

where i represents one of N paths, j represents the number of months, $r^{i,k}$ represents the one-period discount rate for period k of path i, determined using the techniques of Chapter 12. The cash flow of the security for period j of path I is represented by $cf(i, j)$, and s is the OAS. Generally, one solves for the OAS, s, such that the price from equation (13.2) equals the market price. In this way, equation (13.2) is the stochastic generalization of equation (13.1).

COLLATERAL

In Monte Carlo analysis, the model must dynamically compute cash flows for every interest-rate path. The key ingredient to compute security cash flows is determining the cash flows of the underlying mortgage collateral, and the key feature of the collateral that affects cash flow is prepayments. For most reasonable choices of interest-rate models, prepayment assumptions are the most important input into OAS calculation. For a reasonable range of prepayment assumptions, it is possible to get OAS results that vary significantly enough to turn a buy recommendation into a sell recommendation. Due to this sensitivity, it is important for users of OAS to understand the prepayment models, even though the prepayment model operates behind the scenes in the OAS analysis. Unlike yield analysis or total-return analysis, it is difficult to review the path-by-path prepayment assumptions embedded in an OAS model.

A crucial aspect of using prepayment models within an OAS framework is how the prepayment forecasts are linked to the interest rates in the OAS model. Prepayment models generally use three kinds of information: description of the loan, description of the borrower, and description of economic conditions. The description of the loan and the description of the borrower are generally fixed through time. Variations in prepayments arise, for the most part, through variations in economic conditions. Those economic conditions may change as interest rates change. In fact, the leading driver of changes in prepayments is the level of interest rates. Prepayments may also be affected by housing prices, and other economic variables such as gross national product (GNP).

In many prepayment models, the current coupon yield, or the coupon on a hypothetical mortgage pass-through priced at par is used as a driver of prepayment rates. Unfortunately, this rate is not generally a direct output of the OAS model. In Chapter 12, models were created using either the Treasury curve or the swap curve. For many interest-rate models, it is possible to create the full yield curve at every point in the analysis. Therefore, if it is possible to relate the mortgage current coupon to the yield curve, then that relationship can be used to generate current coupon yields to input into the model.

For example, in the Andrew Davidson & Co. models, we use a combination of 2- and 10-year swap rates to forecast the mortgage current coupons. We use different blends for different mortgage products (see Table 13.6).

These weightings produce relatively reliable forecasts of mortgage current coupons (see Figure 13.8).

For other economic variables the situation is more complex. It is difficult to create models for economic variables such as home-price appreciation and changes in GNP based solely on interest-rate levels. For these variables, sensitivity analysis, where the input levels are varied and the change in value of the instruments are assessed, may be an appropriate tool.

TABLE 13.6 Weightings of 2- and 10-Year Swap Rates

		Par Swap			Zero Swap		
Maturity	Agency	2-Year	10-Year	R Squared (%)	2-Year	10-Year	R Squared (%)
5	FHG	0.56651	0.43349	95.04	0.61794	0.38206	94.85
7	FNMA	0.34450	0.65550	97.70	0.41912	0.58088	97.27
	FHG	0.36634	0.63366	93.61	0.43865	0.56135	92.99
15	FNMA	0.17570	0.82430	93.80	0.27112	0.72888	93.13
	FHG	0.19701	0.80299	91.31	0.28708	0.71292	90.81
	GNMA	0.18884	0.81116	89.18	0.28787	0.71213	89.07
30	FNMA	0.10213	0.89787	95.40	0.20684	0.79316	95.18
	FHG	0.10206	0.89794	95.17	0.19977	0.80023	94.73
	GNMA	0.09880	0.90120	92.59	0.20272	0.79728	92.43

		Par Treas			Zero Treas		
Maturity	Agency	2-Year	10-Year	R Squared (%)	2-Year	10-Year	R Squared (%)
5	FHG	0.518357	0.481643	82.45	0.55953	0.44047	82.45
7	FNMA	0.504595	0.495405	88.58	0.54015	0.45985	88.55
	FHG	0.510901	0.489099	86.20	0.55953	0.44047	86.02
15	FNMA	0.357817	0.642183	87.63	0.42110	0.57890	87.35
	FHG	0.345772	0.654228	89.72	0.40540	0.59460	89.70
	GNMA	0.335591	0.664409	79.99	0.39987	0.60013	79.85
30	FNMA	0.236148	0.763852	80.24	0.30429	0.69571	80.14
	FHG	0.18466	0.81534	87.04	0.26141	0.73859	87.32
	GNMA	0.18445	0.81555	86.39	0.25495	0.74505	86.62

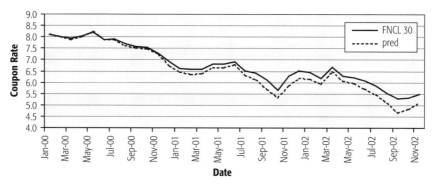

FIGURE 13.8 Actual versus fit current coupon rates

STRUCTURE

Generating the cash flows of mortgage pass-through securities and CMOs is a rather mechanical procedure. Yet there are certain complexities that should be addressed. Given an interest-rate scenario and a prepayment model, it should be straightforward to compute the cash flows of an MBS using the equations of Chapter 8. However, simplifying assumptions are generally required when there are combinations of loans and pools to consider.

The cash-flow process starts with the payments made by the borrowers and then flows through to the payments received by the investors. The flow of funds is shown in Figure 13.9. This process can be even more complicated as large pools could involve thousands of individual borrowers and CMOs can serve as the collateral for other CMOs in the form of re-Real Estate Mortgage Investment Conduits.

Because of the potential complexity of the cash-flow process, there is frequently a trade-off between speed and accuracy. At the first level, there is a choice of whether to model the individual borrowers within a pool as a single loan or use loan-level features. Currently, for agency mortgages, there generally is not sufficient information to produce analysis at the borrower level. For non-agency mortgages, discussed in Chapters 15 and 16, this loan-by-loan analysis is an option. At the CMO level, one must decide whether the cash flow for each pool that is used as collateral should be generated separately or if the characteristics of the pools should be combined into a single pool. Some analytical systems also offer intermediate levels of aggregation that allow similar pools to be combined for the purpose of generating cash flow.

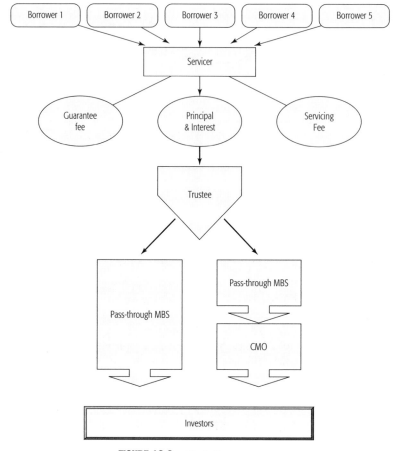

FIGURE 13.9   Cash-flow process.

RESULTS

With OAS tools in hand there is quite a variety of analysis that can be performed. The challenge presented by OAS is deciding what analysis should be performed determining when the results are and are not meaningful.

Value

As a result of the OAS analysis, we now have several different measures of spread available for investment decisions. Table 13.7 shows the results of these measures for a GNMA 30-year, 6 percent MBS as of November 1, 2002.

The first spread measure is the static spread. This represents the difference between the yield on the MBS and the benchmark security assuming the average prepayment speed, which is 371 PSA. The second spread is the

TABLE 13.7   Spread Results for GNMA 30-Year 6 Percent MBS, Price 102.78

Spread		Difference Between Spreads	
Static spread	203		
		68	Prepayment and curve adjustment
Spread to zero curve			
	135		
		29	Forward Cost
Spread to forward curve			
	106		
		84	Option Cost
Option-adjusted spread	22		

Measure	PSA	WAL	Yield
Static	371	4.16	5.20
Zero	371	4.16	5.15
Forward	200	6.99	5.47

WAL = weighted average life.

spread to the zero curve. For this spread, prepayments are generated using the prepayment model with mortgage rates held constant. The zero-curve spread equals 135 basis points, and is substantially lower than the static spread. The zero curve is 68 basis points less than the static spread. The timing of prepayments coupled with the slope of the yield curve make the simple static measure unreliable for this instrument. The difference between the spread to the curve and the spread to a single swap rate accounts for about half of the difference, while the use of a prepayment model, versus a single static prepayment speed, accounts for the remainder of the difference.

The next spread measure is the spread to the forward curve. This measure uses the same discount rates as the spread to the curve, but the prepayment forecasts are altered by allowing the mortgage rate used to generate the prepayment forecasts to vary with forward rates. In this case, the average prepayment speed drops to 200 PSA and the average life extends from 4.16 years to 6.99 years. The forward spread is 29 basis points lower than the current coupon spread, representing the cost of extension risk in a steep yield-curve environment. The difference between the current curve and the forward curve analysis is called the **forward cost.**

The final spread is the OAS. The OAS for this bond is 22 basis points. After adjusting for prepayment effects, yield-curve effects, and volatility the GNMA 6 only offers a 22-basis-point advantage over investing in swaps. The difference between spread to the zero curve and the OAS is called the **option cost.** Sometimes, option cost is presented including other components that we have separated out here. Option cost, as presented here,

TABLE 13.8   Analysis of GNMA MBS

Net Coupon	WAM	Price	OAS	Current Curve			
				Yld	WAL	Sprd	PSA
5.0	327	98.16	44	5.36	7.51	102	160
5.5	346	100.84	24	5.34	6.30	116	223
6.0	348	102.78	22	5.15	4.16	135	371
6.5	345	103.88	30	4.59	2.47	121	610
7.0	344	105.00	36	4.13	2.04	89	718
7.5	333	106.28	64	4.08	2.12	89	627

WAM = weighted average maturity.

represents the theoretical value of the embedded options in the MBS. It can also be thought of as the cost to hedge the options in perfect markets, that is, where there is unlimited buying and selling of the relevant instruments with no transaction costs.

Many mortgage investors have attempted to earn the static spread available from MBS without hedging all of the yield curve and prepayment risks. Unfortunately, these strategies usually fail as changes in market conditions move the embedded options in and out of the money; the resulting price and duration changes are too great for an unhedged strategy to bear.

Table 13.8 shows the analysis of a broad spectrum of GNMA MBS on the same date as the previous GNMA 6. Despite a broad range of static spreads, the range of OAS is much more narrow. Based on static spread, the GNMA 6.5s seem to offer the greatest spread advantage versus swaps. Yet on an OAS basis, they are not the most favored investment.

Figure 13.10 shows the spreads graphically. Static spreads increase into the coupons with the greatest prepayment risk and then decline. Forward spreads can be higher or lower than the static spreads. When the forward spread is greater than the current curve zero-coupon spread, then the security has hedge value; that is, if rates follow the forward rates the security will increase in value. This is most true for securities with high prices that will benefit from slowing prepayments. It is also generally true of Interest Only (IO) securities. The OAS is relatively consistent across instruments.

Risk

The fact that OAS provides relatively consistent results across a variety of disparate securities demonstrates the strength of the approach. However, these securities offer substantially different risk profiles. Table 13.9 shows the risk measures from the securities shown in Table 13.8. **Effective duration** is calculated as in Chapter 10 and represents the change in price of the MBS

Forward Curve				Static		
Yld	WAL	Sprd	PSA	Yld	Sprd	WAL Yld Spread
5.33	8.62	82	128	5.36	103	125
5.39	8.36	89	151	5.35	126	172
5.47	6.99	106	200	5.20	165	203
5.44	5.04	118	293	4.71	182	231
5.29	3.98	115	376	4.27	160	209
5.30	3.83	127	368	4.17	134	195

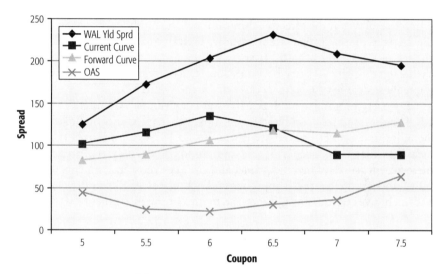

FIGURE 13.10 Comparison of spreads.

TABLE 13.9 Risk Measures Based on Table 13.8

Net Coupon	Effective Duration	Modified Duration	Effective Convexity
5.0	4.70	5.42	−1.14
5.5	3.97	4.63	−1.77
6.0	2.87	3.26	−2.00
6.5	1.98	2.11	−1.49
7.0	1.61	1.83	−0.81
7.5	1.93	1.91	−0.19

TABLE 13.10 Summary of Measures

	Static	Scenario	Option-Based
Income	Yield	Total return	OA-yield (not commonly used)
Value	Yield spread	Return profile	OAS
Risk	Weighted-average life Cash-flow duration	Effective duration	OA-duration OA-convexity

for a 100-basis-point change in interest rates, holding OAS constant. The lowest coupon has the highest duration, while the higher coupons have shorter durations. **Modified duration** is a cash-flow duration and does not include the impact of changing prepayments on price risk. This duration is primarily used as a measure of sensitivity to changing yield spreads. The difference between the effective duration and the modified duration reflects the impact of the prepayment option. **Effective convexity** measures the change in duration for a 100-basis-point change in rates. Negative convexity means that the security becomes shorter as rates fall. The security with the highest degree of negative convexity is the GNMA 6.

A variety of tools to analyze MBS were described in Chapters 7, 10, and 13. These same tools can be used for most other fixed-income investments including most asset-backed securities. Table 13.10 summarizes these risk measures for static, scenario, and option-adjusted analysis. In each case, there are measures of income, value, and risk. For most instruments it is useful to understand all three approaches. Each has strengths and weaknesses and each gives unique insight into the nature of the instruments.

EXERCISES

Simple OAS Analysis

In this section we construct a very simple Monte Carlo model to calculate the OAS of a security. The usual four-step process is followed (see Table 13.11). Table 13.12 provides the template for the calculation for each path. The OAS analysis consists of a set of sheets, one for each path. We go through the step-by-step process for each path.

Bond Assumptions

Coupon	11
Maturity	4 years
Volume	2%
OAS	100

TABLE 13.11 Monte Carlo Within the Four-Step Process

Methodology	Collateral	Structure	Results
Create interest rate paths consistent with current Treasury rates	Generate prepayment forecasts using model	Produce cash flows for MBS or CMOs	Calculate OAS, option cost, effective duration, convexity
Step 1. Use additive interest-rate process	Step 3. Calculate spread of mortgage to current rate.	Step 5. Calculate interest and principal cash flows	Step 6. Calculate the price for each path.
Step 2. Coin toss process to choose paths.	Step 4. Look up prepayment rate in table.		Step 7. Calculate average price and OAS.

TABLE 13.12 OAS Calculation Template

Period	0	1	2	3	4
Coin			Heads	Tails	Heads
Rate		9%	11%	9%	11%
Prepay		40%	5%	40%	
Ending balance	100	60.00	57.00	34.20	0.00
Interest		11.00	6.60	6.27	3.76
Total cash flow		51.00	9.60	29.07	37.96
Present value	100.62	59.68	57.24	33.89	

Prepayments

Spread	Prepay
–5%	5%
–1%	5%
0%	5%
1%	15%
2%	40%
3%	60%
4%	70%

Step 1. Choose an interest rate process. Here, we are using an additive interest-rate process. The initial rate is 9 percent and the step size is 2 percent per year.

Step 2. Choose random numbers. Here, we use a coin-toss method. Toss a coin once for each time period. Record the results heads or tails. Heads means an up-rate path, tails means a down-rate path. Our coin produced a result of heads, tails, heads. This produces an interest rate path of 9 percent, 11 percent, 9 percent, 11 percent.

Step 3. The prepayment model for this example is a look-up table with the input equal to the spread between the mortgage coupon and the discount rate. The mortgage coupon equals 10 percent. For each period calculate the spread.

Step 4. Determine the prepayment rate from the table. The spreads are 2 percent, 0, 2 percent, 0. The prepayment rates are 40 percent, 5 percent, 40 percent. The final prepayment rate does not matter, because the bond matures in year four.

Step 5. Calculate interest and principal cash flows. The interest cash flows equal the coupon times the beginning balance. The principal cash flows equal the prepayment rate times the ending balance from the previous period. The balances are 100, 60, 57, 34.2, and 0. The interest cash flows are 11, 6.6, 6.27, 3.76.

Step 6. Calculate the price for this path assuming an OAS of 100 basis points. The discounting process is accomplished by starting from the last cash flow and then discounting backward. The discount rate is calculated by adding the OAS (in percent) to the current interest rate. The cash flow in year four is 37.962 and the discount rate is 12 percent (11% +1%). The present value of that cash flow in year three is 33.89. The sum of the present value of the year four cash flow and the cash flow from year three is 62.96. The present value is 57.24 using a 10 percent discount rate. The process is repeated for year two and then for year one. The calculated present value is 100.62. This process can be represented in general by Equation 13.3.

$$PV_i = \sum_{j=1}^{WAM} \left(\frac{\text{cash flow}_{ij}}{\prod_{k=1}^{j}(1 + r_{ik} + OAS)} \right) \tag{13.3}$$

Where cash flow$_{ij}$ is the cash flow of the bond in path i for period j and r_{ik} is the discount rate for path i and period k.

Exercise 13.1 Repeat Steps 1 through 6 for the antithetical path tails, heads, tails.

Period	0	1	2	3	4
Coin			Tails	Heads	Tails
Rate		9%			
Prepay					
Ending Balance	100				0.00
Interest		11.00			
Total Cash Flow					
Present Value					

Bond Assumptions

Coupon	11
Maturity	4 years
Volume	2%
OAS	100

Prepayments

Spread	Prepay
–5%	5%
–1%	5%
0%	5%
1%	15%
2%	40%
3%	60%
4%	70%

Step 7. Calculate the OAS. Since there are three periods in which the rates can change, there are eight possible paths. Assuming a 100-basis-point OAS, the values for each path are as shown in Table 13.13. The average value is 101.32. This calculation is shown in Equation (13.4). The OAS level can be calculated for a given price through a trial and error method. Table 13.14 shows the average values for various OAS levels. If the market price equals 101.32, then the correct OAS is 100.

TABLE 13.13   Price Given OAS

Path	Price
up up up	97.54
up up down	98.86
up down up	100.62
up down down	101.54
down up up	102.49
down up down	102.79
down down up	103.26
down down down	103.43
Average	101.32

TABLE 13.14   Average Values for Various OAS Levels

OAS	Price
50	102.26
75	101.78
100	101.32
125	100.85

$$\text{Model Price} = \frac{1}{N} \sum_{i=1}^{N} PV_i \tag{13.4}$$

Vary the OAS in equation (13.4) until model price equals market price.

Option Cost

Option cost represents the difference between the yield of the instrument and the OAS. Calculate option cost using the following four steps.

Step 1. Assume constant interest rates.

Step 2. Follow steps 3 through 5 under Simple OAS Analysis.

Step 3. Calculate the spread for that one path.

Step 4. Subtract the OAS from the spread calculated in the previous step, which gives you the option cost.

Exercise 13.2   Calculate the option cost for this security assuming a price of 101.32.

Price	
Yield	
Spread	
OAS	
Option cost	

Exercise 13.3   How many nodes and how many paths are there for a 30-period model?

Exercise 13.4   How does the antithetical-path method work to reduce variance? Does it ensure accurate mean interest rates? Accurate cross-sectional volatilities? What are the features of a good variance-reduction technique?

Exercise 13.5   If two firms are offering the same security and firm A says the OAS is 20 basis points higher than firm B, would it be better to buy from firm A? What if firm A has a higher price than firm B?

Exercise 13.6   If you want a low-risk, high-return bond, should you buy bond A with an OAS of 350 and an effective duration of 15 or bond B with an OAS of 90 and an effective duration of 3?

Exercise 13.7   If you buy a CMO with a high OAS, and hedge it with Treasuries based on the CMO's effective duration, are you guaranteed a profit?

CHAPTER 14

Comparing Investment Alternatives

U p to this point, we have introduced many types of investments and presented a number of analysis tools. This chapter shows how these tools
can be used to analyze various investments. In doing so, we also see the wide
range of investment performances that mortgage-backed instruments can
provide. This chapter also demonstrates why careful analysis of mortgages
is essential.

MORTGAGE-BACKED SECURITIES

Pass-through mortgage-backed securities (MBS) are the building blocks of
the mortgage investment world. Pass-throughs may have a variety of investment characteristics. Table 14.1 shows summary risk and value measures for
Ginnie Mae and Fannie Mae 30-year pass-through mortgages. The instruments ranging from the lowest coupons to the highest are offered at increasing prices. They offer investors a wide range of spread and average-life
combinations.

Option-adjusted spread (OAS) provides a measure of value. In this
analysis the higher-coupon loans show the highest OAS. However, these results are very sensitive to prepayment assumptions. The various instruments
also exhibit a range of price performance as shown by their effective durations and convexities. The 5.5s and 6.0s have the highest durations, but they
also have a high degree of negative convexity, which would limit price performance in falling interest-rate environments.

Yield and average life provide a static view of the securities. OAS and
effective duration provide a view that takes into account the wide range
of performance possible. Total-return analysis provides insight into the
performance in changing rate environments. Figure 14.1 shows the total return analysis for the pass-throughs in Table 14.1. Note that the lines in

TABLE 14.1 Investment Characteristics of Agency Pass-Throughs

Security	Coupon	Price	Yield	WAL	Spread	OAS	Eff. Dur.	Eff. Conv.	CPR
GNMA	5.5	101.31	5.22	5.88	117	24	3.90	−2.04	14
	6.0	103.41	4.84	3.67	119	17	2.73	−2.26	23
	6.5	104.34	4.26	2.32	94	25	1.86	−1.52	35
	7.0	105.64	3.85	2.08	64	31	1.63	−0.69	38
	7.5	106.52	3.91	2.09	77	65	1.96	−0.19	38
	8.0	107.48	4.35	2.38	116	101	2.30	−0.01	34
FNMA	5.5	101.47	5.09	4.92	133	26	3.57	−2.12	17
	6.0	103.14	4.66	3.01	124	26	2.43	−2.23	28
	6.5	103.84	4.15	2.02	102	39	1.73	−1.24	39
	7.0	104.81	3.90	1.85	88	55	1.67	−0.52	42
	7.5	105.92	3.40	1.67	60	54	1.66	−0.09	46
	8.0	107.17	4.34	2.31	130	112	2.28	−0.04	35

Notes: WAL = weighted average life. Prices as of December 11, 2002.

the figure appear in pairs because comparable coupons between Fannie Mae and Ginnie Mae pass-throughs provide comparable but not identical profiles. Investors may make value decisions and move between programs without significantly altering the risk characteristics of their portfolios.

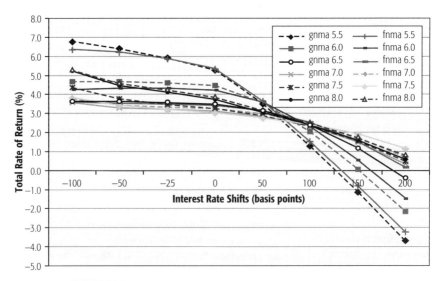

FIGURE 14.1 Total return analysis of agency pass-throughs.

The wide range of investment results is clearly demonstrated by the chart. The lower coupons have returns that are very sensitive to interest-rate levels, whereas the higher coupons show more stable profiles. The impact of negative convexity is clearly visible as the upward movement in returns is limited.

INTEREST ONLY AND PRINCIPAL ONLY SECURITIES

Structuring offers the opportunity to significantly alter the investment characteristics of MBS. Interest only (IO) and principal only (PO) securities are a special example of the power of structuring. Splitting MBS into their principal and interest components produces two new instruments that have very different investment profiles from the underlying collateral.

Figure 14.2 shows the total-return profiles of IO and PO securities created from the Fannie Mae 6 percent MBS shown in Table 14.1 and Figure 14.1. The PO is a very bullish security that benefits greatly from falling interest rates, while the IO is a bearish security that benefits from rising interest rates.

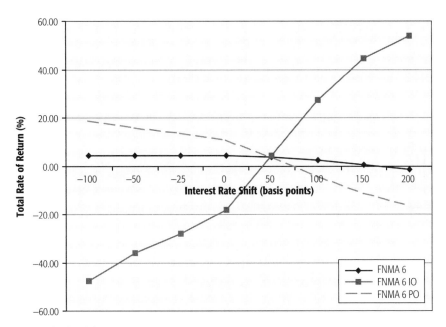

FIGURE 14.2 Total-return profiles of agency pass-through IOs and POs.

The return sensitivity of the IO and PO securities is significantly greater than the sensitivity of the underlying MBS. Even their convexity characteristics are different. In the falling-rate environment, the PO has negative convexity, whereas the IO has positive convexity. In the rising-rate environment, those characteristics reverse.

Even among IOs and POs there is a range of possible performance characteristics. Table 14.2 shows summary results for a set of IOs and POs. The IOs and POs each show a large range of effective duration and convexity. IOs and POs show a wide range of OAS. This wide range of spreads reflects the sensitivity of IO and PO OAS results to changes in prepayment assumptions. There may also be theoretical reasons why IOs tend to price at high OAS levels and POs price at low OAS levels. Market participants sometimes adjust their analyses to reflect the patterns of IO and PO OASs. They may assume that IOs will change with changing interest rates, or they may adjust their prepayment models to produce more stable OAS profiles.

The varying performance of IOs and POs can also be seen using total-return analysis. Figure 14.3 shows the total returns of the IOs and POs listed in Table 14.2. The instruments show a wide range of bullish and bearish profiles. They also show varying degrees of negative convexity.

One interesting feature of IOs and POs is the wide range of returns in the stable-rate case. Bearish instruments (instruments that perform better when rates rise) tend to have lower returns in the stable-rate case (as shown in Figure 14.3). These instruments are said to have **hedge value**. Hedge value means

TABLE 14.2 Investment Characteristics of IOs and POs

Security	Coupon	Price	Yield	WAL	Spread	OAS	Eff. Dur.	Eff. Conv.	CPR
IOs
FNT 329	5.5	26.13	0.44	4.92	−370	101	−31.37	−19.87	17
FNT 328	6.0	22.45	−6.10	2.87	−1050	12	−39.95	−0.69	29
FNT 321	6.5	16.34	−7.77	1.94	−1193	217	−38.48	14.48	41
FNT 320	7.0	15.92	−10.12	1.72	−1406	206	−28.63	15.29	45
FNT 317	8.0	16.19	4.99	2.36	194	1191	−10.27	7.30	35
POs
FNT 328	6.0	80.81	9.10	2.87	613	26	14.40	−2.36	29
FNT 321	6.5	87.53	8.07	1.94	528	−28	9.70	−4.21	41
FNT 320	7.0	88.95	7.72	1.72	507	−7	7.42	−3.45	45
FNT 317	8.0	90.89	4.33	2.36	129	−151	5.72	−1.72	35

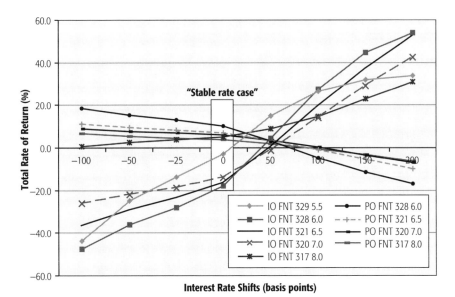

FIGURE 14.3   Total-return profile of IOs and POs.

that these instruments can act to reduce the price sensitivity of a portfolio of fixed-income assets. In an upward-sloping yield-curve environment, investors are willing to pay for this protection. While the mix of IOs and MBS is a tempting hedge strategy, many firms have floundered by relying on this strategy, since the correlation between IO values and MBS values cannot always be maintained.

The PO securities with negative convexity and a high degree of price risk have the highest returns in the stable-rate scenario. These instruments are being compensated for price risk as well as negative convexity. In other market environments, the IOs may have greater negative convexity and then would offer higher yields and higher returns in the stable-rate scenario.

COLLATERALIZED-MORTGAGE OBLIGATIONS

Collateralized-mortgage obligations (CMOs) offer virtually an unlimited range of investment choices. The range of choices is clearly shown when comparing the investment characteristics of various agency CMO securities contained in Table 14.3. The table shows various types of CMO classes issued from five different CMO transactions, each backed by different collateral. The examples range from a planned amortization class (PAC), support,

TABLE 14.3 Investment Characteristics of Agency CMOs

Security	Coupon	Price	Yield	WAL	Spread	OAS	Eff. Dur.	Eff. Conv.	CPR
FNR 2002-76 PY (PAC II)	3.4	101.09	2.49	1.54	51	−12	1.08	−1.06	24
FNR 2002-76 CZ (Z, Supp)	6.0	96.59	8.28	1.44	660	−41	8.04	−6.60	23
FNR 2002-76 SI (Inv, IO)	3.1	20.97	25.97	8.07	2,302	−152	5.63	−16.39	19
FNR 2002-87 NR (PAC II)	5.0	101.94	4.39	3.77	139	32	2.67	−1.65	22
FNR 2002-87 ZB (Sup)	5.5	91.48	11.29	1.55	959	−74	11.81	−4.90	23
FHR 2520 NR (PAC II)	5.0	99.95	5.01	4.10	188	84	3.31	−1.03	20
FHR 370 FD (Sup)	6.0	101.61	3.54	0.75	209	−75	−0.27	−1.59	37
FHR 2520 JB (PAC II)	5.1	101.63	1.52	0.51	8	27	0.03	−0.46	48
FHR 2290 D (Seq)	6.0	102.19	2.72	0.75	105	86	0.43	−1.11	46

Note: Pricing as of December 11, 2002.

sequential bonds to inverse floating bonds. **PACs** are bonds that have a planned amortization schedule. **Sequential** bonds are bonds whose principal is paid down first before principal is paid to other classes of bonds. **Support** bonds are created in conjunction with PAC bonds and receive the remaining principal payments. **Inverse-floating IOs** (**Inverse IOs**) are bonds whose coupons move inversely with an index.

Figure 14.4 shows the average life and prepayment profiles of the collateral underlying four different CMO transactions. The characteristics of the collateral backing these five transactions are summarized in Table 14.4. Two of the transactions are backed by FNMA collateral with a 5.5 percent coupon and the remaining transactions are backed by FHLMC collateral with 5.5 percent and 6.0 percent coupons. Prepayment variability in various interest-rate environments is measured along the left axis in terms of conditional prepayment rate (CPR) and along the right axis in terms of WAL for each respective CMO collateral group. Figure 14.4 shows that prepayment variability is lower for lower-coupon collateral groups over the range of interest rates depicted. Notice that the collateral groups with lower coupons have slower prepayment speeds across different interest-rate environments.

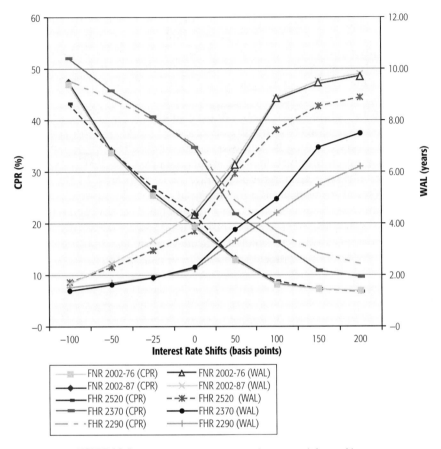

FIGURE 14.4   CMO: Prepayment and average-life profiles.

TABLE 14.4   Characteristics of CMO Collateral

Transaction	Issuer	Gross Coupon	Net Coupon	Current WAM (months)	Current Age (months)
FNR 2002-76	Fannie Mae	6.1062	5.5	348	4
FNR 2002-87	Fannie Mae	6.1244	5.5	357	3
FHR 2520	Freddie Mac	6.0700	5.5	358	2
FHR 2370	Freddie Mac	6.7103	6.0	338	18
FHR 2290	Freddie Mac	6.6997	6.0	295	52

The figure also shows a greater dispersion of WALs, which is attributable to differences in coupon rates. Over the relevant range of interest rates depicted in the figure, the dispersion of WAL is lower for the lower-coupon collateral because the incentive to refinance is lower for mortgages with lower interest rates. The lower coupon provides a certain degree of call protection.

Figure 14.5 shows the total return performance for the PAC, sequential payer, support, and inverse-floating IO classes of CMOs identified in Table 14.2. The inverse-floating IO and two support bonds have higher and more variable total rates of return than the sequential payer and PAC classes. The higher total rates of return in the stable-rate scenarios offered by the inverse-floating IO and support bond are compensation for the adverse price performance of these securities as interest rates change. The PAC and sequential payer classes of CMO have lower duration, less negative convexity, and less variable price performance, which is reflected by the fact that the lines are relatively flat across the range of interest rates examined.

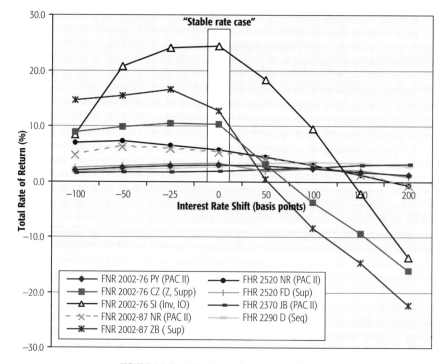

FIGURE 14.5   CMO total-return analysis.

MBS provide a wide range of investment profiles. Utilization of a variety of analytical techniques helps investors make appropriate investment decisions. In considering these techniques, investors should understand the strengths and weaknesses of each measure. In the end, investing still requires the judgment of the portfolio manager to develop and implement the portfolio strategy that will best meet the investment objectives.

EXERCISES

Exercise 14.1   What are the strengths and weaknesses of the various analytical tools?

Exercise 14.2   Which are the most attractive investments in Table 14.2. Why do the instruments with the highest spreads have some of the lowest OAS values?

Non-Agency Mortgage-Backed Securities and Analyzing Credit Risk

CHAPTER 15

Non-Agency Mortgage-Backed Securities

Non-agency mortgage-backed securities (MBS) or **private-label MBS** are securities whose underlying collateral does not conform to the guidelines set forth by government-sponsored enterprises (GSE), such as Fannie Mae (Federal National Mortgage Association) or Freddie Mac (Federal Home Loan Mortgage Corporation) and therefore do not carry the implicit or explicit guarantee of the GSEs. Agency MBS, discussed in Chapter 6, refer to securities whose underlying loans adhere to loan size and underwriting guidelines established by a government agency, Ginnie Mae (Government National Mortgage Association), or a GSE. The GSE guarantees generally provide for the timely payment of principal and interest. Since non-agency MBS do not carry guarantees from a government agency or GSE, some form of credit enhancement is required in order for them to receive investment-grade ratings. The term non-agency MBS and private-label MBS are generally used interchangeably in the mortgage industry.

HISTORICAL OVERVIEW OF THE NON-AGENCY/PRIVATE-LABEL MARKET

Of the $4.7 trillion of mortgage-related securities outstanding in 2002, $694 billion or 6 percent comprised the non-agency or private-label market. As illustrated in Figure 15.1, the overall size of the private-label market has more than doubled since 1994, which is shown by the solid vertical bars. Annual issuance, shown by the patterned vertical bars, has also risen significantly. The reason for the drop in annual issuance in 1999 and 2000 can be explained by rising interest rates, represented by the dotted line.

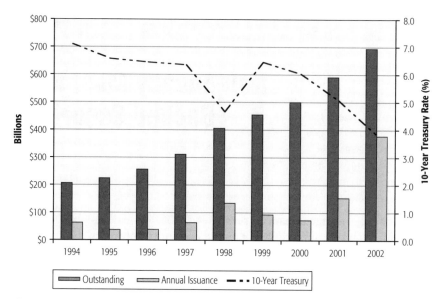

FIGURE 15.1   Private-label MBS outstanding volume and annual issuance for 1994–2002.

Source: 2003 Mortgage Statistical Annual and 2002 Bloomberg LP.

PRIVATE-LABEL MORTGAGE-BACKED SECURITIES COLLATERAL TYPES

Private-label MBS are collateralized by mortgage loans that do not meet GSE standards. These types of mortgages have been traditionally referred to as "nonconforming" because their loan sizes exceed GSE limits or because they do not meet the credit quality standards of the GSEs. There are a wide variety of nonconforming loan types that collateralize the non-agency MBS market.

Jumbo mortgages, one of the most common types of collateral used to back private-label MBS, have loan balances that exceed GSE guidelines ($322,700 in 2003) and are loans generally made to high-quality or "prime" borrowers. In 2001, approximately $211 billion of private-label MBS were collateralized by jumbo mortgages.

Home equity loans are another common collateral type used to back private-label MBS. The home equity loan (HEL) market is quite heterogeneous because it encompasses second-lien mortgages, first-lien mortgages with high loan-to-value (LTV) ratios, home improvement loans (HIL), revolving home equity lines of credit (HELOC), and subprime mortgages. The HEL market was once synonymous with traditional prime "second mortgages," but has evolved into a product area mainly focused on subprime or lower-credit-quality borrowers often labeled as "B," "C," or "D" grade. Only a small portion of HELs consist of true second-lien mortgages today. The HEL market is still a nascent product area and is discussed in more detail in Chapter 17.

Alt-A or Alternative-A represents another large segment of the private-label MBS market. Alt-A generally consists of loans to borrowers who have good credit, but do not meet the standard criteria for determining credit-worthiness. This could be because the borrowers have incomes that are not easily verified, as in the case of the self-employed. Alt-A loans may be within or may exceed the conforming loan limits. Alt-A borrowers generally pay higher interest rates than prime borrowers. With the advent of automated underwriting, the distinction between prime and alt-A borrowers has been blurred. Fannie Mae and Freddie Mac have also increased their securitization of these types of loans, so that many Alt-A loans are now contained in agency pass-throughs. A prospectus supplement for a sample transaction can be found on the CD.

CREDIT ENHANCEMENT

Mortgage credit risk encompasses short-term delinquencies as well as unrecoverable losses due to borrower default. The GSEs eliminate mortgage credit risk from the securities they issue by guaranteeing the timely payment of principal and interest. Non-agency MBS must rely on a variety of credit enhancement techniques, which can be categorized according to whether they are internal or external to the security structure. **Internal credit enhancement** techniques rely on the reallocation of cash flow within the structure, whereas **external credit enhancement** techniques can be provided by the issuer or a third party.

Rating agencies, such as Standard & Poor's, Moody's, and Fitch determine the level of credit support required for non-agency MBS, based on the collateral characteristics, the rating of any parties who play a significant role in the ongoing transaction, and the rating desired for the security itself. In general, the required credit enhancement levels are independent of the form of credit support (e.g., through a reserve fund, third-party guarantees, subordination, etc.). Until the early 1990s, triple-A rated MBS generally required 4 to 5 percent loss coverage for 15-year fixed-rate collateral, 6 to 8 percent for 30-year fixed-rate collateral, and 10 to 12 percent for adjusted-rate mortgage (ARM) collateral. In recent years, these levels have declined due to a combination of tighter underwriting standards and a longer historical

TABLE 15.1   Standard & Poor's Average Credit Enhancement Levels by Quarter (in percent)

	1Q 2001	2Q 2001	3Q 2001	4Q 2001	1Q 2002	2Q 2002	3Q 2002
Prime 15-Year Fixed-Rate Mortgage							
AAA	2.13	1.87	1.59	1.48	1.24	1.54	1.24
BBB	0.72	0.52	0.30	0.28	0.27	0.30	0.25
B	0.18	0.16	0.11	0.10	0.10	0.11	0.10
Prime 30-Year Fixed-Rate Mortgage							
AAA	3.35	3.44	3.26	3.16	3.10	2.92	2.87
BBB	1.04	0.96	0.66	0.64	0.64	0.59	0.56
B	0.27	0.25	0.21	0.20	0.21	0.20	0.19
Prime ARMs							
AAA	3.33	3.28	3.32	3.34	3.40	3.63	3.57
BBB	0.99	0.86	0.72	0.66	0.77	0.75	0.74
B	0.27	0.25	0.23	0.22	0.28	0.26	0.25

Source: Standard & Poor's, Trends in Residential Mortgage Products 2001 and 2002.

experience, all of which has improved the rating agencies' ability to predict credit losses on mortgage pools.

Table 15.1 shows Standard & Poor's average credit enhancement levels for residential MBS by quarter starting in 2001. Notice how dramatically AAA and BBB-rated classes for 15- and 30-year collateral have fallen in such a short time frame. For example, AAA-credit enhancement levels have fallen by 42 percent since first quarter 2001 for 15-year mortgage collateral. The average BBB-credit enhancement levels have fallen even more for the same 15-year fixed-rate collateral.

Rating agencies determine the required credit enhancement level by estimating both a foreclosure frequency and loss severity for each individual loan in a pool. By taking the product of foreclosure frequency and loss severity, they arrive at the required credit enhancement level for each loan. The resulting credit support levels for each loan are then added together to arrive at the overall required credit support for the pool.

In Table 15.2 we perform a sample calculation of the loss coverage amount for an individual loan. The base foreclosure frequency for the desired rating of BBB is 6.0 percent. The adjustment factors are listed in the far right column. The base foreclosure frequency is then multiplied by the adjustment factors to arrive at an adjusted foreclosure frequency for the sample calculation.

TABLE 15.2 Foreclosure Frequency Calculation

	Individual Loan Characteristics	Foreclosure Frequency Adjustment Factor
Borrower credit quality	Subprime (C-grade)	3.6
Loan amount	$170,000	1
Property value	$200,000	n/a
LTV	85%	1.5
Property type	Single-family detached	1
Loan purpose	Purchase	1
Occupancy status	Owner-occupied	1
Seasoning	65 months	0.75
Pool size	300 loans	none
Loan maturity	30 years	1
Loan documentation	No employment verification	1.5
Interest rate types	Fixed	none
Balloon mortgage	No	none
Lien status	First	none
Foreclosure frequency calculation		
Base BBB FF	6.00%	
Adjusted FF	$= 6.0\% \times 3.6 \times 1.5 \times .75 \times 1.5$	$= 36.5\%$

The adjustment factor for **borrower quality** is 3.6 because borrowers below A-grade are typically penalized in a residential MBS transaction. In this particular example, a C-quality borrower is 3.6 times more likely to default than an A-quality borrower.

Loan amount is another factor directly correlated with foreclosure risk. Jumbo loans are considered higher risk because they tend to suffer larger market declines than conventional loans during economic downturns, thus resulting in higher loss severities. In this example, the loan is below GSE limits ($322,700 in 2003) and therefore the adjustment factor is 1.0.

The adjustment factor is 1.5 for the **LTV** ratio. LTV refers to the ratio of the loan amount to the property value. Historically, LTV ratios have proven to be important predictors of foreclosure. Higher LTV loans have a higher risk of default.

The adjustment factor for **property type** is 1.0 because single-family detached properties are generally regarded as the safest category by rating agencies because of the high and stable demand for this type of property. Other categories include low-rise condominium and high-rise condominium. Single-family attached, low-rise condominiums, which can include row houses and townhouses, are viewed as somewhat riskier because there is generally less demand for this category of housing.

The adjustment for **loan purpose** is 1.0 because loans used to purchase property or for refinancing at more favorable rates and terms are not generally penalized. Only a "cash-out" refinance in which a borrower increases the loan amount in order to take equity out of his or her property is penalized since the new loan results in a higher LTV, making it more difficult for the buyer to make his or her debt service payments during economic downturns.

Occupancy status is another important indicator of foreclosure risk. The adjustment factor in this example is 1.0 because the property is **owner-occupied**. Mortgages for nonowner-occupied residences are considered riskier than owner-occupied homes, because a home owner is more likely under economic hardship to forfeit a second home than his or her primary residence. Moreover, rental properties have an additional risk in that owners rely on rental income to make their mortgage payments, which can suffer lapses.

Seasoning refers to the age of the mortgage loan. Generally, defaults peak within the first few years of the life of loan. The risk of default tends to decline as loans become more seasoned. Since the loan in this example is well over 5 years, the risk of default has declined. The seasoning adjustment factor for this example is 0.75.

No adjustment was made for the **size of the loan pool** because this loan pool contains more than 300 loans, which is considered large enough statistically to diversify away systematic risk.

Loan maturity has a direct impact on foreclosure risk of a loan. Mortgages with 15-year maturities are less risky than 30-year mortgages by the very nature that principal is repaid more quickly with a shorter term. The adjustment factor for the loan maturity is 1.0. While the particular loan in this example was not penalized for a 30-year term, a term less than 30 years would have been rewarded with a factor less than 1.0.

Loan documentation refers to the level of documentation provided by a borrower to support claims about employment and income. There are several levels of documentation types, which range from no employment or income verification to full documentation of assets, employment, and income. Since this loan was underwritten without verification of income and employment, an adjustment factor of 1.5 is assigned.

Interest-rate type also plays an important role in determining default risk. ARMs have considerable amount of risk because of the potential payment shock that can arise from a rising index. Various factors are assessed in determining the magnitude of the risk, including the frequency of interest-rate adjustments, the amount of increase allowed during each period, the potential rate increase over the life of the loan, and the volatility of the index. Because the loan in this example has a fixed rate of interest, no adjustment is necessary.

Balloon mortgages are loans that do not fully amortize on maturity. After some specified period (5, 7, 10 or 15 years), the balance of the loan becomes due in one lump-sum payment. The ability to refinance is not necessarily a given. The ability of a borrower to repay the balloon mortgage depends on his or her earning capacity as well as his or her ability to refinance under favorable circumstances, which is sometimes out of the borrower's control due to market forces such as interest-rate moves or market declines. In this example, the loan is not a balloon mortgage and therefore does not have any adjustment factor for this category.

Lien status refers to the position of seniority of the loan in the case of bankruptcy or default. The loan in consideration is in a first-lien position so no adjustments were made. A second lien would be a subordinated loan. In the case where there is a second lien, a combined LTV ratio (CLTV) would be calculated and an adjustment factor assigned depending on the CLTV.

The loss severity calculation (shown in Table 15.3) is based on rating agency assumptions about the property's market value decline and foreclosure costs. The foreclosure cost assumption of 25 percent includes brokerage, taxes, and legal fees as well as unpaid interest. The resulting loss severity for this example is 39 percent.

TABLE 15.3 Loss Severity Calculation

BBB Rating	
Purchase price of home	$200,000
Loan amount	$170,000
Market value decline (27.2% of purchase price)	$ 54,400
Market value at foreclosure sale	$145,600
Market loss	($24,400)
Foreclosure costs (25% of loan balance)	$42,500
Total loss	($66,900)
Loss Severity = Total Loss/Loan Amount	= $66,900/$170,000 = 39%

The required credit enhancement at a BBB level is found by taking the product of the foreclosure frequency and the loss severity (36.5 percent × 39.4 percent), which is equal to 14.3 percent of the principal balance of the loan or $24,385. In order to calculate the required credit support for the entire pool, the same calculations are performed for each loan in the pool. The resulting credit enhancements in dollar terms are then added together to arrive at the overall credit enhancement level.

Once the level of credit support has been determined for a particular mortgage pool, the issuer must decide on the most cost-effective form of the credit support. The various internal and external credit enhancement techniques are discussed here.

Internal Credit Enhancement

Internal credit enhancement techniques allocate a portion of the collateral cash flow to certain senior classes of a particular security, which in turn safeguard senior security holders against potential losses. Internal credit enhancement techniques include **reserve funds, spread accounts,** and **overcollateralization.** The most popular form of overcollateralization is the **senior/subordinated** structure.

Overcollateralization (OC) is a form of subordination and represents the difference between the balance of outstanding securities and the underlying collateral balance. An original OC amount is established when a transaction is issued. For example, if $100 million worth of bonds were secured by $102 million of collateral, the OC amount would be equal to $2 million ($102 million minus $100 million). Stated another way, the transaction is overcollateralized by 2 percent. Therefore, this transaction can withstand losses equal to the OC plus any excess spread available before senior classes incur any losses.

In a typical transaction, in addition to the initial OC level, a target OC level is predetermined. Additional OC can be created while the securities are outstanding by accelerating the amortization of the certificate balance relative to the underlying collateral balance. In any given period, excess interest is used to pay down the certificate balance until the desired target level is reached. As long as the OC target is maintained, excess interest is paid to the holder of the residual interest. If at any time the OC level falls below the target, excess interest is used to pay down the certificate balance to restore the OC level.

In a **senior/subordinated structure,** one or more subordinate classes are created to protect the senior classes from the risks of default. The subordinate classes effectively act to provide overcollateralization to the more senior classes. The original senior/subordinated structures were composed of two classes: A senior ("A") class, which is protected against credit losses by the subordinate ("B" or "junior") class in a first-loss position. If a loss were to occur on an underlying mortgage loan, funds that would normally be allocated to the subordinate class would be redirected to the senior class. If these funds were insufficient to cover the loss and if no funds were available from a reserve fund, spread account, or other form of credit enhancement, payments otherwise due to the subordinated class would be diverted to the senior class until the shortfall was paid off.

In current structures, the senior class is protected from losses until the subordinated B class is exhausted. In early senior/subordinated transactions, however, protection was limited to a prespecified subordinated amount, which applied to the actual cash amount diverted from the subordinated to the senior class. In either case, prepayment risk makes the total amount of available interest cash flow uncertain, so the rating agencies have generally required the total amount of loss coverage in the form of principal. Thus, the subordinate class size must be at least as large as the initial required coverage amount. For example, a $100 million 30-year fixed-rate pool that requires an initial 8 percent loss coverage would need a subordinate class of size $8 million to provide sufficient loss coverage to receive a triple-A rating on the senior class. In structures that have a subordinated class, the total amount of credit support will equal the principal balance plus all interest payments diverted to the senior class, thus providing more than the required 8 percent.

In the early senior/subordinated transactions, the issuer was required by tax regulations to hold the subordinate class. This requirement was eliminated in 1987 by the Real Estate Mortgage Investment Conduit (REMIC) regulations, but investors were not generally sufficiently comfortable with mortgage credit risk to purchase a leveraged first-loss position in a mortgage pool. In 1989, a three-class senior/subordinated structure appeared that divided the subordinated class into a "senior-subordinated" or "mezzanine" class, which was investment grade (generally triple-B), and an unrated "junior-subordinated" first-loss class commonly referred to as the **residual** class.

In 1991, in response to conservative investors' concerns about mortgage credit in a generally weak economic environment, the senior class was divided in the same way to produce a "super-senior" class on top of a regular triple-A senior class. This "belt and suspenders" structure was short-lived, and the market soon settled on a structure with triple-A senior classes, double-A mezzanine classes, and a series of tiered subordinate classes rated from single-A down to single-B. The senior classes were further structured into a variety of tranches such as planned amortization class (PAC) support structures or floater-inverse floater structures, suiting the needs of a diverse investor population.

The senior/subordinated concept can be implemented in many different forms, and for a while it seemed as if issuers and Wall Street dealers were intent on trying every one at least once. However, all of the structures can be understood in terms of a single general principle: the structure must preserve the availability of sufficient credit support to satisfy the general loss-coverage requirements stipulated by the rating agencies. These requirements can be accomplished with a subordinated class alone or in combination with a reserve fund, spread account, or third-party guarantees.

The earliest senior/subordinated transactions used a specific type of reserve fund structure, but since about 1989 the structure of choice has been the so-called shifting-interest structure. An alternative structure that is increasingly used with high-margin (i.e., the spread between the mortgage interest rate and the MBS interest rate) collateral combines a subordinated class with a spread account that provides a measure of first-loss protection.

Excess interest or **excess spread** is the difference between the coupon or interest rate paid by borrowers and interest rate paid to certificate holders. Generally the interest rate paid by borrowers is higher than the interest rate paid to the certificate holders. This difference is available to cover any losses that occur during that period. Thus, if a loan defaults, the excess interest could be used to make payments to the certificate holders.

Excess interest can also be used to create **spread accounts**, which accumulate excess interest over time to cover current losses of the underlying loan pool. Once a deal has reached its target level, any remaining excess interest is distributed to the residual holders.

For some private-label MBS transactions, the collateral can consist of mortgages with distinctly different loan characteristics. For example, both fixed-rate and ARMs can be used to collateralize a single non-agency MBS transaction. Cash flows from the fixed-rate loans would most likely be allocated to the fixed-rate MBS classes, while cash flows from the adjustable-rate loans would most likely be designated for the adjustable-rate MBS classes. However, in instances whereby one collateral type may be experiencing delinquencies or defaults, the excess interest from the other collateral type may be used to **cross-collateralize** all senior MBS classes regardless of security type (fixed or adjustable) before being directed to more subordinate securities.

For all of the forms of internal credit enhancement defined here, the full amount of credit support must be available at or soon after the start of the transaction (the cutoff date), and the initial requirement remains in force for an extended period of time: it is not reduced as the pool balance declines over time—at least for the first several years. Initially, the pool balance is reduced almost exclusively by prepayments as opposed to amortization. However, the rating agencies take a conservative view that only good loans prepay early, because weaker borrowers cannot qualify for a refinancing. Thus, although the pool balance has declined, the pool's credit risk has not.

This view of early prepayments and their negative effect on credit risk is called "adverse selection." To counteract the effects of adverse selection, rating agencies require that the initial loss coverage be maintained until the pools are sufficiently seasoned to ascertain their performance character. This period is generally 5 years for fixed-rate loans, 10 years for ARMs, and 15 years for negatively amortizing ARMs. During this period, the credit support grows as a percentage of the outstanding pool balance. After this period, the loss-coverage requirement steps down over the next few years, provided that the delinquency and loss experience of the pool do not exceed certain levels, known as triggers. During the step-down period, the amount of credit support is gradually reduced, but may continue to grow as a percentage of the pool balance—it just grows at a slower rate. The step-down schedule generally runs for 4 years, after which the credit-enhancement requirement becomes simply a fixed percentage of the outstanding pool balance, which varies depending on the structure and, in most structures currently in use, on the historical paydown experience of the pool.

Coverage for short-term delinquencies, also known as liquidity coverage, is now generally provided by the servicer's agreement to advance delinquent payments to investors, backed by a highly rated entity—most commonly the master servicer or trustee—who provides this service for a fee. In older transactions or when the assets are particularly unconventional, this coverage is more often included with the loss coverage, which is sized appropriately to include the liquidity requirement. The rating agencies generally require that any third party providing delinquency coverage be assessed no lower than one level below the desired rating on the security or, alternatively, have a sufficiently high short-term credit rating.

Although the rating agencies vary in the methods in which they assign security ratings, all of their methodologies are based on a review of the risk characteristics of the underlying mortgage collateral and the security's structure.

External Credit Enhancement

External credit enhancement can take many forms. Some form of external credit enhancement is present in most transactions, in the form of insurance on the individual mortgage loans. Other forms of external credit enhancement would apply to the entire deal or to specific bonds.

Primary Mortgage Insurance and Other Insurance

Prior to any structural considerations—before any decision is made as to whether a loan is to be retained, sold, or securitized—lenders require the borrower to provide standard hazard insurance, and most require primary mortgage insurance (PMI) if the LTV ratio is above 80 percent. PMI is usually written to cover 20 percent to 25 percent of the original loan balance. Normally, when the LTV ratio falls below 80 percent, PMI insurance is no longer required. Flood insurance is required in government-designated flood plains, but earthquake insurance is not required in seismic risk areas.

Pool Insurance

Pool insurance normally covers losses due to borrowers' economic circumstances, and specifically excludes (carves out) losses that result from bankruptcy, origination fraud, and special hazards. The amount of pool insurance purchased for a transaction is determined by the rating agencies as described in the previous section.

A bankruptcy bond provides coverage against a court order that modifies the mortgage debt by decreasing the interest rate or reducing the unpaid principal balance. Such a reduction in mortgage debt is known as a **cramdown**. Individuals can file for bankruptcy under Chapter 13 and Chapter 7 of the Internal Revenue Code. Chapter 13 bankruptcy filings allow individuals to retain their assets while restructuring or forgiving debts. Under Chapter 7 bankruptcy filings, personal assets are liquidated to pay debts; cramdowns are not allowed. In the 1993 case of *Nobleman* v. *American Savings*, the U.S. Supreme Court disallowed cramdowns under Chapter 13 filings as well. While cramdowns are allowed under Chapter 11 bankruptcy filings, Chapter 11 is primarily used by businesses. Thus, given the relatively unlikely event of bankruptcy, most rating agencies would normally require as little as $100,000 to $150,000 of loss coverage on a $250 million pool of high-quality mortgages.

Because pool insurers will not cover losses stemming from fraud during the loan application process, rating agencies require fraud coverage of 1 percent to 3 percent of the original pool balance. Fraud coverage is allowed to decrease over the first 6 years of a transaction, because the risk of losses due to fraud declines as the loans season.

Sources of special hazard insurance have largely dried up since the 1989 and 1994 earthquakes in California. This lack of insurance has become more or less moot, however, as subordination has now almost universally supplanted pool insurance in non-agency MBS transactions. In the period after 1989, however, many pool-insured transactions included a small subordinated class specifically for special hazard loss coverage. These classes found a few willing buyers (and mostly did very well in the wake of the 1994 quake), and were thus arguably the first securitization of earthquake risk, predating the currently popular earthquake bonds.

Letters of Credit

The issuer of a whole-loan security or a third party with a sufficient rating can provide a letter of credit (LOC) in the amount required by the rating agencies to enhance the entire deal or in a lesser amount designed to complement or upgrade other forms of credit enhancement. To protect the investor from event risks, some LOCs are designed to convert to cash if the LOC provider is downgraded.

Bond Insurance (Surety Bonds)

Traditionally insurers of municipal bonds, Capital Markets Assurance Corporation (CapMAC), Financial Guarantee Insurance Corporation (FGIC), Financial Security Assurance (FSA), and Municipal Bond Insurance Association (MBIA) are also active in the MBS arena. Typically, bond insurers will not take the first-loss position in the credit support structure and thus require at least one other form of credit support, usually subordination, to bring the underlying assets up to an investment-grade (usually triple-B) rating. Since surety bonds generally provide 100 percent coverage for all types of losses unconditionally, they are often used to "wrap" existing transactions that are extremely novel or otherwise off-putting to investors regardless of their structural enhancements. For a time in the early 1990s, several extremely conservative investors would demand (and pay for) a "surety wrap" around an already triple-A transaction.

Corporate Guarantees

Corporate guarantees cover all losses and can be used as stand-alone credit support or in conjunction with other forms of credit enhancement to provide the loss coverage required to obtain a particular rating. However, if the primary credit support is provided by a rated entity, the security is subject to reevaluation, and potentially downgraded, if that entity is downgraded. For example, when Citibank was downgraded in the early 1990s, all but the most highly seasoned of the MBS guaranteed by Citibank were downgraded as well.

Because of concerns about the ratings of third-party credit support providers, and because of the more stringent capital treatment of issuer recourse for financial institutions, the use of external credit-enhancement techniques has declined substantially since the 1980s. For example, in 1987, 70 percent of non-agency MBS were externally credit enhanced. The types of credit-enhancement techniques relied on by non-agency MBS are shown in the bar chart in Figure 15.2. The share of external credit-enhancement

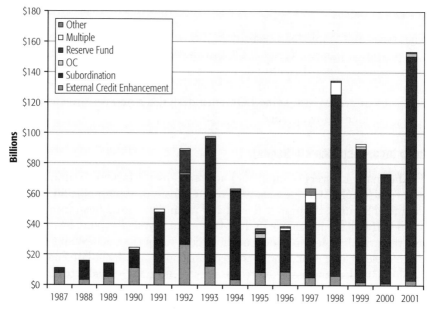

FIGURE 15.2   Private-label MBS production by credit-enhancement type.
Source: 2002 Mortgage Statistical Annual.

techniques reached a low point of 5 percent ($3.5 billion) in 1994. However, in recent years, surety bond use has increased, primarily as a result of the rapid growth in home equity loan-backed security issuance, which is classified as part of the asset-backed securities (ABS) market. In the traditional A-quality jumbo market, however, the senior/subordinated structure is by far the most widely used credit-enhancement technique.

The three main types of collateral for non-agency MBS, or private MBS, are jumbo loans, alt-A loans and subprime loans. Jumbo loans are generally of very high credit quality, but have larger loan sizes than agency-qualifying loans. Alternative A or alt-A loans do not meet the standard underwriting requirements of the agencies, but may still have excellent credit quality. Subprime loans generally do not meet the standard underwriting requirements of the agencies and have greater likelihood of default.

In the absence of the guarantee provided by the agencies, non-agency or private MBS have alternative forms of credit enhancement to protect senior investors from credit risk. Credit enhancement can be either internal or external. Through the ratings process, the rating agencies are the primary determinant of the sufficiency of credit enhancement. Senior/subordinate structures are currently the most popular form of credit enhancement.

EXERCISES

Exercise 15.1   What is the difference between internal credit enhancement and external credit enhancement? If the type of loans in the deal has stable default characteristics with extensive history, which will be better, internal or external credit enhancement?

Exercise 15.2   If the loans are not well understood by the market, what is the advantage of external credit enhancement?

Exercise 15.3   Using the data on the CD, compute the loss coverage for a "BBB" class for a sample transaction. Assume there is no adjustment factor for pool size since the sample transaction contains more than 300 loans. All other adjustment factors and base foreclosure frequencies are contained in the data file for Exercise 15.3 on the CD.

Exercise 15.4   What is the impact on investors in senior securities of lower loss coverage amounts?

Exercise 15.5   If a trigger event occurs that prevents a reduction in over-collateralization levels, what will be the effect on the holder of the residual?

CHAPTER **16**

Collateral Performance

COLLATERAL CASH FLOWS

The price, risk, and return of mortgage-backed securities (MBS) are based substantially on the payments that investors expect to receive over time. The amount and timing of future payments of MBS are uncertain and dependent on the changes in the principal and interest payments passed through from the loan pools that collateralize the issue. The primary determinants of future collateral cash flows are the rates of prepayments, delinquencies, defaults, and credit losses exhibited by the loan collateral. Consequently, investors seeking to estimate MBS price, risk, or return rely on forecasted collateral cash flows adjusted by projections of these variables.

Agency MBS are guaranteed for timely payment of interest and princi- pal from the underlying loans. Thus, the rates at which the loan collateral experiences delinquencies, defaults, and credit losses have little bearing on the amount and timing of the cash flows. With agency-issued MBS, the pri- mary factor responsible for changes in future cash flows is prepayments. In- vestors seeking to estimate the price, risk, or return of agency MBS must forecast the future cash flows adjusted for expected prepayments.

Private-label MBS bear no agency guarantees. Consequently, their fu- ture cash flows vary more with changes in the rates of delinquency, default, and credit losses exhibited by the loan collateral. Investors seeking to esti- mate the price, risk, and returns offered by private-label MBS must forecast the future cash flows they are likely to receive adjusted for their expectations of all of these factors.

MODELING COLLATERAL CASH FLOWS

A set of standard collateral cash-flow-modeling formulas and procedures is contained in a manual published by the Bond Markets Association (BMA). A generalized example of modeling collateral cash flows is shown in Table 16.1.

TABLE 16.1   Generalized Example of Modeling Collateral Cash Flows

Parameter	Amount	Calculation
Beginning Balance	$100,000.00	Last Balance – Scheduled Principal – Prepays – Defaults
Payment	$632.07	Mortgage Constant × Begin Balance
Interest Payment	$541.67	6.5%/12 × Begin Balance
Principal Payment	$90.40	Payment – Interest Payment
Servicing Fee	$41.67	.50%/12 × Begin Balance
Prepay SMM	2.37%	$1 - (1 - CPR)^{1/12}$
Prepayments	$2,366.70	CPR SMM × (Begin Balance – Sched Prin Pmt)
Defaulted Loans	Loss Curve	Default SMM × (Begin Balance – Sched Prin Pmt)
Default SMM	Loss Curve	$1 - (1 - CDR)^{1/12}$

Note: SMM is single monthly mortality, CPR is conditional prepayment rate, CDR is conditional default rate.

In simple terms, monthly collateral cash flows consist of principal and interest payments net of servicing costs and reductions from defaulted loans. Monthly principal payments are calculated by reducing the collateral beginning principal balance each month by scheduled principal payments, prepaid principal, and defaulted loans. Monthly interest payments are a function of the loan rates on the underlying mortgages less a servicing fee. Cash flows available from the collateral each month are reduced by credit losses, which are a function of the conditional default rate (CDR) and loss-severity rate applied. Several of the key calculations used to calculate the cash flows in Table 16.1 are presented later.

The collateral cash flows in Table 16.1 were based on forecasts for prepayments, delinquencies, defaults, and credit losses. The assumptions used to forecast these factors have substantial effects on the timing and amounts of payments to the various classes of MBS issued. The discussion that follows provides guidance with respect to formulating these assumptions.

Mortgage Delinquencies

Mortgage borrowers who fail to make payments as scheduled are considered as delinquent. Typically, for the pools of mortgage loans that collateralize MBS, the amounts of delinquent loans are monitored and categorized by totaling the principal balances of loans that are classified as 30 days delinquent, 60 days delinquent, 90 or more days delinquent, loans in foreclosure, bankruptcy, or loans held as real estate owned (REO).

Often, loans that are delinquent 90 days or more default and are liquidated, which ultimately results in credit losses. Credit losses reduce the principal and interest payments available to debt service all the MBS issued and
can result in payment shortfalls. The extent to which a particular class of
MBS or collateralized-mortgage obligation (CMO) is exposed to credit
losses depends on the magnitude of expected credit losses and the position
of the bond class in the cash-flow waterfall. Senior classes of MBS are much
less exposed to credit losses than subordinated classes of MBS.

Delays in MBS payments because of delinquent loans should have a
negative effect on the cash flows payable to the MBS over time. However,
most MBS are administered by a servicer that advances delinquent principal
and interest payments to investors. In return for a monthly servicing fee, the
servicer performs the advancing function, undertakes MBS record keeping,
and transfers the timely payments collected from the loans underlying mortgage pools to the MBS investors of record. The direct effects of delinquencies on the MBS cash flows are minimal when the MBS class benefits from
advances.

Generally, the amounts of loans that become delinquent are related to
the credit quality of the borrower, loan to value (LTV) ratio, the characteristics of the loan, the type of mortgaged property, location of the mortgaged
property, economic conditions, and other factors. Loans pools consisting of
mortgages made to borrowers with lower-credit quality such as subprime
loans experience higher amounts of delinquent loans than pools of loans
consisting of mortgages made to borrowers with high-credit quality such as
fixed-rate, jumbo A-grade loans.

For many types of mortgage loans, a substantial history exists establishing the pattern of delinquencies that typically occur as the loans age. This
history increases the reliability of delinquency forecasting for MBS. Historically, delinquency rates have been very low for private-label MBS backed by
high-quality jumbo-A collateral, averaging 1 percent or 2 percent of the outstanding principal balance. However, delinquency rates for private-label
MBS backed by subprime mortgages or home equity loans can be substantial. With subprime mortgages loans that are 60 or more days delinquent including loans in foreclosure, bankruptcy, and REO, can reach 10 percent to
25 percent of outstanding percent of the outstanding principal balance of the
loan pool within 24 months.

Figure 16.1 shows delinquency rates experienced for the prime jumbo
loans backing MBS transaction NASC 1996-1 and for the subprime loans
backing MBS transaction TMSHE 1996-A. The data show that for both
loan types delinquencies rise with loan age to a peak level in the years following origination. With the subprime loans, the amounts of loans in the 90-
days delinquent category alone are multiples of the prime jumbo loans

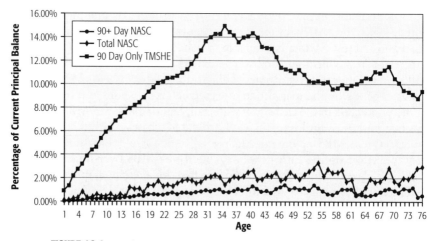

FIGURE 16.1   Delinquencies: Prime jumbo and subprime collateral.

delinquent in all categories (30 days, 60 days, 90 days, loans in foreclosure, and loans held as ROE).

Historical delinquency rates are positively correlated with defaults and credit losses. Consequently, historical delinquency rates should be a primary factor considered when formulating credit-loss assumptions.

Delinquency rates are often tied to delinquency triggers featured within the MBS or CMO structure that alter the amount of overcollateralization and credit enhancement provided to the senior bonds by the most subordinate bonds issued. When delinquencies exceed specified trigger levels, excess cash flow otherwise payable to the most subordinate bonds issued is generally redirected to accelerate reductions in the principal balance of the most senior MBS issued. For holders of the most subordinate classes of MBS issued, high delinquency rates and active delinquency triggers can have substantial and negative effects on the timing and amounts of cash flow investors can expect to receive.

Defaults and Credit Losses

If a loan continues to be delinquent more than 30 days, 60 days, or perhaps 90 or more days, the loan may be considered in default. If default persists the mortgage lender may initiate foreclosure proceedings. Foreclosure proceedings frequently result in the sale of the mortgaged property by the lender in order to recoup the unpaid delinquent payments owed and the remaining loan amount owed. If the proceeds the lender receives from a foreclosure sale turn out to be less than the delinquent payments, the unpaid loan balance, and the foreclosure expenses owed to the lender, a credit loss occurs.

Credit losses that occur with mortgage loans contained in the loan pools that collateralize MBS will reduce the cash flow payable to the MBS. Most private-label MBS issued are structured with credit enhancements intended to mitigate the adverse effects of credit losses on the amounts of cash flows that the more senior MBS classes expect to receive over time. Most private-label MBS use subordinate classes whose cash flow is the first to be reduced by credit losses that occur on the underlying loan collateral. Consequently, investors in subordinated MBS have a substantial interest in assessing and modeling the credit losses they expect mortgage loans to experience.

Generally, the amounts and timing of the credit losses exhibited by the loan pools underlying an MBS are related to the credit quality of the borrower, the LTV, the characteristics of the loan, the property type, the location of the property, loan size, economic conditions, home prices, and several other factors. Loan pools consisting of mortgages made to borrowers with lower-credit quality experience higher amounts of credit losses than pools of loans consisting of mortgages made to borrowers with high-credit quality. Historically, there is a strong positive relationship between the amounts of loans within a mortgage pool that are 90 or more days delinquent or in foreclosure, and the amounts of credit losses that occur within the mortgage pool. For many types of mortgage loans, a vast history exists establishing the pattern of rates of defaults and credit losses that typically occur for mortgage loan pools over time. This history increases the reliability of credit-loss forecasting for MBS. It also contributes to the existence of various credit-loss-forecasting models available for MBS.

The ability of the borrower to pay, and the value of the mortgaged property relative to the loan balance, have a substantial influence on the default rates and credit losses exhibited by mortgage loans. If the financial status of the borrower deteriorates to the point where the loan payment is unaffordable, the likelihood increases that the property will be sold and the loan will terminate. If real estate values are stable or rising and the value of the property is substantially above the loan balance, the borrower can recapture equity by selling the home and repaying the principal balance of the loan. No default or credit loss occurs in this circumstance as the loan terminates as though it were prepaid. However, if real estate prices are equal to or lower than the loan balance at the time the borrower experiences affordability problems, the borrower can exercise the option to default and effectively "put" the property to the lender in order to satisfy the obligation to repay a loan balance that exceeds the property value. Thus, mortgage delinquencies, defaults, and credits losses are most likely to occur when borrowers experience income and employment decay when property values have declined.

To a significant extent, the diverse types of mortgage loans that exist in the market today are a function of the efforts of mortgage lenders to maximize cash flows received after defaults or credit losses. A range of mortgage loans exists that reflect various combinations of LTV and ability to pay. Subprime mortgage loans represent a loan type intended to mitigate the higher default rates imposed by weak borrowers with the lower risk of default and loss associated with lower LTV loans. High LTV loans represent a loan type intended to balance the increased default frequency typical of high LTV loans with the lower probability of default associated with affluent borrowers. Prime jumbo loans are a loan type that mitigates the potential for large losses related to big loans with the lower risk of default associated with wealthy borrowers and modest LTV. To date, subprime mortgage loans with weak borrowers have produced the highest credit losses and the lowest cash flows after losses, while prime jumbo loans with strong borrowers have produced the lowest credit losses.

Credit loss rates for the pools backing MBS are frequently measured and forecast using a CDR and a loss severity. The CDR represents the percentage of the mortgage loans that default annually. The loss severity estimates the share of defaulted loan principal lost each month, and not recovered through the foreclosure and liquidation process. Another measure of the amounts of credit losses that occur within mortgage pools is the cumulative default rate or cumulative loss rate. Cumulative default rates are used to measure the total, lifetime amounts of defaults and credit losses that have occurred for a mortgage pool in total on a life-to-date basis. Cumulative, lifetime default rates are a function of the annual CDR and loss severity experienced.

Standard Default Assumption

The PSA (now BMA) standard default assumption (SDA curve) illustrates the assumption used to model defaults and credit losses for a pool of mortgage loans. Figure 16.2 shows a benchmark time series of annual default rates using multiples of the base 100 percent, SDA. The shape of the SDA curve is intended to approximate the tendency of mortgage pools to experience defaults that increase with age initially, then stabilize for an interim period, and ultimately decline as time passes. With the SDA curve, default rates peak in 30 months, stabilize, and then decline after month 60.

The cumulative default rates resulting from the application of the SDA curves are depicted in Figure 16.3. Cumulative default rates show the total amount of loans that default over the lifetime of the pool stated as a percentage of the original principal balance of the pool. It is important to note that the SDA curves represent only one functional example of the relationship between mortgage defaults and loan age. Investors use a variety of default functions to relate their subjective view of expected defaults and credit losses to loan age that vary by loan type, underwriting criteria, borrower, property type, geography, and many other factors.

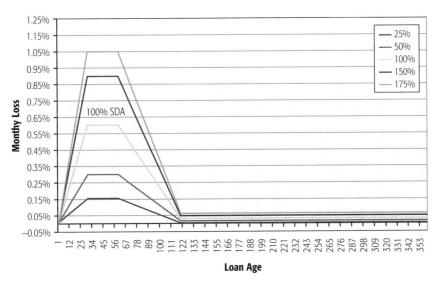

FIGURE 16.2 Standard default assumption.

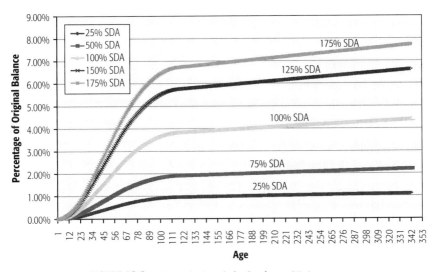

FIGURE 16.3 Cumulative defaults from SDA curve.

Figure 16.4 shows cumulative losses as a percent of the original pool balance. Losses are derived by converting the annual default rate of the SDA curve to a monthly rate and multiplying the monthly default rate by the loss severity. Loss severity represents the loss estimated to occur when a mortgage defaults and the property is sold. This method of estimating a

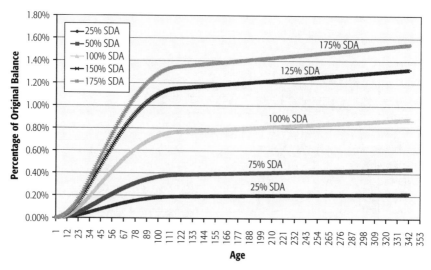

FIGURE 16.4   Cumulative losses from SDA curve.

distribution of default rates and multiplying them by loss severities is the standard process used to forecast the reductions in MBS cash flows due to credit losses.

The cumulative credit losses derived from the SDA curves are depicted in Figure 16.4. The SDA curve implies that 24 percent of cumulative defaults will occur by month 30, 51 percent of cumulative defaults will occur by month 60, and about 86 percent of total defaults will occur before the end of year 10 (120 months).

Office of Federal Housing Enterprise Oversight Benchmark Loss Experience

By looking at the Office of Federal Housing Enterprise Oversight (OFHEO) benchmark loss experience, we can see an example of the amount of loss possible for mortgage loans in a stressed environment. OFHEO has developed risk-based capital regulations for FNMA and FHLMC. OHFEO applies a stress test to gauge the capital adequacy of FNMA and FHLMC that subjects each entity to very large credit losses on the mortgages it owns or guarantees. The OFHEO stress test is based on historical credit losses experienced in various distressed economic regions of the United States and provides a benchmark, worst-case credit-loss scenario for conforming agency mortgage loans.

The benchmark OFHEO stress test is based on the losses experienced by Fannie Mae and Freddie Mac on 30-year fixed-rate loans originated from

1979 to 1993. The default rates and loss severity used by OFHEO represent the highest rates of default and loss severity of unseasoned mortgages observed in contiguous areas of the United States containing 5 percent or more of the U.S. population for a period of two or more consecutive origination years. Default rates represented cumulative defaults over a 10-year period following origination. The OFHEO benchmark loss experience is summarized in Table 16.2. The OFHEO loss rates excluded the proceeds of mortgage insurance on loans with LTV of 80 percent or more. OFHEO estimated that such mortgage insurance reduced losses on the benchmark loans by one-quarter.

OFHEO compared its benchmark loss rate to the losses experienced in Texas in the early 1980s and to other benchmark loss experiences. Using its methodology and data OFHEO identified the worst loss rate measured in Texas as 7.3 percent for the loans originated in 1982 and 1983. In the areas of Houston and Beaumont, Texas, OFHEO estimated the loss rate was 11 percent, while the El Paso and West Texas area loss rates were 9.8 percent. OFHEO estimated that the aggregate loss rate for the continental United States from 1979 through 1985 was 2.1 percent, which is less than 25 percent of the OFHEO benchmark. OFHEO noted that the benchmark default rate for FHA loans originated in the United States in 1981 was 19.1 percent.

TABLE 16.2 OFHEO Benchmark Loss Experience

States	U.S. Population (%)	Origination Year	Loss Rate (%)
Arkansas	5.3	1983	9.40
Louisiana		1984	
Mississippi			
Oklahoma			

	Default Rate Loss (%)	Severity (%)	Cumulative Loss (%)
<= 60 LTV	2.2	43.5	1.0
>60 LTV <= 70	3.5	46.2	1.6
>70 LTV <= 75	7.9	50.1	4.0
>75 LTV <= 80	9.4	58.9	5.5
>80 LTV <= 85	12.0	55.0	6.6
>85 LTV <= 90	17.7	60.2	10.7
>90 LTV	26.4	69.0	18.2
Average	14.9	63.3	9.4

OFHEO applied its loss methodology to a pool of loans graded by the ratings agencies using their loss-coverage methodology. The OFHEO method resulted in a benchmark loss rate of 6.2 percent for the hypothetical agency prime loan pool. OFHEO noted that its loss rate was similar to the loss coverage required by the ratings agencies to attain a AA rating on the mortgage pool.

Impact of Loan-to-Value Ratios and Home Price Appreciation

The OFHEO results clearly demonstrate the impact of LTV ratios on losses. Borrowers default on their loans when they are unable or unwilling to make payments. The value of the home relative to the value of the loan is one of the chief determinants of default. For the typical high-quality loan, the risk of default is small. The loan is generally created with a LTV ratio less than or equal to 80 percent. As the loan ages, generally home prices increase. Even if home prices stay constant or decline, the balance of the loan is declining. Only if home prices decline significantly will a newly originated loan experience negative equity.

Figure 16.5 shows the balance on a loan versus the value of a home at various rates of home-price appreciation. Note that the greatest risk of negative equity occurs from about 2 years to 5 years into the life of the loan. Figure 16.6 shows the probability of negative equity for different LTV ratios. As the LTV ratio increases, the probability of negative equity increases. Note the similarity of the results of the theoretical model to the actual OFHEO results.

Mortgage Prepayments

In general, borrowers (mortgagors) have the right to make principal payments in advance of scheduled principal over the term of the loan. The terms of most residential mortgage loans permit these principal prepayments to occur at any time without penalty. Other mortgage loans may require that borrowers pay a penalty if they prepay the principal balance of the loan within an initial period of time. In general, prepayments of the full mortgage loan balance occur when a borrower sells the home or refinances the loan. Borrowers also make partial prepayments of their loan balance.

Amounts of prepaid principal collected from the mortgage pools that collateralize MBS are generally paid to MBS pass-through investors as they occur. More complex, multiclass types of MBS exist that split mortgage prepayments among the various classes of mortgage security in order to alter the rate at which each class is redeemed. The prepayments rates exhibited by the loan pools that collateralize MBS have a substantial influence on the

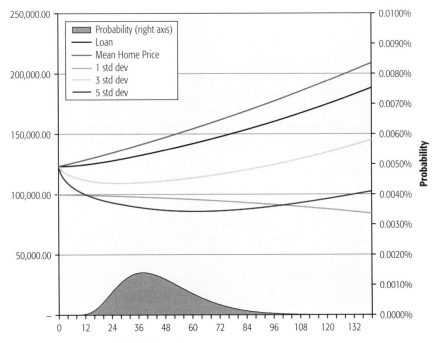

FIGURE 16.5 Home value versus loan value.

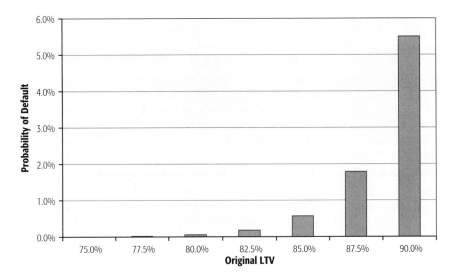

FIGURE 16.6 Probability of negative equity.

timing of principal payments that MBS investors can expect to receive from MBS. Changes in prepayment rates can cause substantial changes in the present value or investment value of an MBS. In general, prepayments are positively related with present value with MBS that bear lower coupon interest rates, and negatively related to the present value of MBS with negative coupon interest rates.

Prepayment rates for mortgage loan pools are often measured and forecast using a conditional prepayment rate (CPR). CPR measures on an annual basis the percentage of the principal balance of the mortgage loan pools that prepays.

Prepayment rates for residential mortgages vary by loan type, borrower demographic, property type, loan purpose, location, loan age, interest rates, property value, economic conditions, and many other factors. For many types of mortgage loans, a vast history of prepayments exists that increases the reliability of prepayment forecasting for MBS.

Dynamic Prepayment Model

Andrew Davidson & Co., Inc., has constructed prepayment models for private-label MBS backed by a variety of collateral types. The following discussion summarizes the prepayment model used to forecast prepayments for fixed-rate, residential, nonconforming jumbo loans, which are characterized by both their large original balances taken out by affluent borrowers and their lack of any private or government-sponsored mortgage insurance.

The prepayment characteristics of jumbo fixed-rate loans are similar to conforming mortgage loans, differing primarily in degree. However, for jumbo loans additional loan-level variables are available for analysis. A jumbo loan prepayment model can incorporate these variables that are not available for conforming loans.

The jumbo model uses mortgage data described on a loan-level basis versus a pool-level basis to forecast jumbo prepayments. While pool-level models are sometimes simpler to develop, loan-level models reveal additional sources of prepayments, allow for a greater degree of flexibility in the modeling process, and are more predictive when loan pools are heterogeneous. Another benefit of loan-level data is that there simply are more of them. Instead of thousands of observations at the pool level, we commonly work with millions of loan-level observations. This amount of data allows us to develop more accurate models that can capture the intricate nonlinear relationships that affect prepayments. From a modeling point of view, it is always desirable to have loan-level data.

AD&Co. relied on the prepayment histories of individual jumbo loans from a database of over 250,000 nonconforming jumbo loans tracked over several years through various interest-rate environments for over 9.5 million observations. This database provided a unique opportunity to model the complex prepayment behavior of jumbo loans using loan instead of pool data. Table 16.3 shows the loan counts for selected loan characteristics for 15- and 30-year loans.

Separate models were developed for 15- and 30-year fixed-rate nonconforming, owner-occupied single-family residential jumbo loans. Estimating a joint 15- and 30-year model was not possible because the experience modeling other types of loans shows that the 15-year and 30-year amortization

TABLE 16.3 Loan Counts for Selected Loan Characteristics for 15- and 30-Year Loans

Coupon Rate

	5–6%	6–7%	7–8%	8–9%	9–10%	10–11%	11–12%
15 Year	86	19,540	25,147	3,471	312	39	6
30 Year	17	15,126	138,799	44,869	6,006	629	149

State

	5–6%	6–7%	7–8%	8–9%	9–10%	10–11%	11–12%
15 Year	86	19,540	25,147	3,471	312	39	6
30 Year	17	15,126	138,799	44,869	6,006	629	149

Loan Amount

	≤250K	250–300K	300–350K	350–500K	>500K
15 Year	11,025	13,737	8,000	10,926	4,913
30 Year	56,143	62,175	32,934	39,600	14,750

Origination Year

	1989	1990	1991	1992	1993	1994
15 Year	33	14	39	742	19,715	8,415
30 Year	328	264	371	1,522	64,478	36,420

	1995	1996	1997	1998	1999	2000
15 Year	2,219	2,618	3,829	6,886	3,813	274
30 Year	17,003	12,692	16,078	34,028	19,779	2,581

subgroups exhibit distinctly different prepayment behaviors. Therefore, separate 15-year and 30-year models were estimated. In addition, it was observed that within the 15- or 30-year loan groups, discount and premium loans also have different prepayment behaviors; so additional submodels were developed.

The result is a rather sophisticated "survival analysis" model that segments the data into four subpopulations and captures the unique prepayment characteristics of each.

Following are factors that affect prepayments in the jumbo loan model:

- Discount/premium effect
- Aging effect
- Interest rate effect
- Burnout-effect
- Loan-size effect
- Loan-quality effects
  - Spread
  - Original LTV ratio
  - Home price appreciation
- Geography
- Seasonality effect

Discount/Premium Effect   A discount loan exhibits distinctly different prepayment behavior than a premium loan. In general, the discounts have slower prepayment rates compared to premiums and a less severe ramping-up period. In addition, they are not subject to the burnout effects that are characteristic of premium loans, yet they show some seasonality. Figure 16.7 shows the aging curves when the loans are segmented into discounts and premiums.

Aging Effect   A prominent feature observed in jumbo loan prepayment rates is the aging effect. Very well-defined, accelerated prepayments during the early months of the loans can be observed, followed by complex behaviors for the remaining lives of the loans. These behaviors are indications that other variables are affecting prepayments. We can control for these variables by using econometric techniques and separating out a "pure" baseline aging effect. This effect is seen as the diamond series in Figure 16.8. The complex behavior in the actual prepayments (triangle series) masks the true baseline aging effect. The true effect is a gradual increase followed by a slow decline in prepayment rates over time. The aging curve shapes, however, have very different characteristics, depending on whether or not the loan is a discount or premium.

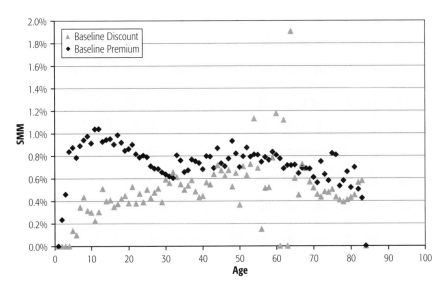

FIGURE 16.7   Premium/discount effect.

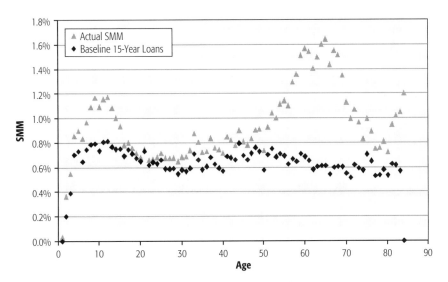

FIGURE 16.8   15-year jumbo loan baseline (SMA).

Interest Rate Effect   The interest-rate effect on prepayment rates is captured by a refinancing-incentive variable. This variable changes over time as interest rates vary and affects prepayments through the refinancing it induces. The refinancing incentive variable changes over time and is the ratio of the loan's current coupon to the coupon on a similar, new loan. Prepayments generally increase as this incentive increases because new loans are now at more attractive lower rates. However, this relationship is quite complex and needs to be modeled using nonlinear econometric techniques. Figure 16.9 shows that the interest-rate effect for discount loans is rather gradual compared to the very strong effect for premium loans.

Burnout Effect   Another variable affecting prepayments is the cumulative refinance ratio, which is used to capture the burnout effect. This variable summarizes a loan's cumulative exposure to refinancing incentives and captures the burnout experienced by seasoned premium loans. Figure 16.10 shows that for larger values of the variable, the prepayment rates are slower.

Loan Size Effect   Loan size also affects prepayments. Larger initial balances result in slightly higher prepayment rates. This may be due to the fact that large balances are associated with better-credit quality borrowers and improved opportunities to refinance. Figure 16.11 shows the gradual increase in prepayment rates with loan size. The effect for premium loans is much stronger than for discounts.

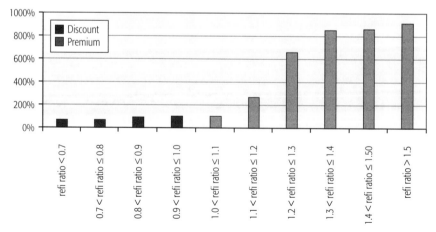

FIGURE 16.9   30-year whole loan model refinancing risk multipliers.

Loan-Quality Effect   The credit quality of the loan has a significant impact on prepayment rates. Since this data did not contain explicit information on the credit grades of the loans, AD&Co. investigated several proxies that proved to have good explanatory value.

The spread, defined as the difference between the coupon rate and the mortgage index rate, is a proxy variable that captures the credit quality of the loan. Typically, the greater the spread the lesser the quality of the loan,

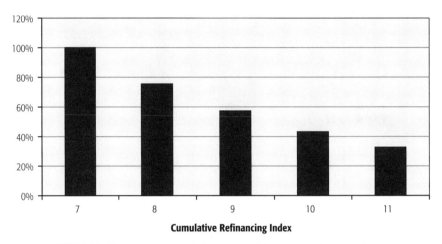

Cumulative Refinancing Index

FIGURE 16.10   30-year whole loan model burnout risk multipliers.

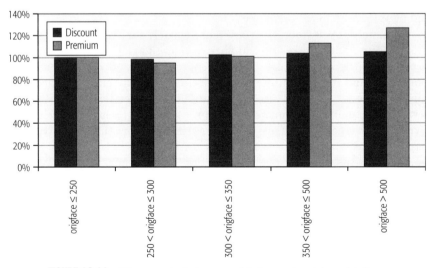

FIGURE 16.11   30-year whole loan model: Loan size risk multipliers.

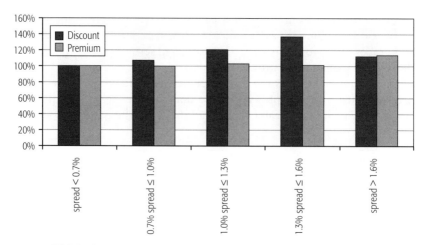

FIGURE 16.12 30-year whole loan model: spread risk multipliers.

which leads to faster prepayment rates due to the "credit-curing" effect; that is, as the borrower's credit improves, he or she can refinance into a more favorable loan. Figure 16.12 shows this effect through the risk multipliers estimated for the spread variable. As the spread increases, the prepayment rates increase. However, this effect is much more pronounced for discount loans than for premiums.

Original LTV is another proxy that captures the credit quality of the loan. In our models the relationship between original LTV and prepayments is complex. The very high LTV loans are often associated with better-credit borrowers and therefore those less likely to credit cure and refinance into lower-rate loans. There is also less equity in the properties, which implies fewer opportunities to refinance so the prepayment rates are relatively low. Very low original LTV loans, however, actually show slightly lower prepayment rates than the average 75 percent to 80 percent LTV loans. Figure 16.13 shows the risk multipliers for the original LTV effect.

The change in the home price index (HPI) is the last proxy for collateral quality. The HPI is a proxy for home price appreciation. The greater the increase in the HPI, the faster the prepayments. Figure 16.14 shows that this tends to make the collateral more secure, and thus the loans are more likely to refinance to get cash out and so forth.

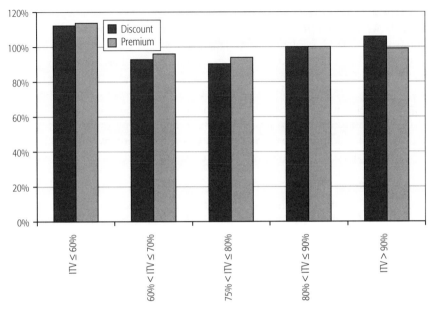

FIGURE 16.13   30-year whole loan model: LTV risk multipliers.

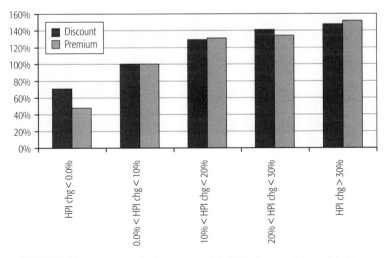

FIGURE 16.14   30-year whole loan model: HPI change risk multipliers.

Geography Effect   Prepayments are also affected by the location of the collateral. As aforementioned, this is dubbed the geography effect. Certain states on average have faster prepayment rates than other states, even after correcting for the influence of other explanatory variables. This may be due to localized differences in the degree of difficulty in refinancing, their associated costs, and other market imperfections. Figure 16.15 shows the geography effect for several states and makes clear that this effect is also dependent on whether or not the loan is a discount or premium loan. For example, Florida loans prepay faster than California loans when they are discounts, yet slower when they are premiums.

Seasonality Effect   The final effect in the prepayment model is seasonality. This effect is present in the model for discount loans only. We observed a well-defined cyclical trend in prepayment rates based on the month of the year. Peak prepayments occur in September and decline 6 months later in March. Figure 16.16 shows the seasonality effects estimated for the discount loans.

   In general we find three characteristics that affect prepayments and defaults:

1. Characteristics of the loan.
      Term or maturity
      Fixed versus floating
      Rate relative to prevailing market rates
      Loan size

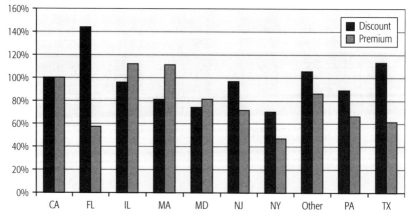

FIGURE 16.15   30-year whole loan model: Geography risk multipliers.

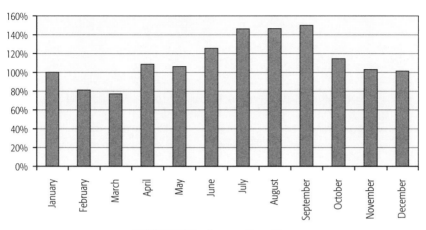

FIGURE 16.16   Seasonality effect.

2. Characteristics of the borrower.
   Income
   Wealth
3. Characteristics of the home.
   Value of the home
   Change in value of the home

Using loan-level models, it is possible to differentiate pools of loans from diverse types of borrowers. As borrower characteristics become more diverse, loan-level modeling will become more widespread in the mortgage industry.

EXERCISES

Exercise 16.1   Why is LTV correlated with losses?

Exercise 16.2   What is the difference between loan-level modeling of prepayments and pool-level modeling?

Exercise 16.3   If rates fall 50 basis points, is a $100,000 loan or a $500,000 loan more likely to prepay? Assume that the fixed costs of refinancing are the same for both borrowers.

CHAPTER 17

Home Equity and Subprime Loans

The home equity loan (HEL) market was once synonymous with traditional prime second mortgages, but has evolved into a product area mainly focused on subprime or lower-credit-quality borrowers. HEL asset-backed securities (ABS) today are primarily backed by subprime mortgages, high loan-to-value (LTV) loans, home improvement loans (HILs), and home equity lines of credit (HELOCs). Only a very small portion of the entire HEL ABS market consists of prime second mortgages. The first half of this chapter provides a historical overview of the HEL ABS market, and the second half focuses on the collateral and structural features distinct to the subprime sector.

HOME EQUITY LOAN ASSET-BACKED SECURITIES ISSUANCE

The HEL market has experienced explosive growth since the mid-1990s. Figure 17.1 shows that in 1995, HEL ABS issuance was only $17 billion or 16 percent of the entire ABS market. By the end of 2001, issuance of HEL ABS represented the largest ABS sector, totaling more than $100 billion. By November 2002, HEL issuance reached approximately $125 billion. However, the growth that occurred during the entire period was not always steady or continuous. Figure 17.2 shows a dramatic slowdown in HEL ABS issuance in 1998 and a reduction in the volume of issuance in 1999 and 2000. The reason for the sudden reversal can be explained by the important changes that took place in the HEL market.

Since the early HEL securitizations in the late 1980s, the HEL sector has undergone a dramatic evolution from the traditional A-quality second-mortgage product to include a broader range of collateral that share a common denominator of lower-credit-quality borrowers (B&C quality).

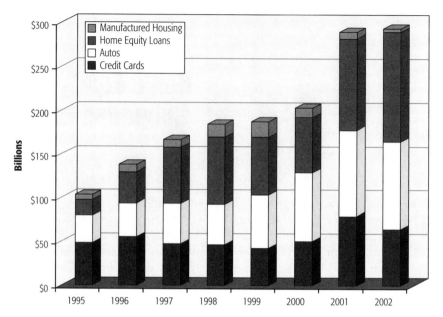

FIGURE 17.1   ABS production volume by collateral type from 1995 through November 2000.

Source: 2002 Mortgage Market Statistical Annual and 2002 Bloomberg LP.

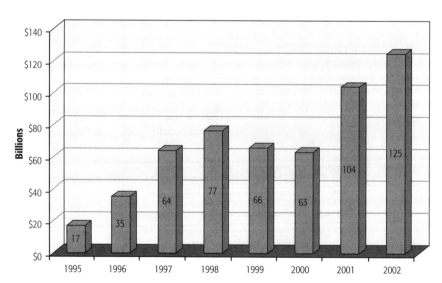

FIGURE 17.2   Home equity loan ABS production volume from 1995 through November 2002.

Source: 2002 Mortgage Market Statistical Annual and 2002 Bloomberg LP.

Unfortunately, the term HEL no longer accurately describes this ABS sector. There tends to be considerable confusion about the HEL sector because subprime lending or B&C lending are also used interchangeably to describe the HEL market.

The HEL market today comprises subprime mortgages, traditional prime second mortgages, high-LTV (125s) loans, HILs, and HELOCs. Subprime lending (HEL ARM and FRM) dominates the home equity market as illustrated by Figure 17.3, which shows the composition of HEL ABS issuance by product type as of October 2002. Subprime loans consist of first-lien mortgages made to credit-impaired borrowers. HELOCs represent the second largest product type, while high-LTV loans/HILs constitute a very small proportion of the market. High-LTV loans can either be first- or second-lien loans whose LTV ratios are in excess of 100 percent when combined with first liens on the same property. A large number of high-LTV loans are made to home owners overburdened with credit-card debt, who

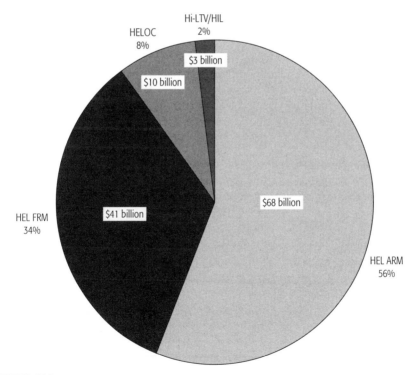

FIGURE 17.3 Home equity loan ABS issuance by product type through October 2002.

Source: J.P. Morgan Chase Global Structured Finance Research.

seek to consolidate their debts at lower interest rates while cashing out on some of the equity in their homes. High-LTV loans can have LTV ratios as high as 125 percent, which is why they are also referred to as 125s in mortgage parlance. HELOCs represent the smallest category in home equity securitizations. HELOCs are revolving loans that home owners access by writing checks against the equity in their homes. They resemble credit-card debt in that balances fluctuate and can be paid down before the term of the loan and drawn down again.

In 1998, the asset quality of the HEL sector deteriorated dramatically. This was caused by more relaxed underwriting standards that resulted from fierce competition among lenders to increase their lending volume to subprime borrowers. By the end of 1998, many subprime mortgage lenders experienced higher prepayment rates than expected, and many were forced to write down their assets. Aames Financial Corporation was the first to announce a write-down in 1998, and was quickly followed by Cityscape, Green Tree Financial, Mego Mortgage, and United Companies Financial. By October of 1998, Southern Pacific Financial Corporation had filed for bankruptcy.

Since 1997, there has been considerable consolidation of the subprime lending market as evidenced by a dramatically different landscape of players in 2001 (shown in Table 17.1). Many of the top ten subprime lenders that existed in 1997 either went bankrupt or were acquired by other lenders. For example, Conti Mortgage and FirstPlus, who appear in Table 17.1, filed for bankruptcy. The majority of other lenders found strategic partners or buyers. Table 17.2 provides a list of subprime players active in the mid-1990s that were either acquired or went bankrupt. In addition to the con-

TABLE 17.1 Top Ten Subprime Lenders

1997	$Billions	2001	$Billions
Associates First Capital	7.0	City Financial	19.0
The Money Store	5.9	Household	15.3
IMC	5.9	WAMU/Long Beach	8.1
Conti Mortgage	5.5	Bank of America	7.8
FirstPlus	4.5	GMAC/RFC	7.5
GMAC/RFC	3.8	Option One	5.3
AMRESCO	3.6	Countrywide	5.2
Household	3.5	First Franklin	4.4
Green Tree	3.5	New Century	4.2
Advanta	3.5	Ameriquest Mortgage	3.0

Source: 2001 Mortgage Statistical Annual.

TABLE 17.2 Where Are They Now?

Subprime Lender	Status as of 1Q2002
Conti Mortgage	filed for bankruptcy
First Plus	filed for bankruptcy
United Companies	filed for bankruptcy
Southern Pacific Financial Corporation	filed for bankruptcy
Cityscape	filed for bankruptcy
Advanta	acquired by Chase
Green Tree	acquired by Conseco
Long Beach	acquired by WAMU

Source: Moody's Investor Service and Bloomberg LP.

solidation that occurred in the subprime sector, mortgage lending in 1999 and 2000 was curtailed due to rising interest rates during that period.

Collateral and Loan Characteristics

HELs can be divided into two main categories: closed-end loans and revolving lines of credit. Table 17.3 contains a list of specific HEL products that fall under these categories.

Closed-end HEL products are fully amortizing, level-paying loans with terms ranging between 15 and 30 years. The majority of subprime loans (64 percent) tend to have adjustable rates of interest. Adjustable rate mortgage (ARM) subprimes tend to be first-lien loans, whereas fixed-rate mortgage (FRM) subprimes can have first or second liens. High LTVs, 125s

TABLE 17.3 Home Equity Collateral Characteristics

Closed-End Loans	Coupon	Term	Lien Status	Borrower Quality
Subprime	ARM	15–30 years	1st	A- to D
Subprime	FRM	15–30 years	1st or 2nd	A- to D
High LTV (125s)/HILs	ARM or FRM	15–20 years	1st and 2nd	A- to D
Traditional second mortgage	ARM or FRM	15–20 years	2nd	A-quality (prime)

Revolving Lines of Credit	Coupon	Term	Lien Status	Borrower Quality
HELOCs	ARM	10–15 years	2nd	varies

and HILs can have either first- or second-lien status, whereas traditional HELs are true second mortgages generally made to A-quality borrowers.

HELOCs, however, fall under the revolving-credit-line category. They closely resemble revolving-credit cards because loan balances tend to fluctuate with purchases made by borrowers. There is generally a revolving period in which borrowers draw down their loan balance, followed by an amortization period or balloon payment. HELOCs differ from consumer loans in that they are collateralized by real estate. Subsequently, interest rates on HELOCs tend to be lower than comparable consumer loans because of higher-quality collateral. HELOCs are also more attractive than consumer debt because interest payments are tax deductible and maturities are longer, ranging between 10 and 15 years.

ENVIRONMENT

In a recessionary environment with rising unemployment, subprime borrowers are more likely than prime borrowers to default on monthly mortgage payments. In addition, recoveries may be considerably lower compared to prime borrowers because many subprime borrowers may have very little equity or even negative equity in their homes.

At the time of writing, the economy was heading toward a double-dip recession. Unemployment claims were on the rise, consumer spending was falling, and consumer confidence was plummeting. As a result, delinquency rates of HEL ABS began to rise, particularly for newer loan pools.

PREPAYMENT

Although ABS are generally less sensitive to prepayments than agency mortgage-backed securities (MBS), there is some degree of prepayment risk that results from turnover, refinancing, defaults, and partial prepayments of HELs. Credit cards and auto loans tend to be the least sensitive to interest rate changes; however, HELs exhibit a higher degree of interest-rate sensitivity and thus experience higher prepayment rates. According to the Andrew Davidson & Co. HEL fixed-rate prepayment model, HELs exhibit faster prepayment ramps in a stable-rate environment compared to agency MBS. Only in a falling interest-rate environment do HELs exhibit more stable prepayments compared to agency MBS.

Research has shown that prepayments tend to be correlated with the credit quality of the borrower. The higher the credit quality of the borrower, the more the prepayment behavior of the HEL resembles an agency mortgage, which shows a high degree of interest-rate sensitivity. Thus, lower-credit-quality loans (i.e., B and C grade loans) tend to have more stable prepayments compared to higher-quality loans. Impaired credit histories often prevent B and C grade borrowers from qualifying for lower interest-rate loans. The opportunity for lower-credit-quality borrowers to refinance often results from an improvement in credit scores rather than from a declining interest-rate environment. The improvement of a borrower's credit score, referred to as credit curing, often occurs early on in the pool of HELs. HEL borrowers also refinance to consolidate their debt or to work out a new payment schedule when they are having difficulty repaying a loan. These types of refinancing are uncorrelated to interest-rate movements.

The convention for expressing HEL prepayments is the home equity prepayment (HEP) curve developed by Prudential Securities. The HEP curve reflects the observed behavior of $10 billion of historical HEL data. For example, for the 25 percent HEP curve shown in Figure 17.4, prepayment rates start at zero and rise to a peak speed of 25 CPR in the 10th month and remain constant thereafter.

HOME EQUITY LOAN ASSET-BACKED SECURITIES

Two main structures are used in securitizing HELs, depending on whether the loans are closed-end or revolving. **Closed-end amortizing structures** are generally secured by closed-end loans such as subprime first-lien mortgages, HILTVs, and 125s. The closed-end HELs are sold to a trust either by the

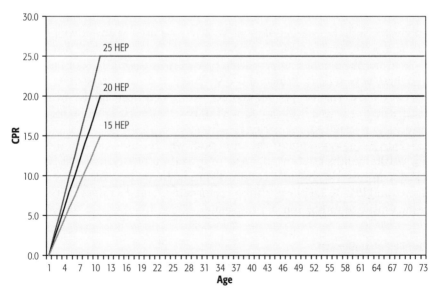

FIGURE 17.4 Example of HEP curves.

seller directly or by a special-purpose entity. The residual interest in the trust is usually retained by the seller, servicer, or related entity. These transactions can consist of single- or multiple-class securities. Principal payments may be distributed sequentially or in some other order, depending on the terms of the individual transaction. See the CD for a sample transaction.

Money-market tranches were a structural innovation of the HEL ABS market. These tranches have final maturities of less than 1 year and are sized according to the historical prepayment experience of the underlying collateral. Principal, prepayments, and excess spread are used to pay down the money-market class before any other certificate class receives principal.

Revolving-trust structures are secured by HELOCs and share many of the same features as credit-card ABS. The assets or loan balances of the HELOCs as well as the future cash flows associated with these lines of credit are deposited into a trust. The trust then issues investor certificates, which can consist of multiple classes with varying maturities, as well as seller certificates retained by the issuer.

Like credit-card ABS, there are three distinct phases: a revolving or funding period, a planned amortization period, and a rapid amortization period. During the revolving period, investor certificate holders only receive interest payments. Any principal collected from the underlying loans is deposited into an account used to finance additional draws on the credit lines. For example, a home owner may only draw on part of his or her line of credit and then repay the loan so that his or her balance goes back to zero. These funds are then available if the same home owner or other home owners in the pool want to draw on their credit lines again. At the end of the revolving period, the amount of money collected is used to pay down principal of the investor certificates.

During the planned amortization phase, investors receive both principal and interest payments. Principal is distributed as a percentage of net principal collected during the period. In other words, certificate holders would not receive any principal if the amount of draws on the HELOCs exceeded the principal collected for the period.

During the rapid amortization period, which can occur any time from 48 to 100 months after the planned amortization phase, investors receive a fixed share of all principal collected during the period regardless of any draws on HELOCs. Poor portfolio performance and default events can also trigger rapid amortization of principal.

Credit Enhancement

In 1995, the majority of home equity securitizations were insured or "wrapped" by a bond insurance policy, which guarantees timely receipt of interest and ultimate repayment of principal. That percentage has come down considerably in 2002. Only about half of all deals are now insured by a third-party guarantee. The other half rely on internal credit enhancement, primarily subordination. The presence of bond insurance has been favorable for issuers and investors because it has reduced the required amount of internal credit enhancement, mitigating widening spreads for subordinate tranches and achieving tighter spreads for AAA-rated tranches. Bond insurance also allays investors concerns about unrated originators and servicers and any structural risks present in the transaction.

Most home equity deals rely on some form of internal credit enhancement in addition to bond insurance. Typically a combination of subordination and overcollateralization (OC) is used in home equity deals. In a typical subordinated transaction, the rights of junior classes of investors to receive principal and interest are subordinated to the rights of the senior classes. More importantly, the junior classes are in a "first-loss" position and shield senior classes from potential principal and interest shortfalls resulting from defaults or credit losses.

OC is the difference between the certificate balance (sometimes referred to as bond balance) and the underlying loan balance. OC is created by accelerating the amortization of the certificate balance relative to the underlying collateral balance. For example, if $100 billion of bonds are secured by $102 billion of HEL collateral, the OC amount would be equal to $2 billion ($102 billion minus $100 billion). Another way of stating this is that the transaction is overcollateralized by 2 percent, which means that this transaction can withstand losses equal to the OC plus any excess spread available before investors incur any losses.

In a typical transaction, an OC target level is set. In any given period, excess interest is used to pay down the certificate balance until the desired target level is reached. As long as the OC target is maintained, excess interest is paid to the holder of the residual interest. If at any time the OC level falls below the target, excess interest is used to pay down the certificate balance to restore the OC level.

Spread Accounts

The use of excess spread is also a very common form of internal credit enhancement for the home equity transactions. In contrast to OC, excess spread is deposited into an account that accumulates over time to cover any current losses of the underlying pool. Once a deal has reached its target level, any remaining excess spread is distributed to the residual holders as opposed to certificate holders in the case of OC.

Prepayment rates play a critical role when assessing the ability of a transaction to withstand losses. Higher than expected prepayment rates reduce the principal balance of the securitized pool and consequently the balance on which interest payments are based. As a result, less excess spread is available in the transaction, reducing protection against future losses. Prepayments represent a double-edged sword for HEL ABS. On one hand, they have a positive impact because losses cannot occur on loans that are already prepaid in full. On the other hand, higher-quality borrowers tend to prepay, leaving a greater concentration of riskier borrowers compared to the original loan pool.

Rating Agency Criteria

Rating agencies generally apply the same methodology for HELs as for residential MBS transactions. Rating agencies first estimate an expected loss rate of the underlying HELs by conducting a loan-by-loan analysis. Each loan that deviates from the characteristics of a benchmark pool is assigned a risk adjustment factor in determining the ultimate level of credit enhancement required. The risk adjustment factors for each loan are expressed as a multiple of expected losses and are then aggregated to determine the overall risk of the entire loan pool. One of the most critical loan characteristics is the LTV ratio because of the strong correlation with expected losses. The higher the LTV ratio, the less equity is available in a property. As a result, there is a higher probability of default. Other benchmark loan characteristics include the following:

- Geographic diversity
- Fixed rate
- Owner-occupied
- Full documentation
- Newly originated
- Single-family residence
- Properties of average value
- A-quality borrowers
- Purchase versus refinance

In addition to quantitative loan factors, rating agencies also take into account qualitative factors such as the lender's or servicer's track record and structural features of the transaction. Additional risk adjustments are made to account for these qualitative factors. Rating agencies then assign a final credit rating that reflects the transaction's ability to withstand losses.

Valuation Methods

The industry convention used to measure relative value for HEL ABS is to quote a static spread to the swap curve. Some dealers also quote spreads to

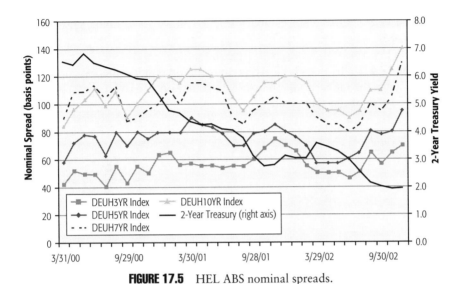

FIGURE 17.5   HEL ABS nominal spreads.

the Treasury curve. Figure 17.5 shows Deutsche Bank's indexes for nominal spreads of various maturity HEL tranches. As one would expect, the longer-maturity HEL ABS trade at a wider spread compared to shorter maturity instruments.

Because prepayment variability is an important aspect of HEL ABS, especially as the credit quality of borrowers improves, the use of static spread is a deficient measure because it fails to capture the embedded prepayment option present in a HEL ABS. Until option-adjusted spread (OAS) analysis becomes more widespread in the industry, investors should at the very least perform scenario or total-return analyses to see how the price performance is affected by changes in the timing of cash flows, especially for residual tranches that are highly sensitive to performance triggers.

EXERCISES

Exercise 17.1   What explains why HEL ABS exhibit lower prepayment sensitivities compared to agency MBS pass-throughs? Why do prepayments represent a double-edged sword for HEL ABS investors?

Exercise 17.2   What are the two main types of structures used in HEL ABS transactions and when are they used?

Exercise 17.3   What features does HEL ABS have in common with credit-card ABS?

Exercise 17.4   Why does HEL ABS require credit enhancement compared to agency pass-throughs? Explain how subordination and overcollateralization are two sides of the same coin.

CHAPTER 18

Analysis of Credit-Sensitive Mortgage-Backed Securities

Through securitization, the mortgage market protects most investors from the risk of default on the underlying loans. Credit risk is borne primarily by mortgage insurance companies, Fannie Mae, and Freddie Mac, the U.S. government through FHA and VA, and the holders of lower-rated and un-rated, subordinated classes of private pass-throughs. In many cases, the orig-inating lender retains the subordinated classes, particularly the riskiest first-loss piece. (Lenders may also bear credit risk due to the representations and warranties they make to buyers of securities.)

Because default risk is concentrated among relatively few players, the analysis of the valuation of credit risk is not as well developed as the analy-sis of interest-rate risk and prepayment risk. In fact, many leading analytical systems provide limited ability for investors to assess credit risk. Further-more, much of the analysis that does exist is proprietary.

In this chapter we describe a framework for analyzing credit risk that mirrors the scenario analysis and option-adjusted spread (OAS) approaches used to assess interest-rate risk and prepayment risk.

Within mortgage-backed securities (MBS) credit markets, credit en-hancement levels have changed dramatically since the inception of the mar-ket, reflecting the developing credit performance of the various loan types that collateralize sub-MBS. Under such dynamic conditions, the static yield spread measures most commonly applied to evaluate sub-MBS provide little information regarding changes in the net returns available from subordi-nated MBS after expected credit losses. Return measures such as OAS, typ-ically applied to measure the cost of options such as the MBS credit option, have yet to evolve popularly within the market for lower-rated MBS. Con-sequently, the expected returns available within subordinated MBS-markets, after adjusting more fully for the inherent default costs, are not as visible as desirable.

Andrew Davidson & Co. has developed a simple credit loss adjusted return measure called Default Adjusted Spread (DAS). DAS is similar to OAS conceptually and is useful for gauging the expected returns available from subordinated MBS after credit losses, across ratings and collateral types. A nice feature of DAS is that it can be measured relative to each investor's unique leverage and cost of capital, reflecting his or her unique earnings and risk tolerances.

METHODOLOGY

The fundamental question that needs to be addressed in assessing credit risk is what is the amount of losses that an investment may experience due to credit losses. Answering that question involves the four-step approach described in Chapter 3. First, it is necessary to establish a methodology. Generally, market participants use either yield spreads or stress scenarios to assess credit risk. Here, we describe a probability-driven approach. Next, it is necessary to assess the risk of the collateral. To measure default risk it is necessary to understand all aspects of the collateral that will affect the securities created with the loans. Generally, this means that prepayments, defaults, losses, and delinquencies need to be considered.

Based on an analysis of the collateral, the cash flows of the securities can be generated following the specific rules for that deal. This chapter includes a sample senior/subordinated transaction to demonstrate some of the important issues in structuring.

The DAS framework uses a theoretical construct similar to that used to derive OAS. Calculating DAS involves estimating the cost of the default option, adding the cost of the default option to offered price of the subordinated MBS, calculating the new yield at the offered price plus the default-option cost, and subtracting the yield from cost of capital to get the DAS.

A key part of the DAS framework is that it uses a simple approach to estimating the dollar cost of the default option. The cost of the default option is estimated as the difference between the sub-MBS price at zero losses, and an *expected* sub-MBS price that is calculated as a probability weighted average of the sub-MBS prices calculated in various credit-loss scenarios. For a given class of sub-MBS being analyzed, scenario prices are calculated using the cumulative loss rates that would wipe out the subordination and cause default for each of the AAA, AA, A, BBB, BB, B, and NR classes of MBS. The discrete probabilities used to weight the MBS price calculated in each credit-loss scenario are derived quickly and simply using the cumulative density function given a mean credit-loss rate and a variance. The expected price of the sub-MBS class is calculated by summing the products of scenario prices and probabilities.

Finally, results can be generated that reflect the amount and probability of loss. These results may provide insight into relative value between bonds within a transaction, between bonds from different deals, and between different asset classes.

COLLATERAL

Prepayment Risk

Evaluating collateral involves an analysis of prepayment risk and default risk. Generally, collateral that has greater default risk has reduced prepayment risk. Figure 18.1 shows the relative prepayment speeds of several MBS with

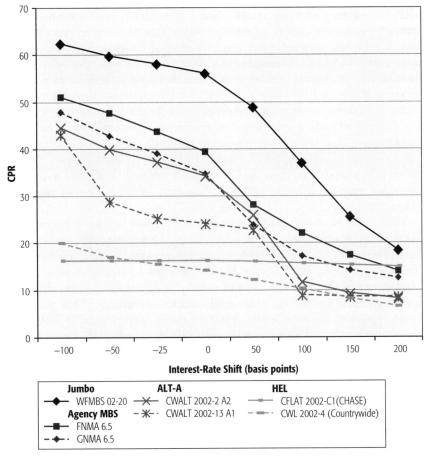

FIGURE 18.1 Prepayment forecasts.

different kinds of collateral. It is clear from the chart that there is an interaction between credit risk and prepayment sensitivity at the collateral level. The high-quality jumbo loans and agency MBS exhibit greater prepayment sensitivity than Alt-A and lower quality home equity loan (HEL) collateral.

The creation of senior/subordinate can alter the relationship between prepayments and default risk. Junior classes from high-credit-quality collateral may still be subject to prepayment risk and have concentrated credit risk. However, for most of these structures, prepayment risk is reduced since the subordinated classes are typically priced at a discount, so accelerating prepayments will improve value.

Credit Risk

For the remainder of this chapter we focus primarily on the credit risk of MBS. The valuation method described in this chapter requires an understanding of the dispersion of possible losses as well as the mean expected losses. To assess this probability distribution of losses, information about ratings upgrades and downgrades as well as the ultimate default percentages by initial rating class are valuable. While each individual loan and each pool of loans may have its own unique credit situation, rating agencies strive to create consistency across ratings classes. Thus, the default probability by rating class can provide insight into the distribution of potential losses of a pool of loans.

The rating agencies publish statistics on ratings changes. Ratings changes reflect upgrades or downgrades. A security that defaults generally has passed through a series of downgrades prior to default. Table 18.1 is a sample transition matrix from Standard & Poor's (S&P).

The S&P probability transition matrix defines the percentages of an MBS that migrated from one credit rating to another over a 10-year period. For example, of the securities whose original rating was AAA, 98.49 percent remained AAA securities, and 1.38 percent were downgraded to AA, 0.10 percent were downgraded to A, and so on. The last column, labeled D, represents the probability of the original security defaulting. While no AAA-rated securities in the sample defaulted, 5.63 percent of the BBB-rated securities defaulted. This table represents only securities that existed for 10-year periods during 1978 to 2001. In order to include more securities, it is possible to use 1-year transition matrices and compound the results, using matrix multiplication to produce results for longer time periods.

Figure 18.2 shows the probability of loss for various ratings categories. The three sets of bars represent the 10-year mortgage transitions, the 10-year corporate bond transitions, and an implied 10-year transition for mortgages, based on compounding of 1-year transition results.

TABLE 18.1   Ratings Transitions (%)

Start	End AAA	10-Year Transition 1978–2001								
		AA	A	BBB	BB	B	CCC	CC	C	D
AAA	98.49	1.38	0.10	0.02	0.01	0.01	0.00	0.00	0.00	0.00
AA	45.68	43.08	8.00	1.54	0.64	0.57	0.10	0.07	0.00	0.30
A	27.50	21.45	39.26	6.70	1.66	0.76	0.41	0.38	0.02	1.90
BBB	13.84	15.66	16.45	34.24	6.07	6.72	0.98	0.96	0.05	5.63
BB	4.17	5.35	11.65	18.10	28.81	8.53	1.82	2.57	0.09	18.43
B	1.41	1.21	2.67	6.96	13.60	37.11	2.56	3.63	0.13	30.68
CCC	0.00	0.00	0.00	0.00	0.00	0.00	0.08	4.66	0.01	95.25
CC	0.00	0.00	0.00	0.00	0.00	0.00	0.00	5.86	0.00	94.14
C	0.00	0.00	0.00	0.00	0.00	0.00	0.00	0.00	0.00	100.00
D	0.00	0.00	0.00	0.00	0.00	0.00	0.00	0.00	0.00	100.00

Source: Standard & Poor's Rating Transitions 2001.

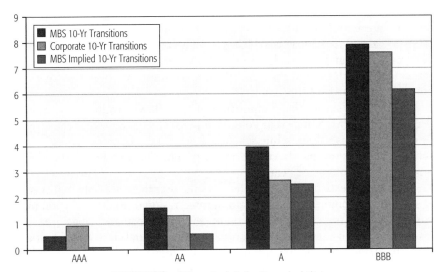

FIGURE 18.2   Historical default probabilities.

For different types of collateral these ratings categories may relate to different amounts of credit enhancement. Thus 1 percent credit enhancement on high-quality collateral may produce the same rating as 4 percent credit enhancement on lower-quality collateral. Overall, we would expect that similarly rated instruments would have approximately the same probability of default. Once prepayment and defaults have been assessed, the structure of the transaction can be evaluated.

STRUCTURE

Just as the collateralized-mortgage obligation (CMO) structure can allocate prepayment risk, the senior/subordinated structure can allocate credit risk. The modeling of senior/subordinated securities can be quite complex, due to the shifting priorities of cash flows depending on the performance of the collateral. Accurate modeling of deal cash flows may also depend on documents and information that is not readily available.

Senior/Subordinated Example

In order to understand more fully how a senior/subordinated structure works to protect senior security holders from default risk, we created a very simple senior/subordinated transaction. Let us assume that we start out with collateral of $100 million in mortgage loans. The weighted-average coupon (WAC) is 12.0 percent and the weighted-average maturity (WAM) is 360 months. We assume a constant prepayment rate (CPR) of 25. We assume defaults are zero for the first year, increase at a constant rate over the second year, and peak at an annualized rate of 6.0 percent. Defaults remain constant until month 60 and then decline at a constant rate over two years to half the peak rate or 3.0 percent.

Figure 18.3 shows the composition of cash flows produced by the underlying collateral. Notice that voluntary prepayments represent the largest proportion of cash flows while scheduled principal payments represent the smallest proportion, barely visible on the graph. The area below the x-axis represents the volume of defaults.

The example assumes for simplicity's sake that there are only two classes of securities, a senior (A) class and an unrated residual (B) class. As you may remember from the earlier discussion of senior/subordinated structures, the residual class is in a first-loss position so that the residual class would first absorb any defaults in the underlying mortgage loans, before there would be losses to the senior class. Residual class holders would be entitled to excess funds, if any, after paying any amounts due to senior bondholders for principal and interest, including maintaining the proper level of overcollateralization (OC), and after paying servicing fees and other expenses.

If the initial credit enhancement is equal to 2.0 percent of the mortgage collateral balance (.02 × 100 million = 2.0 million), then $98 million of senior securities can be issued against $100 million of collateral. The remaining $2.0 million is the size of the subordinate or residual class. This $2.0 million is also equal to the **subordinated amount** or **overcollateralization amount**,

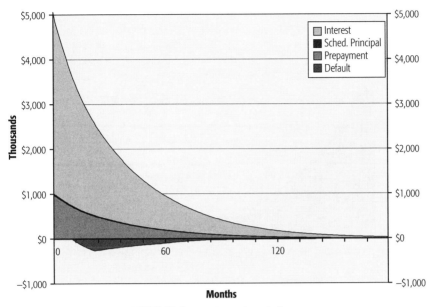

FIGURE 18.3   Collateral cash flow.

which is simply the difference between the collateral balance and the balance of outstanding senior securities.

Figure 18.4 compares the balances of the outstanding senior securities and OC amount. Notice that the initial OC level starts at $2.0 million in month 0, gradually rises to $5.0 million and remains at that level until about month 30, because in this example the target OC level is set at 5.0 percent of the original collateral balance or $5.0 million. Any excess interest that would otherwise be paid to residual holders is used to pay down the principal of the senior class until the OC amount reaches the target level of $5.0 million. It is a common feature of senior/subordinated transactions to require that initial OC requirements increase to a target level and then remain at that level over a specified period because of the problem of "adverse selection" created by prepayments early on in a transaction's life. The reason the OC level drops in month 30 is that we have allowed a step down to occur after 30 months as long as the OC level does not fall below a minimum of 0.50 percent of the original collateral balance or $500,000. In many senior/subordinated transactions, the step-down period occurs after several years as long as delinquencies and defaults do not exceed performance triggers.

Figure 18.5 shows the monthly cash flows paid to the senior class. What stands out the most on this graph is that principal payments, which include both scheduled principal and voluntary prepayments, represent the largest

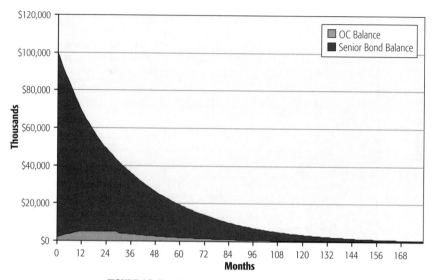

FIGURE 18.4   Senior bond and OC balance.

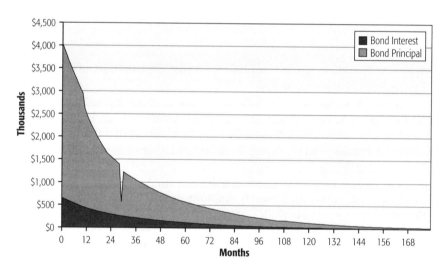

FIGURE 18.5   Cash flow to senior class.

proportion of monthly cash flow to the senior class. The sharp dip in principal cash flows around month 30 can be explained by the fact that the target OC level has been reached and excess interest can now be directed to the residual class, so long as the OC level does not fall below the required amounts.

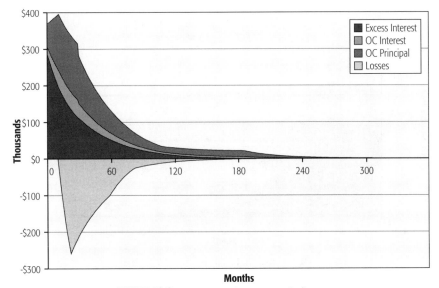

FIGURE 18.6   Sources of excess cash flow.

The cash flow available to the residual will depend on the exact formulation of each individual transaction. This sample transaction provides some indication as to the sources of cash flow. Excess cash flow created by the structure can be used to increase OC levels, or to make payments to the residual holder if the OC requirement has been met. The sources of excess cash flow consist of excess interest and the principal and interest payments on the current balance of OC, whereas negative cash flow results from defaults or credit losses as shown in Figure 18.6.

Figure 18.7 shows the residual cash flow and the OC balance over time. The available excess cash flow is first used to build the OC balance until the OC requirements are met. The first spike in residual cash flow occurs when the target OC level has been reached and excess interest can now be diverted from paying down the principal of the senior class to the residual class. The reason for the drop around month 20 is that defaults have reached their peak rate and the amount of excess cash flow has declined. The second spike occurs in month 30 because of the step down in target OC level.

This simple example provides only a hint as to the complexity of an actual transaction. In most cases there are several layers of subordinate bonds. There may also be complex provisions related to insurance and servicing. Analysis of subordinated transactions requires a detailed review of all relevant deal documents and careful analysis of deal cash flows.

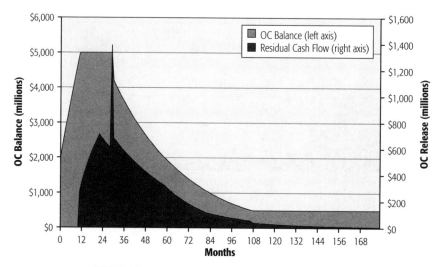

FIGURE 18.7 Residual cash flow and OC balance.

RESULTS

Table 18.2 shows a sample calculation of DAS. The bond has a default option cost of 2.4 points and a resulting DAS of −16 basis points. The following discussion provides a step-by-step description of the DAS calculation.

Step 1. Calculate a weighted-average cost of capital (WACC). WACC is used for discounting the MBS cash flows and as a benchmark hurdle rate against which DAS is quoted. WACC is calculated as a simple weighted average of the cost of the debt and equity used to finance the subordinated MBS investment.

$$r_{wacc} = \lambda_d \times r_d + \lambda_e \times r_e \qquad (18.1)$$

where λ_d, λ_e represent the weights of debt and equity and $\lambda_d + \lambda_e = 1$, and r_d, r_e represent the cost of debt and cost of equity, respectively.

WACC changes with the risk of the sub-MBS and the leverage applied. In general, the lower-rated, riskier classes of subordinated MBS that are more highly capitalized have a higher WACC and require commensurately higher yields to generate equivalent DAS.

Step 2. Calculate the zero-loss price of the sub-MBS. This price equals the net present value (NPV) of the sub-MBS cash flows at zero losses discounted at the WACC.

$$P_0 = \sum_{k=1}^{n} \frac{cf_0(k)}{(1 + r_{wacc})^k}$$

TABLE 18.2 DAS Calculation for Generic BBB Security, 2001

Rating	Cumulative Loss (%)	Probability (%)	Price ($)
No Loss	0.000	0.00	93.94
NA	0.031	14.51	93.94
NA	0.125	37.12	93.94
B	0.250	25.22	93.94
BB	0.500	13.84	93.94
BBB	0.850	5.80	90.94
A	1.350	2.41	34.69
AA	2.200	0.88	22.48
AAA	4.000	0.22	15.33
Price at zero losses			93.94
Expected price		*less*	91.54
Default option			**2.40**
Market-offered price			92.06
Default option		*less*	2.40
Default-adjusted price			**94.46**
Default-adjusted yield			7.79%
WACC		*less*	7.95%
Default-adjusted spread (bp)			**(16)**

where the cash flows are calculated using zero losses.

Step 3. Calculate the expected MBS price. The expected MBS price is a probability weighted average of MBS prices calculated at various credit loss rates.

$$E(P) = \sum_i (p_i \times P_i)$$

where p_i is the probability of credit loss rate i and P_i is the price for credit loss rate i given by

$$P_i = \sum_{k=1}^{n} \frac{cf_i(k)}{(1 + r_{wacc})^k}$$

Each scenario MBS price is calculated as the NPV of MBS cash flows at a prescribed cumulative credit-loss rate, discounted using the WACC. In

Table 18.2, credit losses were distributed across time in each scenario in accordance with the standard default assumption (SDA) curve. For a given class of sub-MBS being analyzed, scenario prices are calculated using the cumulative loss rates that would wipe out the subordination and cause default for each of the AAA, AA, A, BBB, BB, B, and NR classes of MBS. Table 18.3 shows the cumulative loss rates modeled.

The discrete probabilities used to weight the MBS price calculated in each credit-loss scenario are derived using a cumulative density function given a mean credit-loss rate and a variance. Loss rates are assumed to be lognormally distributed. Figure 18.8 shows the probability functions derived at several different means and variances for illustrative purposes.

A particular combination of expected losses and standard deviations will roughly reflect the rating agency-implied probabilities of default. Figure 18.9 shows the match of the probability densities to the ratings for the right-hand tail of the distribution.

Figure 18.10 shows the scenario MBS prices depicted in Table 18.2 and the probabilities related to each credit-loss scenario. A mean loss of 15 basis points and a standard deviation of 1.25 were used to derive the probabilities. The expected MBS price that results is $91.54. The figure also demonstrates the optionlike features of credit risk. For low levels of losses, the bond experiences little or no credit loss. Once losses on the collateral exceed a threshold, the value of the bond drops dramatically. This chart also shows why yield-based analysis based on a single scenario would not be a useful tool.

Investors can view the expected MBS price as the price they should be willing to pay for the sub-MBS at a given capitalization and WACC, assuming the distribution of cumulative losses given by the cumulative density

TABLE 18.3 Cumulative Loss Rates and Credit Enhancement

Sample MBS Credit Enhancement Requirement	Percent
AAA	4.0000
AA	2.2000
A	1.3500
BBB	0.8500
BB	0.5000
B	0.2500
CCC	0.1250
CC	0.0313

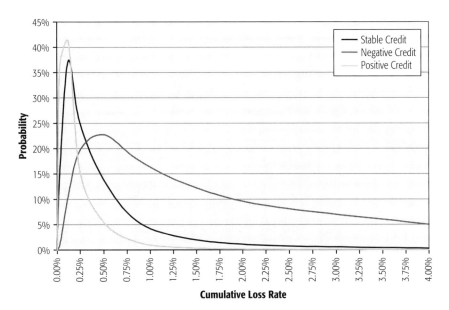

FIGURE 18.8   Probability distributions of cumulative losses.

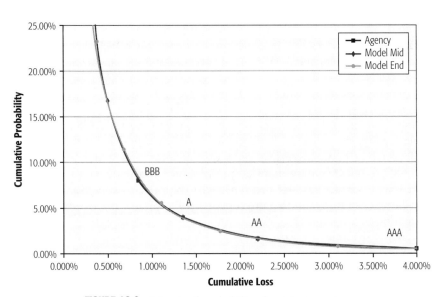

FIGURE 18.9   Match of probability densities to ratings.

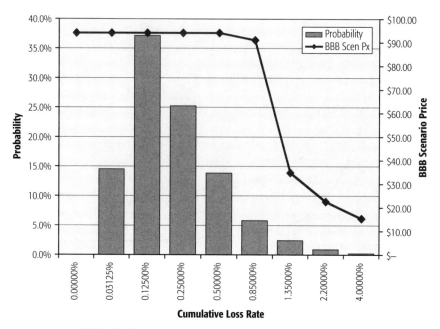

FIGURE 18.10   BBB scenario prices and loss probabilities.

function, mean, and variance applied. At offered prices above the expected MBS price, investors would expect not to earn their WACC. At offered prices below the expected MBS price, investors would expect to earn more than their WACC.

Sensitivity analysis can be used to better understand the price risk of various sub-MBS classes as mean loss rates and the volatility of mean loss rates change. For example, the differences between the expected MBS price at cumulative loss rates that are high and narrowly distributed and the expected MBS price at cumulative loss rates that are low and widely distributed should provide meaningful price performance information to investors. Likewise, investors can use the expected MBS price to solve for the mean and variance of loss rates that are consistent with offered prices, revealing information implied in the market's implied pricing of sub-MBS.

Step 4. Estimate the cost of the default option. The expected MBS price is equivalent to an average, loss-adjusted price. The difference between the expected MBS price and the MBS price at zero losses represents an estimate for the cost of the default option.

$$P_{option} = P_0 - E(P)$$

Step 5. Estimate the default-adjusted price, which is the MBS offered price plus the cost of the default option. In essence, this defaulted-adjusted price represents the price of a theoretical default-free bond as if an insurance premium equivalent to the default option cost had been added to the offered price of the sub-MBS class.

$$P_{da} = P_{mkt} + P_{option}$$

Step 6. Estimate the default-adjusted yield, which is simply the static MBS yield calculated at the default-adjusted price or the default-free price. In essence, this yield represents that expected yield to maturity of the sub-MBS adjusted for the expected cost of the default option. The difference between the zero-loss yield and the default-free yield is a measure of the expected default-option cost in terms of yield to maturity.

$$P_{da} = \sum_{k=1}^{n} \frac{cf_0(k)}{(1 + r_{da})^k}$$

Step 7. The last calculation is the DAS itself. Subtracting the WACC from the default-adjusted yield results in the DAS. The DAS is a measure of the return likely to be earned in excess of the WACC.

$$DAS = r_{da} - r_{wacc}$$

Sub-MBS with various ratings from BBB to unrated can be compared using the DAS to compare which sub-MBS class offers the highest yield after expected credit losses. Likewise, bonds backed by different collateral types can be compared using DAS.

As shown in Table 18.2, the expected or probability-weighted price in this example is 91.54 and the price at zero losses was 93.94. The difference, 2.40, is equal to the theoretical price of the default option. Adding 2.40 to the market price of 92.06 results in a default-adjusted price of 94.47, which approximates the theoretical price of a default-free bond. Then yield of the default-free bond referred to as the default-adjusted yield is shown in Table 18.3 to be 7.79 percent. When compared to the investor's WACC, the DAS is negative. This suggests that if the loss rates and defaults by rating observed S&P over time continued in the future, the BBB-rated sub-MBS would not meet or exceed the investors WACC, given the financing mix and leverage employed. The same analysis could be employed with other types of sub-MBS and for classes with other ratings to see if the DAS offered by other sub-MBS offered better relative value.

The simple mean, variance approach utilized by DAS uses the expected sub-MBS price to estimate default costs in terms of both dollars and yield. This approach provides quick and interesting insights into the dispersion of sub-MBS prices as credit losses vary. It also provides a measure of return to MBS credit risk that considers more rationally the expected cost of the short default option. The benefit of DAS is that it is a quick, simple, and consistent measure that allows investors to compare securities across time regardless of changes in rating agency criteria. Note, however, that the approach described in this chapter does not take convexity (value of the prepay option) into account. It is possible to extend the method in a multidimensional setting to address prepayment risk and default risk simultaneously.

EXERCISES

Exercise 18.1   If higher losses are generally accompanied by slower prepayment speeds, will the DAS method understate or overstate the value of the default option?

Exercise 18.2.   Why might some investors seek to invest in loans with moderate amount of credit risk?

Exercise 18.3   What mechanism is used by the rating agencies to equate ratings categories across asset classes? That is, how can the probability of default be similar for different transactions with different underlying collateral?

Asset-Backed Securities

Auto-Loan Asset-Backed Securities

Auto loan asset-backed securities (ABS) are securities whose underlying collateral are automobile loans. While auto leases, agricultural machinery loans, and car dealer floor-plan securitizations are often included under the umbrella of auto ABS, this chapter focuses exclusively on loans made to retail purchasers of automobiles. This chapter provides a general overview of the auto ABS sector as well as a description of the distinct features of auto loans that make the securitization process different from other collateral types.

AUTO ASSET-BACKED SECURITIES ISSUANCE

With close to $190 billion outstanding at the end of 2001, auto ABS make up the second largest nonresidential ABS sector. The primary players in the origination of these securities are: (1) the captive finance wings of the big three automakers, (2) banks, (3) specialty finance companies such as Advanta and Capitol One, and (4) other captive finance companies. The big three automakers dominated this market during the time period 1996–2001 as shown in Figure 19.1.

COLLATERAL AND LOAN CHARACTERISTICS

Several characteristics of the underlying loans and assets distinguish auto loans from residential mortgage-backed securities (RMBS). For one thing, auto-loan terms are significantly shorter than mortgage-loan terms. Terms typically range from 3 to 5 years, with some origination in the 6- to 8-year maturity range.

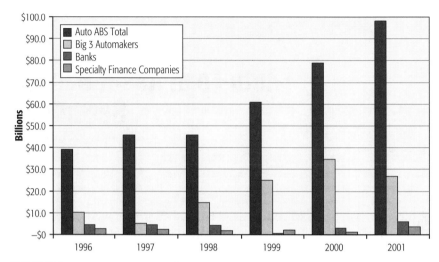

FIGURE 19.1   Auto ABS issuance by issuer type, 1996–2001.
Source: 2002 Mortgage Market Statistical Annual.

For another thing, automobiles are depreciating assets, which has important consequences for refinancing behavior, default, and recovery of losses. For a refinancing to occur, the future lender must see some equity left in the vehicle, or the borrower must put up additional cash. In addition, since equity in the vehicle can become negative, the default option is more attractive to borrowers. If a default occurs, recovery levels can be low.

The likelihood of negative equity depends on two principal factors: the depreciation curve of the vehicle and the interest rate on the loan, which determines the rate of principal payoff. In addition to the impact on refinancing, cars that depreciate quickly would have low recovery levels in the event of default. These factors increase in importance in the subprime auto sector, with its higher interest rates, longer loan maturities (necessary to achieve lower monthly payments), and lower-credit-quality borrowers.

As with residential home loan rates, auto-loan rates at a particular origination date can vary greatly. There are several reasons for this variation. First, there is a significant difference between rates on new and used cars. Second, there is a large spread between prime and subprime borrowers. In addition, because many of the originating institutions are captive-finance companies, special-incentive programs can result in loan origination in the 1.99 percent to 3.99 percent range.

TABLE 19.1 Auto Loan Obligor Quality

	Credit Grade	Avg. Pool Losses (% OPB)[a]	Loan Terms	Sample Interest Rates (%) (as of July 2002)
Prime	A+ to B	0.83	36–60 months	6.79–6.95[b]
Near Prime	B– to C+	1.0–6.0	36–72 months	7.0–10.0
Subprime	C+ to D–	6.0–25.0	36–72 months	13.95–20.95

Source: Moody's Investor Service, JPMorgan, E-Loan, Intelligent Life, Bloomberg LP.
[a]OPB = original principal balance.
[b]National average for a 36- and 48-month term as of 2Q 2002.

More recently, the market has begun to divide borrowers into prime, nonprime, and subprime categories. These gradations are highly subjective and are not consistent across lenders. Furthermore, the distinctions between borrowers are becoming increasingly blurred as heightened competition targets more and more lower-credit-quality borrowers. Table 19.1 characterizes some of the (inherently fluid) categories and provides an example of loan rates and terms for each credit grade.

ENVIRONMENT

In a recessionary environment with rising unemployment, borrowers unable to make monthly payments will begin to default. In addition, recoveries may be even lower since demand for used autos may simultaneously wane, lowering used-car auction prices.

Auto ABS have only become popular since the late 1990s, and until recently, this market was not subject to a recession. Thus, default models cannot be built with the same attention to historical data, as they are in the RMBS prime and subprime sectors.

At the time of writing, the economy had recently emerged from a prolonged recession in 2001 but continued to be plagued by sluggish growth in 2002 through the first quarter of 2003. Increased sales of new autos in 2002 at extremely low rates may also lead to an eventual glut in the used-car market, depressing the values of recoveries from defaults that may occur. In this environment, understanding the structure backing a deal and the levels and forms of overcollateralization (OC) are even more crucial.

358 ASSET-BACKED SECURITIES

Auto Asset-Backed Securities Structures

An auto loan securitization can currently take one of three forms: a **grantor trust**, an **owner trust**, or a **financial asset securitization trust (FASIT)**. Grantor and owner trusts are the most commonly used structures for auto-loan receivables. Although FASITs were created to repackage cash flows from a variety of assets, they have not been used to date for auto loans because of the immediate taxable event they create for issuers. The various trusts serve as bankruptcy-remote vehicles that hold collateral on behalf of investors and administer the distribution of cash flows. Therefore, even if an issuer becomes insolvent, the trust is a separate entity that will continue to pay proceeds to investors.

A grantor trust is the simplest auto ABS issuer, but is rarely used with newer transactions. A grantor trust is a pass-through structure that requires a pro rata share of principal and interest from the underlying collateral to be passed through to investors. Investors, often referred to as certificate holders, are entitled to all of the cash flows from the auto-loan receivables. A pass-through can be structured as a single tranche or multiple tranche security. In a senior/subordinated structure, principal and interest are allocated proportionally according to original tranche sizes. For example, in a 5 percent subordinated deal, 95 percent of the principal collected each period is used to pay down the senior bonds, while the remaining principal pays down the subordinate bonds. Both senior and subordinate classes are repaid at the same rate unless the subordinate class is written down because of credit losses. Therefore, in a grantor trust, the average life and principal windows are the same for both senior and subordinate tranches, assuming no credit losses have occurred.

In contrast, **owner trusts** are designed to be more flexible than grantor trusts, which explains their popularity among issuers. Because auto loans are self-amortizing as mortgages are, principal is returned over the entire life of the security. This feature allows issuers to carve out multiple tranches with varying risk characteristics, much like collateralized-mortgage obligations (CMOs) in the mortgage-backed securities (MBS) sector. For example, an issuer might create several different bonds against a particular collateral pool such that each bond would correspond to a different average life and principal repayment window. The classes of securities that can be created for owner trusts are very similar to CMO classes such as sequential-pay, total rate of return, money market, and floating rate. A glossary of definitions is contained in the sidebar.

DEFINITIONS

Sequential-Pay Classes: In sequential-pay structures, all scheduled principal and prepayments are repaid by class, starting with the class with the earliest stated maturity. For example, an owner trust might comprise four senior classes of bonds with varying average lives. The bond with the shortest average life will be retired before any principal is paid to the bond with the next shortest maturity. This process continues until all the bonds are retired.

Total Rate of Return Classes: Total rate of return classes are a specialized form of sequential pay tranches that have long interest-only periods and tight principal payment windows varying between 12 and 18 months.

Money-Market Classes: Rule 2a-7 of the Investment Company Act of 1940 prohibits money-market funds from buying securities with maturities longer than 13 months. By structuring one or more sequential pay bonds with a maturity of 13 months or less, issuers can create a suitable security for money-market funds.

Floating-Rate Classes: Floating-rate classes can also be created in auto ABS structures. The coupon can adjust periodically based on an index with a margin.

Prepayment Rates

The absolute prepayment rate (ABS) is the standard measure of prepayment rates in the auto-loan sector. ABS measures the monthly rate of loan prepayments as a percentage of the original pool balance. ABS is defined by the following formula where SMM refers to **single monthly mortality,** which measures the percentage of dollars prepaid in a given month expressed as a percentage of the scheduled loan balance.

$$ABS = (100 \times SMM)/100 + (SMM \times (AGE - 1))$$

The ABS measurement differs from conditional prepayment rate (CPR) used in the mortgage industry, which measures prepayment as an annualized percentage of the current pool balance.

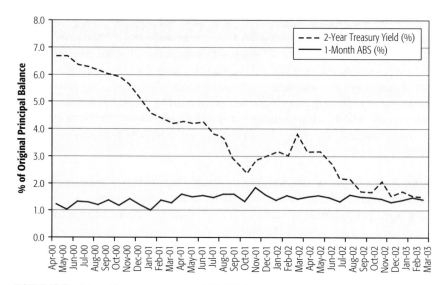

FIGURE 19.2   Monthly prepayments of FORDO 1999-A versus two-year Treasury.
Source: 2002 Bloomberg LP.

Most prepayments on auto loans result from either defaults or trade-ins. Borrowers rarely refinance existing car loans because interest rates tend to be higher for used cars than new cars. A loan resulting from a refinancing would be considered a used-car loan. Thus, auto-loan prepayments tend to be fairly predictable and not highly correlated with interest-rate changes as shown in Figure 19.2.

Rating Agency Methodology

Credit support is a form of insurance designed to protect investors against a shortfall of cash flows from the underlying collateral. Credit support can take one of two forms: internal or external. Subordination, excess interest, and OC are examples of internal-credit support. Letters of credit (LOC) and bond insurance are examples of external-credit support.

In determining the appropriate amount of credit support for a particular securitization, rating agencies take into account both qualitative and quantitative considerations. Some of the **qualitative** considerations include:

- Company history
- Experience of management
- Overall financial health

- Originator's relationships with car dealers
- Underwriting standards
- Quality of loan servicing

Company History　A strong, proven track record in the auto-lending industry is an important factor in determining the level of required credit support. The rating agencies look at the number of years a company has been in business and the company's historical performance over the past 3 to 5 years. Companies with shorter track records and weaker loan portfolios may find that they have to obtain external bond insurance to lower their all-in cost of issuance.

Experience of Management　The experience and integrity of management is also critical. Rating agencies may investigate the background of the principals of the company to assess their integrity and character.

Overall Financial Health　A company's financial survival is key, particularly for newly established auto finance companies, which may not have adequate capital and sources of liquidity to fund a rapidly growing loan portfolio.

Originator's Relationship with Car Dealers　The risk of a transaction tends to increase if an originator depends too heavily on a concentrated car-dealer network. A broadly diversified car-dealer base with emphasis on manufacturer-franchised new-car dealerships as opposed to used-car dealerships and a rigorous selection process for soliciting car dealerships tend to produce better transactions because of lower incidence of dealer fraud and better creditworthiness of borrowers.

Underwriting Standards　Consistent underwriting and tight monitoring controls are of utmost importance in determining the creditworthiness of a pool of borrowers. Credit history, stability with respect to employment and residence, debt and income ratios of borrowers, and credit scores are some of the important characteristics evaluated by rating agencies.

Quality of Loan Servicing　Strong servicing is vital for a successful transaction, especially if the collateral is of lower credit quality. The quality of servicing can make all the difference between a delinquent loan and unrecoverable loss. Aggressive collection procedures help ensure that defaults do not result in higher-than-expected credit losses, particularly for lower-credit-quality collateral. For example, subprime borrowers typically need early and continuous payment reminders because this class of borrowers tends to make late payments.

Rating agencies also take **quantitative factors** into account when determining the required credit support for a securitization. Rating agencies start out by deriving an expected cumulative loss curve for a base-case scenario. The rating agencies examine the following factors for the securitized pool in question:

- Static pool performance of existing originations
- Historical portfolio performance
- Pool selection criteria
- Comparative analysis and credit scores
- Delinquency methodology
- Charge-off policy

Static Pool Performance   Rating agencies rely heavily on static pool analysis to forecast cumulative net losses. The rating agencies examine on a monthly basis the historical loss performance of pools by year of origination (vintage). They also examine both newly originated and seasoned loan pools at least 18 to 24 months old.

Historical Portfolio Performance   Rating agencies also require 3 to 5 years of historical performance data disaggregated by origination, delinquencies, repossessions, gross and net losses, and recoveries. Losses tend to be understated during periods of high growth of the portfolio; therefore, annual losses are adjusted by dividing the outstanding balance in the previous year. Standard and Poor's calculates expected cumulative losses by multiplying expected annual losses by weighted-average life (WAL). The WAL estimate used in the cumulative-loss calculation assumes zero defaults and low prepayments.

Pool Selection Criteria   Rating agencies place a lot of emphasis on the consistency of loan characteristics between the securitized and aggregate portfolio of the firm. The relevant characteristics include:

- APR
- Contract amount
- Loan-to-value ratio
- Original maturity
- Remaining maturity
- Composition of new/used car mix
- Model year and vehicle mileage

- Amortization method
- Geographic concentration

Comparative Analysis and Credit Scores   Rating agencies also assess the credit quality of the borrower by examining the following characteristics and by doing a comparative analysis of prior loan pools and industry peers.

- Gross income
- Monthly debt service
- Debt to income
- Down payment to manufacturer's suggested retail price(MSRP)
- Years of credit history
- Credit scores
- Past credit problems
- Housing status (rent versus own)
- Stability of residence and employment

Delinquency Methodology   The method a company uses to calculate delinquencies will determine the accuracy of the reported number. The preferred method by rating agencies is based on the contractual definition. For example, if a borrower misses one payment but is current on subsequent payments, the loan continues to be classified as 30-days delinquent. Under the **recency of payment** method, the same loan would be classified as current regardless of whether the borrower has failed to make one payment.

Charge-Off Policy   The timing of losses as well as the methodology of estimating losses can vary widely among issuers. Any delay in recognizing losses could result in negative carry if interest payments from the underlying collateral are insufficient to meet interest payments to bondholders. Therefore, the sooner a charge-off is recognized the better. Most issuers charge off receivables between 120 and 180 days, although some wait until a vehicle is repossessed and make an estimate of the recovery value before the car is actually auctioned off. This practice is generally discouraged by rating agencies because of the risk that recoveries turn out to be less than expected, thus requiring a large upward adjustment to losses.

Losses can be measured as a percentage of either gross or net receivables. Gross receivables include accrued but unearned interest on the receivable. Standard & Poor's prefers losses to be calculated based on net receivables because that method eliminates distortions created by including unearned income using the gross method.

VALUATION

The industry convention in the auto ABS sector is to quote ABS products either as a spread to some point on the swap curve (generally 2 or 3 year, based on the average life of the tranche) or to quote Z-spreads. Recall that the Z-spread is the single spread that, when added to the zero-coupon curve (described in Chapter 13), provides discount factors that match the net present value (NPV) of bond cash flows to the market price (this is equivalent to option-adjusted spread (OAS) in a zero-volatility world). In addition, some dealer commentaries include spreads to the Treasury curve.

Figure 19.3 shows nominal spreads of short-maturity auto ABS tranches to the 2-year swap curve from March 2001 to July 2002. Each of the four securities corresponds to a different issuer: CarMax Auto (CARMX 2001-1-A2), Chase Manhattan (CMAOT 2000-A A3), Ford (FORDO 2001-A A4), and Capital Auto Receivables Asset Trust, the GM captive finance company (CARAT 2000-2 A4). Table 19.2 compares the characteristics of specific tranches of deals and their average prepayment behavior. All four deals were quoted over the 2-year swap rate.

Table 19.2 shows that the gross weighted-average coupon (WAC) varies considerably between the deals, ranging from the subprime CARMX WAC of 11.7 to the 4.45 CARAT WAC. The prepayment assumptions made at

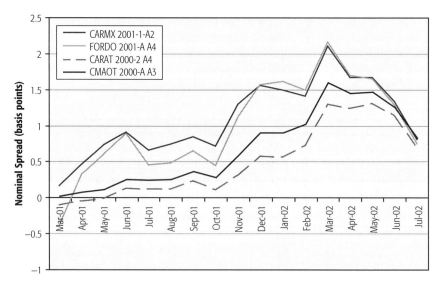

FIGURE 19.3 Auto ABS nominal spreads versus 2-year swap curve.
Source: 2002 Bloomberg LP.

TABLE 19.2 Comparison of Deal Characteristics

Deal	Tranche	Tranche Maturity	OWAL	ABS Assumption at Origination	WAC	Net Coupon	Actual 12-month ABS	Rating
CARMX 2001-1	A2	10/15/2003	1	1.5	11.70	5.39	1.60	Aaa
CMAOT 2000-A	A3	12/15/2004	2	1.5	9.77	6.21	1.74	Aaa
FORDO 2001-A	A4	8/15/2004	2	1.5	8.72	LIBOR + 9bps	1.51	Aaa
CARAT 2000-2	A4	7/15/2006	2	1.0	4.45	6.46	n/a	Aaa

Source: 2002 Bloomberg LP.
OWAL = original weighted-average life.

deals issuance ranged between 1.0 ABS to 1.5 ABS. The actual prepayment experience measured by 12-month ABS in Table 19.2 shows that while there was some deviation from the original assumptions, the magnitude of the deviation was not substantial. Since all the tranches are rated Aaa, spreads over the 2-year swap rate are minimal and any variations between the deals may be due entirely to slightly different weighted-average lives (WAL).

Because prepayment variability is not associated with interest-rate movements for auto ABS, an OAS-type analysis is not performed. However, prepayments and defaults can vary based on other variables, and it is useful to perform at least scenario and total-return analyses in which prepayment and default assumptions are stressed, together with changes to the yield curve, to see how price performance and the timing of income may differ from expectations.

EXERCISES

Exercise 19.1   What are the distinguishing characteristics of auto loans that make them behave quite differently from residential mortgages?

Exercise 19.2   Why are auto-loan prepayments not highly correlated with interest-rate changes?

Exercise 19.3   Explain how the measures ABS and CPR differ.

CHAPTER 20

Credit-Card Asset-Backed Securities

Credit-card asset-backed securities (ABS) are securities whose underlying collateral are credit-card receivables. Unlike other classes of ABS, there are no hard assets or physical property backing these securities, just individual promises to repay a financial obligation. This chapter focuses on the unique features of credit-card receivables and how they drive the securitization process.

CREDIT-CARD ASSET-BACKED SECURITIES ISSUANCE

Figure 20.1 shows credit-card ABS origination since 1995. With $79 billion originated in 2001, and a total of $433 billion originated between 1995 and the third quarter of 2002, the credit-card sector is one of the three largest sectors within the ABS market. The first credit-card deals were issued in 1987 by banks with the intent of diversifying their sources of funding.

There are two primary types of credit-card accounts that make up credit-card ABS. General purpose credit cards are those issued by Visa, MasterCard, American Express, and Discover. Their respective shares of this market in 2000, for example, were 46 percent, 37 percent, 9 percent, and 8 percent. The other type is generally referred to as **affinity cards**—those used by members of a particular affinity group, such as American Airlines frequent flyers, or alumni of universities. MBNA and First USA are the two largest issuers of such cards.

The primary originators of credit-card ABS are banks, specialty finance companies (such as MBNA, Providian), and retailers such as Sears, which may carry their own line of charge cards or co-brand with MasterCard/Visa.

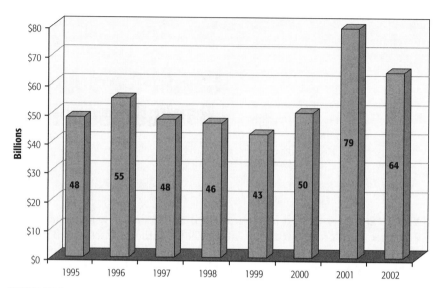

FIGURE 20.1   Volume of credit-card ABS issuance, 1995 through November 2002.
Source: 2002 Mortgage Market Statistical Annual, 2002 Bloomberg LP.

Institutional features differentiating commercial banks from the specialty finance companies (SFCs) include:

- SFCs do not borrow via checking/savings accounts (though a number do
  borrow retail using CDs).
- SFCs do not have branches; therefore there is much less overhead.
- SFCs have thus far not entered business lending.

Loan Characteristics

Credit-card loans have several features that distinguish them from both residential mortgage-backed securities (RMBS) and from ABS such as auto
loans, home equity loans (HEL), and manufactured housing loans (MH).
These features tend to lead to differences in structure, defaults, and recoveries. First, in contrast to auto, HEL, and MH, there is typically no physical
underlying asset to most credit-card loans. Therefore, the concept of loan-to-
value (LTV) makes no sense, and defaults cannot be offset by recoveries
from liquidating the underlying asset. Instead, defaulted accounts can be
sold off to specialists in the recovery/renegotiation of credit-card debt.
   Second, there is no set amortization schedule to a credit-card loan, and
the balance on any given loan fluctuates as charges are made and some per-

centage of the balance is paid off. Therefore, there is no natural amortization schedule for credit-card securities, and the structure needs to address fluctuating balances.

Another consequence of the lack of an amortization structure at the loan level is that there is no natural concept of loan prepayment in the way that it exists for HELs, for example. Although borrowers can pay off their entire balance using other credit cards (which would roughly correspond to a mortgage refinancing), we see that the revolving nature of credit-card structures imply a different impact. There is, however, a concept of early amortization, which is discussed in the structure section.

An additional issue to be aware of regarding credit-card loans is the relationship of credit quality to **secured credit cards**. Lower-credit-quality borrowers or brand new ones with no credit history (especially older borrowers who are immigrants) may get started with a secured card. A secured card is essentially a savings account or CD held as collateral by the originating institution. The account earns interest while the borrowers develop or improve their credit history; in the event of default the bank can claim the cash in the account. Over time, the ratio of required collateral to credit-card charge limit may be lowered until the borrower qualifies for a regular card. Although this type of card may have higher delinquency or default rates, the collateralized feature may actually make it a more attractive loan type.

Environment

In a recessionary environment with rising unemployment, borrowers unable to make monthly payments will begin to default. In contrast to home equity, manufactured housing loans, and auto loans, there is no hard asset underlying the loan unless it is a secured card. Therefore recoveries exist to the extent that borrowers who are in default can be coaxed (or threatened, as the case may be) into paying some portion of their balance.

The period in which credit-card ABS have become popular has not included a recession until very recently. Therefore, the same issues that were relevant to the use of auto-loan default models based on historical data pertain to credit-card ABS.

CREDIT-CARD ASSET-BACKED SECURITIES STRUCTURES

To create a credit-card ABS, an issuer establishes a bankruptcy-remote trust and then sells the outstanding receivables of a designated group of credit-card accounts to the trust. The receivables include both the current balances of credit-card accounts and any future cash flows associated with these accounts.

Prior to 1991, the **stand-alone trust** was the predominant vehicle for credit-card ABS issuance. In this type of vehicle, an issuer would transfer receivables from credit-card accounts into a single trust and issue a single security or several classes of securities off the designated collateral pool. For subsequent securities, the issuer would create an entirely new pool of receivables as collateral.

Since 1991, the **master trust** has been adopted as the vehicle of choice for credit-card ABS issuers. The master trust is much more flexible than the old stand-alone trusts, because it allows issuers to sell multiple securities from the same trust. In other words, one pool of credit-card receivables cross-collateralizes a series of distinct securities. For example, an issuer transfers $1 billion dollars worth of credit-card receivables to a trust and issues a multiclass security. The issuer transfers an additional $1 billion of receivables from new credit-card accounts to the same trust and issues another set of securities. All of the securities issued from the trust are now supported by the entire $2 billion in receivables. See prospectus and supplement on the CD.

There are several advantages of the master trust structure. First, the cost of setting up and maintaining one trust is less than creating a new trust for each new security. Second, the pool of receivables tends to be much larger than in stand-alone trusts and therefore more diversified in terms of seasonal or demographic characteristics. Third, principal and excess spread may be shared among series within the same group (i.e., fixed-rate, floating-rate).

Two types of securities are issued off the collateral pool: investor certificates and seller certificates. Investor certificates are sold to ABS investors, whereas seller certificates are retained by the issuer. The seller certificate is the unrated residual interest in the trust designed to absorb any fluctuations in the total outstanding principal amount of the portfolio. The seller's participation must remain above a minimum percentage of the receivable balance. If it falls below the minimum requirement, the seller is required to add additional accounts to the trust on approval of rating agencies. If additional accounts cannot be added, early amortization will occur. More detailed discussion follows later. The seller certificate also serves as an incentive for issuers to maintain the credit quality of the pool. The seller certificate is entitled to all finance-charge cash flows after payment of investor certificate coupon, servicing fees, charge-offs, and trust expenses.

Collateral-Invested Amount Owner Trusts

Collateral invested amount (CIA) is a popular form of credit enhancement used in credit-card securitizations. The CIA class is the most subordinated interest and thus in a first-loss position. In earlier credit-card securitizations, issuers typically issued three tranches out of a master trust, a Class A, Class B, and CIA Class. More recently, major issuers have created a new **owner trust** structure within the master trust framework. This owner trust structure allows issuers to transfer the interest, principal, and excess cash flow entitlement to the CIA class into a trust from which notes are issued. These notes are collateralized and payable only from cash flows allocated to the owner trust. The main advantage of the CIA owner trust structure is that issuers have been able to expand its investor base dramatically to include ERISA (Employment Retirement Security Act) restricted investors, since notes are treated as debt from an accounting standpoint.

Revolving and Amortization Phases

Credit-card ABS have two distinct phases, the **revolving period** and the **principal-amortization period.** During the revolving period, investors only receive interest payments monthly, quarterly, or semiannually. The interest is paid from finance charges, discount-option funds, or drawn from credit enhancement if necessary. Any principal repaid by credit-card holders during this period is used to purchase additional receivables in order to maintain a constant level of receivables to support the investor certificates. The risk of early amortization provides adequate incentive for the seller to maintain its participation well above the minimum requirement. The revolving period usually ranges between 18 and 48 months, but can be any predetermined length of time.

At the end of the revolving period, securities are retired during the amortization period, which generally lasts about 12 months. The principal is retired in one of two ways, either through a controlled amortization or a bullet payment.

In a controlled amortization, principal is repaid to investors and sellers according to a planned schedule, very similar to a sinking-fund corporate bond structure. Typically, principal is repaid in 12 equal installments. If credit-card holders make principal payments in excess of the predetermined principal schedule, the excess is used to purchase additional receivables for the pool.

For bullet credit-card securities, interest is repaid on a periodic basis and the entire principal is returned in one single payment on the expected maturity date. An initial revolving period is followed by a principal accumulation phase in which principal payments are deposited into a trust account or principal funding account (PFA) and held until the final maturity date. These funds are invested in short-term, highly rated investments. The revolving and accumulation phases are indistinguishable to investors because investors continue to receive the same periodic interest payments in both periods. On the expected maturity date, the entire accumulated principal amount is paid to investors. If the funds collected in the PFA are insufficient to repay investors on the expected payment date, principal will continue to pass through to investors until the legal final maturity date, at which time the trust would sell any remaining receivables to repay investors.

There are two types of bullet securities, hard and soft. Hard bullet securities have longer accumulation periods and often have third-party guarantees. Soft bullet securities are the most common type used for credit-card ABS. The expected maturity on a soft bullet is 1 to 3 years earlier than the legal final maturity. The length of the soft bullet's accumulation phase is based on average payment rates for comparable collateral. For example, an accumulation period of 12 months would require an 8.33 percent (100 percent/12) principal repayment rate by credit-card holders in order to accumulate sufficient principal to repay the bullet. If repayment rates were less than 8.33 percent, then the accumulated principal would be paid out on the expected maturity date and additional principal repayments would be passed through to investors through the legal final maturity date.

Early Amortization

While conventional loan prepayments do not exist for credit-card ABS as they do for mortgage-backed securities (MBS) and auto-loan ABS, *early amortization* or early tranche prepayment can occur. All credit-card securities have provisions that allow amortization ahead of schedule in the event that the trust fails to generate sufficient income to cover expenses. One or more of the following events may trigger early amortization:

- Failure or inability to make required deposits or payments.
- Failure or inability to transfer receivables to trust when necessary.
- False representations or warranties that remain unremedied.
- Certain events of default, bankruptcy, insolvency, or receivership of the seller or servicer.
- Excess spread disappears due to reduction in portfolio yield or increase in loss rates.
- Monthly payment rate (MPR) falls below specified minimum.
- Seller's participation falls below required minimum.
- Portfolio principal balance falls below invested amount.

In the event of early amortization, principal is no longer used to purchase new receivables. Principal received from credit-card holders is used to repay investors. Once senior investors are fully repaid, principal is used to repay subordinate investors. In order to accelerate repayment of investor certificates, principal distributions normally allocable to seller certificates are redirected to investor certificates. Only three deals in the history of credit-card securitization have experienced early amortization events, and none of these deals suffered any losses.

RATING AGENCY CRITERIA

There are two main approaches that rating agencies take in determining the appropriate level of credit enhancement for credit-card ABS transactions: the **steady state/static pool** approach and the **expected loss** approach.

Steady-State Approach/Static Pool Analysis

In the steady-state approach, rating agencies start out by determining the steady state of key performance variables through examination of historical performance and volatility of these indicators. The key variables that determine credit-enhancement requirements include portfolio yield, charge-offs, MPR, purchase rate, and type of investor coupon. Once the steady state has been established, the variables are stressed in order to withstand certain levels of losses for the desired credit rating.

Tables 20.1 and 20.2 contain the stress-test guidelines from Fitch IBCA and Standard & Poor's, respectively. Table 20.1 shows that in order to obtain a BBB rating from Fitch IBCA for a fixed-rate coupon security, Fitch IBCA would require 4.01 percent of credit enhancement, given the steady-state

TABLE 20.1 Fitch IBCA Stress Scenarios

Variable	Steady State Assumption (%)	AAA	A	BBB
Yield	17.0	35.0%	25.0%	20.0%
MPR	12.0	45.0%	35.0%	30.0%
Charge-offs	7.0	4.5X	3.0X	2.3X
Purchase rate	100	0	0	0
Credit enhancement (fixed-rate coupon)		12.95%	6.91%	4.01%
Credit enhancement (floating-rate coupon)		15.13%	8.22%	4.18%

Source: Fitch IBCA, ABCs of Credit Card ABS, *Structured Finance*, April 4, 2001.

TABLE 20.2   S&P General Guidelines for BBB Stress Test

Security must be able to withstand the following combination of stresses without loss of principal:

Key Variable	
Yield	Decrease to 75% of expected case over 18-month period
Charge-offs	Increase to 1.5 to 2X expected case over 18-month period
Payment rate	75% of expected case
Purchase rate	Flat portfolio for investment grade originators/servicers and declining portfolio for below investment grade originators/servicers
Coupon rate	Actual fixed-rate coupon; increase of 75% of worst-case portfolio yield over 18 months for floating-rate coupon.
Excess spread	Lower of current level and highest excess triggers

Source: Standard & Poor's, Credit Card Criteria 1999.

assumptions in the last column. This level of credit enhancement corresponds to a scenario whereby investors are repaid 100 percent of principal and interest even if the portfolio yield were to fall instantaneously by 20 percent, MPR were to decrease instantaneously by 30 percent, and charge-offs were to increase by 2.3 times over a 6-month period. Securities rated AAA and A are subject to more severe stress tests, as indicated in Table 20.1.

Table 20.2 also shows the general stress test guidelines for a BBB rating from Standard & Poor's. Notice that the stress tests and key variables differ somewhat from Fitch IBCA's ratings methodology. For example, loss multiples for a BBB-level range between 1.5X and 2.0X base-case losses compared to Fitch's multiple of 2.3X base-case losses.

DEFINITIONS

Portfolio Yield: Total monthly payments attributable to annual percentage rate (APR) charges, annual fees, late-payment fees, recoveries from charge-offs, and interchange as a percentage of outstanding receivables. APR accounts for the majority of portfolio yield. Increasing APR, cash advances, account balances, and a reduction in convenience users results in higher portfolio yields.

Charge-offs: Loans written off as uncollectable by issuer. Most issuers are required to charge off accounts at 180 days of delinquency and 30 days after notification of bankruptcy of obligor.

MPR: Monthly Payment Rate is the total payment, including both principal and finance charges, made by cardholder each month as a percentage of the total outstanding balance.

Purchase Rate: Monthly purchases made by cardholders as a percentage of the previous month's outstanding principal balance. Higher purchase rates accelerate repayment of principal to investors and require lower credit-enhancement levels.

Coupon for Floating-Rate Transactions: Annual interest paid to investors of floating-rate investor certificates. The basis risk resulting from a rapid rise in interest rates may require 2.5 to 4.0 percent additional credit enhancement.

Interchange: Percentage of fees paid to credit-card issuer by merchant for taking credit risk and funding receivables. The amount varies between 1 and 2 percent annually.

Principal Payment Rate: Monthly principal payments by cardholders as a percentage of prior month's outstanding balance.

Excess Spread: Difference between the interest earned from receivables less interest owed to investors, servicing fees, and trustee expenses.

Expected-Loss Approach

Another approach used to determine the necessary level of credit enhancement focuses on expected losses. Expected losses refer to average credit losses that an investor would experience under many scenarios. Expected losses are derived from probability distributions, which measure average credit losses and the variability of those losses around a center/mean. Higher expected losses and larger variances will result in lower credit ratings and vice versa. While the shape and position of the probability distribution influence the required level of credit enhancement, structural features of the transaction are critical in the rating process. Structural features include treatment of excess spread, cash collateral loans, letters of credit (LOC), insurance, CIA.

Excess Spread Excess spread is the first line of defense in the event of credit losses. Excess spread represents the difference between interest earned from receivables less interest owed to investors, servicing fees, and trustee expenses. Any excess is deposited into a spread account. Spread accounts can be prefunded at the closing of a transaction or built up over time. Rating agencies give more credit to transactions in which spread accounts are pre-funded because they provide immediate protection against potential losses.

Cash Collateral Account   A cash collateral account (CCA) is a segregated trust account, funded at the outset of a transaction. This account can be drawn down to cover shortfalls in interest, principal, or servicing fees if excess spread has been depleted. The account is typically funded by a bank loan or cash contribution from the issuer. The CCA is repaid after all classes of certificates have been retired in full. The cash in the account is invested in highly rated short-term investments. Withdrawals from CCAs can be reimbursed by future excess spread.

Letters of Credit   LOCs are third-party obligations that ensure timely payment of principal and interest. LOCs are no longer used today because, historically, the ultimate credit rating depended so heavily on the LOC provider. LOCs were precursors to CCAs.

Insurance   First-time issuers, particularly issuers specializing in the subprime sector, use surety bonds to guarantee timely payment of principal and interest to investors. Bond insurance is typically used for senior/subordinate structures.

Subordination

Senior/subordinate structures are designed to provide varying degrees of protection to investors. The subordinate classes of securities are designed to absorb losses for senior classes. For example, consider a transaction with three classes of securities A, B, and C. Class C absorbs all losses not already covered by excess spread and CCAs before losses are allocated to A and B tranches. Once Class C has been depleted, Class B absorbs all losses before they are allocated to Class A.

Valuation

The industry conventions used in the credit-card ABS sector are similar to those used for auto ABS. The two most common conventions are a spread to a point on the swap curve (generally 2, 3, and 5 year for senior/intermediate tranches, 7 and 10 year for the subordinated tranches, based on the base-case average life of the tranche) or Z-spreads for fixed-rate tranches. In addition, some dealer commentaries include spreads to the Treasury curve. For floating-rate tranches the natural quote is in basis points over LIBOR.

Figure 20.2 shows Deutsche Bank's index for nominal spreads of short-maturity credit-card ABS tranches to the 2-year swap between July 2001 and June 2002. We can see that spreads (generally on the AAA-rated senior

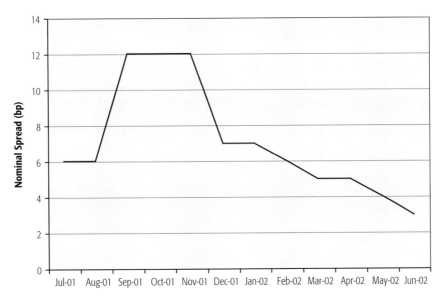

FIGURE 20.2 2-year ABS credit-card spread versus 2-year swap curve.
Source: 2002 Bloomberg LP.

tranches) over the 2-year swap ranged from 2 basis points to a high of 12 basis points right after September 11, 2001. For most of 2001–2002, however, it appears that the normal range is 5 to 7 basis points.

Because credit-card loans do not have an amortizing structure as do home equity, manufactured housing, or auto loans, prepayment variability is not an issue. However, defaults can vary based on a variety of variables, and it is useful to perform at the very least scenario and total-return analyses to see how price performance and the timing of income may differ from expectations based on events that would trigger early amortization. This would especially be an issue for B and C pieces, which tend to trade at 10 to 25 basis points over the 5-, 7-, or 10-year points on the swap curve.

EXERCISES

 Exercise 20.1 What is the main distinguishing characteristic of credit-card ABS that sets them apart from other ABS sectors such as autos, home equity loans, and manufactured housing? How does that characteristic affect the resulting structure used for credit-card ABS transactions?

Exercise 20.2   Why are the concepts of loan-to-value and prepayments not relevant for credit-card ABS?

Exercise 20.3   Briefly explain the most common structure used to structure credit-card ABS transactions and list the events that are likely to trigger early amortization.

CHAPTER 21

Manufactured-Housing Asset-Backed Securities

Manufactured housing asset-backed securities (ABS) are securities backed by residential dwellings commonly known as mobile homes. The manufactured-housing (MH) ABS sector has recently experienced the most severe downturn in its history. This chapter provides an overview of the unique features of MH collateral, loans, and borrowers in order to explain the current state of the MH ABS sector.

MANUFACTURED-HOUSING ASSET-BACKED SECURITIES ISSUANCE

Figure 21.1 compares MH ABS issuance against the three major ABS sectors from 1995 through the second quarter of 2002. MH ABS reached a peak in 1999 with about $17 billion in issuance. Figure 21.2 shows that the volume of issuance declined precipitously in 2000 and continued to be moribund in 2002. A number of factors contributed to the decline, including the general economic slowdown during the period, declining MH sales, and an exodus of major players from the sector.

Up until the end of 2001, Conseco Finance and GreenPoint Credit were the largest issuers of MH ABS, accounting for $3.3 billion combined or 44.0 percent of the sector. Table 21.1 shows a breakdown of MH ABS volume by issuer. On January 3, 2002, GreenPoint Credit announced that it was closing its MH lending business. According to Bloomberg News, GreenPoint's CEO stated that the decision was driven by "the most severe downturn in the manufactured-housing business that has ever occurred." In addition, on August 9, 2002, Conseco announced that it would be missing some bond interest payments and asked lenders to restructure $6.5 billion in debt. The next week, a variety of Conseco deals were put on negative-ratings watch by S&P and its shares were suspended from NYSE trading with a likely delisting.

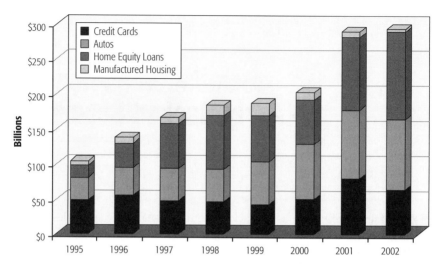

FIGURE 21.1   Volume of ABS issuance, 1995 through November 2002.
Source: *2002 Mortgage Market Statistical Annual*, 2002 Bloomberg LP.

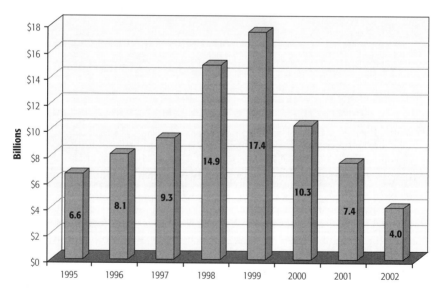

FIGURE 21.2   Volume of MH ABS, 1995 through November 2002.
Source: *2002 Mortgage Market Statistical Annual*, 2002 Bloomberg LP.

TABLE 21.1 Volume of Manufactured Housing ABS by Issuer

Issuer	Volume (in $billions)	
	2000	2001
Conseco Finance Corp.	4.01	2.58
GreenPoint Credit	2.10	0.70
Oakwood Homes Corp.	1.11	0.74
Vanderbilt Mortgage & Finance	0.35	0.78
Other	2.72	2.63

Source: Standard & Poor's, "U.S. Manufactured Housing ABS Hit Turbulent Times," May 30, 2002.

The MH sector has been plagued by continued deterioration of delinquencies, foreclosure frequency, and losses. Table 21.2 shows that all the major issuers have experienced increasing delinquencies since 1998, with GreenPoint Credit experiencing the greatest increase of 72.0 percent. Overall credit losses have also trended upward for the same issuers as shown in Table 21.3. In 2001, losses had almost doubled for GreenPoint Credit. The overall deterioration has been particularly pronounced for loan pools securitized in 1999 and 2000.

The departure of GreenPoint Credit (and other active players that have since shut down their MH-lending businesses) can be traced to aggressive lending practices adopted in 1995, fueled by fierce competition due to a barrage of new entrants to the market (Access Financial Lending Corp., United

TABLE 21.2 Manufactured Housing 30+ Day Delinquencies

Issuer	Percent of Outstanding Contracts at Year End			
	1998	1999	2000	2001
Conseco Finance Corp.	2.56	2.99	3.93	3.84
GreenPoint Credit	n/a	2.99	4.40	5.13
Oakwood Homes Corp.[a]	4.10	5.10	4.50	6.10
Vanderbilt Mortgage & Finance[b]	3.34	2.07	2.19	2.59

Source: Standard & Poor's, "U.S. Manufactured Housing ABS Hit Turbulent Times," May 30, 2002.
[a]Fiscal year ends September 30.
[b]Fiscal year ends June 30.

TABLE 21.3 Manufactured Housing Credit Losses

	Percent of Principal Balance at Year-End			
Issuer	1998	1999	2000	2001
Conseco Finance Corp.	1.05	1.16	1.57	2.17
GreenPoint Credit	n/a	2.16	2.36	4.19
Oakwood Homes Corp.*a*	1.46	1.66	1.96	2.15
Vanderbilt Mortgage & Finance*b*	0.84	1.37	1.44	1.77

Source: Standard & Poor's, "U.S. Manufactured Housing ABS Hit Turbulent Times," May 30, 2002.
*a*Fiscal year ends September 30.
*b*Fiscal year ends June 30.

Financial Companies, Bombardier Capital Inc., INDYMAC Inc., and Oakwood Acceptance Corp). MH loan originations, starting from 1995 and onward, changed dramatically because of looser underwriting standards that allowed 5 percent down payments (compared to 10 percent down-payment requirements), higher loan-to-value (LTV) ratios, and longer loan terms.

In order to further understand why the two largest MH ABS issuers left the business, it is important to understand MH collateral, loans, and borrowers and the impact of a weakening economy on them. These topics are presented in the following section.

COLLATERAL AND LOAN FEATURES

Manufactured homes are different from typical residential dwellings in several important ways. First, MH is a permanent housing structure that sits on cement pads and has wheels and a chassis. In the past, these structures were referred to as mobile homes, but most are never actually moved from their original location. In fact, the entire home is constructed in a factory and then transported to its final location. In addition, manufactured homes are the only type of home with a national building code that regulates design, construction, fire safety, and so forth.

The MH market consists of single-section (48 to 72 feet by 12 to 14 feet) and multisection (36 to 70 feet by 24 to 28 feet) homes, sometimes referred to as singlewides and doublewides. The median price of MH is approximately $44,000 compared to $137,000 for site-built homes.* The land is

---

*Standard & Poor's, Manufactured Housing Criteria, January 2000.

typically rented in MH parks. Given the cost differential, MH demand has typically been from low-income borrowers. To some extent, demand for MH is countercyclical: When rates rise, borrowers who might buy either manufactured or site-built homes tend to buy manufactured homes because of the cost savings.

The more common way to purchase a manufactured home is via a retail sales contract (as an installment payment). The typical contract ranges from 10 to 25 years with higher interest rates than mortgage and home equity loans but with lower rates than most credit cards. The second way to finance MH, growing in popularity as somewhat higher-income borrowers enter this market, is as real property including land. The loan terms can range from 5 to 30 years for this type of financing.

Because of small loan balances, loan-servicing costs are a much higher percentage of interest income; therefore, servicers typically require on the order of 100 basis points rather than 25 basis points of loan balance as a servicing fee. In addition, there is typically a relationship between the length of the contract, borrower credit quality, and loss severity. First, borrowers with lower disposable income (caused either by low-income itself, or in conjunction with a high-debt burden) will prefer longer loan maturities to bring down monthly payments. This leads to a slower principal amortization schedule along with a longer time period in which a default can occur.

Finally, while there are differences in depreciation between land-and-home and home-only assets (as well as a small difference between single and multiple section), MH is a depreciating asset. This feature is significant with respect to how frequently defaults occur. In a typical 15- to 30-year loan, most of the loan payments in the early years consist of interest. As a result, the collateral depreciates faster than the loan principal amortizes, which raises the LTV ratio of the loan. It can take up to 8 years before the borrower builds up equity in his or her home. Therefore, there is a strong incentive for borrowers to default on MH loans during the initial period of the loan.

MANUFACTURED-HOUSING ASSET-BACKED STRUCTURES

Early MH securitizations were issued as single-class pass-throughs with third-party protection, but have evolved more recently into multiclass, senior subordinated structures with principal lockout periods. The majority of MH securitizations are structured as real estate investment conduits (REMICs), which are commonly used in mortgage-backed securities (MBS) transactions. REMICs allows for multiple classes of securities to be offered,

TABLE 21.4   Conseco 2002–2

Class	Size (millions)	Percent of Deal	Rating	Orig. WAL
A1	46.3	8.0	AAA	0.36
A2	300.0	51.8	AAA	5.23
AI0	117.7	20.3	AAA	
M1	38.8	6.7	AA	8.61
M2	28.8	5.0	A	8.61
B1	28.8	5.0	BBB	5.22
B2	18.8	3.2	BB	9.86

Source: 2002 Bloomberg LP.
WAL = weighted-average life.

which has created a broader investor base because of the wide range of risk characteristics available. Table 21.4 shows the structure of a Conseco MH securitization, which is representative of the industry. As one can see, investors have a wide variety of credit ratings and average-life profiles from which to choose. In addition to broad investor appeal, a multiple-class offering is also advantageous from the standpoint of credit enhancement, because subordinated securities provide credit protection to more senior securities. See the CD for a sample prospectus.

Within the REMIC framework, one will often see a *shifting interest cash flow* structure designed to provide additional protection to senior classes. In this structure, subordinate certificates receive no principal during an initial lockout period, which typically ranges between 4 to 5 years. During this lockout period, all principal goes to repay senior classes. Theoretically, losses would have peaked by the end of the lockout period, thus reducing the senior classes' exposure to potential losses. At the end of the lockout period, all classes receive a pro rata share of principal as long as collateral is performing adequately and has not violated any performance triggers.

PREPAYMENTS

MH prepayments are measured both in conditional prepayment rate (CPR) and the manufactured housing prepayment (MHP) curve. The base MHP curve, shown in Figure 21.3, starts at 3.7 percent CPR in the first month and rises at 0.1 percent CPR each month to 6.0 percent by the end of month 24. Therefore, 200 MHP is simply twice the base MHP vector.

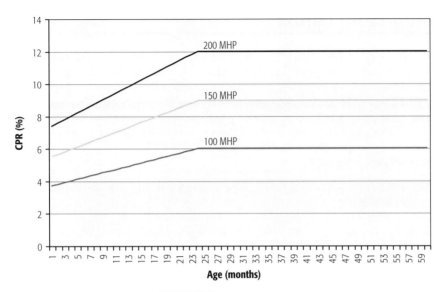

FIGURE 21.3 MHP curve.

MH prepayments result from many of the same factors that lead to pre-payments in residential MBS: refinancings, housing turnover, and defaults. One of the most salient features of MH ABS is that prepayments tend to be stable for MH contracts compared to conventional residential mortgages be-cause MH owners tend to be less sensitive to interest-rate changes com-pared to conventional home owners. A change in interest rates would not significantly impact an MH owner's monthly payment since loan balances tend to be significantly smaller compared to conventional home mortgages ($44,000 versus $137,000 median price). For example, if an MH owner were to refinance from a 15-year loan of $30,000 at 9.0 percent interest rate into an 8.0 percent interest-rate loan, he or she would only save $17.58 per month. In contrast, a conventional home owner would be much more in-clined to refinance because the monthly savings would be more significant for a larger loan balance.

Refinancing options are also limited for MH owners. MH owners tend to be lower-credit-quality borrowers and would not necessarily qualify for alternative financing. In addition, the MH unit is a depreciating asset. Dur-ing the initial years of an MH contract, the depreciation of the housing unit may exceed amortization, thus leaving the MH owner in a negative equity position. Therefore, LTV may rise to a level that is unacceptable or too risky for lenders.

RATING AGENCY CRITERIA

In determining the level of credit support for an MH transaction, rating agencies focus on expected cumulative net losses of the underlying collateral like other ABS transactions. In order to quantify the cumulative net loss for a particular MH pool, rating agencies estimate the **foreclosure frequency** and **loss severity** by conducting a static pool analysis.

Foreclosure Frequency

The main determinants of foreclosure frequency or the rate at which defaults occur include:

- Original LTV (OLTV)
- Term of loan
- Coupon rate
- Seasoning (age of loan pool)
- Collateral characteristics
- Borrower demographics

Original LTV is an important indicator of how aggressive a finance company is and how much it stands to lose on repossession of an MH unit. Higher LTV ratios can lead to higher foreclosure frequencies. Rating agencies will look at the weighted-average LTV of the pool and compare it to the maximum limit as stipulated by the issuer's underwriting standards.

Loan term is another predictor of foreclosure frequency. Longer-term contracts tend to have higher defaults because obligors are exposed to potential losses for a longer period of time. Most lenders provide terms ranging in maturity from 5 to 30 years. Typically, lenders offer 15-year terms for single-section units and 20-year terms for multisection units. Because MH units depreciate immediately after a sale, there is often a period when the borrower has negative equity in the MH unit, increasing the incentive for an MH owner to default on his or her loan.

Higher coupon rate loans tend to result in higher foreclosure frequencies. A borrower with a riskier credit profile will typically pay a higher interest rate on his or her contract compared to a higher-quality borrower.

Most defaults occur early in the MH contract, which is consistent with the negative equity position of the borrower that occurs due to the depreciation of the MH unit following its purchase. As loans *season*, home owner equity begins to rise because of principal amortization. Moreover, borrowers who remain in the pool and have consistently made their loan payments are less likely to default in the future. Therefore, fewer defaults are expected for collateral pools, which are more **seasoned.**

Foreclosure frequency is also directly related to the **characteristics of the collateral,** such as the size, location, and type of MH unit. Units come in two sizes, singlewide or doublewide. Generally, doublewide units are associated with borrowers of better credit quality, except when the doublewide units are located in housing parks. The risk is that the monthly rent for the land is twice that for a singlewide unit and that the associated expenses such as utilities, taxes, and insurance are also higher. Units can either be located on privately owned land, privately leased land, or land rented in a housing park. MH units on privately owned land tend to reflect the highest-quality borrowers. Land ownership tends to convey income stability and a longer tenure in the MH unit. Contracts that finance both the purchase of land and housing unit tend to perform better than MH-only contracts because the land/home combination does not depreciate like a stand-alone MH unit. Most lenders finance both new and used MH. Generally speaking, financing of new MH have lower foreclosure frequencies.

Geographic concentration has a significant impact on the loss severity of a pool. Pools that have geographic concentrations of more than 10 percent in any state or 1 percent in any one MH park, will need more credit support.

Borrower demographics are important determinants of borrower creditworthiness. Important borrower attributes that can influence default frequency include debt-to-income ratio, payment-to-income, purchase versus refinance, employment period, employment status, borrower age, and existing versus first-time home buyer.

Loss Severity

Once the foreclosure frequency has been determined by evaluating the factors described previously, recovery rates are estimated. The recovery rate is the percentage of the outstanding loan balance realized on liquidation of the MH unit. Recovery rates are directly related to the age and condition of the unit, dropping rapidly in the first 2 years and gradually flattening, as the unit gets older.

Another important determinant of loss severity is the method of liquidation. Servicers that have access to retail distribution channels for repossessed homes generally have higher recovery rates compared to wholesale disposition. Access to retail distribution channels requires strong dealer relationships and only services with active loan origination are able to achieve significantly higher recoveries of repossessed MH units.

RECENT PERFORMANCE IN CONTEXT

Having reviewed borrower, loan, and deal characteristics, it is possible to speculate on the combination of factors that led to such a severe downturn in the MH lending industry. For ordinary home owners, the bite of the 2001–2002 recession was to a great extent mitigated by high levels of home price appreciation. Many borrowers tapped the increased home equity. Those who may have had to sell their homes due to losing their jobs would largely still have been able to realize a profit by selling their homes and therefore would not have been motivated to default.

For MH, due to property depreciation, there was no such effect. However, lower-income borrowers appear to have been particularly hard hit by the manufacturing-led recession. In addition, loose underwriting standards and a high level of interlender competition will continue to contribute to the deterioration of the sector. Without significant regulatory oversight, lenders with the loosest standards will grow the fastest—as long as the economy is also growing at a rapid pace.

EXERCISES

Exercise 21.1 What do auto-loan ABS and MH ABS have most in common?

Exercise 21.2 What explains why prepayments tend to be more stable for MH ABS compared to home equity loan ABS and residential MBS?

Commercial
Mortgages

Commercial Loans

T he success of commercial mortgage-backed security products, just as with residential mortgage-backed securities products, depends on the success of their underwriting. Unlike residential lending, the area of commercial mortgage financing involves a detailing of specialties within both the field of mortgage lending and real estate sales. As with residential property, both the borrower's credit history and the characteristics of the property are important.

TYPES OF INCOME-PRODUCING PROPERTIES

There are a wide variety of income-producing property types. The following are general categories:

- Acquisition and development (A&D)
- Multifamily conventional (new and existing construction)
- Multifamily-FHA insured (new and existing construction)
- Mobile home tracts
- Commercial (shopping centers, office buildings, motels, bowling alleys, etc.)
- Industrial

Within each of these categories, the size differences between projects creates specialization, for example, a $500,000 project versus a $20,000,000 development. Savings and loan associations, a large provider of funds in single-family mortgages, generally will be less involved in these more specialized areas. However, commercial banks will be more involved at least on the short-term A&D and construction loans. The permanent loan on either existing or new construction can be placed again, depending on the size involved and the length of time required for development, with a savings and loan, commercial bank, life insurance company, real estate investment trust (REIT), or one of the many other new sources (pension funds, foreign loans). There are many mortgage banking operations that specialize or have a special department for these types of financing. Based on a feasibility study and appraised value, the mortgage banker or broker will attempt to find the required lenders to handle the project.

GENERAL RISK EVALUATION

In analyzing the risk of an income-producing property, a lender concentrates on three general areas:

1. The financial feasibility of the property and capacity to sustain mortgage payments.
2. The credit and financial condition of the individuals or corporations behind the loan, their character, history, and experience.
3. The collateral behind the loan via an appraisal and general locational risk.

Financial Feasibility of the Property

In submitting a loan package of all the information required by the lender to analyze the loan, the first step is a market analysis reviewing the demand, supply (competition), and general need for the project. From the market analysis, estimates of projected gross rent and vacancy are derived. Next, a financial analysis involves an estimation of all of the operating expenses projected on the property. Putting these two analyses together results in net operating income, as follows:

> Gross possible income (GPI)
> Vacancy and collection allowance (VCL)
> Effective gross income (EGI)
> Operating expenses (OE)
> Management expenses (EXP)
> Maintenance and repair (REINV)
> Other expenses (OTH)
> Net operating income (NOI)

The **net operating income** is the amount of money generated by the property that is available for debt servicing (the repayment of mortgage loans). A given financing proposal (loan-to-value ratio, term, interest rate, etc.) can now be analyzed for the ability of the property to cover the payments. Note that a projection of NOI should span several years and incorporate the expected growth (or decline) rates in income, vacancies, and expenses.

Financial Ratios

There are several important financial ratios used by lenders to analyze risk.

Debt Service Coverage   The debt service coverage (DSC) ratio is defined as the NOI divided by the debt service (DS):

$$DSC = \frac{NOI}{DS}$$

If the DSC is 1.10, that means the debt payments are covered 1.10 times or that NOI could decline 10 percent relative to current debt service and the property could still sustain mortgage payments.

As a general rule, lenders like to see commercial properties have a DSC of 1.25 or more. If the property is deemed riskier, a lender might require a DSC of 1.5 or 1.6. If the property is considered very stable, with long-term high-credit tenants and very predictable expenses, then a lower DSC may be acceptable. If the first- or second-year projection involves a low DSC, the borrower may consider keeping some cash in escrow at the lending institution to provide additional assurance that mortgage payments can be made.

Operating Expense Ratio   The operating expense ratio (OER) reflects the annual operating expenses as a percentage of gross possible income:

$$OER = \frac{OE}{GPI}$$

A common rule of thumb used by lenders on residential income properties is that these expenses should range from 33 to 40 percent of effective gross income in order to properly maintain a property in the condition necessary to provide rents projected for the property. Borrowers, if they could, might try to skimp on their estimate of expenses to increase the NOI figure, which effectively raises the debt coverage ratio and might make for a strong argument for a larger loan. However, lenders are aware of this possibility and for this reason examine the operation ratio closely.

Breakeven Cash-Flow Ratio   Breakeven cash flow ratio (BER) is another ratio used by lenders that tells them the vacancy rate a property can tolerate before owners cannot make mortgage payments from operating income. This ratio is usually calculated as follows:

$$BER = \frac{OE + DS}{GPI}$$

If BER = .811, then this ratio calculation tells us that the project could tolerate a total vacancy rate of 19.9 percent before the owners would have difficulty meeting the mortgage payment from operating income. This calculation is very important, particularly for newly constructed projects that must "rent up" from scratch.

Operating Return on Asset   Operating return on asset (ROA) is the same ratio as a capitalization rate in income appraisal:

$$r = \frac{NOI}{V}$$

As a general rule r should exceed the cost of financing, unless significant price appreciation is expected on the property. If no appreciation is expected, the r should always exceed the cost of the debt, otherwise the lender is receiving a higher return on the investment with a lower risk position than the property equity owner.

Gross Rent Multiplier   Another simplistic rule of thumb is the gross rent multiplier (GRM), which is the property value divided by gross possible income:

$$GRM = \frac{V}{GPI}$$

The GRM should be in line with similar properties in the area and is used as a quick appraisal check. The net income multiplier (NIM), which is the price or value over the NOI, can be used in a similar manner if the NOI on similar properties and their recent prices are known.

   Example: Assume a 20-unit apartment complex is being considered for purchase by an individual who has had the property appraised for $280,000 ($220,000 building, $60,000 land) by a competent appraiser. Based on operating statements constructed from those presented to her by the present owner, she provides the following information to a lender (see Table 22.1). The borrower would like to obtain a 75 percent loan on the property. Current interest rates are 14 percent requiring a loan of $210,000, assuming a

TABLE 22.1 Operating Statement

Gross Possible Income	$50,000	
− Vacancy & Collection Loss (7%)	3,500	
= Effective Gross Income		$46,500
Operating Expenses:		
Management	2,800	
Utilities	500	
Maintenance	2,400	
Repairs	1,900	
Insurance	900	
Taxes	2,800	
Other Expenses	2,000	
Reserve	1,100	14,400
Net Operating Income		$32,100

purchase price of $280,000 and a monthly mortgage payment of $2,527.90 or $30,334.80 per year.

The DSC is too low, which means either the investor will have to place more cash down, or lower the price, or both, if the interest rate is fixed. A longer-term mortgage loan would help a little. Another option would be to place several thousand dollars in escrow for a year or two to provide greater protection for the lender.

The OER appears to be a bit low, but would be acceptable if the property were new, in excellent condition, and required low maintenance. The BER is fair at almost 90 percent, which means the property could suffer a 10 percent vacancy rate and still break even. The market trend will be important in reviewing the acceptability of this ratio. The r appears low when compared to the finance cost of 14 percent. Thus, strong appreciation trends should be demonstrated in order to justify the low r. The GRM and NIM cannot be analyzed without data on similar property in the area for comparison. If similar property GRMs were equal to or above 5.6, then a GRM of 5.60x might be acceptable. If they were below 5.6, it would be a danger signal (see Tables 22.1 and 22.2).

Credit and Financial Condition of the Borrower

If the property does not generate enough income to cover mortgage payments, the borrower must have the ability to do so. If the borrower is an individual or a partnership, then the financial analysis of the borrower is similar to that for a single-family mortgage. If the borrower is a corporation, then several financial statements, preferably audited, will be required. In

TABLE 22.2   Results of Analysis

(1) **Debt Service Coverage (DSC)**

$$DSC = \frac{NOI}{DS} = \frac{\$32,100}{\$30,334.80} = 1.058\% \text{ or } 1.06\%$$

(2) **Operating Expense Ratio (OER)**

$$OER = \frac{OE}{GPI} = \frac{\$14,400}{\$50,000} = 0.288\% \text{ or } 28.80\%$$

(3) **Breakeven Cash Flow Ratio (BER)**

$$BER = \frac{OE + DS}{GPI} = \frac{\$14,400 + \$30,334.80}{\$50,000} = 0.8947 \text{ or } 89.47\%$$

(4) **Operating Return on Asset (ROA)**

$$r = \frac{NOI}{V} = \frac{\$32,000}{\$280,000} = 0.1146 \text{ or } 11.46\%$$

(5) **Gross Rent Multiplier (GRM)**

$$GRM = \frac{V}{GPI} = \frac{\$280,000}{\$50,000} = 5.60x$$

analyzing the income statement, the lender desires a stable or positive trend in net income with a sufficiently large dollar amount to handle mortgage payments, if need be. In reviewing the balance sheets, the larger the net worth relative to total assets the better. The preferable type of assets are liquid; cash, securities, and bonds that are easily converted to cash. Current assets over current liabilities should be 2.5 or better or typical for the specific industry. Preferable debt is the long-term stable payment type as opposed to short-term prime plus type of notes. The size of the net worth is also compared to the size of the mortgage loan desired.

In the case of a large property with only one or a few major tenants on long-term leases, a similar analysis may be required of the tenants, especially if the property is of a special purpose type (which was uniquely adapted to the tenant). This analysis of the tenant is because it may be difficult to lease the property if the tenant went out of business. Because of these concerns, the lender needs to review the leasing clauses and arrangements on all major tenants (not residential type).

Other than the credit and financial condition of the borrower, their experience in real estate and their past track record are very important factors to most lenders, especially if the property is new. The background and experience of each major participant in the investment decision process will be reviewed.

The Collateral

The last resort for a lender when default occurs is always the foreclosure process, but that possibility requires a sound analysis of the collateral behind the loan. In general, sound analysis of the collateral means a competent appraisal report with some emphasis on locational analysis and future trends. If future trends are uncertain, the lender may want to make the loan on a callable basis, that is, in 10 years, even though the payments are based on 25 years.

It goes without saying that characteristics including location, design, accessibility, and local market demand for rental property as well as trends in neighborhoods are of obvious importance to the lender. These characteristics will influence the appraised value and the income-producing capability of a property. The appraised value in our discussion means value as determined by the financial institution.

LEASES

The vast majority of commercial loans secured by real property include leases. The leases are between the tenant (lessee) and the property owner (lessor). Leases can be quite simple, as in the case of multifamily properties (which are typically month-to-month or annual), or they can be complex as in retail leases, which include revenue or profit sharing as part of lease-rate determination.

Leases can be created that are either fixed (no change in rent over the life of the lease) or graduated (where the rent changes over time according to a schedule). Leases can be revalued based on changing market conditions. Also, rents can be calibrated to an index to control for inflation (such as the consumer price index) in an effort to protect the property owner against a deterioration in purchasing power from inflation.

The lease rate (and the value of the lease) can be impacted by a number of market and tenant-related factors:

■ *Location Specific.* The location of a specific property can impact the rents that the lessor can charge. For example, properties with poor highway access have trouble attracting (and keeping) tenants, so rents tend to be lower.

- *Credit Quality of Lessee.* The desireablilty and rent charged to a tenant is a function of the tenant's credit quality. Clearly, property owners would prefer AAA-rated tenants with national exposure. However, competitive forces in the market make those tenants scarce and shopping malls often include local or regional tenants with less than stellar credit ratings (but at a higher rent, of course).
- *Lease Term.* The length of the lease can impact the rent charged.
- *Terms of the Lease.* The specifics of the lease can impact the rate that is charged as well. The specifics include any covenants, assignment (sublet) rights, concessions (e.g., tenant improvement allowances, free rent) and other details. Also, care should be taken in identifying whether the lease is based on gross leaseable space (GLA) or net leaseable space (NLA); GLA is the total square footage of the space, whereas NLA is the total square footage less unusable space such as elevator shafts.
- *Lease Options.* Commercial leases often contain options to re-lease at predetermined rates.

One of the most important factors determining the lease rate is how the operating expenses of the property are handled. Under a gross lease (or full-service) lease, the landlord pays the operating expenses. Under a net lease (or triple-net leases), the tenant pays operating expenses. Hence, the gross lease carries a higher rental rate than a triple-net lease. Commercial leases often have expense-stops where the tenant pays increases in operating expenses.

VALUING INCOME-PRODUCING PROPERTIES

Income-producing properties (e.g., apartment complexes, office buildings, shopping centers) represent an important segment of the international economy, yet little is known about their value or return behavior. Unlike common stocks, income-producing properties trade on an irregular basis and each trade is transacted between only a few participants. As a consequence, simple valuation models such as capitalization rates can have enormous errors.

Capitalization Rates

The value of an income-producing property is equal to the present value of the future cash flows generated by the property. Without the use of debt financing, the cash flows for each year of operations are assumed to be:

Gross possible income
$-$ Vacancy and collection losses

Gross effective income
$-$ Operating expenses

Net operating income

Example: Assume that an office building can generate $83,333.33 in effective gross income over the next year. The operating expenses for the building are estimated to be $33,333.33. NOI, or rents less operating expenses, is estimated to be $50,000. Suppose that an investor pays $454,545.45 for this property. The resulting capitalization rate or *cap rate* is:

$$r = \frac{NOI_1}{V_0} = \frac{\$50,000.00}{\$454,545.45} = 0.11 \tag{22.1}$$

Note that the cap rate, r, is similar to the earnings-to-price ratio that is often used in common stock analysis. Like the earnings-to-price ratio, the value of the property is assumed to be equal to the present value of the future NOI stream in perpetuity:

$$V_0 = \frac{NOI_1}{\left(1 + r_u\right)^1} + \frac{NOI_2}{\left(1 + r_u\right)^2} + \frac{NOI_3}{\left(1 + r_u\right)^3} + \frac{NOI_4}{\left(1 + r_u\right)^4}$$
$$+ \frac{NOI_5}{\left(1 + r_u\right)^5} + \dots + \frac{NOI_\infty}{\left(1 + r_u\right)^\infty} \tag{22.2}$$

If we assume that net operating income grows at a constant rate g and that:

$$NOI_1 = NOI_0 (1 + g) \tag{22.3}$$

the valuation model becomes

$$V_0 = \frac{NOI_1}{\left(1 + r_u\right)^1} + \frac{NOI_1\left(1 + g\right)}{\left(1 + r_u\right)^2} + \dots \tag{22.4}$$

which compresses to

$$V_0 = \frac{NOI_1}{r_u - g} \tag{22.5}$$

which is finally rewritten as

$$r_u - g = \frac{NOI_1}{V_0} \qquad (22.1a)$$

Note that equation (22.1a) and (22.1) differ by the growth rate g. That is, the observed capitalization rate r is a combination of two separate rates: the required return on real estate *without* financial leverage and the expected growth rate of NOI. Since we have two unknowns, we must be able to identify one of the variables so we can solve for the other.

Fortunately, we have empirical evidence on the required return on real estate *without* financial leverage from both the Russell-NCREIF and equity REIT indexes. Therefore, we can solve for the imputed growth rate for the property in question. Alternatively, one can simply hazard a guess about the expected growth in the area (this technique is called the "Delphi Technique").

IMPACT OF FINANCIAL LEVERAGE

As we observed in the previous section, the value of an income-producing property is equal to the present value of the future cash flows generated by the property. Specifically, the cash flows for each year of operations are assumed to be:

> Gross possible income
> − Vacancy and collection losses
> _____
> Gross effective income
> − Operating expenses
> _____
> Net operating income
> − Debt service
> _____
> Before-tax cash flow

Similarly, the cash flow generated by the sale of the property at the end of the holding period is assumed to be:

> Sales price
> − Remaining loan balance
> _____
> Before-tax cash flow on reversion

Assume that the purchase of the property is financed by both debt and equity. A commonly used measure of investment performance is *cash-on-cash return* (or the equity dividend rate). It is defined as the property's before-tax cash flow (BTCF) in Year 1 divided by the initial equity investment in the property in Year 0:

$$EDR = \frac{BTCF_1}{EQ_0} \qquad (22.6)$$

Of course, this measure of return is identical to the dividend yield on a common stock. It focuses solely on the property's ability to generate cash flow over the next 12 months.

A superior measure of return is *internal rate of return* (IRR) since it includes increases (or decreases) in property value as well as several years of cash flows. Consider a property with an expected holding period of 5 years. The property's IRR is defined as the interest rate (r^*) that equates the present values of future cash flows to the initial equity investment:

$$\begin{aligned} EQ_0 = \; & \frac{BTCF_1}{(1+r^*)^1} + \frac{BTCF_2}{(1+r^*)^2} + \frac{BTCF_3}{(1+r^*)^3} + \frac{BTCF_4}{(1+r^*)^4} \\ & + \frac{BTCF_5}{(1+r^*)^5} + \frac{BTCF_{Sale}}{(1+r^*)^5} \end{aligned} \qquad (22.7)$$

A third measure of investment performance is *net present value* (NPV). With this measure we are attempting to ascertain if returns from a particular property exceed our opportunity cost on investments of comparable risk:

$$\begin{aligned} EQ_0 = \; & \frac{BTCF_1}{(1+r_L)^1} + \frac{BTCF_2}{(1+r_L)^2} + \frac{BTCF_3}{(1+r_L)^3} + \frac{BTCF_4}{(1+r_L)^4} \\ & + \frac{BTCF_5}{(1+r_L)^5} + \frac{BTCF_{Sale}}{(1+r_L)^5} \end{aligned} \qquad (22.8)$$

If V_{EQ} is greater than our initial equity investment, we consider the purchase to have a *positive* NPV. However, if V_{EQ} is less than our initial equity investment, we would not purchase the property since it is a *negative* NPR project.

The discount rate r_L in equation (22.8) can be found by taking the unleveraged expected return on real estate and adding a premium for financial leverage. The equation for r_L in the first year is:

$$r_L = r_u + \frac{LA_0}{EQ_0}\left[r_u - i\right] \qquad (22.9)$$

where LA_0 is the initial loan amount, EQ_0 is the initial amount of equity financing, and i is the riskless rate on debt. It should be noted that r_L declines over the term of the loan. In fact, as the end of the loan term approaches, r_L approaches r_u.

An Example

Consider the property used at the beginning of this chapter where the net operating income for the first year is expected to be $50,000 and the purchase price of the property is $454,545.45. The resulting unlevered expected return is 11 percent. Suppose that the buyer finances the purchase with a mortgage (80 percent of the purchase price); the mortgage is amortized annually over 40 years and the mortgage interest rate is 10 percent. The amortization table for the first 5 years is presented in Table 22.3.

The revenues and expenses are expected to be constant for the next 5 years. As a result, the BTCF from operations is $12,814.76 each year for the next 5 years. In addition, the sales price at the end of the fifth year is assumed to be $500,000; when we subtract the remaining loan balance at the end of the fifth year, the resulting BTCF on reversion (or sale) is $141,379.62 (see Table 22.3).

We now have the cash flows for equation (22.8), but we do not have the discount rate r_L. The discount rate r_L for the first year is:

$$r_L = r_u + \frac{D}{E}\left[r_u - i\right] = .11 + \frac{\$363,636.36}{\$90,909.09}\left[.11 - .10\right] = .15$$

TABLE 22.3 Payments, Interest, and Principal for a Simple Interest Loan: $363,636.36 Loan at 10 Percent over 40 Years

Year	LA-Beginning	Payment	Interest	Principal	LA-Ending
1	$363,636.36	$37,185.24	$36,363.64	$821.61	$362,814.75
2	$362,814.75	$37,185.24	$36,281.48	$903.77	$361,910.99
3	$361,910.99	$37,185.24	$36,191.10	$994.14	$360,916.85
4	$360,916.85	$37,185.24	$36,091.68	$1,093.56	$359,823.29
5	$359,823.29	$37,185.24	$35,982.33	$1,202.91	$358,620.38

TABLE 22.4 Before-Tax Cash Flows from Operations

	1	2	3	4	5
Revenue	$83,333.33	$83,333.33	$83,333.33	$83,333.33	$83,333.33
– OE	$33,333.33	$33,333.33	$33,333.33	$33,333.33	$33,333.33
= NOI	$50,000.00	$50,000.00	$50,000.00	$50,000.00	$50,000.00
– DS	$37,185.24	$37,185.24	$37,185.24	$37,185.24	$37,185.24
= BTCF	$12,814.76	$12,814.76	$12,814.76	$12,814.76	$12,814.76

The discount rate r_L for the second year is:

$$r_L = r_u + \frac{LA_1}{EQ_1}\left[r_u - i\right] = .11 + \frac{\$362,814.75}{\$91,730.70}\left[.11 - .10\right] = .149552$$

since the loan balance has fallen ($363,636.36 - $821.61 = $362,814.75) and the equity position has increased by the amount of the mortgage amortization ($90,909.09 + $821.61 = $91,730.70). The discount rates are presented in Table 22.5:

Equation (22.8) must be modified to allow the discount rate r_L to change over time:

$$EQ_0 = \frac{BTCF_1}{(1 + r_L)^1} + \frac{BTCF_2}{(1 + r_L)^2} + \frac{BTCF_3}{(1 + r_L)^3} + \frac{BTCF_4}{(1 + r_L)^4}$$
$$+ \frac{BTCF_5}{(1 + r_L)^5} + \frac{BTCF_{Sale}}{(1 + r_L)^5}$$

(22.8a)

TABLE 22.5 Discount Rates

Year	r_L
1	0.150000
2	0.149552
3	0.149069
4	0.148548
5	0.147987

We will replace the subscipt L with the appropriate number for the year and expand the discount rate:

$$
\begin{aligned}
EQ_0 = {} & \frac{BTCF_1}{(1 + r_1)} + \frac{BTCF_2}{(1 + r_1)(1 + r_2)} + \frac{BTCF_3}{(1 + r_1)(1 + r_2)(1 + r_3)} \\
& + \frac{BTCF_4}{(1 + r_1)(1 + r_2)(1 + r_3)(1 + r_4)} \\
& + \frac{BTCF_5}{(1 + r_1)(1 + r_2)(1 + r_3)(1 + r_4)(1 + r_5)} \\
& + \frac{BTCF_{Sale}}{(1 + r_1)(1 + r_2)(1 + r_3)(1 + r_4)(1 + r_5)}
\end{aligned}
\tag{22.10}
$$

If we fill in the blanks, we get:

$$
\begin{aligned}
EQ_0 = {} & \frac{\$12,814.76}{(1.15)} + \frac{\$12,814.76}{(1.15)(1.149552)} + \frac{\$12,814.76}{(1.15)(1.149552)(1.149069)} \\
& + \frac{\$12,814.76}{(1.15)(1.149552)(1.149069)(1.148548)} \\
& + \frac{\$12,814.76}{(1.15)(1.149552)(1.149069)(1.148548)(1.147987)} \\
& + \frac{\$95,925.07}{(1.15)(1.149552)(1.149069)(1.148548)(1.147987)} \\
= {} & \$90,909.09
\end{aligned}
$$

What this complicated-looking equation says is that the relationship between cash flows and value are complicated by mortgage amortization. Why? Because as the loan amortizes, the loan-to-value (LTV) ratio declines, leading to a lower expected return on the property.

To illustrate this point, the IRR on this property is 14.9159 percent, which is less than the original 15 percent. Thus, it can be seen that the IRR is a weighted average of the levered discount rates over time.

Case Study: Multifamily

Consider a multifamily apartment complex located in Red Bank, New Jersey, named Navesink View Apartments. The apartment complex contains

100 one-bedroom, one-bath units, 200 two-bedroom, two-bath units, and 100 three-bedroom, three-bath units. The units rent for $550, $650 and $750 per month, respectively. The expected vacancy rate is 6 percent and bad debt expense is expected to be 1 percent. The property management fee is 4.5 percent and annual property taxes per unit amount to $1,500. Annual replacement reserves per unit are $200 and annual additional income per unit from the rental of covered parking spaces is $100. The operating expenses for the apartment complex for 2001 are presented in Table 22.6. The pro forma statement is presented in Table 22.7.

As we can see in Table 22.7, the NOI for the first year is $1,253,336. If we use a capitalization rate (or cap rate) of 9 percent (which we will assume was obtained from an appraiser or market analysis firm), the value of the property is $13,925,956 (or $1,253,336/0.09). If we assume that the buyer decides to finance the purchase with an 80 percent first mortgage loan, this would result in an initial equity position of $2,785,191 (or $13,925,956 × 20 percent) and a first mortgage loan of $11,140,764. If we assume that the buyer will obtain a 30-year, fixed-rate mortgage (amortized annually), the annual mortgage payment will be $989,606, resulting in a BTCF in the first year of $263,730. The pro forma statement including the impact of debt financing and ratios is shown in Table 22.8.

As can be seen in Table 22.8, the DSC ratios exceed 1.25 for the first 5 years, which indicates that the buyer can withstand a 25 percent drop in rental income and still find it advantageous to continue making the payment due on the loan. The other ratios are in line with comparable industry stan-

TABLE 22.6 Navesink View Apartments, Red Bank, New Jersey, Selected 2001 Operating Expenses

	2002 Data	
	Total ($)	Per Unit ($)
Payroll and benefits	225,000	563
Utilities	215,000	538
Repairs and maintenance	195,000	488
Insurance	35,000	88
Landscaping	20,000	50
Marketing	60,000	150
Administrative and general	75,000	188
Legal and accounting	15,000	38
Subtotal	840,000	2,100

TABLE 22.7 Navesink View Apartments, Red Bank, New Jersey, 5-Year Operating Pro Forma Before Debt

	2002 ($)	2003 ($)	2004 ($)	2005 ($)	2006 ($)
Gross potential income:					
1 bedroom, 1 bath	660,000	686,400	713,856	742,410	$772,107
2 bedroom, 2 bath	1,560,000	1,622,400	1,687,296	1,754,788	1,824,979
3 bedroom, 2 bath	900,000	936,000	973,440	1,012,378	1,052,873
Subtotal	3,120,000	3,244,800	3,374,592	3,509,576	3,649,959
Vacancy allowance	187,200	194,688	202,476	210,575	218,998
Bad debt expense	31,200	32,448	33,746	35,096	36,500
Net potential rent	2,901,600	3,017,664	3,138,371	3,263,905	3,394,462
Other income	37,600	39,104	40,668	42,295	43,987
Effective gross income	2,939,200	3,056,768	3,179,039	3,306,200	3,438,448
Operating expenses:					
Payroll and benefits	234,000	243,360	253,094	263,218	273,747
Utilities	223,600	232,544	241,846	251,520	261,581
Repairs and maintenance	202,800	210,912	219,348	228,122	237,247
Insurance	36,400	37,856	39,370	40,945	42,583
Landscaping	20,800	21,632	22,497	23,397	24,333
Marketing	62,400	64,896	67,492	70,192	72,999
Administrative and general	78,000	81,120	84,365	87,739	91,248
Legal and accounting	15,600	16,224	16,873	17,548	18,250
Management fees	132,264	137,555	143,057	148,779	154,730
Replacement reserve	80,000	83,200	86,528	89,989	93,589
Property taxes	600,000	624,000	648,960	674,918	701,915
Total operating expenses	1,685,864	1,753,299	1,823,431	1,896,368	1,972,22
Net operating income	1,253,336	1,303,469	1,355,608	1,409,833	1,466,22

dards that can be found in a number of trade publications (or from Fannie Mae's multifamily lending manuals).

Using the spreadsheet entitled navesink.xls on the CD enables the user to stress test the loan to see which assumptions most impact the financial viability of the apartment complex (and loan). For example, one might test

TABLE 22.8 Navesink View Apartments, Red Bank, New Jersey: 5-Year Operating Pro Forma after Debt

	2002 ($)	2003 ($)	2004 ($)	2005 ($)	2006 ($)
Gross potential income:					
1 bedroom, 1 bath	660,000	686,400	$713,856	$742,410	$772,107
2 bedroom, 2 bath	1,560,000	1,622,400	1,687,296	1,754,788	1,824,979
3 bedroom, 2 bath	900,000	936,000	973,440	1,012,378	1,052,873
Subtotal	3,120,000	3,244,800	3,374,592	3,509,576	3,649,959
Vacancy allowance	187,200	194,688	202,476	210,575	218,998
Bad-debt expense	31,200	32,448	33,746	35,096	36,500
Net potential rent	2,901,600	3,017,664	3,138,371	3,263,905	3,394,462
Other income	37,600	39,104	40,668	42,295	43,987
Effective gross income	2,939,200	3,056,768	3,179,039	3,306,200	3,438,448
Operating expenses:					
Payroll and benefits	234,000	243,360	253,094	263,218	273,747
Utilities	223,600	232,544	241,846	251,520	261,580
Repairs and maintenance	202,800	210,912	219,348	228,122	237,247
Insurance	36,400	37,856	39,370	40,945	42,583
Landscaping	20,800	21,632	22,497	23,397	24,333
Marketing	62,400	64,896	67,492	70,192	72,999
Administrative and general	78,000	81,120	84,365	87,739	91,249
Legal and accounting	15,600	16,224	16,873	17,548	18,250
Management fees	132,264	137,555	143,057	148,779	154,730
Replacement reserve	80,000	83,200	86,528	89,989	93,589
Property taxes	600,000	624,000	648,960	674,918	701,915
Total operating expenses	1,685,864	1,753,299	1,823,431	1,896,368	1,972,222
Net operating income	1,253,336	1,303,469	1,355,608	1,409,833	1,466,226
Debt service	989,606	989,606	989,606	989,606	989,606
Before-tax cash flow	263,730	313,864	366,003	420,227	476,620
Debt service coverage ratio	1.2665	1.3172	1.3698	1.4246	1.4816
Operating expense ratio	0.5339	0.5339	0.5339	0.5339	0.5339
Breakeven cash-flow ratio	0.8473	0.8353	0.8237	0.8125	0.8018
Operating return on asset	0.0900	0.0936	0.0973	0.1012	0.1053
Gross rent multiplier	4.4103	4.2407	4.0776	3.9207	3.7699

the higher-end apartments to see if the property is sensitive to a decline in demand for higher-end apartment units.

Additional Property Types

Of course, commerical loan portfolios and commercial mortgage-backed security deals contain property types other than multifamily residential. These property types include retail (e.g., shopping centers), office, and industrial. The underwriting criteria for each of these property types vary depending on the risk of the property's income stream (which is discussed in Chapter 23).

EXERCISES

Exercise 22.1 Suppose that the borrower in the Navesink View Apartment case requested a 90 percent LTV ratio rather than an 80 percent LTV ratio. Calculate the DSC ratio and other critical measures mentioned in this chapter. As a commercial lender, would you make this loan at a 90 percent LTV ratio?

Exercise 22.2 One of the problems with examining the viability of a commercial loan is the uncertainty of the value of the underlying collateral. Suppose that the cap rate on the property was 10 percent rather than 9 percent—at an LTV ratio of 80 percent, would you make the loan? More specifically, how much would you be willing to lend to the borrower?

Exercise 22.3 Currently, we are in a low-interest-rate environment. Even so, a small change in interest rates can impact the cash flows for a commercial loan dramatically. In the Navesink Apartment spreadsheet, increase the interest rate on the loan by 200 basis points (or 2 percent). How does this change impact the DSC ratio? Does a higher-interest-rate environment dampen the demand for mortgage lending? Discuss.

CHAPTER 23

Commercial Mortgage-
Backed Securities

Commercial mortgage-backed securities (CMBS) represent an interesting departure from residential mortgage-backed securities (MBS). With residential MBS, the underlying collateral is loans on residential properties (1–4 units). With CMBS, the underlying collateral is loans on retail properties, office properties, industrial properties, multifamily housing, and hotels. Unlike residential mortgage loans, commercial loans tend to be "locked out" from prepayment for 10 years. Counterbalancing the reduction of prepayment risk for CMBS is the increase in default risk. As a result, CMBS can be an interesting alternative investment in the mortgage arena.

Both CMBS and real estate investment trusts (REITs) have grown tremendously over the past 6 years as investors' tastes for new real estate-related products have increased. Investment banks were able to take what they had learned from residential MBS and apply that knowledge (with some interesting twists) to the commercial real estate loan market. Not only is the U.S. market continuing to expand, but CMBS is also growing at an ever-increasing rate in Europe (albeit on a much smaller scale). This chapter focuses on the interesting twists that make CMBS such a fascinating product.

COMMERCIAL MORTGAGE-BACKED
SECURITIES: AN OVERVIEW

The attraction of CMBS stems from the unique combination of prepayment dampening coupled with, for the most part, excellent credit quality. Most of the loans underlying CMBS deals have prepayment protection in the form of prepay lockouts and yield maintenance, which boosts the yield of CMBS bonds over those of comparable callable (or prepayable) bonds. As long as the credit quality of the underlying collateral is in the A-rated range, the yield pickup on CMBS bonds can make them quite attractive to institutional investors used to traditional Treasury securities.

A CMBS is formed when an issuer deposits commercial loans into a trust. The issuer then creates securities in the form of classes of bonds backed by the commercial loans. As payments on the commercial loans (and any lump-sum repayment of principal) are received, they are distributed (passed through) to the bondholders according to the rules governing the distribution of proceeds.

Bond Pass-Through Rates

An example of a recent CMBS deal can be used to highlight the distribution of cash flows to the bondholders and the rules governing the distribution. The GMAC 1997-C1 deal, underwritten by Deutsche Morgan Grenfell (now Deutsche Bank), is summarized in Table 23.1. The special servicer is GMAC and the servicer is LaSalle.

The bonds are sequential-pay. The pass-through rate for the first bond, class A-1, is 6.83 percent. The certificate amount is $1,696,984,278, which accounts for approximately 15.41 percent of the underlying collateral amount. The bond is rated as Aaa by Moody's and AAA by Fitch. The other A-class bonds, A-2 and A-3, are junior in priority, but are rated as Aaa by Moody's and AAA by Fitch as well. Since the weighted-average life (WAL) of class A-1 is 4.0 years and the WALs of class A-2 and A-3 are 7.50 and 9.71 years, respectively, we would expect that the pass-through rate on the A-2 and A-3 classes would be greater. In fact, the initial pass-through rate on the class A-2 bond is 6.853 percent and 6.869 percent on the A-3 bond. Together, the A-rated bonds account for 71.50 percent of the total amount of this deal.

The remaining bonds, classes B through K, carry ratings from Moody's and Fitch that are less than Aaa/AAA. The pass-through rates on the B through G bonds rise gradually (although the H through K bonds are lower in terms of initial pass-through rate). Class X is an interest-only class based on the notional amount of the deal.

While each bond receives a share of interest from the underlying pool, the principal payments are disbursed sequentially to classes A1 through K. Prepayment penalties allocated to sequential classes A1 through G are capped at 25 percent. Remaining penalties are allocated to X class.

Commercial Mortgage-Backed Securities Ratings and Subordination Levels

The rating agencies play a critical role in the CMBS market. The role of the rating agency is to provide a third-party opinion on the quality of each bond in the structure (as well as the necessary level of credit enhancement to achieve a desired rating level). Typically, the CMBS issuer submits the underlying portfolio of real estate loans to the rating agencies. The rating agencies then examine critical characteristics of the underlying pool of loans such as the debt

TABLE 23.1   CMBS Deal: GMAC 1997-C1

General deal characteristics	
Deal type	Conduit
Lead manager	Deutsche Morgan Grenfell
Current collateral balance	1,368,918,193
Trustee	LaSalle
# Loans (orig. current)	356, 304
Master servicer	GMAC
Original closing date	9/30/1997
Delinquency (%,#loans)	3.46, 5
Special servicer	GMAC
Mortgage pool characteristics	
Initial pool balance	$1,696,984,278
No. of mortgage loans	355
No. of mortgaged properties	380
Avg. cutoff date balance	$4,780,237
Wtd. avg. mortgage rate	8.62%
Wtd. avg. cut-off date LTV	71.04%
Wtd. avg. DSCR	1.33x
Major property types	
Retail	25.51%
Multifamily	18.79%
Office	18.06%
Industrial	10.21%
Hospitality	9.42%
Skilled nursing	7.13%
Mixed use	4.29%
Self-storage	2.86%
Mobile home park	2.65%
Congregate care/assisted living	0.98%
Other	0.10%
Geographic distribution	
California	17.29%
New York	12.25%
Pennsylvania	7.54%
Connecticut	6.07%
New Jersey	6.01%
Texas	5.41%

service coverage (DSC) ratio and the loan-to-value ratio (LTV). If the target ratios at the asset level are below a certain level, the credit rating of the bond is reduced. Of course, an appropriate credit rating from the agencies is dependent on the quality of information provided by the issuer to the agencies.*

---

*One issuer had a unique approach to reporting LTV ratios to the rating agencies, which led to artificially high ratings for the CMBS bonds.

The credit ratings for the bonds in the GMAC 1997-C1 deals are presented in Table 23.2. Fitch rated the first three bonds (A-1, A-2, and A-3) as AAA. Moody's rates the same bond classes as Aaa. The B through F bonds have progressively lower ratings. The subordination level declines with the bond ratings: 28.5 percent subordination for the AAA bond down to 11.5 percent for the BBB bond.

Prioritization of Payments

The highest-rated bonds are paid off first in the CMBS structure. Any return of principal caused by amortization, prepayment, or default is used to repay the highest-rated tranche first and then the lower-rated bonds. Any interest received on outstanding principal is paid to all tranches. However, it is important to note that many deals vary from this simplistic prioritization assumption.

Loan default adds an additional twist to the structuring. Any losses that arise from loan defaults will be charged against the principal balance of the lowest-rated CMBS bond tranche that is outstanding (also known as the "first loss piece"). For the GMAC 1997-C1 deal, losses are allocated in reverse sequential order from Class K through Class B. After Class B is retired, classes A-1, A-2, and A-3 bear losses on a pro rata basis. As a consequence,

TABLE 23.2 Bonds for GMAC 1997-C1 Deal

Class	Initial Certificate Amount ($)	Initial Spread	Rating Moody's/ Fitch	Percentage of Pool Balance
A-1	261,582,000	48	Aaa/AAA	15.4
A-2	227,661,000	62	Aaa/AAA	13.4
A-3	724,100,000	65	Aaa/AAA	42.7
B	67,879,000	70	Aa2/AA+	4.0
C	50,909,000	75	A1/AA	3.0
D	50,909,000	85	A2/A+	3.0
E	93,334,000	100	Baa2/BBB	5.5
F	25,454,000	118	Baa3/BBB-	1.5
G	84,849,000		BB/BB	5.0
H	59,394,000		B	3.5
J	16,969,000		B-	1.0
K	33,944,278		Unrated	2.0
X	1,696,984,278	Notional	Aaa/AAA	N/A
Total	1,696,984,278			

a localized market decline (such as a rapid decline in the Austin, Texas, real estate market) can lead to the sudden termination of a bond tranche. Hence, issuers seek strategies that will minimize the likelihood of a microburst of defaults.

As long as there is no delinquency, the CMBS are well behaved. Unfortunately, delinquency triggers intervention by the servicer (whose role is discussed later in the chapter). In the event of a delinquency, there may be insufficient cash to make all scheduled payments. In such a case, the servicer is supposed to advance both principal and interest. The principal and interest continue to be advanced by the servicer as long as these amounts are recoverable.

Call Protection

In the residential MBS market, the vast majority of mortgages have no prepayment penalties. In the CMBS market, the vast majority of mortgages have some form of prepayment penalty that can impact the longevity and yield of a bond. Call protection can be made at both the loan level and in the CMBS structure. At the loan level, there exist several forms of call protection: prepayment lockout, yield maintenance, defeasance, and prepayment penalties.

Subordination (%)	Initial Pass-Through Rate (%)	Weighted-Average Life (yrs)	Payment Window
28.5	6.830	4.00	1–75
28.5	6.853	7.50	75–108
28.5	6.869	9.71	108–119
24.5	6.918	9.94	119–120
21.5	6.898	9.96	120–120
18.5	6.997	10.01	120–125
13.0	7.085	11.45	125–158
11.5	7.222	13.53	158–170
6.5	7.414	14.93	170–195
3.0	6.600	17.99	195–235
2.0	6.600	19.78	235–242
0.0	6.600	22.00	242–358
N/A	1.629	N/A	1–358

Prepayment lockout is where the borrower is contractually prohibited from prepaying the loan during the lockout period. The lockout is the most stringent form of call protection since it removes the option for the borrower to prepay before the end of the lockout period. The prepayment lockout is commonly used in newer CMBS deals.

Under **yield maintenance**, the borrower is required to pay a "make-whole" penalty to the lender if the loan is prepaid. The penalty is calculated as the difference between the present value of the loan's remaining cash flows at the time of prepayment and principal prepayment. Yield maintenance was a common form of call protection in older CMBS deals but it is less common in newer deals.

Defeasance is calculated in the same manner as yield maintenance. However, instead of passing the loan repayment and any penalty through to the investor, the borrower invests that cash in U.S. Treasury securities (strips/bills) to fulfill the remaining cash-flow structure of the loan. The Treasuries replace the building as collateral for the loan. The expected cash flows for that loan remain intact through to the final maturity date. Like yield maintenance, defeasance was more popular with older CMBS deals and is less common in newer deals.

With **prepayment penalties,** the borrower must pay a fixed percentage of the unpaid balance of the loan as a prepayment penalty if the borrower wishes to refinance. The penalty usually declines as the loan ages (e.g., starting with 5 percent of the outstanding principal in the first year, 4 percent in the second year, etc., until the penalty evaporates).

Tables 23.3 and 23.4 examine the 40 largest loans underlying the GMAC 1997-C1 deal. In terms of call protection, a variety of methods are used to dampen prepayment. Yield maintenance is the primary form of prepayment protection, although lockout is used quite extensively. Since the majority of the loans are 30-year loans with a 10-year balloon, most of the yield maintenance of lockout only have about 50 months (or 6 years) remaining.

TABLE 23.3   Current Loan Status as of November 2002

Status	Count	Current Asset Balance ($)
In foreclosure	1	2,286,820
Special	9	58,401,924
Grace	122	518,228,843
Perform	171	787,697,534
All assets	303	1,366,615,122

TABLE 23.4 Characteristics of Top 40 Loans in GMAC 1997-C1 Deal: Property Level

Name	State	Property Type	Original Balance	Originator
Crossroads Tower	NY	Office	40,000,000	Deutsche Morgan Grenfell
Circuit City HQ (Deep Run III)	VA	Credit tenant lease	39,951,500	Deutsche Morgan Grenfell
Aggregate Loan Level Information	CT	Nursing care	31,000,000	Deutsche Morgan Grenfell
Gateway Industrial Center	MI	Industrial	26,000,000	Deutsche Morgan Grenfell
Amboy Care Center Rosewood Manor	NJ	Nursing care	23,835,000	GMAC
215 Park Avenue South	NY	Office	22,500,000	Deutsche Morgan Grenfell
Hartford Marriott Farmington	CT	Limited-service hospitality	22,000,000	GMAC
Franklin Commons Apartments	PA	Multifamily housing	21,500,000	GMAC
Fairfield Place Shopping Center	PA	Retail—anchored	20,000,000	Paul Revere
Highland Glen & Highland Ridge	OK	Multifamily housing	20,000,000	Deutsche Morgan Grenfell
Northville Centre	MI	Retail—anchored	19,900,000	Deutsche Morgan Grenfell
Holtze Executive Place	CO	Full-service hospitality	19,250,000	GMAC
Capital Parkview and Manahawin	NJ	Nursing care	19,165,000	GMAC
Continental Plaza	CA	Office	18,900,000	GMAC
Central Valley Plaza Shopping Center	CA	Retail—anchored	18,500,000	ContiFinancial
Aggregate Loan Level Information	IL	Industrial	18,900,000	Paul Revere
Olympia House	NY	Multifamily housing	16,000,000	Paul Revere
1050 17th Street NW	DC	Office	15,250,000	Deutsche Morgan Grenfell
Encino Town Center	CA	Retail—anchored	15,000,000	ContiFinancial
Embassy Tower Apartments	NY	Multifamily housing	14,000,000	Deutsche Morgan Grenfell
Farmer's Market III Office Building	CA	Office	14,000,000	GMAC
369 Lexington Avenue	NY	Office	13,750,000	GMAC

(*continued*)

TABLE 23.4   (*Continued*)

Name	State	Property Type	Original Balance	Originator
Hillsdale Manor Care Center	CA	Nursing care	13,400,000	GMAC
The Atriums Retirement Center	KS	Nursing care	13,250,000	Paul Revere
Holiday Inn Arlington at Ballston	VA	Limited-service hospitality	12,650,000	GMAC
Shelbourne Square Shop Center	PA	Retail—anchored	12,500,000	Deutsche Morgan Grenfell
1400 Marina Way South	CA	Mixed Use	11,950,000	Boston Capital
Winsom Village (Mt. Clemens MHP)	MI	Mobile home park	12,000,000	ContiFinancial
Condyne Freezers Inc.	MA	Industrial	11,800,000	Deutsche Morgan Grenfell
Sunset Village	IL	Mobile home park	11,600,000	ContiFinancial
Aggregate Loan Level Information	NJ	Office	11,400,000	ContiFinancial
Mount Pocono Plaza	PA	Retail—anchored	11,400,000	Deutsche Morgan Grenfell
ShopRite/Grade-A Plaza	CT	Retail—anchored	12,500,000	Paul Revere
Eastgate Pavilion	OH	Retail—anchored	12,000,000	Paul Revere
Monticello West	TX	Congregate care	11,000,000	Deutsche Morgan Grenfell
Builders Square #1310	PR	Retail— unanchored	10,600,000	Deutsche Morgan Grenfell
Vineyard Valley Center	CA	Retail—anchored	10,400,000	Deutsche Morgan Grenfell
CarMax	GA	Retail— unanchored	10,360,460	Deutsche Morgan Grenfell
Avon Marketplace	CT	Retail— unanchored	10,700,000	Paul Revere
Memorial Club Apartments	TX	Multifamily housing	10,300,000	Deutsche Morgan Grenfell

In addition to call protection at the loan level, call protection is available in structural form as well. Since CMBS bond structures are sequential-pay, lower-rated tranches cannot pay down until the higher-rated tranches are retired, which is the exact opposite of default where principal losses hit the lowest-rated tranches first.

Timing of Principal Repayment

Unlike residential mortgages that are fully amortized over a long time period (say, 30 years), commercial loans underlying CMBS deals are often *balloon loans*. Balloon loans require substantial principal payment on the final maturity date although the loan is fully amortized over a longer period of time. For example, a loan can be fully amortized over 30 years but require a full repayment of outstanding principal after the 10th year. The purpose of a balloon loan is to keep the periodic loan payment of interest and principal as low as possible.

Balloon loans pose potential problems for investors due to the large, lump-sum payment that must be refinanced. If there is a change in the quality of the underlying asset (e.g., a decline in the real estate market, increased competition leading to a decline in lease rates, etc.), there is a danger that the loan will not be refinanced, which can result in default. In order to prevent this type of loan failure at the balloon date from occurring, there are two types of loan provisions: the internal tail and the external tail.

THE UNDERLYING LOAN PORTFOLIO

There are two sources of risk relating to the underlying loan portfolio: prepayment risk and default/delinquency risk.

Diversification

A factor that is often considered when analyzing the risk of a CMBS deal is the diversification of the underlying loans across space. The reasoning for what is termed "spatial diversification" is that the default risk of the underlying pool of loans is lessened if the loans are made on properties in different regions of the country. Rather than have the entire portfolio of loans being subject to an idiosyncratic risk factor (e.g., the decline in oil prices and the collapse of the Houston real estate market), the portfolio can spread its risks across numerous economies. Thus, a collapse of the Houston real estate market (which may lead to higher defaults on commercial loans) will be less of a concern if the commercial property markets in Chicago, Kansas City, New York, and Seattle remain strong.

The strategy of spatial diversification can be seen in Table 23.1. Approximately 17 percent of the loans underlying the GMAC 1997-C1 are on properties in California, 12 percent on properties in New York, and 7.5 percent on properties in Pennsylvania. The remaining loans are spread out among other states such as Connecticut, New Jersey, and Texas. Thus, the GMAC 1997-C1 deal has achieved a significant degree of spatial diversification. Although a 29 percent concentration factor for California and New

TABLE 23.5   Characteristics of Top 40 Loans in GMAC 1997-C1 Deal: Loan Level

Name	Gross Coupon (%)	Net Coupon (%)	Current Balance ($)	Rate Type	Remainin Terms
Crossroads Tower	8.99	8.96	38,175,150.03	Fixed 30/360	YM^1(49) O(6)
Circuit City HQ (Deep Run III)	7.83	7.67	35,700,659.93	Fixed act/360	L(206)
Aggregate Loan Level Information	9.01	8.98	28,960,300.54	Fixed 30/360	L(57)
Gateway Industrial Center	8.41	8.38	24,709,319.38	Fixed 30/360	L(50), O(6
Amboy Care Center Rosewood Manor	8.54	8.41	22,177,146.99	Fixed act/360	YM^1(50) O(6)
215 Park Avenue South	8.18	8.15	21,337,172.48	Fixed 30/360	L(53), O(3
Hartford Marriott Farmington	8.35	8.22	20,605,451.04	Fixed 30/360	YM^1(49) O(6)
Franklin Commons Apartments	8.63	8.49	20,432,797.29	Fixed 30/360	YM^1(48) O(6)
Fairfield Place Shopping Center	7.80	7.70	18,353,640.51	Fixed 30/360	YM^1(210 O(3)
Highland Glen & Highland Ridge	8.47	8.44	19,202,072.64	Fixed 30/360	YM^1(63) O(3)
Northville Centre	8.00	7.97	18,837,599.65	Fixed 30/360	L(51), O(5
Holtze Executive Place	9.37	9.24	17,836,322.64	Fixed 30/360	YM^1(47) O(6)
Capital Parkview and Manahawin	8.54	8.41	17,831,972.56	Fixed act/360	YM^1(50) O(6)
Continental Plaza	8.23	8.10	17,366,698.47	Fixed 30/360	YM^1(50) O(6)
Central Valley Plaza Shopping Center	8.46	8.32	17,075,097.09	Fixed 30/360	YM^1(117 O(120)
Aggregate Loan Level Information	9.50	9.49	0	Fixed 30/360	Due
Olympia House	8.85	8.75	14,140,352.47	Fixed 30/360	YM^1(26) O(3)
1050 17th Street NW	8.50	8.47	14,505,223.02	Fixed 30/360	L(53), O(3
Encino Town Center	8.13	7.99	13,767,105.34	Fixed 30/360	YM^1(50) O(6)
Embassy Tower Apartments	8.70	8.67	13,580,213.48	Fixed 30/360	L(49), O(3
Farmer's Market III Office Building	7.99	7.86	12,714,172.68	Fixed 30/360	YM^1(80) O(36)
369 Lexington Avenue	8.94	8.93	0	Fixed 30/360	YM^1(45) O(6)
Hillsdale Manor Care Center	8.76	8.63	12,487,802.15	Fixed act/360	YM^1(31) O(84)

TABLE 23.5 *(Continued)*

Name	Gross Coupon (%)	Net Coupon (%)	Current Balance ($)	Rate Type	Remaining Terms
The Atriums Retirement Center	8.10	8.00	11,731,384.11	Fixed 30/360	YM^1(70), O(3)
Holiday Inn Arlington at Ballston	9.06	8.93	11,661,997.66	Fixed 30/360	YM^1(112), O(60)
Shelbourne Square Shop Center	8.42	8.39	11,868,765.87	Fixed 30/360	L(55)
1400 Marina Way South	8.01	7.95	11,325,867.27	Fixed 30/360	YM(51), O(6)
Winsom Village (Mt. Clemens MHP)	8.37	8.36	0	Fixed 30/360	O(14)
Condyne Freezers Inc.	9.53	9.50	10,968,670.34	Fixed 30/360	L(51), O(3)
Sunset Village	8.91	8.90	0	Fixed 30/360	Due
Aggregate Loan Level Information	9.13	8.99	10,683,917.08	Fixed 30/360	YM^1(13), O(7)
Mount Pocono Plaza	8.24	8.21	10,805,255.98	Fixed 30/360	L(55)
ShopRite/Grade-A Plaza	8.65	8.55	9,147,027.00	Fixed 30/360	YM^1(124), O(4)
Eastgate Pavilion	7.65	7.55	8,094,129.56	Fixed 30/360	YM^1(92), O(5)
Monticello West	8.09	8.06	10,109,241.95	Fixed 30/360	L(54)
Builders Square #1310	8.13	8.10	10,057,939.63	Fixed 30/360	L(54), O(3)
Vineyard Valley Center	8.62	8.59	9,893,281.17	Fixed 30/360	L(55)
CarMax	7.88	7.73	9,210,790.94	Fixed act/360	L(200)
Avon Marketplace	9.65	9.55	8,796,588.60	Fixed 30/360	YM^1(134), O(5)
Memorial Club Apartments	7.68	7.65	9,741,069.44	Fixed 30/360	L(55), O(3)

York is still quite large, it is considerably less than a 100 percent concentration factor (which is often referred to as a "pure-play" strategy).

In addition to spatial diversification, CMBS pools can be diversified across property types. Rating agencies tend to require lower levels of credit enhancement for deals that contain diversification across property types since a pool that is diversified across residential, office, industrial, and retail will likely avoid the potential of a national glut in one of the sectors (such as the retail market).

The degree of property type diversification can be seen in Table 23.1. A more detailed description of individual property names and locations, as well as characteristics for the GMAC 1997–C1 deal can be found in Table 23.5 and Table 23.6. Approximately 25.5 percent of the loans are retail properties,

TABLE 23.6 Characteristics of Top 40 Loans in GMAC 1997-C1 Deal: Performance Level

Name	Cutoff Occupancy	Current Occupancy
Crossroads Tower	0.87	0.93
Circuit City HQ (Deep Run III)	1.00	1.00
Aggregate Loan Level Information	0.00	0.00
Gateway Industrial Center	0.96	0.78
Amboy Care Center Rosewood Manor	0.00	0.83
215 Park Avenue South	0.98	0.94
Hartford Marriott Farmington	NA	0.66
Franklin Commons Apartments	0.96	0.95
Fairfield Place Shopping Center	0.99	0.99
Highland Glen & Highland Ridge	0.86	0.88
Northville Centre	1.00	1.00
Holtze Executive Place	NA	0.89
Capital Parkview and Manahawin	0.00	0.87
Continental Plaza	1.00	1.00
Central Valley Plaza Shopping Center	1.00	0.99
Aggregate Loan Level Information	0.00	1.00
Olympia House	0.99	0.95
1050 17th Street NW	0.94	0.98
Encino Town Center	0.93	0.86
Embassy Tower Apartments	0.96	0.95
Farmer's Market III Office Building	1.00	1.00
369 Lexington Avenue	1.00	0.97
Hillsdale Manor Care Center	0.86	0.70
The Atriums Retirement Center	0.99	0.96
Holiday Inn Arlington at Ballston	NA	0.72
Shelbourne Square Shop Center	0.97	0.97
1400 Marina Way South	1.00	1.00
Winsom Village (Mt. Clemens MHP)	0.81	1.00
Condyne Freezers Inc.	1.00	1.00
Sunset Village	0.86	1.00
Aggregate Loan Level Information	0.00	0.90
Mount Pocono Plaza	1.00	0.99
ShopRite/Grade-A Plaza	0.98	0.98
Eastgate Pavilion	1.00	1.00
Monticello West	0.91	0.65
Builders Square #1310	1.00	0.97
Vineyard Valley Center	0.85	1.00
CarMax	1.00	1.00
Avon Marketplace	1.00	1.00
Memorial Club Apartments	0.97	0.87

Cutoff DSCR	Current DSCR	Cutoff LTV	Servicer Status
1.34	1.41	0.72	Perform
NA	NA	NA	Perform
1.31	1.56	0.80	Special
1.27	1.06	0.80	Grace
1.41	1.17	0.79	Perform
1.26	2.64	0.53	Perform
1.44	1.84	0.69	Perform
1.25	1.80	0.72	Perform
1.30	1.65	0.73	Perform
1.19	1.52	0.82	Grace
1.27	1.37	0.79	Perform
1.40	1.15	0.66	Perform
1.39	2.34	0.79	Perform
1.36	1.79	0.75	Perform
1.25	1.32	0.70	Perform
1.11	0.26	0.66	Matured
1.24	2.70	0.58	Grace
1.27	1.76	0.71	Perform
1.57	1.76	0.55	Grace
1.25	1.44	0.74	Perform
1.11	1.28	0.80	Perform
1.13	0.13	0.71	Prepaid
1.53	0.87	0.64	Grace
1.32	1.65	0.73	Perform
1.33	2.45	0.65	Perform
1.30	1.42	0.75	Grace
1.25	1.50	0.74	Grace
1.18	0.88	0.64	Prepaid
1.40	1.24	0.71	Grace
1.15	0.61	0.69	Matured
1.29	1.50	0.71	Grace
1.28	1.75	0.77	Grace
1.56	1.82	0.52	Perform
1.23	1.35	0.62	Perform
1.45	1.25	0.79	Perform
1.28	1.41	0.79	Perform
1.25	1.78	0.73	Perform
1.00	0.99	0.89	Perform
1.25	1.29	0.65	Perform
1.16	1.48	0.83	Perform

18.8 percent multifamily properties, 18.0 percent office properties, and 10.2 percent industrial properties. The GMAC 1999-C1 deal has reduced the risk of default by not being heavily concentrated in only one of the property groups.

Cross-Collateralization

Diversification of the underlying collateral is one way of reducing default risk. Another way to reduce default risk is to use cross-collateralization. Cross-collateralization means that the properties that serve as collateral for the individual loans are pledged against each loan. Thus, the cash flows on several properties can be used to make loan payments on a property that has insufficient funds to make a loan payment. This "pooling" mechanism reduces the risk of default. To add some additional enforcement penalties to the cross-collateralization mechanism, the lender can use cross-default, whereby the lender can call each loan within the pool, when any one defaults. With regard to the GMAC 1997-C1 deal, there were 355 loans based on 380 properties, which indicates that there may be some cross-collateralization.

Loan Performance

By November 2002, only 303 of the 355 original loans were remaining. Of the 303 loans still remaining, 1 loan was in foreclosure, 9 loans were with the special servicer, and 122 loans were in "grace," while 171 loans were still performing. Of the 52 loans that left the pool, 8 loans had matured and 44 loans had prepaid. As we would expect, the loans that prepaid were primarily those with yield maintenance; no loans with lockout prepaid. Figure 23.1 indicates that the remaining loan balance on the underlying loan pool is declining over time (as a function of prepayments, loan maturing, and loan amortization). Figure 23.2 depicts the 1-month conditional prepayment rate (CPR) (with its jagged spikes) and 90+ day delinquencies.

Stress Testing at the Loan Level

Stress testing the collateral in a CMBS deal is important from both the underwriter's and investor's perspective. By allowing the forecasts on net operating income and value to be varied over time, underwriters and investors can better understand the default and extension risk likelihoods and how these in turn impact CMBS cash flows.

For CMBS markets, stress tests must be performed in a manner that is consistent with modern portfolio theory. While diversification across property type and economic region reduces the default risk of the underlying loan pool, the effects of diversification are negated if the stress test ignores the covariance between the properties. For example, there should be some degree of common variance across all properties (reflecting general economic

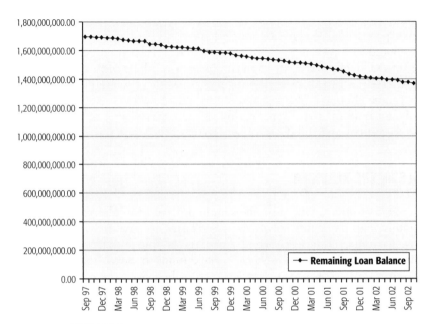

FIGURE 23.1   Remaining loan balance for GMAC 1997-C1.

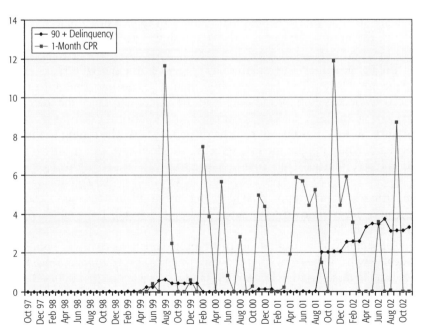

FIGURE 23.2   90+ day delinquency and 1-month CPR for GMAC 1997-C1.

conditions). Furthermore, there should be some degree of common variance across property type and economic regions.

In addition to being able to create a diversification index, the user can construct a default risk/extension risk index as well. As the underlying loans are stressed, a distribution of outcomes in terms of default and extension risk can be obtained. This distribution would allow users to compare CMBS deals not only for the diversification of the underlying loan portfolio, but also to compare CMBS deals for sensitivity to the stress test.

ROLE OF THE SERVICER

The servicer on a CMBS deal plays an important role. The servicer collects monthly loan payments, keeps records relating to payments, maintains escrow accounts, monitors the condition of underlying properties, prepares reports for the trustee, and transfers collected funds to the trustee for payment.

There are three types of servicers: the subservicer, the master servicer, and the special servicer. The **subservicer** is typically the loan originator in a conduit deal who has decided to sell the loan but retain the servicing. The **subservicer** will then send all payments and property information to the **master servicer**. The master servicer oversees the deal and makes sure the servicing agreements are maintained. In addition, the master servicer must facilitate the timely payment of interest and principal. When a loan goes into default, the master servicer has the responsibility to provide for servicing advances.

Unlike the subservicer and the master servicer, the **special servicer** enters the picture when a loan becomes more than 60 days past due. Often, the special servicer is empowered to extend the loan, restructure the loan, and foreclose on the loan (and sell the property). This critical role is of great importance to the subordinated tranche owners because the timing of the loss can significantly impact the loss severity, which in turn can greatly impact subordinated returns. Thus, first-loss investors usually want either to control the appointment of the special servicer or to perform the role themselves. This situation creates a potential moral hazard problem since the special servicer may act in its own self-interest and potentially at the expense of the other tranche holders.

Although CMBS deals tend to be prepayment insensitive, bonds (or tranches) will still be somewhat sensitive to interest-rate changes since lockouts usually dissolve after 10 years. Default risk is a concern with CMBS and the underlying collateral needs to be examined on a loan-by-loan basis.

CREATING A COMMERCIAL MORTGAGE-BACKED SECURITIES MODEL

While there are a number of prepayment models for agency MBS (discussed in previous chapters), the development of models for CMBS is substantially more difficult. The reason for the difficulty is the forecast of credit-related problems on the individual properties underlying the CMBS deals. Furthermore, delinquencies and foreclosures on commercial loans contain idiosyncratic risks that are location specific (hence the need for the diversification strategies discussed previously).

Any model of CMBS should include the following:

- An econometric model of historical loan performance using logit or proportional-hazards models. This method permits a better understanding of property and loan attributes that predict default and prepayment (see Ambrose and Sanders, 2001, for a discussion of hazards models applied to CMBS loans).
- If default does occur, empirical estimates of loss severity by property type and state are needed.
- Database of actual net operating income (*NOI and value volatility*) by property type and geographic location. This step permits the construction of default-risk indicators.
- Monte Carlo simulation of interest rates and NOI paths to estimate foreclosure frequency and prepayment risk.
- Finally, the deal structure (and waterfalls) should interface cleanly with loan-by-loan simulations.

A CMBS model with these features should be able to capture the critical elements of pricing, risk, and return. Of course, exposure to tenant risk (such as Kmart) should be included as well.

THE FUTURE OF COMMERCIAL MORTGAGE-BACKED SECURITIES

Growth in the CMBS market is a function of the ability of the economy to generate new commercial real estate loans. With an economic slowdown and a contraction in the commercial real estate market in terms of new construction, CMBS issuance will be quite cyclical. As the economy rebounds and the inventory of existing properties are absorbed into the market, construction will likely increase again as will the issuance of CMBS products.

Of particular interest is the international CMBS market. This market has lagged behind the American CMBS market; however, there is growing international demand for a CMBS-type market in a number of countries, particularly in European countries and Japan. As China continues to privatize its real estate markets, an excellent opportunity for REIT-type and CMBS-type securities unfolds.

EXERCISES

Exercise 23.1 In the GMAC 1997-C1 deal, the subordination level is 28.5 percent for the triple-A bonds (or tranches), meaning that 28.5 percent of the underlying loans must default before the losses impact the triple-A bonds. For the bonds in the following deal (GMAC 1999-C3), what is the subordination for the triple-A-rated bonds (A-1-a, A-1-b, and A-2)?

Bond	Moody's Rating	Fitch Rating	Original Amount ($)	Coupon	Coupon Type
A-1-a	Aaa	AAA	50,000,000	0.0697	Fixed
A-1-b	Aaa	AAA	190,976,000	0.0727	Fixed
A-2	Aaa	AAA	600,000,000	0.0718	Fixed
B	Aa2	AA	51,840,000	0.0754	Fixed
C	A2	A	57,601,000	0.0779	Fixed
D	A3	A-	20,160,000	0.0779	WAC-0b
E	Baa2	BBB	37,440,000	0.0779	WAC-0b
F	Baa3	BBB-	23,040,000	0.0779	WAC-0b
G	NA	NA	57,601,000	0.0697	Fixed
H	NA	NA	8,640,000	0.0697	Fixed
J	NA	NA	11,520,000	0.0697	Fixed
K	NA	NA	14,400,000	0.0697	Fixed
L	NA	NA	11,520,000	0.0697	Fixed
M	NA	NA	5,760,000	0.0697	Fixed
N	NA	NA	11,524,048	0.0697	Fixed
X	NA	NA	1,152,022,048n	0.0053	WAC/IO
R	NA	NA	0r	0	

Notes: n = notional amount; r = residual.

(◎) **Exercise 23.2**   In the GMAC 1999-C3 deal in Exercise 23.1, only the bonds from A to F are rated, whereas the bonds from G to R are not rated. What is the reason for the lack of bond ratings on the G through R bonds?

(◎) **Exercise 23.3**   In Figure 23.1, the 90+ delinquency and 1-month CPR for GMAC 1997-C1 are depicted. How does the 1-month CPR for a CMBS deal typically differ from a 1-month CPR for an agency MBS pass-through in terms of smoothness of the curve? What does that difference say about pre-payments on CMBS versus prepayments on residential mortgages?

Exercise 23.4   For the underlying loans in Tables 23.4 through 23.6, there are several different originators. How does the loan performance in this par-ticular deal (for the top 40 loans only) vary across originators?

CHAPTER **24**

The Role of Real Estate Investment Trusts (REITs)

Real estate investment trusts (REITs) are essentially closed-end funds that hold real estate in their portfolios instead of stocks and bonds. As a consequence, they represent an alternative form of securitization. REITs can hold real property (e.g., shopping centers, hotels, and office buildings); shareholders in the REIT then share in the cash flows to the REIT as well as capital appreciation (on sale of the asset). Hence, REITs represent one of the earliest examples of securitizing real properties into securities.

BACKGROUND

REITs were made possible by Congress in 1960, when it passed the Real Estate Investment Trust Act. This act enabled companies to raise large pools of funds by selling shares of beneficial interest. These shares could be purchased by small investors who would ordinarily be unable to participate in real property investment because of the large sums involved.

By the 1990s, financial institutions such as pension funds, insurance companies, and corporations found that they could sell their real property to REITs, thereby achieving liquidity. Futhermore, the REITs have a comparative advantage in the management of real property, whereas the insurance companies, pension funds, and corporations have a varying degree of expertise. A number of insurance companies, pension funds, and corporations exchanged their real property with REITs for shares in the REIT. In fact, the 1990s saw a dramatic surge in the number of initial public offerings (IPOs) in part due to the dramatic increase in the number of financial institutions removing relatively illiquid real property from their balance sheets in exchange for (it was hoped) more liquid REIT shares. Thus, REITs represent a slightly different way for financial institutions to securitize their balance sheets.

QUALIFYING AS A REAL ESTATE INVESTMENT TRUST

A REIT is a trust legally established to raise capital from investors (in the form of common stock and bond issuance) and to borrow from lenders in order to buy income-producing properties or make mortgage loans in varying maturities. A REIT is allowed a special tax status; that is, it is only taxed at corporate rates on its retained earnings (annual) if it meets the following three general conditions:

1. A REIT is legally required to pay virtually all of its taxable income (90 percent) to its shareholders every year.
2. A REIT's assets are primarily composed of real estate held for the long term.
3. A REIT's income is mainly derived from real estate.

TAX RAMIFICATIONS FOR REAL ESTATE INVESTMENT TRUSTS

Generally, most REITs will adhere to the above rules to reduce taxes in the event operating income is realized during a particular year.

1. It should be pointed out that since some REITs own properties, they are entitled to depreciate them and consequently may show an operating loss for the year for tax purposes, while producing actual cash available for distribution. However, since REITs are tax-exempt, the value of this deduction is questionable.
2. Tax laws allow REITs to distribute any losses to shareholders to the extent of showing a zero net income for the year.

TYPES OF REAL ESTATE INVESTMENT TRUSTS

There are four different types of REITs, ranging from REITs that invest in real property such as office buildings, shopping centers, and apartment complexes to mortgage REITs that either invest in mortgage-backed securities (MBS) or lend funds to real estate developers or investors for the purchase of real property. As we expect, the return-generating process for the different types of REITs varies quite a bit.

Equity Trusts   The trust's assets are invested in ownership claims to various types of property, such as residential, industrial, commercial property, or vacant land. This type of REIT is the most common, although less so during the 1970s.

Mortgage Trusts   The assets of the trust are invested in mortgages or other claims where interest is the source of income (along with discounts and other commission earned). The mortgages can be in the form of single-family MBS or commercial mortgage-backed securities (CMBS). In addition, these REITs may make loans to real estate developers (see Specialized Trusts) or long-term investors.

Hybrid Trusts   These trusts invest in both equity interests and mortgages, and offer the investor the advantage of offsetting interest income from the flow-through of depreciation. Hybrid trusts offer diversification to investors, although alternative sources of diversification are available elsewhere at a reduced cost.

Specialized Trusts   These trusts invest in development and construction, for example. They may also be involved in sale and lease-back arrangements, or may specialize in making term mortgages of up to 5 years, usually on construction and development projects.

REAL ESTATE INVESTMENT TRUST STRUCTURES

In addition to alternative REIT types, there are alternative REIT structures such as Umbrella Partnership Real Estate Investment Trusts (UPREIT) and DownREITs.* The purpose of these structures is to encourage the transfer of an existing partnership (which is a common form of ownership of real property) to a REIT form of ownership. The UPREIT structure was partially responsible for the dramatic growth of REITs (and its subsequent decline) in the 1990s.

Umbrella Partnership Real Estate Investment Trust

In an UPREIT structure, the partners of the existing partnerships and a newly formed REIT become partners in a new partnership that is termed "the operating partnership." The partners contribute the properties from the existing partnership and the REIT contributes the cash proceeds from its public offering. Typically, the REIT is the general partner and the majority owner of the operating partnership units. The partners may sell their units for either cash or REIT shares (at the option of the REIT or operating partnership).

---

*A DownREIT structure is analogous to an UPREIT and was created for those REITs that did not have an umbrella group.

DownREIT

A DownREIT is structured in a similar fashion to an UPREIT, however, the
REIT owns and operates properties directly rather than only its interest in a
controlled partnership that owns and operates separate properties.

PROPERTY TYPES

Table 24.1 provides a list of REITs by property type. As the table shows, industrial and office properties are the most common category of REIT, consisting of $48.7 billion in market capitalization. The next two largest

TABLE 24.1 Constituent Companies and Relative Weights in the NAREIT Index
for May 1, 2002

Number of REITs	Company Summary by Property Sector and Subsector	Equity Market Capitalization[a]	
		Millions of Dollars	Percent of Total
34	Industrial/office	48,697.1	28.5891
19	Office	29,699.9	17.4362
7	Industrial	9,594.1	5.6325
8	Mixed	9,403.1	5.5204
42	Retail	36,870.5	21.6459
27	Shopping centers	17,815.3	10.4590
10	Regional malls	16,491.7	9.6819
5	Free standing	2,563.4	1.5049
24	Residential	33,350.8	19.5796
19	Apartments	30,822.6	18.0953
5	Manufactured homes	2,528.2	1.4842
20	Diversified	13,747.6	8.0709
16	Lodging/resorts	10,291.2	6.0417
3	Self-Storage	5,864.2	3.4428
12	Health care	8,509.4	4.9957
8	Specialty	6,934.4	4.0711
20	Mortgage	6,069.4	3.5632
13	Home financing	4,247.5	2.4936
7	Commercial financing	1,822.0	1.0696
179	Industry totals	170,334.7	100.0000

Source: NAREIT.
[a]Ranked by property sector/subsector and equity market capitalization in millions of dollars;
April 30, 2002.

categories include retail and residential sectors, representing $36.9 billion and $33.4 billion, respectively. Table 24.2 provides a summary of the largest REITs that exist in the office-property sector. The first two REITs in the list are by far the largest and together account for almost 10 percent of the entire market capitalization. The largest seven REITs in the industrial-property sector are shown in Table 24.3, with ProLogis Trust accounting for the largest REIT at 2.3 percent of market capitalization.

TABLE 24.2 Largest REITs in the Industrial/Office Sector

| Property Sector: Industrial/Office | Ticker Symbols | Equity Market Capitalization[a] | | |
		Millions of Dollars	Percent of Subsector	Percent of Total
1 Equity Office Properties Trust	EOP	11,868.5	39.9616	6.9678
2 Boston Properties, Inc.	BXP	3,538.6	11.9146	2.0775
3 CarrAmerica Realty Corporation	CRE	1,994.0	6.7139	1.1706
4 Mack-Cali Realty Corporation	CLI	1,867.1	6.2865	1.0961
5 Arden Realty Group, Inc.	ARI	1,795.8	6.0466	1.0543
6 Highwoods Properties, Inc.	HIW	1,487.3	5.0078	0.8732
7 Prentiss Properties Trust	PP	1,281.2	4.3139	0.7522
8 HRPT Properties Trust	HRP	1,118.1	3.7645	0.6564
9 SL Green Realty Corp.	SLG	1,054.5	3.5505	0.6191
10 Brandywine Realty Trust	BDN	848.9	2.8583	0.4984
11 Alexandria Real Estate Equities, Inc.	ARE	738.7	2.4873	0.4337
12 Glenborough Realty Trust Incorporated	GLB	618.3	2.0817	0.3630
13 Koger Equity, Inc.	KE	389.0	1.3099	0.2284
14 Parkway Properties, Inc.	PKY	338.8	1.1407	0.1989
15 Corporate Office Properties Trust	OFC	307.0	1.0336	0.1802
16 Great Lakes REIT	GL	267.9	0.9020	0.1573
17 Prime Group Realty Trust	PGE	131.1	0.4415	0.0770
18 AmeriVest Properties, Inc.	AMV	41.2	0.1387	0.0242
19 Maxus Realty Trust Inc.	MRTI	13.7	0.0462	0.0081
19 **Subsector Totals**		**29,699.9**	**100.0000**	**17.4362**

Source: NAREIT.
[a]Ranked by property sector/subsector and equity market capitalization in millions of dollars; April 30, 2001.

TABLE 24.3 Largest REITs in the Industrial Sector

Property Sector: Industrial	Ticker Symbols	Equity Market Capitalization[a]		
		Millions of Dollars	Percent of Subsector	Percent of Total
1 ProLogis Trust	PLD	3,932.7	40.9910	2.3088
2 AMB Property Corp.	AMB	2,360.0	24.5982	1.3855
3 First Industrial Realty Trust, Inc.	FR	1,309.9	13.6535	0.7690
4 CenterPoint Properties Trust	CNT	1,250.1	13.0293	0.7339
5 EastGroup Properties, Inc.	EGP	401.1	4.1804	0.2355
6 Keystone Property Trust	KTR	278.3	2.9003	0.1634
7 Monmouth Real Estate Investment Corp.	MNRT.A	62.1	0.6474	0.0365
		9,594.1	**100.0000**	**5.6325**

Source: NAREIT.
[a]Ranked by property sector/subsector and equity market capitalization in millions of dollars; April 30, 2002.

A BIT OF HISTORY

REITs were one of the hottest investment alternatives in the early 1970s. However, by the second last half of 1973 REITs were one of the fastest declining investments in the United States. What happened?

The rapid decline of REITs was caused by short-term construction and development REITs. These REITs would borrow funds from a bank (say, at 6 percent) and lend to a firm building a shopping center (say, at 12 percent). If the project was successful and the firm paid off the construction loan, the REIT would clear 6 percent. In a booming economy (1971–1973), few projects defaulted and every loan application looked like a winner. However, the oil embargo struck in 1973 and real estate projects ground to a screeching halt. The number of defaults skyrocketed and REITs' values plunged. By 1975, numerous REITs had filed for bankruptcy, leading investors to be wary of using REITs as an investment vehicle. This situation led to construction and development REITs exiting the market and reappearing as equity REITs.

It took several years for investors to regain confidence in the REIT market since the "new" equity REITs contained a large concentration of defaulted properties (such as half-built sites). The real estate recession of the late 1980s and early 1990s (caused by an oversupply of commercial properties, particularly office properties, and an economic slowdown) left financial institutions holding underperforming properties. With the recovering economy, financial institutions found it profitable to securitize their holdings of real property and sell them to REITs (or to use the UPREIT structure to change from a partnership to a REIT form of ownership). Essentially, the attraction of real property securitization led to a dramatic growth in the REIT industry. Figure 24.1 depicts the pronounced bubble in the REIT market during 1993 and 1994.

When securities experience abnormally high growth in returns, mean reversion (the tendency for interest rates and security returns to return to their long-run mean or average) kicks in. Accordingly, the REIT market suffered a sharp decline in 1998 (see Figure 24.2). It is interesting to note that the REIT bubble burst prior to the Russian Credit Crisis of 1998 and the slump continued until the year 2000. However, since 2000, REITs have experienced a resurgence that has outperformed the S&P 500 index.

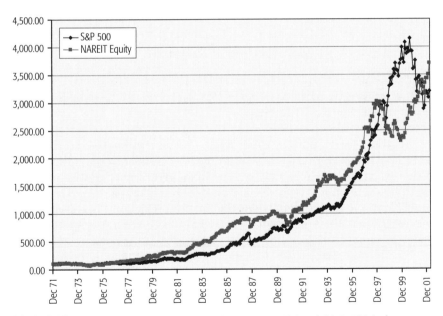

FIGURE 24.1 $100 invested in the NAREIT Equity REIT and S&P 500 indexes at the end of December 1971.

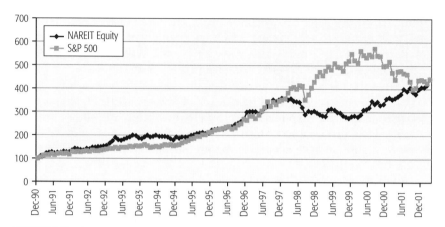

FIGURE 24.2 $100 invested in the NAREIT Equity REIT and S&P 500 indexes at the end of December 1990.

REAL ESTATE INVESTMENT TRUST INITIAL PUBLIC OFFERINGS

As mentioned in the previous section, the bubble or run-up in REIT returns was the result of the recovering property markets in conjunction with the advent of the UPREIT structure. The renewed interest in real estate and REITs led to a boom in IPOs for REITs in 1993 and 1994. In particular, 88 REIT IPOs were brought to the markets in 1993 and 1994 alone. In addition, the initial returns on the REIT IPOs were 2.68 percent and 3.26 percent, respectively, for 1993 and 1994.

As can be seen in Table 24.4, REIT IPO activity slowed in 1995 and 1996 as REIT performance relative to the S&P 500 index diminished. IPO activity increased again in 1997 with an initial return of 7.26 percent. However, the slump in REITs at the end of 1997 resulted in another slowdown in REIT IPO activity with only one IPO in 1999. Thus, REITs are subject to waves. In fact, three noticeable waves have occurred since 1980: 1985, 1993–1994, and 1997.

The bottom line for REITs is that the REIT IPO activity of the 1980s and 1990s has increased the number of REITs available in the marketplace and has increased the liquidity of REITs in the secondary market. However, it is important to note that REIT liquidity is substantially lower than the liquidity for other stocks such as those in the Dow Jones Industrials. However, REITs provide institutional investors with better liquidity than they can receive by direct ownership in the underlying real estate.

TABLE 24.4 REIT IPO History

Time Period	Initial Return (%)	T-stat	Observations	Average First-Week Volume in 1,000s
Entire Sample	2.00	4.34	205	
1980–1988	−1.61	−2.09	49	790
1990–1994	2.70	4.95	98	3,073
After 1994	3.87	3.63	58	5,117
By Year				
1980	−4.69	—	1	—
1981	—	—	0	—
1982	0.62	—	1	786
1983	6.45	—	1	259
1984	−7.82	−1.12	4	317
1985	−2.42	−2.33	21	1,172
1986	−0.26	−0.30	8	389
1987	−0.30	−0.63	5	1,101
1988	0.52	1.38	8	299
1989	—	—	0	—
1990	—	—	0	—
1991	−0.63	−1.00	3	582
1992	1.03	1.10	7	1,525
1993	2.68	3.52	48	3,847
1994	3.26	3.42	40	2,621
1995	2.07	1.25	8	1,627
1996	0.74	0.21	6	3,606
1997	7.26	4.01	25	7,010
1998	1.11	0.71	18	4,104
1999	2.06	—	1	10,012

Source: R.J. Buttimer, D.C. Hyland, and A.B. Sanders, "The Long-Run Performance of REIT IPOs," Dice Center Working Paper, The Ohio State University, October 2001.

INTERNATIONAL REAL ESTATE RETURN PERFORMANCE

While REITs in the United States have performed reasonably well (compared to the S&P 500 index) since 1980, property market companies in other countries have not fared so well. As can be seen in Table 24.5, the average monthly return from 1990 to 2001 for REITs was 1.211 percent with a

TABLE 24.5   International Real Estate Returns, February 1990 to December 2001

Country	Mean	Std Dev	Skew	[p-val]	Ex Kurt	[p-val]
Australia	0.879	4.701	−0.315	0.27	0.522	0.40
Belgium	−0.105	4.859	−0.292	0.28	1.757	0.19
France	0.328	4.618	−0.040	0.47	0.457	0.41
Germany	0.381	6.510	−0.019	0.49	3.525	0.04
Hong Kong	0.909	11.533	−0.066	0.45	2.817	0.08
Italy	0.236	7.693	1.108	0.01	2.652	0.09
Japan	−0.702	10.328	−0.021	0.48	0.904	0.33
Netherlands	−0.065	3.628	−0.214	0.33	0.257	0.45
Singapore	−0.244	12.964	−0.054	0.46	2.733	0.09
Spain	0.108	8.183	−0.304	0.27	0.589	0.38
Sweden	−1.167	10.335	0.039	0.47	4.159	0.02
Switzerland	0.175	5.023	0.289	0.28	0.595	0.38
United Kingdom	0.200	5.369	−0.298	0.28	−0.292	0.44
United States	1.211	4.066	0.148	0.38	0.594	0.38
MSCI Global	0.595	4.079	−0.789	0.06	1.211	0.27

Source: S.A. Bond, G.A. Karolyi, and A.B. Sanders, "International Real Estate Returns: A Multifactor, Multicountry Approach," *Real Estate Economics*, forthcoming.

standard deviation of 4.066. The Pacific Basin countries, Australia and Hong Kong, had average returns slightly below the United States at 0.879 percent and 0.909 percent, respectively. While Australia's standard deviation is similar to the REIT standard deviation (4.701 versus 4.066), Hong Kong's standard deviation is dramatically higher at 11.533. The other Pacific Basin countries, Japan and Singapore, have had relatively poor performance on their property company stocks.

European property companies have substantially underperformed their U.S. counterparts. Each of the European Union countries had average returns below that of the MSCI Global index. Of course, the relatively poor performance of European Union stocks during the same period in part explains the relatively low returns for European Union property stocks.

Table 24.6 depicts the results from a Jensen's alpha test for REIT and property company performance. REITs generated a significantly positive alpha (meaning that REITs outperformed the MSCI Global index) for the 1990–2001 period. Sweden suffered the only significantly negative alpha (indicating statistically significant underperformance). One explanation for Sweden's underperformance was the withdrawl of funds by one of the market's leading investors (from Japan); however, this explanation does not

TABLE 24.6 International Real Estate Returns, February 1990 to December 2001

Country	α_i		β_{iw}		Adj R^2
Australia	0.354		0.559	**	0.23
Belgium	−0.562		0.259	**	0.04
France	−0.143		0.320	**	0.08
Germany	−0.011		−0.032		−0.01
Hong Kong	0.199		1.385	**	0.24
Italy	−0.275		0.499	**	0.07
Japan	−1.349		1.106	**	0.19
Netherlands	−0.523		0.264	**	0.08
Singapore	−1.047		1.799	**	0.32
Spain	−0.492		0.898	**	0.20
Sweden	−1.774	*	0.926	**	0.13
Switzerland	−0.276		0.229	*	0.03
United Kingdom	−0.286		0.384	**	0.08
United States	0.728	*	0.372	**	0.14

Source: S.A. Bond, G.A. Karolyi, and A.B. Sanders, "International Real Estate Returns: A Multifactor, Multicountry Approach," Dice Center Working Paper, The Ohio State University, October 2001.

Notes: Estimates from the single factor mode $R_{it} - R_{ft} = \alpha_i + \beta_{iw} [R_{wt} - R_{ft}] + \sigma_{it}$ are reported. The statistical significance of the coefficients is indicated beside each estimate. ** indicates significance at 1% level and * indicates significance at 5% level.

offer any further understanding as to why other investors did not bid the stocks back up in price.

Despite the lackluster performance of international property stocks, additional property company stocks make their appearance every year. As the popularity of property company stocks increases and the European Union (and U.S.) equity markets make a comeback, the European Union property company stocks should begin to approximate REITs in terms of risk and return.

REAL ESTATE INVESTMENT TRUST VALUATION

Unlike the MBS and asset-backed securities (ABS) products discussed in this book, REITs are valued in a fashion similar to common stocks. Given that REITs typically have a very high dividend yield (90 percent of taxable income must be passed through to shareholders as a dividend), REITs are typically valued at a present value of their expected dividend stream. However, certain adjustments must be made to REIT dividend streams before calculating their present value.

One of the more interesting elements of REIT valuation is the adjustments that must be made. As with most common stocks, the calculation of net income to common shareholder is a straightforward exercise (revenues less expenses). However, since the majority of REITs hold a large percentage of their portfolio in depreciable assets (real property), the typical net income calculation will greatly understate the cash flows. As a consequence, net income has to be adjusted for sales of property plus depreciation and amortization; the resulting calculation generates what is known as **funds from operations** (FFO). Stated differently, FFO is equal to net income, excluding gains or losses from sales of property, and with depreciation added back.

The next step is to calculate cash available for distribution (CAD). CAD is a measure of the REIT's ability to generate cash and to distribute dividends to its shareholders. CAD is derived by subtracting nonrecurring expenditures.

A further refinement on the REIT's cash flow is adjusted funds from operations (AFFO). AFFO refers to a further adjustment by subtracting from FFO both (1) normalized recurring expenditures that are capitalized by the REIT and then amortized, but that are necessary to maintain a REIT's properties and its revenue stream, and (2) "straight-lining" of rents (straight-lining averages the tenant's rent payments over the life of the lease).

An example of a REIT valuation (the actual name of the REIT has been changed to protect the innocent) is presented in Table 24.7. Net income to shareholders is $28,200. Given that depreciation is $23,254, it is clear that the non-cash-flow entry greatly distorts the actual cash flow available.

TABLE 24.7   Income Statement for Asbury Park Properties

Asbury Park Properties

Operating income and expenses		2001 Totals
Revenues:		
	Minimum rents	81,896
	Percentage rents	2,254
	Other rents	712
	Tenant reimbursements	37,215
	Management & leasing fees	2,889
	Development fees	293
	Interest & other	4,457
	Acquisition & development income	759
	Total revenue	130,475

Expenses:

	Property operating & maintenance	(39,135)
	% of total revenue	29.99%
	Management expenses	0
	% of total revenue	0.00%
	Acq. & dev. operating expenses	(220)

Net Operating Income   91,119
 % of total revenue   69.84%

Other Expenses
 General & administrative   (8,326)
             Percent of total revenue   6.38%

 Depreciation &
  amortization   (23,254)
 Other   (715)
 Interest Expense   (32,375)
 G&A from acquisitions
  & developments   (51)
             Total other expenses   (64,722)

 Gain on sale of assets
  (not in FFO)   2,235
 Equity earnings in
  unconsolidated affil.   2,254
 Write-off of development
  costs   0
 Straight-line rent
  adjustment   (1,150)
 Minority interest & other   (1,536)
Net income to common shareholders   28,200

Funds from operations   51,455
 Other   0
 Capital expenditures   (6,633)
 Interest rate adjustment
  (50 Basis Points)   (259)

Cash available for distribution   44,563

Shares outstanding   26,928

FFO per share $1.91
CAD per share $1.65
Dividend per share $1.59
Dividend/FFO   83.21%
Dividend/CAD   96.08%
Interest coverage ratio after Cap-Ex   2.35

Hence, FFO is calculated and is $51,455 (although this figure is adjusted to $44,563 after adjusting for capital expenditures). Therefore, using the FFO and AFFO calculations permit a greater amount of cash flows to be seen by investors as available.

A review of the spreadsheet (asbury.xls on the CD) should give an indication of how important dividends (based on leases) are for a REIT. Given the difficulty of determining the present value of future appreciation on real property, investors and analysts focus on what information is available (and more reliable). Hence, dividends (and the streams that produce them) are examined quite carefully.

It is clear that a REIT (particularly an equity REIT) is a portfolio of lease payments less expenses. Given that leases are a form of fixed income, REITs can be thought of as a portfolio of debt securities (with equity kickers). As a consequence, it is not surprising that REIT returns can largely be explained by changes in the government and corporate bond markets (see Chan, Hendershott, and Sanders [1992] and Karolyi and Sanders [1998] for a discussion of macroeconomic factors that explain REIT returns).

In performing a discounted cash valuation of expected cash flow for a REIT, it is important that the discount rate reflect the underlying nature of REITS: the underlying assets as a portfolio of leases with an equity kicker. Thus, we would expect the discount rate on REITs to be lower than that of typical stocks in the market. This expectation is validated by the beta estimate for REITs in Table 24.6, which was 0.372, indicating that REITs are "defensive" relative to the MSCI Global index. Furthermore, this beta estimate reflects the fixed-income-like performance of REITs, leading some to suggest that REIT performance and valuation should be tied to fixed-income indexes such as the Lehman government bond index rather than the S&P 500 index. In fact, Sanders (1997) demonstrates that long-term government bonds and high-yield corporate bonds explain a significant portion of REIT returns, particularly during certain subperiods.

OTHER FACTORS INFLUENCING REAL ESTATE INVESTMENT TRUST VALUATION AND PERFORMANCE

Other issues that can impact the valuation and performance of REITs are dividend policy, the advisor puzzle, organizational form, and economies of scale issues. The interested reader is advised to read *Real Estate Investment Trusts: Structure, Performance, and Investment Opportunities* by Chan, Erickson, and Wang (2003) for an in-depth discussion of these issues.

EXERCISES

⊚ **Exercise 24.1** Several universities have created student investment management programs where students engage in managing a portfolio of stocks. Fewer universities have programs where the students manage portfolios that include REITs (or manage a portfolio solely composed of REITs). Examine Figure 24.2 and discuss the success of these REIT-related portfolios with regard to when they were started: (1) January 1990, (2) December 1997, and (3) December 1999. Based on your analysis, what would you predict about the performance of a REIT portfolio started in December 1999?

⊚ **Exercise 24.2** A REIT portfolio manager can choose among several benchmarks for determining risk-adjusted performance. One choice is the S&P 500 index as a benchmark. Another choice is the NAREIT equity REIT index. Discuss which index is the most appropriate and why.

⊚ **Exercise 24.3** During the 1980 through 1988 period, REIT IPOs had a negative initial return (see Wang, Chen, and Gau [1992] for further discussion), whereas they had a positive initial return during the 1990–1994 period (see Ling and Naranjo [1999] for further discussion). The initial returns were even more positive after 1994. Can you speculate as to why the initial returns after an IPO have grown over time?

⊚ **Exercise 24.4** In Table 24.7, we calculate the FFO and CAD for Asbury Park REIT (a fictional REIT). Calculate the traditional method for reporting REIT cash flows (prior to FFO) by dividing net income to common shareholders by the number of shares outstanding. Prepare a table showing the difference between net income per share, FFO per share, and CAD per share.

The European
Securitization
Market

CHAPTER 25

Development of a Market

It is important to know the catalyst for a new market in order to understand its development. In the United States, the catalyst for securitization was the U.S. government's target for encouraging home ownership and creating a secondary market for mortgages. The government's purpose was to alleviate regional liquidity crunches. To this end, they set up various government and government-sponsored agencies, as discussed in Chapter 6. One extremely important result of this government intervention was to create a body that could set standards, which provided homogeneity in the mortgage market. Securitization, with the first mortgage-backed securities (MBS) issued in 1970, became a tool for providing liquidity. The investors for early MBS were fairly limited because a monthly paying bond with a maturity of 30 years suited only a small number of investor profiles. The market did not really take off until 1983, when collateralized-mortgage obligations (CMOs), which "structured" mortgage cash flows into different bonds with features more familiar to a larger group of investors, were created.

In Europe, there has been no government body to act as a catalyst for securitization. In most countries, larger commercial banks have issued the first MBS. Their reasons range from regulatory arbitrage to simply seeking a more diverse source of funding, often trying to appeal to international investors. In a few countries, governments have provided an important boost to the securitization market, but in a totally different way from the United States. Governments in Europe have traditionally had a large role in their respective economies, from state-owned utilities to banks, and even a large ownership in commercial and residential property. The increasing strength of the European Union (EU) in the 1990s, the advent of the euro, and the resulting stabilization pacts, have meant that many European governments have been faced with a funding dilemma for their state-owned companies. Their need to reduce balance-sheet debt has meant a large amount of privatization and securitization.

The lack of a large powerful body to provide for homogenization and standards and the differing legal frameworks in each European government provide a very different setting for securitization than in the United States. Europe is able to make use of the U.S. knowledge base, but must alter it to fit specific European needs. Europe does not have a pass-through type MBS market, for example. Almost all MBS have been issued CMO-style, with hedges in place to provide quarterly paying floating-rate bonds, and different types of options to create shorter maturities. Moreover, prepayment risk, a driving factor in the U.S. market, is almost entirely absent in European MBS. Any prepayment risk is either retained by the originator or hedged by third parties.

MBS from different countries, and indeed from different issuers within one country, can be very dissimilar. This makes it difficult to provide benchmarking for investors. Finally, there is a huge lack of statistics on underlying assets, making it necessary to do significant due diligence on each and every MBS and asset-backed security (ABS) issued. The variety and lack of homogeneity on the underlying assets in MBS and ABS have meant that investor focus tends to be on understanding the assets and underlying credit characteristics. The bond structures, while not necessarily simple, tend to be designed to be fairly uniform floating quarterly paying bonds with average lives in the 3 to 7 year range.

A very important but nonquantifiable hindrance to the development of the European securitization market is a suspicion of new financing techniques. There are two major factors behind this suspicion. First, the banking industry has been highly regulated and protected within Europe, resulting in an oligopolistic banking sector within most countries and a captive investor community. Secondly, achieving high returns on equity has traditionally had little importance in Europe. Both of these two factors are changing. EU regulations now allow for any bank regulated in one EU country to provide services in the other EU countries, and thus the banking sector is becoming increasingly competitive. Shareholder pressure is becoming more powerful as the general public increases its participation in the stock market. These two factors should provide a stronger incentive for securitization going forward.

The importance of securitization as part of the fixed-income markets in Europe varies widely and is highly time dependent. In the United Kingdom and Italy in the last few years, securitized debt has been fairly large in comparison to government and corporate debt, mainly because of the different government privatization initiatives and large pressures on the banking sector. Countries such as Sweden and Germany are more typical of Europe, with a large government bond sector, a significant mortgage bond or pantbrief sector, respectively, an extremely small corporate bond sector, and fairly insignificant securitization sector.

SIZE OF MARKET

In the year 2001, new issuance in the European securitization market reached over € 150 billion. While this is the highest level of new issuance in Europe, it is still tiny compared to the market in the United States, with agency MBS new issuance alone at $1.1 trillion. As seen in Figure 25.1, since the first European MBS issued in 1987, the market has grown on average by 61 percent per year. After a sluggish and erratic start, the market has been on a steady growth path since 1996.

The largest issuance in Europe comes from the United Kingdom, with 35.2 percent of the total market in 2001. While the United Kingdom has consistently had the largest share of securitization issuance, the rest of Europe has participated in fits and starts, as illustrated in Figures 25.2, 25.3, and 25.4. In 2000 and 2001, the second largest issuance came from Italy with 12.1 percent and 18.7 percent, respectively, of the market followed

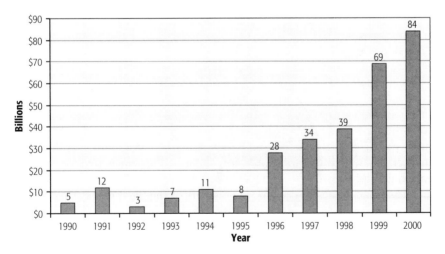

FIGURE 25.1 European ABS issuance, 1990–2000.
Source: Fredell & Co. Structured Finance Ltd.

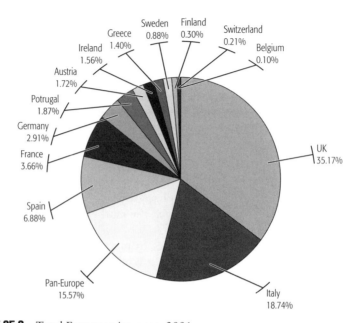

FIGURE 25.2 Total European issuance, 2001.
Source: ISR, issue 65, pg. 23, Feb. 2002 ("Table 1: Total European Issuance (2001)").

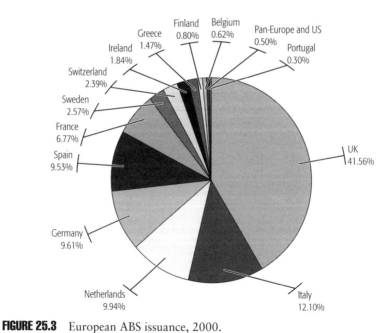

FIGURE 25.3 European ABS issuance, 2000.
Source: ISR, Issue 54, pg. 22, Feb. 2001 ("Table 1: Total European Issuance (2000)").

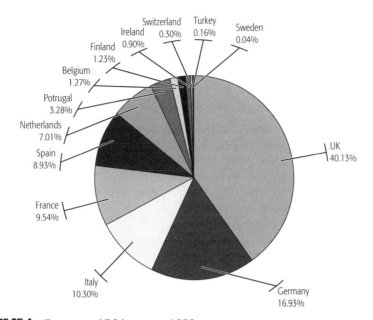

FIGURE 25.4   European ABS issuance, 1999.

Source: ISR, issue 44, pg. 25, Feb. 2000 ("European Lead Managers by Country (1999)").

closely by Pan-European transactions in 2000 (15.6 percent) and the Netherlands in 2001 (9.9 percent). However, in 1999, the second largest issuer was Germany, with 16.9 percent of total European issuance. Because the size of the whole market is still fairly small, a concentrated burst of issuance by one originator can change the country ranking significantly. For example, in 1999, ABN Amro issued $2.7 billion of ABS in the Netherlands, which was 59.3 percent of the total issuance for that year.

The U.K. market, like most other European markets, is dominated by residential MBS with several large financial institutions coming to the market several times a year, including Abbey National, Northern Rock, and Bank of Scotland. In 2000, for example, residential mortgage-backed securities (RMBS) accounted for 61.02 percent of the U.K. market, with over $21.1 billion. In 2001, $21.9 billion of RMBS was issued in the U.K., which accounted for 43.2 percent of all securitization transactions. The U.K. issuance is illustrated in Figures 25.5 and 25.6.

For several years, the euro has been the preferred currency in which to issue securitization deals in Europe. As seen in Figure 25.7, in 2000, 54 percent of all issuance was in euros, with British pounds coming in second (29 percent) and U.S. dollars, third (17 percent).

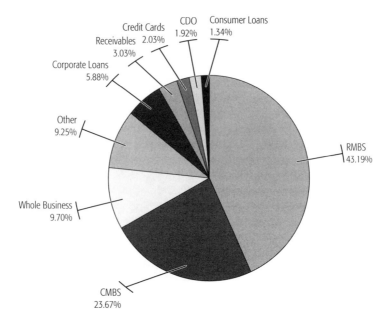

FIGURE 25.5 U.K. issuance, 2001.
Source: ISR, issue 64, pg. 27, Feb. 2002 ("Table 1: European Countries by Asset Class (2001)").

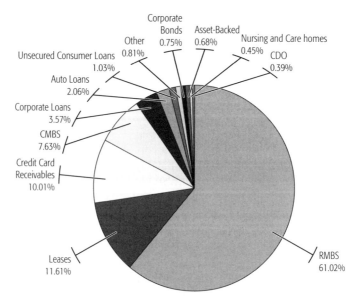

FIGURE 25.6 U.K. issuance, 2000.
Source: ISR, issue 54, pg. 26, Feb. 2001 ("Table 1: European Countries by Asset Class (2000)").

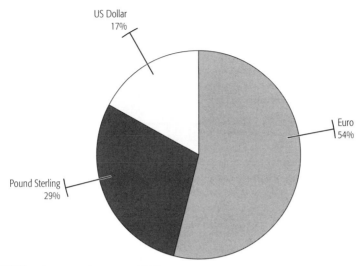

US Dollar
17%

Euro
54%

Pound Sterling
29%

FIGURE 25.7 Currency issuance, 2000.
Source: Fredell & Co. Structured Finance Ltd.

TYPE OF ASSETS

The European securitization market first started in the United Kingdom with MBS issued in 1987. While the market was and still is dominated by residential mortgages, other assets have quickly entered the market, as seen in Tables 25.1 and 25.2. Today, collateralized loan obligations and commercial mortgages are the second and third largest asset classes to be securitized. Whole business securitizations are a European innovation, which was approximately 3.6 percent of the securitization market in 2001.

The European market differentiates itself from the much larger and more developed U.S. market by two things: the diversity of the assets and the direct involvement of the government sector. Even with residential mortgages, the variety of structures can be bewildering to a U.S. investor used to conforming FNMA pools. Within one single transaction, a variety of underlying loan types can be present. Thus, every transaction must be analyzed separately. Governments in Europe play a different role in the securitization market than does the U.S. government. The U.S. government is a large player in the U.S. market given its direct sponsorship of FHA and VA loan programs and its indirect support of Fannie Mae and Freddie Mac through their unique status as government sponsored enterprises (GSEs). These agencies provide credit guarantees for mortgages and play a huge role in terms of standardization and providing a robust secondary market. However, European government involvement is more direct because they are securitizing

TABLE 25.1   European Issuance by Asset Class (2001)

Asset Class	Millions (%)	Breakdown (%)
RMBS	51,898.07	34.38
CLO	19,181.60	12.71
CMBS	16,547.21	10.96
CDO	8,332.77	5.52
Whole business	5,433.61	3.60
Nonperforming loans	5,037.81	3.34
Corporate loans	4,780.85	3.17
Housing loans	4,039.19	2.68
Other	3,938.67	2.61
Consumer loans	3,833.12	2.54
Auto loans	3,824.86	2.53
Lottery receivables	2,685.60	1.78
Corporate bonds	2,154.61	1.43
MBS (mixed pool)	2,118.20	1.40
Future EU receivables	1,797.80	1.19
Eurotunnel junior debt	1,678.31	1.11
Leases	1,511.20	1.00
Social Security contributions	1,465.52	0.97
Equipment leases	1,418.51	0.94
Credit cards	1,382.40	0.92
Health care payments	920.81	0.61
State-related payments	677.40	0.45
Telecom receivables	603.45	0.40
Vehicle	582.26	0.39
Railway loan	540.74	0.36
SACE loan claims	525.00	0.35
Pub revenues	477.68	0.32
IT contract receivables	427.78	0.28
Nursing receivables	389.69	0.26
Housing association rents	338.71	0.22
Reverse RMBS	335.09	0.22
Trade receivables	313.02	0.21
MBS	282.00	0.19
Performing secured personal loans	248.81	0.16
Real estate leases	233.40	0.15
Home loans	230.20	0.15
Credit derivatives	190.20	0.13
Farm loans	184.70	0.12
Aircraft loans	153.05	0.10
Issuer's assets and shares	142.59	0.09
Inventory (diamonds)	100.00	0.07
Total	150,956.49	100.00

Source: ISR, issue 64, pg. 23, Feb. 2002 ("Table 2: European Issuance by Asset Class (2001)").

TABLE 25.2   European Issuance by Asset Class (2000)

Asset Class	Millions ($)	Breakdown (%)
RMBS	41,092.75	48.77
Corporate loans	7,380.89	8.76
CMBS	4,352.03	5.16
CDO	3,787.74	4.50
Credit-card receivables	3,770.48	4.47
Pub leases	2,617.14	3.11
Auto loans	2,069.13	2.46
Nonperforming loans	2,022.65	2.40
Corporate bonds	1,922.63	2.28
Consumer loans	1,713.10	2.03
Future flow receivables	1,243.56	1.48
Secured leases	1,179.12	1.40
Municipal loans	1,147.16	1.36
Insurance premiums	1,140.00	1.35
Asset-backed	730.68	0.87
Trade receivables	700.00	0.83
Lottery receivables	614.50	0.73
Cruise ship contract receivables	583.90	0.69
Mall leases	534.26	0.63
Vehicle real estate leases	525.76	0.62
Credit rights	458.13	0.54
Aircraft leases	436.63	0.52
CMBS/RMBS	405.59	0.48
Champagne receivables	382.42	0.45
Home lease rentals	374.78	0.44
Auto leases	339.80	0.40
Supermarket leases	339.38	0.40
Freight wagon leases	320.61	0.38
Pfandbrief	282.39	0.34
Auto and personal loans	277.79	0.33
Commercial loans	232.50	0.28
Rents/Leases	164.48	0.20
Nursing and care homes	155.20	0.18
Lease payments	145.29	0.17
Consumer/real estate loans	131.94	0.16
Credit default swaps and bonds	129.93	0.15
Ticket receivables	118.00	0.14
Student rents	112.40	0.13
Equipment/auto leases	104.89	0.12
Credit default swaps	67.10	0.08
Equipment leases and loans	59.94	0.07
Repackaged securities	51.65	0.06
Equipment leases	43.63	0.05
Total	84,261.96	100.00

Source: ISR, Issue 54, pg. 22, Feb. 2001 ("Table 2: European Issuance by Asset Class (2000)").

their own assets—from residential and commercial real estate, to lottery revenues, and even future tax revenues. Government securitizations, along with residential mortgages, have often been the catalyst for popularizing securitization as a funding method within their respective countries. For example, in Italy, the government has securitized lottery and future tax revenues, which has provided a huge volume to the Italian market. In Finland, the government-housing agency remains the only securitization issuer, with six issued to date, since the first Fennica transaction in 1995. In Belgium, the first securitization transaction, Atrium 1, launched in 1996, was backed by housing loans with a Flemish government guarantee.

Residential Mortgage-Backed Securities

Within the MBS sector, the largest issuance is for prime mortgages. While almost all European countries have issued prime RMBS, the United Kingdom and the Netherlands are notable for the amount of repeat issuance and relatively standardized deals. Repeat issuers in the Netherlands include SNS Bank, ASR Bank, Delta Lloyd Levensverzekeringen, and ABN Amro. Spain has been increasing its securitization significantly in the past few years and now boasts quite a few repeat issuers such as Caixa D'Estalvis I Pensions de Barcelona, Caixa Catalunya and Banco Santander. Portugal came to the market with a first RMBS in 2001 issued by Canco Comercial Portugues. The Portuguese market has been slow in developing due to tax issues.

However, in the United Kingdom, several subprime lenders are also present with repeat issuance, including Kensington, Mortgages PLC, Preferred, RFC, and Southern Pacific. As seen in Figure 25.8, Italy issued the fourth largest volume of MBS deals, after the United Kingdom, Spain, and the Netherlands. Italian nonperforming residential mortgage loans comprise a total volume of € 4.84 billion in 2001, led by Morgan Stanley's sponsored International Credit Recovery 6 (€ 1.02 billion) and Banca di Roma's Trevi Finance 3 (€ 750 million). All European countries other than the United Kingdom and Italy have issued only prime MBS.

Commercial Mortgage-Backed Securities

The United Kingdom has also been the largest commercial mortgage-backed security (CMBS) player. Issuance has been mainly via large single-borrower securitizations such as Canary Wharf in London and the Meadowhall shopping center in Sheffield. Sale and lease-back securitization of commercial real estate also has been fairly popular recently, including deals from companies such as British Telecom and Marks & Spencer. These deals are largely a result of increasing pressure on corporations to release capital, which can be efficiently achieved through securitization. This sector has been impacted by

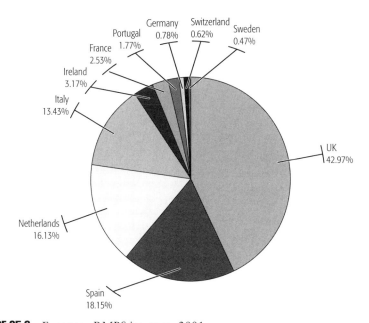

FIGURE 25.8 European RMBS issuance, 2001.
Source: ISR, issue 64, pg. 27, Feb. 2002 ("Table 1: European Countries by Asset Class (2001)").

the events of September 11, 2001, but it is expected to have a more minimal impact in the United Kingdom than in the United States because terrorism insurance is a standard inclusion for commercial property.

In 2001, the United Kingdom led in the issuance of CMBS. There were also a fair amount of Pan-European deals. The first French CMBS since 1998 was issued by Powerhouse Finance and was backed by a portfolio of houses and apartments leased by Electricité de France (the French national electricity utility). The Netherlands also issued its first CMBS in 2001 with Dutch Dream 2001-1, a synthetic issue backed by loans on commercial properties. A breakdown of European CMBS issuance is provided in Figure 25.9.

Corporate Loans

Although the overall volume was fairly small in 2001, the United Kingdom was by far the leader in corporate loan securitization, with over $3.2 billion being brought on the market. This figure is over double the country's 2000 issuance, and accounted for 74.0 percent of Europe's total corporate loan issuance, as seen in Figure 25.10.

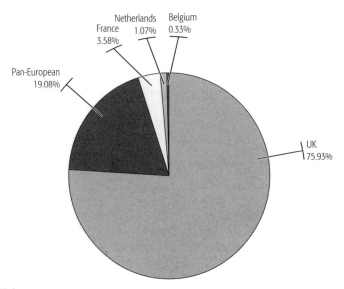

FIGURE 25.9 European CMBS issuance, 2001.
Source: ISR, issue 64, pg. 27, Feb. 2002 ("Table 1: European Countries by Asset Class (2001)").

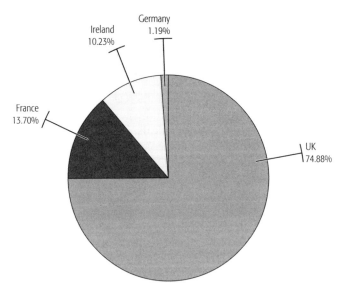

FIGURE 25.10 European corporate loan issuance, 2001.
Source: ISR, issue 64, pg. 27, Feb. 2002 ("Table 1: European Countries by Asset Class (2001)").

Consumer Assets and Leasing

Consumer assets such as credit cards have not seen the large-scale securitization in Europe that they have in the United States. In 2001, Italy led in this type of asset securitization. The United Kingdom is also active, with MBNA, Barclays, and RBS all having set up programs. However, in 2001, only MBNA did any issuance. Again, Italy has been very strong lately with issuance in 2001 of over $2.2 billion, and almost a quarter of European issuance as seen in Figure 25.11. In France, Cetelem has been a long-standing issuer for deals backed by consumer loans with over € 1 billion issued. Auto loans remain a strong sector in France with two new issuers, Socram and Banque PSA Finance.

Whole-Business Securitization

Whole-business securitization is, thus far, unique to the United Kingdom and France. Instead of focusing on cash flows from a single identifiable asset, the entire set of flows generated by a business during its day-to-day

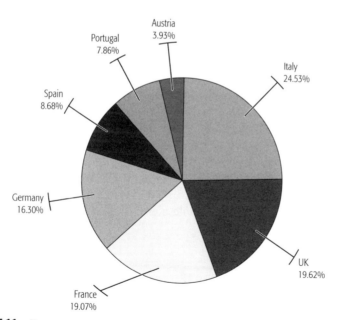

FIGURE 25.11 European consumer asset and leasing issuance, 2001.

Source: ISR, issue 64, pg. 27, Feb. 2002 ("Table 1: European Countries by Asset Class (2001)").

operations is used. The technique uses a variant of the concept of a "secured loan" rather than a true-sale structure. While whole-business securitization to date has only been performed in the United Kingdom and France, the secured-loan structure was actually pioneered on a Swedish deal, St. Erik, issued in 1994, which was backed by rental flows from social housing. The idea is to isolate the cash-flow-producing assets from the originator/borrower, so that, in case of default, the control of the assets is given to the trustee/receiver to be managed and operated for the realization of cash flows over time. Thus, the ultimate credit quality is based on the stability of the operating cash flows rather than the ability to "sell" the assets. This technique has come to be a popular source of funding for corporates but is suitable only for a restricted type of business that can demonstrate very stable historical cash flows.

In 1996, the United Kingdom saw the first secured-loan structure in the Craegmoor Nursing Homes deal, soon followed by two Angel Train securitizations from Nomura. These transactions paved the way for the Welcome Break deal, structured by BT Alex Brown International, which is today regarded as the first whole-business securitization. Other notable transactions include Madam Tussaud's Museum and London City Airport. In 2001, new transactions included GHG, a private hospital, and Isle of Wight ferries, a ferry operator. Although the United Kingdom had 94.8 percent of the whole-business securitization market in 2001, France also completed $282.8 million in whole business securitization.

Other Innovations

Europe continues to provide innovative funding solutions using securitizations, particularly within the government sector. Italy, for example, has raised € 3 billion from future lottery revenues. France has recently securitized receivables owned by France's national railway, SNCF. In Belgium, there have been two transactions, in 1999 and again in 2001, issued by Rosy Blue, a Belgian diamond wholesaler backed by diamond-trade receivables.

SECURITIZATION OUTSIDE EUROPE AND THE UNITED STATES

Outside Europe and the United States, Australia has the most active securitization market. The MBS market in Australia is particularly robust. Other countries have used securitization with success, but usually with one-off deals, rather than repeat issuance.

Australia

After posting a strong year in 2000 with more than $11 billion in new issuance, the Australian market posted the fifth consecutive year of growth in 2001 with total issuance exceeding $14 billion, as can be seen in Table 25.3. Following the trend of the last several years, RMBS, CMBS, and ABS transactions account for the bulk of Australian securitizations in terms of issuance.

Asia and South Pacific

With the exception of Japan, Asia and the South Pacific have been fairly slow in developing their securitization markets. Total non-Japanese issuance in Asia and the South Pacific amounted to little more than $4.5 billion in 2001. The most promising markets appear to be Korea and Singapore, with a combined issuance of over $3.6 billion, or 90 percent of the Asian market, as seen in Table 25.3. Although most attribute the slow growth to the lack of infrastructure and legal systems, it is hoped that the public sector will see securitization as a valuable tool to restructure Asia's debt problems and as a means of reviving the economy.

Japan

After new legislation was passed in 1998, the Japanese securitization market started growing at a formidable pace. After expanding more than 100 percent in 1998 and 1999, total issuance grew over 41 percent between 2000 and 2001. As seen in Table 25.4, issuance reached over $24.6 billion in 2001 with a wide variety of asset classes. As a result of the country's creaking

TABLE 25.3 Australian, Non-Japan Asian, and South Pacific Issuance (2001)

Country	Millions ($)	Breakdown (%)
Australia	14,340.96	76.01
Korea	2,113.80	11.20
Singapore	1,503.70	7.97
Hong Kong	435.35	2.31
Malaysia	325.00	1.72
New Zealand	80.07	0.42
International	68.00	0.36
Total	18,866.88	100.00

Source: *ISR*, issue 64, pg. 24, Feb. 2002 ("Table 1: Non-Japan Asia Issuance (2001)").

TABLE 25.4   Japanese Issuance by Asset Class (2001)

Asset Class	Millions ($)	Breakdown (%)
CMBS	5,810.35	23.55
RMBS	3,845.50	15.59
Equipment lease receivables	3,552.30	14.40
Shopping credit receivables	3,032.90	12.29
Credit cards	2,222.58	9.01
Auto loans	2,109.40	8.55
Lease receivables	1,499.40	6.08
CLO (corporate and municipal loans)	878.60	3.56
Unsecured loans	482.50	1.96
Auto leases	344.10	1.39
CBO	244.30	0.99
ABS equipment	238.40	0.97
Small business loans	203.30	0.82
Shopping centers	64.30	0.26
Truck loans	63.00	0.26
Lease claims	41.80	0.17
Asset-backed loans	39.70	0.16
Total	24,672.43	100.00

Source: *ISR*, issue 64, pg. 24, Feb. 2002 ("Table 1: Japanese Issuance by Asset Class (2001)").

banking sector burdened with bad debt, it is expected that the coming years will see various transactions aiming to securitize the bad loans extended by the banks.

Latin America

The Latin American market is still in its infancy, with $6.7 billion of issuance in 2001 as seen in Table 25.5. Future flow deals backed by U.S. dollar-denominated receivables such as iron ore and oil are the dominant type of issuance, as shown in Table 25.6. Brazil, Venezuela, and Mexico have the majority of securitization activity in the region. Development may be supported by activity from the World Bank and other similar agencies.

The European securitization market can be characterized by its diversity and lack of homogenization. This diversity has also resulted in a high level of innovation and creativity as issuers structure diverse types of cash flows into bonds, which investors can understand. It is a foregone conclusion that the European and other new securitization markets will continue to grow.

TABLE 25.5   Latin American Issuance (2001)

Country	Millions ($)	Breakdown (%)
Brazil	2,550.00	38.04
Venezuela	1,500.00	22.38
Mexico	1,386.04	20.68
Argentina	792.00	11.82
Trinidad & Tobago	150.00	2.24
Jamaica	125.00	1.86
Peru	100.00	1.49
Panama	100.00	1.49
Total	6,703.04	100.00

Source: *ISR*, issue 64, pg. 25, Feb. 2002 ("Table 1: Latin American Issuance (2001)").

TABLE 25.6   Latin American Issuance by Asset Class

Asset Class	Millions ($)	Breakdown (%)
Future flows	2,500.00	37.30
Equipment leases	732.04	10.92
Credit cards	675.00	10.07
Brewery revenues	500.00	7.46
Coparticipation revenues	463.00	6.91
Future flows (electronic)	300.00	4.48
State bank securities	300.00	4.48
Dividend securitization	300.00	4.48
Future worker remittance	250.00	3.73
Hydrocarbon future flows	234.00	3.49
Diversified payment rights	150.00	2.24
Oil & gas revenues	150.00	2.24
RMBS	95.00	1.42
Leases	54.00	0.81
Total	6,703.04	100.00

Source: *ISR*, issue 64, pg. 25, Feb. 2002 ("Table 1: Latin American Issuance by Asset Class (2001)").

However, the development of the markets, while embracing U.S.-style technology, will be distinctly different in order to meet the specific needs of each country's issuers. The harmonization being brought by the European Union and the euro will surely be an important factor in advancing securitization. However, it will take many, many years for Europe to catch up with the homogenization and sheer volume of the U.S. RMBS market.

EXERCISES

Exercise 25.1   Should the government be involved in the securitization market? What about the mortgage market? Should the European Union have the authority to set standards for the mortgage market in Europe?

Exercise 25.2   Why is the United Kingdom the leader over the rest of Europe in terms of securitization volume? Is their leadership because of structural market factors or is it a cultural phenomenon?

CHAPTER 26

European Residential Mortgages

Around the world, residential mortgages constitute one of the largest single sectors of debt in an economy. The size, growth, and credit characteristics of mortgages tend to make them the most commonly securitized asset. In Europe, the volume of mortgages outstanding more than doubled in the 1990s, to stand at around €3.2 trillion at the end of 2000, as shown in Figure 26.1.

The importance of residential mortgages within the economy varies greatly across Europe. As shown in Figure 26.2, in 2000, the Netherlands, Denmark, United Kingdom, and Germany all had an outstanding mortgage

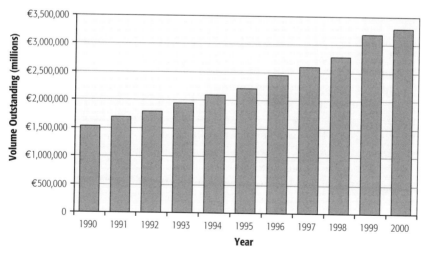

FIGURE 26.1   Residential mortgage loan volume in the European Union and Norway between 1990 and 2000.

Source: European Mortgage Federation.

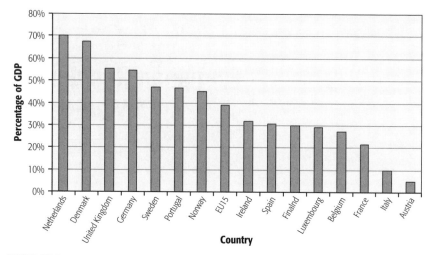

FIGURE 26.2   Mortgage volume as a percentage of GDP by country in 2000.

Source: European Mortgage Federation.

volume greater than 50 percent of gross domestic product (GDP). Italy, Austria, and Greece have outstanding mortgage volumes less than 10 percent of GDP. The wide divergence in market sizes is a reflection of the very different economic, political, historical, legal, and social frameworks in all the European countries. It will not come as a surprise to find that countries with a very large mortgage market tend to have strong methods for funding those mortgages via the capital markets, while smaller markets tend to fund solely with bank deposits.

Generic characteristics for each market, such as average loan size, amount of leverage, and debt maturity also vary greatly across Europe, as shown in Table 26.1. The average loan size in Europe is just over € 100 thousand, contrasting with € 158 thousand for Ireland and only € 45 thousand for Greece. The average loan to value (LTV) ratio is 70 percent in Europe, compared with 80 percent in Denmark, and only 47 percent in Greece. Maturities tend to range from 10 to 30 years. These characteristics may be the direct result of legislation or may simply be a historical convention. For example, in Italy, mortgages legally may not exceed 80 percent LTV. In Germany and Sweden, loans below 60 percent and 70 percent LTV, respectively, are treated differently in terms of regulatory capital for banks. In the Netherlands, loans with 100 percent LTV are very standard because of tax reasons.

Commercial banks are the dominant provider of mortgages across Europe, with a 42 percent market share at the end of 2000. Savings banks

TABLE 26.1 Loan Amounts, LTV Ratios, and Maturity in European Countries (2000)

Country	Mortgage Loan (€)	Loan to Value (%)	Original Maturity (years)
Denmark	107,000	80	30
Germany	176,000	67	28
Spain	45,000	47	15
Luxembourg	67,500	70	16
France	80,000	67	15
Ireland	158,530	90	20
Italy	75,000	50	10
Netherlands	122,000	72	30
Sweden	119,000	70	30
United Kingdom	114,000	69	25
Norway	108,000	70	
Simple Average	106,454	70	

Source: European Mortgage Federation.

and mortgage banks take second and third slots, with 16 and 15 percent market share, respectively. A more detailed breakdown is shown in Figure 26.3.

In 1998, securitization provided only 1 percent of the funding for mortgages in Europe as shown in Figure 26.4, compared to over 50 percent in the United States. This figure is probably slightly increased in 2003, but will still be extremely small compared to the United States. Retail deposits continue to be the dominant funding method, with various kinds of mortgage bonds coming in second. Within different European countries, the funding sources for mortgages can be quite different. Figure 26.5 shows these sources for various European Union countries compared with Japan and the United States in 2000. The United Kingdom, which has the most advanced securitization market, still only used mortgage-backed securities (MBS) for about 5 percent of its mortgage funding. Denmark is rather unique in Europe because all of its mortgages are funded using the capital markets. They have a mortgage bond system that can be thought of as a variant of a securitization, somewhere in between an MBS and the German pantbrief system. Most European countries, however, still rely heavily on deposits for mortgage funding. As the trend of decreasing retail deposits continues, this picture should face some rapid changes in the future.

The great volume of mortgages in Europe and the changing face of the financial industry mean that securitization will become a more important

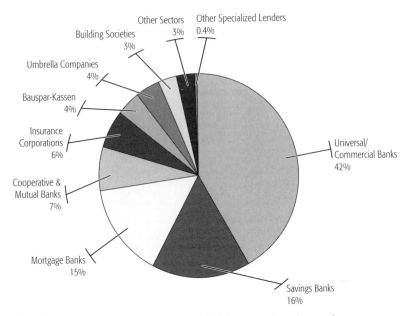

FIGURE 26.3 Mortgage market share in 2000 (percent based on volume outstanding).

Source: European Mortgage Federation.

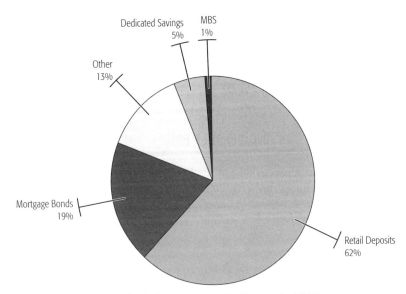

FIGURE 26.4 Funding methods for mortgages in Europe in 1998.

Source: European Mortgage Federation.

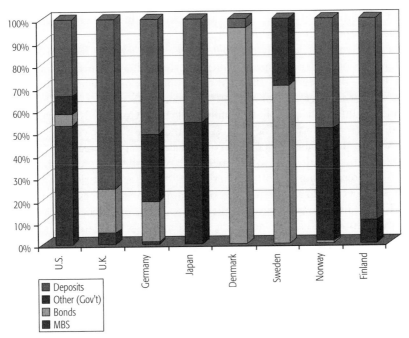

FIGURE 26.5 Funding methods for mortgages, selected countries, in 2000.
Source: Fredell & Co. Structured Finance Ltd.

funding tool for mortgage originators in the future. While it is probable that the European Union and the euro will bring a certain amount of convergence in the mortgage market, any changes will take place slowly. This lack of homogeneity means that any mortgage originator or investor in MBS must be aware of all the similarities and differences in individual European markets.

PROPERTY VALUE LOSS AND DEFAULT RISK

There are distinct differences within the European mortgage markets regarding the risks on potential property-value decline and loan-default rates. These two risk factors have a considerable effect on a securitization transaction.

Assessing default risk and actual losses on foreclosure, although extremely important, is difficult, because data on mortgage defaults and losses in Europe are not publicly available. The ultimate sources of such statistics are the actual banks and financial institutions that originate mortgage loans. However, these institutions frequently regard this information as proprietary or confidential, and therefore do not release the data to the public. Unfortunately, there is no central body that collects and reports on aggregate data.

One can also get an idea of the default rates in different countries through the treatment of those markets by rating agencies. This approach, however, does not give a particularly detailed understanding of the magnitude of the differences within each country. Since mortgage loans generally have fairly low losses, the differences between two countries may be something like a loss rate of 0.5 percent for Country X versus 0.8 percent for Country Y. While Country Y clearly has a higher risk than Country X, this relatively small difference may not be reflected in the rating agencies' stresses for a AAA bond, which assumes property-value declines in the region of 30 to 50 percent and default rates of 10 percent! Nevertheless, comparing rating agency criteria can give you a general idea of the relative risks. Table 26.2 contains a generalized comparison of default and value-loss risks in different European countries based on rating agencies' approaches.

As mentioned earlier, however, the comparison of data in Table 26.2 might not always be very accurate reflections of common belief on markets. For example, although the Netherlands seems to have a normal default-risk status, the country actually experiences mortgage losses of significantly less than 1 percent, which is low by European standards. Germany, too, is indicated as a normal default-risk country. Western and Eastern Germany, however, have extremely different risk characteristics. Various cultural and social barriers to defaulting exist in Western Germany, and it can be said that this area has an overall low default risk. Eastern Germany does not have a culture of property ownership, which results in higher default rates. Establishing property ownership and liens on properties can also be difficult because the municipal property registries still retain much inefficiency. Countries such as Italy are fairly reflected in the rating-agency approach.

TABLE 26.2   European Country Risks

Country	Default Risk	Property Value Risk	Overall Loss Risk
Sweden	Normal	Normal	Low
Germany	Normal	Normal	Normal, East Germany High
Ireland	High	Normal	Normal
Italy	High	Normal	High, because of time to foreclose
Netherlands	Normal	High	Low
Portugal	Normal	Medium	Normal
Spain	Normal	Medium	Normal
United Kingdom	Normal	High	Normal, Southern area high because of property value increases

Italy suffers from high default rates and a weakened willingness to pay, partly due to borrower friendly laws. Additionally, Italy has a lack of rigid underwriting criteria.

Default rates and property-loss values differ greatly in various mortgage markets. The process of property-value loss and default-risk assessment is extremely important for securitization, as they give an indication of the collateral's ability to provide security, and help determine what securitization structure or extra security is needed. It takes knowledge of the markets and considerable research and analysis to accurately identify the extent of these risks.

LEGAL AND TAX ISSUES FOR RESIDENTIAL MORTGAGES

The basic idea of a mortgage loan is the same in most countries, that is, a loan backed by real estate to be held as security. If the borrower does not pay the loan, the lender has the right to be repaid by selling the real estate. Chapter 5 describes the legal mechanics of mortgages in the United States. In Europe, the mechanisms are similar, but, as should be expected, the details differ widely.

The most important factors to consider are:

- The loan contract
- The security (i.e., right to the real estate as collateral)
- Legal foreclosure process
- Taxes

The details of how these four factors relate to each other can have important impacts on credit quality. It is beyond the scope of this chapter to describe these factors for every country in Europe. Instead, major differences or issues will be pointed out, and a detailed example will be given for Sweden.

The Loan Contract

The loan contract spells out the obligations of the borrower and the lender regarding how much will be borrowed, the term in which it will be paid back, and at what interest rate. In most European countries, lenders have standard terms and conditions for a loan contract, which may be a separate contract from the description of the loan or may be part of the loan contract. The terms and conditions normally state the rights of the lender to charge various types of penalties such as late fees and prepayment fees, to terminate the loan early, to change interest rates, to ask for more collateral, and the obligations of the borrower. These terms and conditions are normally based on the legal framework in the country in question. Very often, there are stringent consumer-protection codes that dictate terms and conditions.

There are a few main issues with regard to loan contracts that create problems in Europe for securitization.

A common issue in many countries, such as Ireland and the Netherlands, is notification. If the original lender sells the loan, the borrower by law must be notified. The notification is not necessarily a problem, as it can be included in a monthly payment invoice, but many originators do not want their borrowers to know that they have sold the loan, particularly if they are retaining the servicing. The generally accepted solution to this dilemma is to structure the securitization so that the sale only is completed on some trigger events, such as financial distress of the originator. Once these trigger events take place, then the borrowers must be notified and the sale of the loans will be perfected. Because the sale is not perfected at the outset, care must be taken to ensure that the bankruptcy of the originator would not result in a claw back of the assets. Also, if a bank is interested in regulatory capital relief, regulators must be convinced of the off-balance sheet nature of the transaction.

Another tricky problem to overcome is that in some jurisdictions, the borrower must agree to the loan sale. One common solution is "negative consent." This is often used in Ireland. Here the originator sends out a letter to the borrowers informing them of the sale and asking them to contact the originator within a specified number of days if they do not agree. This type of solution must normally be agreed on with the relevant regulators in order to ensure that consumer rights are not violated.

Consumer privacy laws can sometimes create problems. When structuring a securitization, many parties must have access to very detailed data on the borrowers. This is more a theoretical problem than a real problem. Normally this type of privacy law can be overcome by ensuring that customer names and identification numbers are never given out. However, in some jurisdictions there can be a theoretical risk that a borrower could sue the originator for giving out data.

The Security

The form of the security for the loan, or the mortgage, varies greatly across Europe. There are three fundamental questions to look at:

1. How is the collateral secured?
2. If the collateral is seized, does the borrower still have to pay the loan?
3. How does the lender know that he or she has sole right to the real estate?

The mortgage normally is a contractual agreement, allowing the lender to seize the real estate if the borrower does not fulfill the obligation to pay the debt. In most countries there is one basic way this contract is written. However, in some countries, there can be different types of security that give different outcomes. Germany is a good example of this difference. There are at least four different types of mortgage contracts. The ease of transferability and the registration of the lien is different for all types. For example, the transfer of the mortgage should normally be registered in the real estate register of the district in which the real estate is located. This registration can become costly, because a notary would be involved for certification purposes, with a fee based on the value of the real estate. However, for a mortgage certificate (*grundschuldbrief*), the transfer is executed by simply delivering the certificate to the new owner of the loan. This last type is clearly a preferable method, but will not necessarily be possible if the portfolio to be securitized is an old one, which contains different types of security.

In the United States, it is fairly common that, if the collateral is seized, the borrower has no further duty to pay off the loan, which means that once the proceeds for the sale of the property are realized, if the amount is insufficient to pay off the loan and costs, the lender suffers a loss. However, if the proceeds of the loan sale are higher than the loan, then the lender has made an additional profit. Of course, this last scenario rarely happens, since the borrower would have a strong incentive to sell the property first. In Europe, it is almost universally true that the borrower retains responsibility over the debt if the proceeds of the sale are insufficient. Conversely, the lender can never seize more than the amount of the debt owed and must return the balance to the borrower if there is any gain.

The registration of the mortgage is very important for a lender in order to know that the lender has sole right to the asset (or the correct ranking, in the case of multiple lenders and liens). How the mortgage right is registered can vary from country to country. For example, in Belgium, it is the notary's job to secure that the lender has the first lien on the property. The notary checks the various property registries, and then tells the lender whether or not there is a previous lien. The notary then must submit the lender's lien to the property registry. The notary is personally liable if it should turn out that there is a prior lien or if he or she does not submit the new lien to the property registry. The delay from paying out the mortgage to securing the lien in the appropriate registry varies greatly from country to country and can be a risk factor. In Germany and in Belgium, for example, there can be an extremely long delay of up to 6 months before registration.

A final important aspect is a detailed look at the actual collateral or real estate that is being pledged. Most countries have the concept of a mortgage backed by a building on land, where the right of the mortgage is to sell the entirety of the building and land. However, there can be variations on this right. For example, in Finland, due to tax reasons, many people own their homes through a company rather than directly. The mortgage is then on the shares of the housing company, rather than the real estate itself. In Sweden, a loan on a cooperative apartment, a large part of the housing market, is actually pledged by the transferable right to live in the apartment, but not by the land. The cooperative society has the right to borrow with a mortgage on the land. If the cooperative went bankrupt, the lenders with the mortgage on the land would be senior in priority to those who lent directly to apartment owners. In the United Kingdom, there is a distinction between a freehold and a leasehold. A freehold is when the land is owned with the building. A leasehold is when someone owns the land, which is leased to the owner of the building for a certain number of years, typically with original maturities of 100 years. Property values differ greatly depending on the length of the lease outstanding. These few examples show the diversity of housing systems within Europe, grown out of different historical and regulatory environments.

Legal Foreclosure Process

The foreclosure process whereby the lender seizes real estate collateral in order to obtain payment on a loan is normally detailed in law. However, the strictness of the procedure and the length of time can vary, as shown in Table 26.3. On one side of the spectrum is Sweden, where every step of the process is specified by law and is normally completed within 6 to 9 months, versus Italy, which is notorious for having extremely long foreclosure procedures, with some cases taking over 20 years. Normally, a key factor will be whether or not a court can force the lender to work out terms or negotiations.

Taxes

There are two general areas to consider with regard to taxes: the tax position of the borrower and transfer taxes for the originator. The tax position of the borrower can affect the characteristics of the loan. An extreme example of this is the Netherlands where mortgage interest is tax deductible. This

TABLE 26.3 Estimated Times to Foreclosure in Selected European Countries

Country	Estimated Time to Average Completion of Foreclosure
Belgium	18 months
Finland	12 months
France	36 months
Germany	24 months
Italy	120 months
Netherlands	9 months
Spain	36 months
Sweden	6 months

Source: Fredell & Co. Structured Finance.

has resulted in loan structures that try to maximize interest payments. High sales taxes on real estate can sometimes mean that loan amounts are extended to cover the cost of the tax.

Taxes for the originator can be a large problem for securitization. There are often transfer taxes if loans are sold from one party to another. These kinds of taxes can make it very expensive for originators to use securitization as a funding method, unless some kind of work-around solution can be found, such as a nonperfected sale. Most countries that have enacted specific securitization legislation have addressed this type of problem.

Case Study: Sweden

The loan contract in Sweden is very simple. It consists of three documents: (a) terms and conditions (*villkorsbilaga*); (b) loan description (*skuldbrev*); and (c) mortgage (*pantbrev*). The terms and conditions are generally about two pages and outline the right of the lender to charge late fees, prepayment fees as allowed under Swedish law, and how interest rates will be offered after an interest-rate reset period is ended. The loan description is generally about one page and shows the amount borrowed by the customer, the term of the loan, the amortization type, the interest rate, and the interest-rate reset date. The *pantbrev* is the real estate security for the loan. Swedish loan documentation is extremely sparse compared to many countries, because the rights of lenders and borrowers are extensively set out within the law and thus do not need to be repeated in the contracts (see Chapter 27 for a discussion of different legal systems).

The *pantbrev* (mortgage right) in Sweden is a unique instrument in Europe. The owner of the real estate must apply for a *pantbrev* at the official Swedish property registry (*Inskrivningsmyndigheten*). The *pantbrev* is a certificate that is issued for a certain face value. There is a cost of 2 percent of the nominal amount of the face value for the issuance of a *pantbrev*. The *pantbrev* is a perpetual document and cannot be terminated. Traditionally, a *pantbrev* is a bearer document. However, today most *pantbrev* are electronic and exist only as an inscription in the property registry database (*datapantbrev*). The Swedish property registry keeps track of each *pantbrev* and the priority of the *pantbrev*, because more than one *pantbrev* can be issued on each property or against a loan. The security interest in a property is granted by the titleholder pledging one or more *pantbrev* to the creditor and either physically delivering the *pantbrev* or by registering the lender in the property registry.

Because a *pantbrev* is an instrument that is drawn up independently from the loan, this gives rise to a unique loan structure. Say a borrower builds a new house and borrows 50 against it. The borrower would then take out a *pantbrev* for 50. Ten years later, the borrower sells the house. The house has risen in value over time, so the new owner borrows 80. The borrower must take out a second *pantbrev* with a face value between 50 and 80. In another 5 years, property values have gone up, and the borrower wants to increase the amount of the loan by another 20. So the borrower takes out a third *pantbrev* with a face value between 80 and 100. Over time, it is clear that an older property could have many *pantbrev*, with as many as 10 to 15 being fairly common. Now, say that the borrower wants to refinance his or her loans. There are prepayment penalties in Sweden, so a borrower may choose to have multiple loans, some of which have a floating interest rate, that have no prepayment penalty, and some that are fixed. The borrower will normally take out loans that match the amounts on the *pantbrev*. At this point it starts to get complicated for a lender if a borrower wants a loan of, say, 20 against two *pantbrev* of 10 each, but not in a consecutive order priority. This situation is very common and makes it tricky to calculate LTV figures.

The amount of secured liabilities is mandated by law. Under the loan contract, the lender is entitled to the loan amount, together with any fees and charges, and the interest at the contractual rate. The *pantbrev* entitles the lender to the amount shown on the *pantbrev* plus up to 15 percent of that amount to cover costs resulting from the foreclosure, plus interest from the date of the application for foreclosure.

The foreclosure process is also outlined by law. Once a borrower is late with the loan payments, a lender applies to the Swedish government enforcement agency (*Kronfogdemyndigheten*), which is responsible for carrying out enforcement orders over assets. The lender obtains an enforcement order, which obliges the enforcement agency to carry out the claim. The borrower may challenge the application or appeal the order, which is then referred to the courts. The sale of the property is normally conducted by public auction within 4 months of the enforcement order. The proceeds of the sale are applied in the following priority: first, to satisfy the costs of the enforcement agency, and second, in satisfaction of the claims of *pantbrev* holders in order of priority. Any excess amounts are returned to the borrower. If the amounts are insufficient to satisfy all claims, the excess turns into an unsecured obligation of the borrower.

MORTGAGE COLLATERAL CHARACTERISTICS

The characteristics of the underlying collateral will influence the characteristics of the resulting security. While mortgages tend to have similar characteristics around the world, each individual country will have its own standards. To describe a mortgage, we need to know:

- How the mortgage amortizes.
- How the interest is paid.

- How prepayments are treated.
- How often are payments.
- Any other special characteristics.

Table 26.4 briefly describes the differences in amortization, interest payment types, and prepayment risk per selected European countries. Looking at the table, one might feel that the countries are quite similar, which is both true and untrue. There are standard ways of describing a mortgage that hold for all countries. However, the table ignores many special factors that drive the products in each market. For example, legislation may be a large factor in whether or not a lender can charge prepayment penalties. Taxes, or more

TABLE 26.4   Differences in Mortgage Characteristics per Selected European Countries

Country	Amortization Types	Common Interest Types	Prepayment Risk
Belgium	Annuity, bullet	Fixed, variable with collar	Yes, partial penalty
Denmark	Annuity, linear, bullet	Fixed, variable	Yes
Finland	Annuity, linear	Majority fixed, variable	No, full penalty
France	Annuity, bullet	Majority fixed, variable	Yes, partial penalty (capped)
Germany	German annuity	Majority fixed, variable	Yes, full penalty but normally only for fixed rate over 5 years
Ireland	Annuity, bullet	Fixed, variable	Yes (not for variable)
Italy	Annuity, bullet	Fixed, variable, capped	Yes, as stipulated in contract
Netherlands	Annuity, bullet, linear	Fixed, variable	Yes, partial penalty
Spain	Annuity, bullet	Fixed, majority variable	Yes, depending on amount repaid and mortgage type
Sweden	Linear, bullet	Fixed, variable,	No, full penalty
United Kingdom	Annuity, bullet	Majority variable, fixed	Yes, potential penalties vary across lender

Source: Fredell & Co. Structured Finance.

importantly, tax relief can also have a fundamental impact on product design. Thus, it is necessary to take a look at each country in detail to understand the mortgage products and their inherent risks.

PRINCIPAL PAYMENT RULES

The three standard mortgage amortization styles around the world are annuity (level payment), linear, and bullet (interest only). In this section, we describe these amortization styles, as well as local deviations. We discuss the impact of different amortization profiles on credit and securitization.

Annuity Mortgages

Around the world, annuity-style or level-payment mortgages are among the most traditional. The reason for this popularity is that this amortization style provides a good blend of security for both the borrower and the lender. First, an annuity is self-amortizing, which means that by the end of the loan maturity, the loan's principal is fully paid. A lender appreciates this feature because it lowers the credit risk of the loan, while a borrower may like it for the security it brings. Second, the level payments are stable, so it is easy for a borrower to budget his or her costs into the future.

Annuity-style or level-payment mortgage calculations, where the amount of interest and principal remains constant over the life of the loan, were discussed in Chapter 5.

Annuity Calculations on Old Mortgages   Unlike in the United States, European mortgage securitizations are frequently done using old or seasoned portfolios of mortgages. The reason for this is simply that the market is fairly new and there are many banks entering the securitization market for the first time, lifting their old mortgage book off the balance sheet. Old portfolios can have loans that are 20 or even 30 years old. For portfolios of this age, a common amortization profile will be an annuity, calculated assuming annual payments. However, the actual payments on the mortgages are monthly. To arrive at a monthly payment, the annual payment is simply divided by 12. This method, of course, means that the interest rate on the mortgage is misstated, because the calculation does not take into account compounding interest.

Linear Mortgages

Linear mortgages (also called constant-amortizing mortgages), like annuity mortgages, are self-amortizing and are very easy to calculate. You simply divide the total principal amount by the number of payment periods.

An advantage of a linear amortization is that it is very easy to calculate and to understand. A disadvantage, from the point of view of the borrower, is that the payments decrease over time, which is exactly the opposite of the income profile over time of the average person. When a person is young, his or her income is normally at its lowest. As he or she ages and gains more experience, his or her salary increases. So a person might prefer to have a mortgage (since a home is usually an investment over a lifetime) with payments that increase over time, rather than decrease. From the lender's point of view, the credit risk on a linear mortgage is even less than on an annuity since the mortgage is paid off even sooner than with an annuity. However, because linear mortgages are fairly unpopular with borrowers, this kind of amortization type is rarely used in the United States. In Europe, linear mortgages are more common. For example, in Sweden, linear mortgages are the prevalent type. Linear mortgages are also available in Finland and the Netherlands, although to a lesser degree than in Sweden.

Bullet or Interest-Only Mortgages

Interest-only mortgages (also called constant-interest mortgages or bullet loans) are the easiest type of amortization profile to calculate since, in fact, there is no amortization. Instead, the principal is paid off in its entirety at maturity.

From a lender's point of view, bullet loans are the most risky. Since the loan does not amortize, the credit risk stays the same throughout the life of the loan, rather than decreasing as it does with an amortizing loan. There is also a large risk that at the maturity of the loan, the borrower will not have the funds to pay back the principal amount.

From the borrower's point of view, bullet loans can be very desirable. First, the payments are lower than for an amortizing loan since there is no principal portion of the payment. However, more importantly, bullet loans are frequently the most tax-efficient loans. Many countries have tax incentives for home owners. A frequent tax perk is that interest on a mortgage is fully tax deductible. In high-tax countries, it can be very beneficial to keep the amount of interest paid as high as possible. The Netherlands is a prime example of a country where tax concerns drive mortgage origination. Two very popular products in the Netherlands are saving mortgages and investment mortgages.

Savings Mortgage   A savings mortgage has two parts: a bullet loan and a savings account. Every month, a borrower pays the interest on the mortgage and deposits a small amount into a savings account on which the borrower receives interest at the same rate as the mortgage. By the end of the maturity of the mortgage, the amount in the savings account is exactly the amount of the mortgage, so the borrower can use the built-up savings to pay off the mortgage. The savings account is linked to the mortgage so that if the borrower defaults on the loan, the lender can take the accumulated savings in order to help pay back the loan. (See Savings Mortgage Calculator.xls on the CD.)

Careful readers might have noticed the similarity between this type of mortgage and an annuity. In fact, economically, this is an annuity-style mortgage. However, from a tax point of view, the borrower receives the maximum tax advantage from the bullet loan, while maintaining the security of an annuity.

Investment Mortgage   An investment mortgage, again, is a combination of a bullet mortgage and a savings account. Here, however, the money in the account is invested in a mutual fund or some kind of stock portfolio. The idea behind the mortgage is to allow borrowers to benefit from a higher rate of return in the stock market, as well as to maximize tax advantages. However, unlike the savings mortgage, the investment mortgage adds another element of risk, that is, stock market risk. The lender and borrower both take the risk that the investment portfolio does not develop as expected.

German Annuity

The German annuity calculation starts with assuming how much principal should be paid down in the first year of the loan contract. Then it calculates the monthly payment based on this principal paydown and a given interest rate. Given the monthly payment, one can then solve for the maturity of the loan. This process involves some iteration.

   Input Variables:

   ■ Coupon: Monthly compounding interest rate expressed as an annual rate
   ■ Loan amount
   ■ Percent of principal to be paid off in first year

   Result:

   ■ Monthly payment
   ■ Maturity

   Step 1. Calculate total principal and interest to be paid off in first year.

$$\text{First Year Payment} = (\text{Coupon} + \text{Percent Principal}) \times \text{Loan Amount} \qquad (26.1)$$

For example, assume

Coupon = 5%
Loan amount = 200,000
Percent of principal = 1 percent

Then, the first-year payment = 6 percent times 200,000 which equals 12,000.00.

Step 2. Calculate the monthly payment.

$$\text{Monthly Payment} = \frac{\text{Annual Payment}}{12} \tag{26.2}$$

In this example, the monthly payment would be 1,000.

Step 3. Calculate the maturity.
In order to calculate the maturity, you basically use the standard annuity calculation and then solve for maturity to result in equation (26.3).

$$\text{Monthly Payment} = \frac{\text{Loan Amount} \times \text{Coupon}/12}{1 - (1 + \text{Coupon}/12)^{-\text{Maturity in Months}}} \tag{26.3}$$

Equation (26.4) gives maturity in months from standard annuity.

Maturity in Months =

$$\text{Absolute Value of } \frac{\ln\left(1 - \dfrac{\text{Loan Amount} \times \text{Coupon}/12}{\text{Monthly Payment}}\right)}{\ln(1 + \text{Coupon}/12)} \tag{26.4}$$

In this example:

Coupon = 5%
Loan amount = 200,000
Monthly payment = 1,000

The maturity equals 431 months, rounding to the nearest month.

Step 4. Recalculating the monthly payment.
If you take the maturity, put it back into equation (26.3), and calculate the monthly payment, you will not get exactly the monthly payment calculated in Step 2 using equation (26.2). Furthermore, if you project out the monthly

cash flows in the standard annuity style, the borrower will not pay the exact percent principal amount in the first year as assumed in Step 1, because Steps 1 and 2 are approximations, and also due to rounding error. So, we must then take our maturity and calculate the correct monthly payment, according to the standard annuity calculation.

Assuming:

Coupon = 5%
Loan amount = 200,000
Maturity = 431

Plugging these numbers into equation (26.3), the monthly payment equals 999.93. Rounding to the nearest integer gives 1,000.

One of the problems with this mortgage style is that the lender's portfolio is longer or shorter, in terms of maturity, depending on the interest rates charged. Further, the maturity is not expressed in "clean" figures such as 25 or 30 years. It is very difficult, then, for a lender to price mortgages based on maturity, which is more or less a convention in most countries. (See German Annuity Calculator on the CD.)

INTEREST PAYMENT RULES

Most mortgages in Europe have fairly straightforward interest-rate payments. However, there are very few countries that have fixed interest rates for an entire 30-year maturity as is common in the United States. The longest fixed interest rate tends to be about 10 years. Variable-rate loans are normally not pegged to any interest-rate index. Thus, if a borrower has a loan with a 5-year fixed interest-rate period, but with a 30-year legal maturity or amortization period, the lender would normally be obliged to offer the borrower a new 5-year interest rate after the first rate period has ended, but that new rate would be completely discretionary. Long-term fixed rates are fairly uncommon. One of the reasons for this is that most European countries do not have a government-bond benchmark longer than 20 years. Thus, pricing of long-term loans is made more difficult.

A survey of several major countries shows the diversity of interest-rate types.

Belgium

Contrary to the generally short interest reset periods common in Europe, Belgian mortgages are typically fixed for up to 25 years. However, in recent years, products such as 10-5-5, which refers to a 10-year fixed rate, and then a 5-year fixed rate thereafter has become more popular. Belgium is one of the few countries that has extremely detailed legislation regarding the types of loan products that one can give. The interest rates for variable-rate mortgages must be pegged to a particular index of Belgian government bonds. Further, there is a collar on the resets of a maximum of up or down by 3 percent. In Belgium, lenders must be given permission by the government supervisory agency to offer any new products. Therefore, mortgage-product innovation is fairly low. A further complication in Belgium is that, like many European countries, there are various types of state-subsidized loans. These loans may have fairly obscure rules regarding interest rates. For example, mining was once a huge industry in Belgium. As this industry has been phased out, the government provided loans for old miners with very advantageous interest rates. The problem when analyzing the return on such loans is that the interest rates depend on the length of time that the borrower was a miner, and the adjustments for this depend on a series of charts, rather than a mathematical formula.

France

Over half of the mortgage loans in France are variable rate, often with caps. Many banks offer flexibility for borrowers to choose between increasing their mortgage payments, if interest rates go up, or increasing the maturity of the loan. This situation poses considerable challenges in terms of trying to project future cash flow.

The French government offers various loan subsidies. There are many possibilities. A few of the most popular are outlined here.

Plan-épargne-logement. This saving plan is state-subsidized, where the French state bears part of the interest paid out to the client during the saving phase. Once the client uses this saving plan to finance the purchase of his or her main residence, the interest rate applied to the mortgage loans is also subsidized by the French state. This *plan-épargne-logement* and the related mortgage loans might be taken out by any borrower, which means that it is a highly popular product.

Zero percent interest rate. Depending on the level of revenues of the borrower, and provided the borrower purchases a newly built property, the French state or regions will grant a loan at zero percent, distributed by all the banks. This loan amount is often capped, so an additional loan is needed.

One percent *employeur.* This is a fund in France is funded by all the employers. This fund also helps subsidize property loans.

United Kingdom

Historically, U.K. lenders tend to have variable-rate mortgages, which do not reset on a schedule but at the complete discretion of the lender. This has, of course, been extremely profitable for lenders, as they have avoided the hedging problems facing U.S. lenders such as maturity mismatch. It has also

---

Monetary Policy Hits Home

An interesting side effect of U.K.-style variable mortgages is that any change in the country's overall interest-rate levels is very quickly and directly passed onto consumers, which poses a challenge for government monetary policy. Decreases in the Bank of England's rates will normally mean a decrease in mortgage rates for both new and existing borrowers. This policy can be very positive, as we saw in 2001 and 2002 where, despite a bleak economic environment, home sales and property values remained steady due to attractive mortgage interest rates. Conversely, an increase in rates will also be fed through to most mortgage holders in an increased mortgage payment, creating an immediate dampening effect on consumer spending. Thus, the Bank of England must tread more carefully than most central banks because consumers feel the effects of its policies both immediately and directly in terms of their discretionary income.

---

worked, at times, to the benefit of the borrowers, particularly in declining interest-rate environments. Prepayments have not been a large issue since any decline in interest rates would normally be reflected (more or less) in a new rate on the mortgages. However, today many lenders also offer fixed-rate products with prepayment penalties that vary depending on the lender.

Sweden

The most popular products in Sweden today are quarterly floating interest rates. However, various fixed rates are offered, up to 10-year fixed. The products are very straightforward, with no caps, floors, or collars.

PREPAYMENTS AND OTHER RISKS

In Europe, prepayment risk is highly dependent on local legislation. Some countries have exact methods of dealing with prepayments within the law, whereas others rely on market conventions or the discretion of the lenders. Most European countries with high prepayment risk are still in the very early stages of understanding and quantifying those risks. One reason for this situation is because, historically, most markets have not been very price transparent. Thus, customers have had little incentive to refinance their mortgages. Another reason is that the lenders themselves have not understood prepayment risk. Until very recently most European banks have funded themselves almost exclusively with short-term deposits, and hold a maturity mismatch between their mortgage assets and deposit liabilities. If there were prepayments, then the banks simply made less profit. However, less profit has not been quantified as a loss due to the prepayments. As Europe turns more to securitization, prepayment risk is becoming recognized. However, to date there is very limited data and modeling of prepayment risk is practically nonexistent. Some investment banks have attempted U.S.-style models. However, these models basically take a U.S. framework and are crudely adapted to the limited European data available. At this stage, these models probably have very little predictive value.

Investor focus for European MBS is concentrated on credit risk. Most MBS deals issued in Europe are quarterly floating. If the underlying assets are fixed rate, then the prepayment risk is normally sold to another counterparty, usually via the swap agreement. It is very common, in fact, for the originator of the mortgages to keep the prepayment risk rather than sell it to a third party. As the market in Europe matures, prepayment risk will undoubtedly become an area of extensive research.

The fairly detailed analyses described in Chapters 9, 10, and 13 are rarely used in the context of European MBS. Finding the correct maturity benchmark for MBS with prepayment risk is generally based on a simple average-life calculation. A static prepayment assumption is used in the calculation. This assumption is usually based on a historical average prepayment rate for the originator in question. The data set is rarely more than 5 years. The "standard assumption" on prepayments for calculating the average life is usually set in the first MBS deals that come to market in the relevant country. This assumption is then used for all following deals.

In the following sections, the legal framework regarding prepayments for some European countries is discussed as well as the impact of that framework on the mortgage market and prepayment risk.

Sweden

At one end of the spectrum is a country such as Sweden where there is very little prepayment risk. Prepayments are allowed but lenders may charge a full penalty to cover the interest-rate risk if a borrower should break a contract. However, because of the high prepayment penalties as well as other historical factors, the market has developed such that most borrowers take out a number of smaller loans on their property, each with different fixed interest-rate periods. For example, a typical borrower may have three or more loans. The first loan may have a 10-year fixed interest rate, while the second loan has a 2-year fixed interest rate, and the last loan is quarterly floating. There is a high rate of refinancing for loans with short fixed interest-rate periods, while longer-term interest-rate loans have extremely low prepayments.

Germany

German legislation allows for prepayment penalties on loans with fixed interest-rate periods of 5 years or greater. Penalties are forbidden on loans with shorter interest-rate terms. A direct result of this legislation is that lenders offer products with either quarterly floating rates, which have limited prepayment risk, or with fixed rates of 5 and 10 years where the lender is fully compensated for prepayments.

Belgium

The maximum prepayment penalty allowed by law in Belgium is equal to 3 months of interest. Historically, prepayment statistics have been fairly low in Belgium. This is due to extremely low price transparency as well as to the fact that lenders do not mark a loan as "prepaid" if the borrower refinances with the same lender. In recent years, as the market has become more competitive, Belgium has seen huge prepayments. In May 1999, prepayments reached a peak of between 80 and 100 percent conditional prepayment rate (CPR) for many of the MBS deals issued on the market. These prepayments on securitized loans have forced lenders to realize losses, which they have blamed on securitization, rather than on prepayments. This had a dampening effect on the Belgian residential MBS market, with no deals being issued in the last few years.

France

For fixed interest-rate loans, the maximum prepayment penalty a lender may charge is equal to 6 months of interest capped at 3 percent of the outstanding principal balance at the time of the prepayment. Further, the vendor is not allowed to charge a prepayment penalty if the reason for the prepayment is because of a job change (whether voluntary or not) or death of the borrower or the borrower's spouse.

Netherlands

There is no specific legislation in the Netherlands regarding prepayments. Lenders are free to charge penalties if they desire. However, there are strong market conventions. Most mortgage contracts allow for 10 percent of the principal balance outstanding to be paid back free of penalty per year. Any prepayment beyond this 10 percent would be liable to penalties. The types of penalties charged can vary from a true-loss calculation to a more arbitrary penalty. The variety of penalties and the penalty-free clauses make modeling Dutch prepayments extremely challenging. The data available are generally aggregate in nature, so it is difficult to know which prepayments were subject to penalties versus partial prepayments that take advantage of the annual penalty-free amounts.

United Kingdom

In the United Kingdom, prepayment penalties on the standard variable product are increasingly being dropped due to the growing popularity of flexible mortgage products. The offering of "teaser" rates—encouraging borrowers not to prepay—results in an indirect punishment for the borrower. Fixed-rate and capped-rate products, however, are normally subject to a direct prepayment penalty, which vary depending on the lender.

EXERCISES

Exercise 26.1   Create a calculator in Excel that will project the cash flows of a mortgage loan with either a bullet, linear, or annuity-style amortization. From the cash flows, calculate average life. Which style amortization has the longest average life? Which has the shortest average life?

Exercise 26.2   Assume a German annuity mortgage with the following characteristics and calculate the monthly payment and the maturity. (See German Annuity Calculator on the CD.)

	Example 1	Example 2	Example 3
Balance	€ 100 thousand	€ 100 thousand	€ 100 thousand
Coupon	6.5%	10%	6.5%
Percent paydown in first year	1%	1%	5%

Exercise 26.3   What are some of the potential difficulties for an originator of German annuities in regard to pricing the mortgages?

Exercise 26.4   If you own a portfolio of Belgian loans, how much prepayment risk is covered by the 3-month interest-rate penalty?

Exercise 26.5   You have a portfolio of old mortgages, some originated over 20 years ago. The monthly payments are stated in the contract. However, the monthly payments were calculated with rounding errors. Thus, at the end of the contract, the actual yield on the loans will be different from the stated coupon. You cannot reverse engineer the rounding errors, so you cannot estimate the errors in any mathematical way. How do you project the cash flows for the portfolio?

CHAPTER 27

European Securitization Legislation

In the United States, it is easy to focus solely on mathematics and value because the breadth and maturity of the U.S. market means that most legal issues with regard to securitization have long since been settled. However, in Europe, the legal setup of a deal is crucial, complicated, and is the main up-front cost for originators. It is wise to remember that a bond is simply a contractual agreement; and in the case of securitization results in a stack of documents a meter high! A really excellent model that forecasts cash flows will not help you in a bankruptcy situation, if, due to sloppy drafting, your assets and cash flows are not properly secured.

There are three general areas to think about in regard to legislation:

1. Type of law: Napoleonic, Anglo-Saxon, or Germanic.
2. Securing the assets and cash flows.
3. Local framework for securitization.

In the United States, legal discussions regarding securitization tend to focus on how the asset is secured because the type of law (Anglo-Saxon) and framework for securitization are taken for granted. However, in Europe, all three aspects must be given close scrutiny and nothing should be assumed.

TYPE OF LAW

The main types of law prevalent in Europe can be broadly categorized into Anglo-Saxon, Germanic, and Napoleonic (see Table 27.1). The financial markets tend to assume Anglo-Saxon law because the United States and the United Kingdom are among the largest financial centers in the world.

Please note that this chapter contains a general discussion of legal matters and has not been prepared by lawyers.

TABLE 27.1 Countries According to Legal Type

Country	Legal Type
United Kingdom	Anglo-Saxon
Belgium	Napoleonic
Spain	Napoleonic
France	Napoleonic
Luxembourg	Napoleonic
Portugal	Napoleonic
Sweden	Germanic
Denmark	Germanic
Finland	Germanic
Norway	Germanic
Austria	Germanic
Netherlands	Germanic
Germany	Germanic

However, when dealing with European assets, an understanding of the basic types of law will prevent confusion and numerous arguments with lawyers.

Anglo-Saxon Law

Anglo-Saxon law, originated in England, is contractually based. Laws are intended to establish a broad framework under which individuals can make their own agreements. The details of any agreement between parties will rarely be governed by specific laws and are open to many interpretations. The outcome of a disagreement can usually only be predicted based on case law or precedent (i.e., the outcome of actual disputes that have gone to court that are similar to the case in question). But note that there are statutes that might provide guidance.

The positive aspect of this type of law is the large degree of flexibility it affords since parties can agree to almost anything that they can think up, because very little is specifically illegal. This is extremely beneficial for the financial markets where creation and new solutions are the name of the game. The negative aspect of this type of approach is that one must try to think of all possible aspects and consequences of an agreement and ensure that everything is specifically included in the contract. This makes for a lot of paper, lengthy conversations with lawyers, and large legal bills (mainly because lawyers in Anglo-Saxon countries tend to have the highest fees*).

---

*A nonrigorous survey of legal costs suggests that Anglo-Saxon lawyers are on average twice as expensive as continental lawyers. Today, a partner at a major law firm in the United Kingdom or United States will bill at around € 700 to 900 per hour, compared to a Swedish or Belgian partner at rates around € 300 to 400 per hour.

Germanic Law

Germanic law, in its various local versions, is prevalent in Northern Europe in countries such as Germany, Sweden, Finland, the Netherlands, Austria, Denmark, and Norway. Germanic law tends to be the extreme opposite of the Anglo-Saxon legal system. Laws are very detailed regarding many areas of the economy, including the financial sector, and also with regard to contracts between parties. The positive result of a Germanic law framework is that legal documents can be shorter because detailed law governs many aspects. There is less room for interpretation of agreements and fewer possibilities for different outcomes of a disputed contract.

For example, a loan agreement for a mortgage in Sweden will rarely be longer than two pages, whereas in the United Kingdom the document may run to over 20 pages (and in very small type!). In Sweden most of the aspects of a loan agreement between a bank and a consumer are governed by very specific laws, including how interest is charged, the rights of the borrower and the bank, what happens if a borrower does not pay, including detailed default and foreclosure procedures, and prepayment rights and penalties. In the United Kingdom, all of these aspects must be specifically described and agreed on. The negative aspect of Germanic law is that it is not flexible, which is especially relevant in finance since new structures often arrive faster than regulators can amend laws to keep up. For example, reverse mortgages (also called home equity conversion mortgages whereby a home owner borrows against the equity in his or her home and receives regular monthly tax-free payments from the lender), are popular in the United Kingdom, yet are not possible in Sweden because it is illegal to create an option over real estate.

Napoleonic Law

Napoleonic law lies somewhere in between Germanic law and Anglo-Saxon law. Many areas of Napoleonic law are detailed, depending on the country, but on the whole, there tends to be more flexibility and room for interpretation than in a Germanic law system. Countries in this category include France, Belgium, Luxembourg, Spain, and Portugal.

SECURING THE ASSET

Securitization is about obtaining a legal ownership or right to a revenue-producing asset. It is this right that differentiates a securitization from other forms of debt.

True Sale

Obtaining the legal right to the asset is often done via a "true sale." This means that the asset in question is sold by the originator/owner of the asset to a special-purpose vehicle (SPV) set up solely for the purpose of owning the asset. The purpose of the true sale is to avoid other creditors having access to the collateral in a bankruptcy of the originator. The sale also avoids delays in obtaining collateral from a liquidation/receivership/Chapter 11-type scenario. However, the concept of true sale can be misleading because it is often thought that without a true sale, there can be no real securitization. The point is not to have a true sale but to have the cleanest possible right to the assets in question. Figure 27.1 presents the basic structure of a securitization transaction.

It helps to start by thinking about the asset that is to be securitized because the collateral can have multiple layers of security. For example, for a residential mortgage-backed securities (MBS), the asset is a loan that is backed by a mortgage on real estate. The "true sale" is on the loan, not the underlying real estate, which remains owned by the borrower. In Europe, in many jurisdictions, there is a sale or assignment of the loans to a SPV but the perfection of the sale is often postponed until various trigger events occur in order to avoid complicated borrower notification laws.

Compare the MBS with a commercial mortgage-backed security (CMBS): The asset in question can either be a portfolio of loans given from a creditor to various companies that own real estate or the asset could be one or more loans given from the SPV directly to the real estate owner. In the first case, the credit structure and analysis would be similar to a residential MBS but in the second case, the credit structure and exposure would be very different.

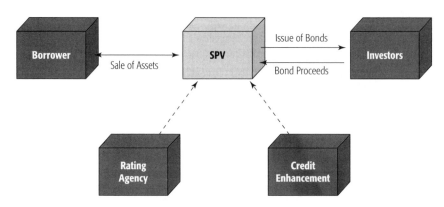

FIGURE 27.1   Securitization structure.

Traditionally, many in the field have felt that in the case of commercial real estate, unless there is a large diversified portfolio of borrowers, the second case is not a true securitization but simply a corporate bond backed by real estate. This simple analysis would be missing the point.

The current popularity of whole-business securitization is a good case to think about. Many argue that if the business goes bankrupt, investors are exposed to large corporate credit risk and thus the securitization was useless, amounting to just a corporate bond. However, the entire point of a whole-business securitization, as well as CMBS structured as a secured loan structure (i.e., secured by a loan or several loans to one or a small number of real estate owners), is that the structure of the deal should assume a default/bankruptcy of the borrower on the first day the deal starts. If this is done correctly, then the asset, whether it be commercial real estate or pubs, should pass cleanly through to the SPV in the transaction, be able to be managed by a third party, and thus continue to produce cash flows that can pay off the debt to investors. It is clear that not all businesses will have assets that can fulfill this stringent profile, but that does not mean that securitization is not a valid funding method for those that do and should provide added value for the owners of those businesses as well as investors. As a matter of fact, analysis has shown that a BBB corporate credit could enhance to a AAA credit using securitization.

Framework for Securitization

In Europe, the legal framework for securitization in any given country is a large factor in how much activity can be seen in that country. The standard structure for a securitization in Europe is somewhat different from the U.S. "pass-through" (see Chapter 2). The United States uses various trust structures whereby the trust owns the assets such as the mortgage loans, and the investors have a direct ownership interest in the trust. In Europe, this concept does not exist. All deals use a variant on the following structure: The originator/owner of the asset sells the asset to an SPV. The SPV then issues a bond, which is purchased by various investors, backed by the assets owned by the SPV. This SPV is, in many jurisdictions, simply a company, subject to normal company law, but restricted in activity and may be exempted from certain taxes. This structure can be much more costly than a U.S. trust structure because on continental Europe it is very common to have a minimum amount of share capital necessary to set up a company. For example, in Belgium, the minimum is € 62 thousand, in Sweden it is SKr 100 thousand, and in the Netherlands € 20 thousand. For a bank intending to issue multiple deals per year, these small equity stakes can start to add up. The United Kingdom tends to be the most popular jurisdiction for SPVs because there is

no minimum share capital necessary. Countries such as Belgium, which have
the ability to divide the SPVs into bankruptcy-remote compartments (see details on Belgium later in this chapter), also allow issuers to save costs.

Although most countries have different approaches to legislating this
fairly new financial technique, attempts are being made to facilitate the
process, while simultaneously ensuring that the transactions are transparent,
safe for investors, and using overall sound and acceptable practice. Some
countries rely on older laws not explicitly addressing securitization to inform
parties on the preferred, expected, or required processes and requirements,
whereas other countries have been implementing legislation specifically
aimed at controlling securitization activity.

Belgium   Belgian legislation is seen as one of the most securitization-friendly
in Europe. In addition to allowing for fairly easy transfer of assets, Belgian
law has some features not seen in other jurisdictions.

Belgian legislation has provided the legal framework for the establish-
ment of a *Vennootschap voor Belegging in Schuldvorderingen naar Belgis-
che recht* (VBS). The VBS is a public or private SPV that is limited to the
acquiring and financing of receivables. A VBS can acquire all types of receivables, including future receivables. There are, however, certain types of
receivables that are subject to additional formalities or requirements as to
the status of the assignee. A VBS may issue pass-through securities and debt
obligations in different tranches or series of securities to finance its activities.
It may also attract funding through credit lines provided by banks or financial institutions.

A special feature under Belgian legislation as a result of the law of December 4, 1990, is the possibility for a VBS to create different "compartments." Creating compartments means that the company is internally
divided into different subdivisions that are legally considered to each be a
separate group of assets corresponding to a separate group of liabilities. The
result is as if each compartment of assets and liabilities were to constitute a
separate company. The liabilities of a compartment are exclusively backed
by the assets of such compartment and are not available for the creditors of
another compartment whose rights have not been allocated to the first compartment. Compartments could therefore be described as a statutory mechanism of ring fencing. All public VBS are authorized and monitored by the
Belgian Banking Commission, and there are specific rules regarding the administration of the VBS, safe custody of assets, and other counterparties; all
of which are designed to provide comfort to investors.

Netherlands   There is currently no legislation in the Netherlands aimed
specifically at regulating the securitization market. This, in combination

with the fact that assets such as consumer and mortgage loans or credits are considered receivables under Dutch law, results in the required application of the Netherlands Civic Code to securitization transactions.

There are a number of aspects of the Dutch legislation that can create hurdles to a securitization transaction, although these can be surpassed. One such hurdle is the issue of notification. Under Dutch law, the originator must in most cases notify the debtors of the transfer of the receivables. This proved to be problematic, as originators are not keen on informing their clients of such transactions. Therefore, securitization structures outline certain notification events. Only if these events (usually pertaining to the financial status of the originator) occur, are the debtors notified. Another issue that must be addressed is the fact that, in many cases, it is not possible to vest security rights in a trustee. This requires additional special provisions in the transaction structure. Additionally, differences between contractual aspects of a receivables assignment and real estate-related regulatory ("in rem") aspects require some maneuvering, which entails mostly the application of Dutch and/or foreign laws to the aspects of the assignment.

Under the Netherlands Act on the Supervision of the Credit System 1992, all credit institutions are subject to banking supervision and require a license. In 1993, a regulation was implemented allowing for exemptions to this law. SPVs that met certain criteria were exempted from the 1992 act, thereby facilitating the securitization process. In September 1997, the Dutch National Bank published a memorandum on securitizations and supervisions. This memorandum established conditions imposed on banks participating in securitizations regarding the true-sale principle, servicing issues, transparency of the transaction, credit enhancement, underwriting, and the administrative organization.

France   France, together with the United Kingdom, has one of the most advanced legislative frameworks when it comes to securitization. The legislation was implemented by the act of December 23, 1988. This act, completed by the decree of March 9, 1989, has been amended several times since, continuously improving the framework and addressing new concerns and concerns not previously addressed.

The act of 1988 made it possible for credit institutions to securitize certain types of assets through the use of a *Fonds Commun de Créances* (FCC), a tax-transparent vehicle. The FCC is an SPV dedicated exclusively to securitizations. Its assets consist only of receivables and the cash flows deriving from them. It is created at the initiative of a management company (*société de gestion*) and a depositary (*dépositaire*). Both founders' rights and obligations are specifically set forth in the 1988 act. While management is responsible for the administration of the FCC, the depository is in charge of the custody of the assets, as well as the monitoring of the management. Currently there are over 140 FCCs in France by the way of public offerings. The act also addresses issues such as receivable types, parties eligible for securitizations, investor protection, and so forth.

Most recent amendments to the 1988 act and 1989 decree include the October 6, 1997, and November 6, 1998, decrees, the July 2, 1998, act, and the June 25, 1999, decree. These amendments all address the market practitioners' concerns and requests.

The October 6, 1997, decree allowed for different types of receivables to be acquired by the FCC, eliminating the need for different FCCs for different receivable portfolios. The decree also permitted for the securitization of future receivables that arise from future completed agreements. Additionally, thanks to the 1997 and 1998 decrees, receivables could be acquired in different currency denominations, which at the time prior to the euro, was seen as a great leap forward. Additionally, the FCC could issue units in currencies other than the currency of the receivables.

Most notably, the July 2, 1998, act allows commercial companies to securitize receivables through the French FCCs, while they were previously only allowed to securitize receivables through offshore SPVs or by selling them to credit institutions, which would then securitize them. The June 25, 1999, decree enabled the creation of umbrella FCCs that allow for the classification of different receivable types, each being financed by a specific class of units.

Secured loan structures can be difficult to structure in France, however, due to the legislation regarding security and priority right on assets such as real estate acting as collateral.

Germany   There are several aspects of German law that create complications for securitizations in Germany. This explains in part why the German market has been fairly active in Europe in the synthetic securitization market, but less active in other areas.

There are some favorable aspects of German law with respect to securitization. For example, there is no requirement for the notification to the debtors of the transfer of assets. Even though some underlying contracts explicitly prohibit the transfer of receivables, it is still possible to assign monetary receivables that came into existence after July 30, 1994, under the German Commercial Law.

However, various other laws apply to securitization transactions in Germany that make transactions more complex. Regulatory capital requirements are set out in the circular of March 19, 1997, of the BAKred, but might become more rigorous in the future. Restrictive German insolvency regulations apply to all insolvency proceedings, including those in a securitization context. Transactions can also be subject to corporate and trade tax regulation.

According to German law, assignments only become effective after the receivable has come into existence. Therefore, structuring tools are required to address this issue for future flow transactions.

As for servicing, it is possible that the servicer, if not the purchaser of the receivables, might require a license to carry out its duties. This also applies if the servicer is the originator of the receivables. Although not always clear if necessary due to inconsistencies, the license costs are minimal within the context of a securitization.

Luxembourg Luxembourg is currently preparing new legislation to facilitate securitization. It is expected to be similar to the Belgian and French framework, although updated and simplified. If this resulting legislation is simply cheap and effective, Luxembourg could become a popular jurisdiction for securitization vehicles since Luxembourg is already a common jurisdiction for stock exchange listing purposes.

Sweden Under Swedish law, practically all asset classes are securitizable, as they are transferable. However, until recently, there was no legislation aimed specifically at securitization. Prior to the summer of 2001, an SPV was considered simply to be a company, which conducted a financing business, thus, it was subject to the licensing and capital adequacy requirements established by the Swedish Act on Financing Operations. This explains why all securitizations in Sweden have used offshore or non-Swedish SPVs.

In the summer of 2001, legislation was passed that exempted the SPV from the requirements under the Swedish Act on Financial Operations, particularly for mortgage securitization. This exemption aims to reduce the costs incurred with this form of financing. Additionally, this legislation makes it easier to achieve off-balance-sheet treatment by allowing parties to securitize a specific "security pool" of loans to "qualified borrowers," thereby giving bondholders priority rights over assets in case of bankruptcy or similar procedures. Nonetheless, the new legislation is vague in that it exempts entities (e.g., SPVs) from the requirements if the entity acquires claims or assets only on a "few occasions," and that it does not "continuously" raise financing from the public. It is hoped that these vague terms will be clarified as the securitization market expands.

Finland Finnish law allows for the securitization of almost any receivable type. However, there are some considerations, such as balance-sheet consolidation and true-sale issues. Additionally, industry-specific legislation relating to matters such as banking secrecy and confidentiality could create some hurdles. Additionally, debtors are usually legally required to be notified of assignments of receivables.

The main legislation regarding securitization in Finland includes the Act on Promissory Notes of 1947, the Companies Act of 1978, and the Act on Credit Institutions of 1993. All three, although not directed specifically at securitization, have implications, and have been occasionally amended since. Additionally, the Finnish Financial Supervisory Authority issued a Guideline on Asset Transfer and Securitization.

Finnish SPVs are also subject to taxes. However, there is some uncertainty whether the taxes applied should be as business income according to the Act on Taxation of Business Income, or as other income according to the Act on Income Taxation. This, combined with the fact that securitizations have been aimed at attracting foreign investors, result in most Finnish securitization transactions being carried out through an SPV situated abroad.

Italy   Although Italy has implemented securitization legislation, there are still several concerns regarding certain points not addressed or specified in the law. However, this has not stopped Italy from being one of the most active markets in Europe. It is anticipated that future legislation will address the shortfall of the current framework

The main legislation governing the securitization activity in Italy is Law No. 130 of April 30, 1999. This law's main purpose is to set out the provisions for the creation of an SPV for securitizations, guidelines for the transaction, and the SPV's relationship to other parties such as creditors and debtors. The Bank of Italy takes a supervisory role as to the activities of the SPV. Additionally, the SPV is not allowed to engage in any other activities other than those performed to ensure sufficient cash flows to pay off the issued notes, unless the parties involved in the transaction are willing to risk the rating of the transaction. In other words, the SPV can only purchase money credits, including future receivables resulting from normal course of business, issue notes, and ensure the payments on these notes.

One major issue that some see as an area that needs consideration in future legislation or amendments is the fact that the SPV is not by law constituted as a bankruptcy-remote entity. Nonetheless, great progress has been made through the implementation of Law No. 130, and this in combination with the current flurry of activity gives hope that future legislation will provide solutions to any current outstanding issues.

Spain   Although securitization laws go back quite a way, the Spanish regulation changes in May 1998 have encouraged both the securitization of a wide range of assets and the participation of new banks in the asset-backed market.

The *Ley* (law in Spanish) 19/1992 of July 7, 1992 (regime for property investment funds and mortgage securities), allowed for the creation of *fondas de titulizacion hipotecaria* or mortgage securitization funds. Its main limited purpose was to assist in providing cheaper loans for the acquisition of homes. This first step, however, was insufficient to extend or apply the financing of securitization to loans other than mortgages.

The royal decree-law 3/1993 dated February 26, 1993, enabled the government to extend the scope of the system for securitization of mortgage bondholding to cover loans and credit rights. In 1994 the process of mortgage securitization was adapted to new types of credits and loans and, more importantly, provisions were introduced to allow for the adaptation of regulations and the legal system so that both mortgage securitization funds and asset securitization funds could be administered and managed. The latest royal decree 926/1998 was enacted on May 14, 1998, and provides for the regulation of nonmortgage assets through asset securitization funds (ASF) and securitization fund management companies.

Portugal   Until 1999, Portuguese securitizations of all asset classes occurred in a legal environment where there was no specific legislation addressing securitization. However, in 1999, legislators passed a decree that was aimed at guiding securitization activity. This law cleared up many of the regulatory and tax obstacles, and was inspired by Spanish and French legislation.

The Decree Law 453 of November 5, 1999, established the legal framework for Portuguese securitization transactions. This law is directed mostly toward mortgage securitization. In short, the law addresses the issue of the transfer of credits to entities that issue securities to finance the acquisition of those credits.

Two types of entities can perform securitizations. One of these is the credit securitization fund, or *Fundo de Titularização de Créditos* (FTC), which can be fixed- or variable-asset funds. These funds can offer securities in different categories. The second entity is known as a credit securitization company, or *Sociedad de Titularização de Créditos* (STC). The STC is a financial company that acquires and manages credits and issues bonds to finance the acquisitions. Both entities have specific requirements and limitations as to their establishments and operations.

Although the law established the legal framework for securitization, the tax framework was flawed, and most securitization transactions occurred through old offshore vehicles or structures. In August 2001, legislation was presented to solve this problem, but did not go far enough, according to analysts. This flaw in the legal framework translates into fairly high costs, and has therefore kept the Portuguese securitization activity level fairly low. However, it is believed that the government will soon loosen its grip, and that new legislation will address these concerns in the near future.

Basel Accords

Capital requirements are intended to provide a credit buffer for a bank's lenders, that is, the depositors and the investors in bank bonds. Because a bank traditionally holds assets on the balance sheet, any credit losses from those assets have to be taken by the bank. Capital requirements are governed country by country. However, the Basel Committee of the Bank for International Settlements (BIS) has developed general guidelines for the minimum level of capital for member country banks. These guidelines are specified in terms of the ratio of bank capital to risk-weighted assets. All assets held by banks are assigned risk levels ranging from 0 percent to 100 percent. A 100 percent risk-weighted asset means that the bank would have to hold a minimum of 8 percent of capital, whereas a 50 percent risk-weighted asset would require a minimum of 4 percent capital. These guidelines are only recommendations. Each country then decides how it will use the guidelines for its own banks. If capital requirements are set to the minimum levels set by BIS, then a residential mortgage is 50 percent risk-weighted (i.e., a 4 percent capital requirement) and a commercial mortgage is 100 percent risk-weighted (i.e., an 8 percent capital requirement).

Securitization generally allows a bank to lift assets off of the balance sheet, and thus eliminates the capital requirements on those assets. However, the extent to which securitization can achieve this is dependent on each country's regulations. The Basel Committee on Banking Supervision is in the process of developing new guidelines for assessing bank capital adequacy. It is believed that these new guidelines will be the most rigorous and strict imposed since the Basel Accord of 1998.

The accords will allow for an internal rating-based (IRB) approach to risk-weighting assets. This approach comes in two forms. The institution in question will internally determine risk, or external ratings will be used. This proposal is mostly to limit or remove regulatory capital arbitrage, while not creating incentives or disincentives for securitization. Nonetheless, increased capital will have to be held against retained or purchased subordinate tranches of securitization transactions. Although this is the main issue addressed, the accords also provide guidelines for the treatment of revolving securitization structures, synthetic securitizations, and different operational requirements. Currently, there is still interaction with the industry in order to determine what the final guidelines should reflect. It is hoped that the accords will be implemented sometime during 2006.

International Accounting Standards

Accounting standards set the rules by which an institution can account for its assets, and determine whether those assets are either on- or off-balance sheet and the profits that those assets generate. Every country has its own individual accounting standards. However, the International Accounting Standards (IAS) will become the European Union standards in 2005. Many large corporations have already initiated their preparations for the new regulations and are therefore currently looking at any implications in following the new standards. There are some direct implications in regard to securitization, specifically the accounting treatment of SPVs of the originating company.

The relevant international standards concerned are:

- IAS 27: Consolidated Financial Statements and Accounting for Investments in Subsidiaries.
- SIC 12: Standing Interpretation Committee on Consolidation of Special Purpose Entities.
- IAS 39: Financial Instruments: Recognition and Measurement.

The comparable relevant standards in the United States are FAS 140, and in the United Kingdom FRS 5. The main issue for concern is the implicit requirements on consolidation of SPVs by the originator outlined in IAS 27, and its interpretation SIC 12. In accordance with most regulations of consolidation, also mentioned in IAS 27, ownership of more than 50 percent of the voting rights of the entity automatically implies that it should be consolidated with its parent company.

However, according to IAS 27 and SIC 12, ownership is neither sufficient nor necessary to determine whether to consolidate an SPV. Instead, they focus around the concept of "control" of the entity. IAS 27 defines control of a company as *"the power to govern the financial and operating policies of an enterprise so as to obtain benefits from its activities."* In SIC 12, control is defined as *"contributing to or benefiting from the risks and the rewards of the SPV,"* not necessarily by ownership or voting rights. Yet another aspect of control according to SIC 12 is *"predetermination of the activities of the SPV so as to receive benefits from its operation."* Hence, these rules challenge the off-balance-sheet objective of a typical securitization.

The setup of most multiseller conduits, that is, SPVs created and sponsored by one entity, and used by several originators, appears to provide for an off-balance-sheet solution under the IAS regulation, which mainly reflects the fact that the conduit is under "control" of the sponsor, and not the originators. However, it still requires an elaborate approach to the legal and financial structuring to make sure that the risk of the assets is properly transferred to the conduit.

There is no doubt about the fact that the IAS and specifically SIC 12 implies that somewhat stricter rules must be taken into account during the structuring of a securitization. First of all, the new IAS rules clearly indicate a need to revise the setup of each transaction individually, which is why the arranger would play a crucial part in detailed discussions with the audit firm of the originating company in order to make sure that they understand and agree to any given structure, and, if necessary, propose mitigation for satisfying the auditor.

Looking ahead, future securitization transactions will demand careful arranging and structuring in order to achieve off-balance-sheet treatment of assets sold to an SPV. The IAS regulations clearly indicate that there is not one definite answer on when to consolidate an SPV.

EXERCISES

Exercise 27.1 Should securities law be harmonized over all European jurisdictions? How might this help or hamper the development of the securitization market?

Exercise 27.2 With the spectacular fall of Enron, SPVs are objects of distrust. Companies such as General Electric, who make heavy use of SPVs in securitization, have come under criticism in the press. Is this criticism justified? Should assets held in SPVs be consolidated under the sponsoring entity's balance sheet?

CHAPTER 28

Structuring Asset-Backed Securities in Europe

As in many financial fields, structuring mortgage-backed securities (MBS) and asset-backed securities (ABS) is both an art and a science. On a basic level, one has to understand mathematically the underlying cash flows from the asset, be able to model the flows, and transform those flows into bonds with characteristics to please the originators and the investors. But it is not enough to take a mathematical approach to structuring. An ABS is bound by legislation relating to the collateral that can impact both the structure of the bonds as well as the credit worthiness of the collateral. Regulations pertaining to the originators, particularly financial institutions, can create incentives for various types of structures. Finally, the needs of the originator and investors can have a large impact on the characteristics of the final bonds. Juggling all of the various aspects that can enter into a deal is the art of structuring. Structuring in Europe takes particular creativity because of the differences between legal jurisdictions and simply because the market is still relatively new and the assets are very heterogeneous.

The main objectives and methodology for structuring an ABS in the United States and Europe are the same, as previously outlined in Chapter 2. The point of this chapter is to explain how structuring differs in Europe because of the nature of the legal system, collateral, and relative immaturity of the market.

THE EUROPEAN APPROACH

When structuring a deal in Europe, you start with the most fundamental question: Why securitize? The objectives and motivations for securitization have been covered already in Chapter 3. The difference between the United States and Europe is that, in the United States, securitization is looked on as one of the standard weapons in a chief financial officer's funding arsenal. In

Europe, securitization is still greeted with suspicion. However, the key motivations for securitization in Europe remain the same as in the United States:

- Selling risks
- Cheaper funding
- Diversification of funding sources
- Balance sheet optimization
- Regulatory and/or tax arbitrage

There continues to be a heavy debate in Europe regarding the validity of securitization, and convincing the originator of the benefit is half the battle to completing a deal. Once the originator has decided to move forward with a securitization, the motives for that decision are the start in deciding how the assets should be transformed into a bond. For example, if the originator's main motive is balance-sheet optimization, special care must be taken to ensure that the sale of the assets to the special-purpose vehicle (SPV) will be characterized as a true sale and that the relevant regulators are satisfied that the risks to the originator have been sold with the assets. If the originator views the transaction as simply a financing, then the true sale character may not be an issue at all, and the focus will be on minimizing credit enhancement in order to obtain the best levels of financing. Whatever the motivations, structuring in Europe is an open field for innovation.

ASSESSING THE COLLATERAL

The first step to structuring a securitization deal is to scrutinize the assets. Your three goals are to: (1) understand the asset and assess risk factors; (2) model the cash flows; and (3) quantify risk factors via stress tests or other techniques.

Understanding the Asset

Every type of collateral will have its own individual features, and your job is to find out what these are. The first step to understanding the collateral is to get data regarding the collateral. The depth of the due diligence at this stage is critical in order to have a smooth transaction and rating result. Table 28.1 lists some common collateral types and the main statistics necessary to understand the asset, along with the main risks that must be assessed. These data are by no means exhaustive but are simply a starting point for analysis.

TABLE 28.1 Main Statistics and Risk per Collateral Type

Type of Asset	Main Statistics	Main Risks
Residential Mortgages	Original and current loan amount Assessed market value Interest rate and type Amortization type Original and current maturity Debt-to-income ratio or other applicable figures Loan-to-value ratio Historical portfolio arrears, default, foreclosure, and loss rates Historical prepayment rates Characteristics of borrower Characteristics of property Purpose for loan Sample loan contracts Underwriting criteria	Credit risk on borrower Geographical concentration Product type risk Property value risk Prepayment risk
Commercial Mortgages	Original and current loan amount Assessed market value Interest rate and type Amortization type Original and current maturity Debt-to-income ratio or other applicable figures Loan-to-value ratio Historical portfolio arrears, default, foreclosure, and loss rates Historical prepayment rates Characteristics of borrower Operating history of property Purpose for loan Sample loan contracts Lease/rental agreement terms	Small number or concentration of loans or debtors Geographical location Limited second-hand market or use for property Vacancy Property value risk Prepayment risk Rental loss and delinquency risk Tenant financial status Debtor industry concentration Currency risk

(continued)

TABLE 28.1   (*Continued*)

Type of Asset	Main Statistics	Main Risks
Commercial Mortgages (*cont.*)	Property management characteristics Rental income and expenses Resale value Environmental aspects Industry/competition characteristics Maintenance costs Underwriting criteria	
Trade Receivables	Pool size Receivables size Historical losses, delinquency, and dilution on receivables Origination volume Maturity of receivables Industry characteristics Company performance (historical and forecasts) Lessee or renter Underwriting criteria	High percentage of receivables pertaining to small number of debtors Industrial concentration risk Currency risk Carrying cost issues Dilution risk Delinquency risk Servicing issues Commingling risk Obligor default risk
Credit Cards	Eligible principle outstanding Gross principle outstanding (including finance charges, etc.) Asset type and contract terms Payment terms Underwriting criteria Servicing and collection Recovery rates Delinquency and default rates Interest rates and portfolio yield Servicing fees Originator characteristics and performance Market conditions	Geographical concentration Economic and industry trends Cardholder type concentration Delinquency and default risk Dilution risk Low recovery risk Market performance risk Purchasing/economic downturn risk Insolvency risk

(*continued*)

TABLE 28.1 (*Continued*)

Type of Asset	Main Statistics	Main Risks
Future Flows	Originator/borrower characteristics and performance Originating company's (implicit) rating (to limited extent) Nature of future receivables Type of asset or operation generating cash flow Historical and expected cash-flow generation Jurisdiction Industry characteristics Obligor characteristics Size of issuance/loan Maturity of receivables Maturity of loan Collection characteristics	Originator/borrower performance risk Commercial and operating risk Receivable generation/ fluctuation of cash-flow risk Obligor risk Exchange rate risk Sovereign risk Delinquency, default, and loss risk
Airplanes/Ships	Asset type (lease, loan, etc.) Aircraft or vessel model and characteristics Market conditions Asset life, write off, and depreciation Assessed market value Rental/charter income (if applicable) and other cash-flow generation Charter/lease/rental contract terms Cost, fees, and expenses Maintenance costs Loss rates of vessel or aircraft Loan-to-value ratio Historical default/loss rate of income Operator of vessel or aircraft characteristics Country of origin	Resale value or second-hand market Lessee concentration Aircraft or vessel type concentration Geographical concentration Date of lease/charter/rental expiration concentration Loss of income/default risks Servicing issues Recession or industry downturn risk

(*continued*)

TABLE 28.1   *(Continued)*

Type of Asset	Main Statistics	Main Risks
Auto Loans	Original and current loan amount Asset age, type, and value Interest rate and type Amortization type and payment method Original and current maturity Debt-to-income ratio or other applicable figures Loan-to-value ratio Company/borrower income Historical portfolio arrears, default, delinquency, and loss rates Historical prepayment rates Loan contract terms Company/borrower history, characteristics, and performance Originator's dealer network Down payment requirements Underwriting criteria Insurance characteristics for vehicles Repossession costs	Credit risk on borrower Geographical concentration Product type risk Prepayment risk Servicing issues Resale value of asset Loss severity (increases with length of contract) Repossession issues

The purpose of the initial data analysis is to get an idea of the parameters of the asset. As background, understanding the nature of the business is essential. If the business is lending, then knowing the standard characteristics of the market is important to evaluate the relative riskiness of the pool in question compared to the norm. If the business is receivables, then one must understand the market position of the originator, the customer segment, and the future viability of the business. The type of business will give you many important clues as to the potential risks in the asset. For example, if you were to do a securitization of loans on gas station franchises, a very important consideration, which would not necessarily be revealed in the loan data, would be environmental issues. However, a familiarization with the business would tell you that environmental concerns are a standard part of any due-diligence process. Potential leakage of gas, oil, or other industrial materials could invite major lawsuits. In fact, if those gas stations were in the United States, under the environmental protection laws, the lender (or bond-holder!) potentially could be liable for any environmental cleanup or penalties. However, this would be mitigated to a bearable risk if the tanks that hold gasoline and other toxic materials were new and had sophisticated leak-monitoring systems. Further research would reveal, that, historically, the environmental costs for replacing tanks and cleaning up damage are actually quite low for gas stations.

Are we dealing with a pool of loans with maturities of 5 years or 30 years? Will the bond amortize over its life or be a bullet bond? What kind of credit is the asset providing? These are just some of the questions that must be answered. For many assets, there can be multiple layers of credit. For example, for any kind of loan backed by real estate, the first layer of credit is the ability of the borrower to pay back the loan. The second layer of credit is the value of the real estate. If the real estate is commercial, then the value of the real estate may be further split into the potential revenues from the real estate in terms of rental or other income, and then finally the resale value of the real estate.

One large problem in Europe is lack of computerized data. If one is trying to do a residential mortgage deal with thousands of loans originated up to 20 years ago, it is very likely that the originator will have collection data available, but limited borrower or collateral information, except on physical files. The perfect solution would be to go through all the physical under-writing documentation and put those data in a computerized database or spreadsheet. This process can, of course, be very costly and time consuming. There are a number of creative alternative ways one could try to solve this dilemma. For example, underwriting guidelines can be used to assess the general credit quality of the pool of loans. If the originator has good loss statistics, then it may not be necessary to know the exact loan-to-value (LTV) and debt-to-income (DTI) statistics on each individual loan. Another potential solution could be to do a physical file audit and compute averages based on a sample. The chosen solution will depend on how the rating agencies view the pool, and the potential costs for the solution versus the potential decrease in credit enhancement (and therefore in funding costs) that increased data accuracy will bring. Although rating agencies prefer as much data as possible, securitization in Europe would be impossible if every originator had to produce perfect historical statistics for 10 years. Thus, rating agencies are generally open to other methods for identifying the riskiness of the collateral. If the issuer is of sufficient credit quality, a legal solution via a representation and warranty from the originator guaranteeing the underwriting quality of the assets might suffice.

Once you have identified the asset as much as possible with the given data, the next task is to try to model the cash flows from the asset. Here, the type of asset will greatly dictate how you try to model.

Modeling the Cash Flows

There are four different approaches to modeling:

1. Generic modeling as one loan
2. Bucket modeling
3. Loan-by-loan modeling
4. Business-type modeling

In the United States, for residential mortgage portfolios, a generic approach will usually suffice; you can assume that the entire portfolio can be described, more or less, as you would describe one loan. This modeling can be done when you are securitizing a portfolio that has been originated in a short time frame, with exactly the same amortization and interest-rate types and when the maturity and coupons are a small range. This type of model is discussed in Chapter 8.

In Europe, this kind of homogeneous portfolio is rare. Most securitizations are done on a fairly heterogeneous pool. Depending on how the pool looks, one can try to "bucket" the portfolio into similar types, and then project, for example, 10 loan types. However, the work required for this bucketing may be fairly extensive and may also be difficult to readjust if the pool is changing. Thus, it may be more effective to simply project the cash flows of the pool by modeling each loan and adding up the cash flows. This is not something that can be done easily with a spreadsheet and requires a database with some programmed cash-flow generators.

When the asset in question is commercial real estate, toll-bridge revenues, or some other kind of flow originating from an operating business, the modeling will resemble a financial business plan or profit-and-loss forecast in order to generate cash flows and stresses. For example, the type of modeling for a deal backed by commercial mortgages will depend greatly on whether the asset is a pool of diversified loans on real estate or whether you are looking at the revenues backed by a single or small number of properties. In the first case, if the pool is sufficiently diversified, it may be sufficient to simply model the loan characteristics. This type of model would be similar to the models you would produce for residential mortgages or consumer loans. Usually commercial mortgage-backed securities (CMBS) deals rely on various kinds of rental streams to produce the cash flow. In this case, the model will be very different from the kind of mortgage cash-flow calculators as shown in Chapter 8. Instead, the analysis will look much more like a company profit-and-loss statement, as described earlier in Chapter 22. The difference between U.S. and European CMBS transactions is mainly in the different legal structures regarding bankruptcy, standard lease terms, and the norms regarding yields on income-producing real estate. For every different type of business that produces assets, different factors will have to be taken into account in order to produce potential future cash flows, and different types of stresses will be made.

Quantify Risk Factors via Stress Tests or Other Techniques

Once the cash flows have been calculated, they will be stressed in order to assess the strength of the flows. The type of risk factors will depend on the asset in question. Some typical risk factors for different collateral types were presented in Table 28.1.

The rating agencies play an important role in determining the stress tests that are applicable for the type of asset. Although the stresses will be different for each type of asset, it is worthwhile to understand the terminology and concepts as applied to residential mortgages. The same kind of analysis can then be applied to all asset types, albeit with different parameters.

The three large rating agencies, Moody's, Standard & Poor's, and Fitch IBCA, may use different terminology in their rating approaches but the concepts are more or less the same. The basic idea is to try to determine, based on historical loss and default statistics, a stress on the cash flow that is commensurate with a rating level. The rating scale starts at AAA, which indicates the strongest credit available that should withstand almost any adverse economic shock, to AA, A, and BBB, which is the last of the investment-grade ratings. After BBB come the speculative grade ratings, BB, B, and so forth. Residential mortgage portfolios typically have the highest rating, AAA, because residential mortgages are a relatively safe asset. In order to obtain this rating, the cash flows and bond structure must withstand losses at a scale that is the absolute worst-case economic scenario, historically speaking.

The two standard indicators of the risk level of any kind of loan, including residential mortgages are DTI and LTV. **Debt to income** indicates the affordability of a loan to its borrower, or, in other words, the ability of the borrower to pay his or her mortgage payments. **LTV** indicates how much equity a borrower has in his or her home. A larger LTV means less equity and reduces the incentive of the borrower to try to maintain loan payments in an adverse environment. LTV also indicates the buffer the lender has on the collateral if the borrower does default. These two indicators must then be translated into a stress of how much total loss the bond must withstand and still pay back the bond.

The first step is to calculate the **default probability** (also termed **default frequency**) of the pool of assets, that is, the percent of borrowers who will stop paying their loan payments. Intuitively, the higher the DTI and LTV, the less ability the borrower has to pay the loan, and less cushion the borrower has against an adverse shock such as unemployment. The rating agencies take historical statistics and assign default probabilities that must be withstood for each rating level. These probabilities are adjusted for different factors, including loan types (i.e., floating-rate loans are riskier than fixed-rate loans), amortization types (bullet loans are riskier than fully amortizing loans), employment status of the borrower, and the quality of the underwriting.

Once a loan has gone into default, one must calculate the lender's probable losses, called **loss severity**. For a mortgage, the lender has recourse to the borrower's home, which will be sold in order to pay off the debt. If the price of the home when sold is less than the debt, the lender will experience losses. To make this calculation, one must make an assumption regarding property prices. For an AAA security, the rating agencies will want the bond to withstand a substantial **market value decline**. This assumption will be based on historical trends in housing prices and will normally differ based on geography. Once a lender has to foreclose on a property, there will be associated costs to pay for legal and administrative fees, called **repossession costs** or **foreclosure costs**. There is also a cost associated with the time it takes from the first day the borrower defaults until the lender finally realizes the money from the sale of the house, typically termed a **carrying cost**.

Let us take an example. Say we have a portfolio of loans in Holland, which we want to rate AAA. The weighted-average LTV on the loans is 65 percent, while the weighted-average DTI ratio is 45 percent. The rating agency assigns this portfolio with a base default probability of 11 percent, that is, over the life of the portfolio of loans, 11 percent will default. These loans have interest-rate resets that expose the borrower to potential interest-rate risk, and thus are considered more risky than a fixed-rate loan. Thus, the rating agency applies a factor of 1.15 percent to the base rate. The quality of the underwriter is considered normal, so a factor of 1 percent is applied. The default probability for this portfolio is then calculated:

$$\text{Default Probability} = 11\% \times 1.00 \times 1.15\% = 12.65\%$$

Next we have to calculate the loss severity. Let us assume a portfolio with a current loan balance of 195 million. The assumed market-value decline for the region of this portfolio, South Holland, is set by the rating agency at 45 percent. The loss due to market-value decline equals:

$$
\begin{aligned}
\text{MVD Loss} &= \text{Appraised Market Value} \times \text{MVD} \\
&= \text{Loan Balance} / \text{LTV} \times \text{MVD} \\
&= 195 \text{ million} / 65\% \times 45\% \\
&= 135 \text{ million}
\end{aligned}
$$

The repossession costs are assumed to be 5 percent of the portfolio loan balance:

$$\text{Repossession Costs} = 5\% \times 195 \text{ million} = 9.75 \text{ million}$$

It is assumed that it takes as long as 12 months for the property to foreclose, and the coupon on the mortgages is 9 percent.

$$
\begin{aligned}
\text{Carrying Cost} &= \text{Coupon} \times \text{Foreclosure Months}/12 \times \text{Loan Balance} \\
&= 9\% \times 12/12 \times 195 \text{ million} \\
&= 17.55 \text{ million}
\end{aligned}
$$

Thus, we must calculate the amount that the lender recovers, taking into account all costs:

$$
\begin{aligned}
\text{Recovery Value} &= \text{Appraised Market Value} - \text{MVD Loss} \\
&\quad - \text{RepossessionCosts} - \text{Carrying Costs} \\
&= 137.7 \text{ million}
\end{aligned}
$$

Thus, the loss the lender experiences on this portfolio is 57.3 million, and the loss severity can be calculated as:

$$
\begin{aligned}
\text{Loss Severity} &= (\text{Loan Balance} - \text{Recovery Value})/\text{Loan Balance} \\
&= 29.38\%
\end{aligned}
$$

The final step is to calculate the potential credit enhancement needed to cover these losses:

$$
\begin{aligned}
\text{Credit Enhancement Required} &= \text{Default Probability} \times \text{Loss Severity} \\
&= 12.65\% \times 29.38\% \\
&= 3.7\%
\end{aligned}
$$

This is a raw credit-enhancement figure and does not include any structuring factors such as capturing excess spread, losses due to arrears, or timing delay factors. The actual structure of the bond will be a factor in determining the final credit-enhancement figure.

The previous example was specific to mortgages. However, the same type of analysis applies for any kind of asset. The idea is simply to quantify the level of losses by calculating the probability that the borrowers will default, and the losses due to selling the collateral under adverse market conditions.

ISSUES IN BOND STRUCTURING

Structuring a securitization, particularly in Europe, is not something that can be explained in one chapter of a book. The methodology and the final goal is dependent on many factors, such as the client's wishes, the type of asset, the attitude of the rating agencies, the availability of data, and the investor appetite for the transaction. Typical structures and analysis for different kinds of collateral have been discussed in earlier chapters in this book. This information holds true, regardless of whether the deal is in the United States or Europe. Thus, the intent of this section is to point out various issues in structuring, particularly where conventions that are used in the United States are either not used or used in a different manner in Europe.

Timing Issues

As the saying goes, time is money. Nowhere is this truer than in a securitization transaction. In Chapter 8, you saw how to calculate the conventional delay factors in U.S. MBS transactions. The same types of delays exist in Europe. However, the conventions that price and account for the delays do not exist. In the United States, the pass-through convention means that cash flows are passed through to the bondholders when they are received from the servicer and the servicer normally has a number of delay days in which to calculate what he or she has received before passing the cash to the bondholders. These delay days are compensated for in the price that the investor pays for the bond. In Europe, no such convention exists. Because MBS issuers tend to be very large banks that retain their own servicing, the cost of delay is normally offset, to a certain extent, by the float on those funds, which is also retained by the bank. Thus, delay costs are almost never directly calculated. However, those delays are nevertheless issues that must be addressed in the structure of any deal.

Reporting delays arise because servicers can rarely instantaneously report what cash has been received categorized into interest, principal, prepayments, and fees. Normally, it will take between 10 and 30 days to get this reporting.

In Europe, the reporting tends to be available more quickly than in the United States. The reason for this is that in the United States servicing consumer loans, such as mortgages, credit cards, or personal loans, involves manual check processing. The checks must be received, opened, booked, deposited, and a confirmation received that the check was honored. In the majority of European countries, most customers pay bills via electronic transfers, where either the customer sets up an automatic payment or where the service "pulls" the payment electronically from the customer's account. These methods mean that the processing is much faster. The exception to this rule is the United Kingdom, where checks are still widely used, although this is changing.

Once the servicer has reported on the monthly collection period, the cash that each bond within the transaction should receive must be calculated, respecting all the rules created in the bond structure. This calculation will normally take a few days and can be called a calculation delay.

Let us assume that all monthly mortgage payments are made on the last day of the month. Then let us assume it takes 15 days for the service to provide reporting on the collections, and then a further 5 days to calculate the bond amounts, for a total delay between the borrower's payment and reporting of 20 days. The cost of this delay is 20 days of interest that the bondholder is due but that is not paid by underlying borrowers. In the United States, bondholders of a pass-through MBS would simply receive their bond payments 20 days late, the cost of the delay having already been taken into account in computing the yield on the bond.

One other difference between the United States and Europe is that in the United States, the servicer holds the collection funds during the delay period in its own bank account. Thus, the servicer retains the float on the delay period. In Europe, it is often true that the servicer collects the funds directly into the bank accounts of the SPV. Thus, the SPV can capture the float on the delay period, which does not mean, however, that there is no cost for the reporting delay, since the money cannot be paid out to bondholders until the servicer reports on it.

In Europe, bond payments are rarely made on a monthly basis. The convention is for quarterly payments, although semiannual and annual payments are sometimes used. Thus, the monthly collections must be held in a bank account until the quarterly bond payment date. If the bank account pays the same interest as the borrowers pay on the mortgage, then everything is fine. However, this is rarely the case. In order to maximize the interest on the bank account and minimize the cost of holding monthly collections for quarterly bond payments, a guaranteed investment contract (GIC) is normally used. A GIC is basically a bank account with restrictions on withdrawals and deposits, with a rate that is guaranteed. With a GIC, the cost of the mismatch in payment periods can be calculated exactly.

So taking the assumptions made earlier regarding delay and assuming a monthly mortgage collection but a quarterly bond payment, we must then think about what happens when we try to make the first bond payment. Say the bond begins on the 1st of January. The first bond payment is then due one quarter later on the 1st of April. By the 1st of April, we have had 3 months of collections on the last day of January, February, and March. However, although we have the cash from the March collections, we will not be able to calculate what is interest and what is principal until April 20th. Thus, the first bond payment will only be able to use two months of collections, with the third being held in a GIC account until the second bond payment. This delay in payment will repeat itself throughout the life of the bond. The total cost then has two items:

1. The cost to hold monthly payments in a GIC until quarterly bond payments are made. The size of the cost will depend on the difference between the interest rate on the mortgage and on the GIC account
2. The cost resulting from the reporting delay and the resulting mismatch in the principal outstanding on the bond versus the mortgages.

Risk Issues

The structure of any bond must address the various risks inherent in the assets. These risks must be either mitigated or passed onto investors. The techniques of structuring remain similar regardless of the jurisdiction of the assets. Credit risks can be mitigated by senior/subordinate structures, over-collateralization, reserve funds, and credit wraps or other types of guarantees. Interest-rate and currency exposures can be hedged using fairly standard swaps. However, the treatment of prepayment risk is very different in Europe than in the United States.

In the United States, as we saw in Chapter 9, analyzing prepayment risk, which is normally borne by investors, is the name of the game when investing in residential mortgage-backed securities (RMBS). In Europe, prepayment risk is rarely borne directly by the investors. The main reason for this is that prepayment data are very scarce, making it difficult to analyze the risks. Also, the degree of prepayment risk differs from country to country, as discussed earlier in Chapter 26.

The common ways to handle prepayment risk in Europe are:

■ Sell it entirely to a third party, normally via a swap. This method is rarely used because there are not many counterparties in Europe who have sufficient expertise to value prepayment risk. There have also been a few transactions, notably ones originated from the Netherlands, that have sold the prepayment risk directly to investors.

- Use a banded swap where the swap is allowed to amortize between two bands. This method has been commonly used, particularly in Belgium. The danger is, of course, that if prepayment rates go above the higher band, investors will bear the brunt of the risk.
- Use a so-called total-return swap whereby the swap bears the prepayment risk. This method is always done via a back-to-back swap with the original lender. Thus, the lender is simply retaining the prepayment risk. This method is probably the most common. These total-return swaps are also used to hide small risks such as mismatches in interest-rate indexes and timing delays. Although this kind of solution is not necessarily negative from the point of view of the investor, any analysis of the strength of the originator/seller should take into account the possibility of this type of hidden off-balance-sheet risk. This is not a large issue for originators today, because the portion of securitized assets tend to be relatively small.

Credit Enhancement and Rating

As discussed generally in Chapter 2, the desired rating on a transaction will have a large impact on the structuring process. Rating agencies will determine the level of credit support or enhancement in order to receive the required rating level. Providing the credit enhancement, whether via internal or external means, is the task of the structurer. The name of the game is to provide the least amount of credit enhancement for the highest rating level possible, which will normally provide the lowest cost of funds. The methodology behind ratings is basically the same, regardless of whether one is structuring in the United States or in Europe. The breadth and depth of the market in the United States means that repeat structures where the credit enhancement is more or less known at the outset is the norm, whereas in Europe, the precedents are less, which means more uncertainty regarding the credit enhancement. The idea of credit enhancement is that the calculations by the rating agency should be based on a mathematical analysis based on the historical performance of the asset in question. Most rating agencies publish matrices of their assumptions and explanations for their calculations. However, while the start of any analysis is mathematics, in Europe, particularly because good historical data is scarce, there is a certain amount of discretion exercised by the rating agents to ask for more or less enhancement than their base numbers would suggest, which means that when structuring a security, a certain amount of negotiation with rating agencies regarding the credit enhancement is necessary.

Particularly for ABS, it is way beyond the breadth of this chapter to discuss in detail the rating process for each type of asset and to catalogue the difference between similar transactions in the United States and Europe.

Suffice it to say that industry characteristics that differ in Europe from the United States must be taken into account in the structuring and rating process, but the methodology for both will be the same regardless of jurisdiction. However, for MBS, where there are many more conventions, it is worthwhile to point out how a few conventions differ in Europe.

Chapters 2 and 15 provide a discussion on structuring MBS in the United States; the concepts described there hold also for Europe. The two main mathematical ratios, discussed earlier in this chapter, used by all the rating agencies, which provide a good indication of the credit quality of a mortgage, are LTV and DTI. The LTV ratio tells you the degree of leverage of the borrower, and the degree of protection the lender has if the borrower is unable to pay the monthly payments. The lower the LTV, the higher the probability that the borrower will be able to simply sell the house in order to repay the lender; and also the higher incentive for the borrower to try to continue making the mortgage payments. The DTI ratio signals how much of the borrower's usable earnings will be used to pay off the debt. The lower the DTI, the easier it is for the borrower to pay off the debt, making it more unlikely that the borrower will be unable to pay the mortgage. In Europe, different jurisdictions may use similar terms but with slightly different meanings, which makes comparisons much more challenging.

LTV ratios are fairly straightforward and have the same meaning in most jurisdictions. Any discrepancies are, of course, to be found in the "value" part of the ratio. Most commonly, the value is a market value at loan origination, either an appraised figure or the sale price paid for the property. However, it is important to verify which value is being used. For example, in the Netherlands, the most commonly used value is not the market value but a liquidation value that tends to be somewhere around 80 percent of the market value. Thus a 100 percent LTV in the Netherlands would normally translate into an 80 percent LTV in U.S. terminology. However, the Dutch also use another LTV figure, which is a figure adjusted by a property price index, in order to try to reflect a current LTV rather than an LTV at origination. It is also very common in many jurisdictions to include in the loan an amount to pay for taxes, loan costs such as notary bills, or insurance. These amounts can be high, sometimes amounting to 5 to 10 percent of the purchase price of the property. The taxes will not be reflected in the price of the property, but are a standard cost. Thus, an LTV of 105 or 110 percent, as is rather common in the Netherlands, does not usually reflect the borrower receiving cash, but rather payments for taxes and insurance.

DTI ratios are the most difficult to compare across jurisdictions, and indeed even between banks in the same country. Generally, the ratio should mean the debt (normally the monthly or annual payment of the mortgage) divided by the income of the borrower. Sound simple? Well, it is not. When calculating the income figure, what income should be used? The first factor to consider is taxes. Normally, the relevant figure should be net of taxes, since these are taken directly from the borrower. This factor is particularly important in Europe since tax rates of 50 percent are quite normal for an ordinary person. Because tax rates are so high, it may also be important to calculate the tax benefits of having a mortgage and add that amount back into the income. In Sweden, for example, this calculation is straightforward and is always performed by lenders. In Belgium, in contrast, this calculation is very complicated and thus may not be included. The second factor to consider is other long-term debts or commitments of the borrower, such as car payments, other loans on homes, or alimony. Finally, one should consider the costs of maintenance on a home, including, for example, insurance payments. If these last two items are subtracted from the income, it is normally termed discretionary income. If one compares DTI ratios from two different originators, one may be using a simple net income versus another using a discretionary income. In order to make the comparison, one would have to obtain the details on how each bank makes its calculations.

A final observation regarding the differences in structuring in Europe versus the United States is the approach regarding geographic diversification. The idea behind geographic diversification is that if loans are spread relatively evenly across an entire country, an economic shock to one region of the country will have relatively less impact on the entire portfolio than if the whole portfolio is located in that one region. Certainly, the concept is valid in Europe. However, it is a truth with modification.

Take, for example, Sweden. What is the relative riskiness of a portfolio with the great majority of loans on property in Stockholm versus a portfolio that is spread around the entire country? Intuitively, one would prefer the portfolio that is diversified across the country. However, consider that Sweden has a population of roughly 8.9 million. Of that amount, 1.8 million or 20 percent of the population live in the greater Stockholm area. However, in terms of economic power, the influence of Stockholm is much greater than 20 percent. One could say without too much exaggeration that Stockholm is the center of all Swedish business other than agriculture. Thus, an economic shock to Stockholm would basically be equivalent to an economic shock to all of Sweden. Further, population movement in Sweden is toward Stockholm and out of the smaller towns where there is little work. Thus, on balance, a Stockholm portfolio versus a geographically diverse portfolio may be equivalent risks. This type of analysis would hold for such countries as Finland, Denmark, Norway, Ireland, and Belgium, where the capital cities have an overwhelming economic importance in the economy. Geographical diversity will be more relevant in countries such as France, Germany, Spain, and Italy, which have two or more important cities. As with many things, the devil is in the details. When we begin an analysis, we can start with basic assumptions and rules of thumb, but in order to truly understand the risk profile, one must learn the details regarding the environment, whether it be legal consequences, economic trends, or cultural factors. It is then the structurer's job to convince the rating agency of any mitigating factors that would benefit the rating of the transaction.

LEGAL PROCESS AND COUNTERPARTIES

A securitization is composed of a number of agreements between different parties, which outline the collateral, and the legal rights to that collateral, the bond's financial structure, and the various counterparties that will provide services to the SPV to enable the transaction to function. Different jurisdictions will have slightly different terms and arrangements.

The documents that make up a securitization transaction can be roughly divided into three different types: (1) the legal arrangements for the collateral; (2) counterparty support roles; and (3) bond description and structure.

Some of these categories may overlap. For example, in the case of a swap, the entity providing a swap is a counterparty, but the swap itself is part of the collateral of the deal as it provides an essential component of the structure of the deal. The same would be the case for an outside guarantor.

Collateral Arrangements

The legal arrangements for the collateral start with a **sale agreement** whereby the **originator/owner** of the assets sells those assets to an SPV. The entity that originates the assets is usually the owner of the assets before the securitization. For example, in the case of an RMBS, the originator is normally a bank or other financial institution. For a receivables deal, the originator would be the corporation that is generating the receivables through the sale of products or services. However, the originator is not always the owner of the assets. For example, Bank X could purchase the mortgage portfolio of Bank Y, in which case Bank X would be the seller but Bank Y would be the originator. The SPV is normally the entity called the **issuer** of the deal, that is, the counterparty that is issuing the bonds. It is common, however, to speak of the seller of the assets as the issuer. In fact, the terms originator, seller, and issuer are often used interchangeably to mean the entity sponsoring the securitization.

These assets are then pledged to the bondholders via a **pledge agreement** and/or a **deed of charge**. The pledge agreement contains a description of the lien on the assets and also the priority of payments, which is a list that describes who should be paid, when, and in what order.

Any outside credit enhancement such as **third-party guarantees, letters of credit,** or **liquidity facilities** would all have contracts and would be part of the collateral pledged to the bondholders. These guarantees can range from a guarantee on the entire credit of the bond, normally termed **credit wraps,** to a guarantee on a single aspect of the bond. A liquidity facility is not a credit guarantee, but a credit line, which would be available to cover temporary shortfalls in cash. Repayment of a liquidity facility would generally come before bondholders. Any counterparty providing guarantees or liquidity facilities would generally have to have high credit ratings itself, similar to the highest credit rating of the bond in question.

Various types of swaps are fairly standard in European transactions. Standard swaps might be used to convert fixed-rate flows into floating and also to cover currency risks. In RMBS deals, so-called total-return swaps are quite normal, whereby the **swap counterparty** promises to pay the interest on the bond in return for receiving the interest on the underlying collateral. These types of swaps are evil little creatures covering up all sorts of risks such as index mismatches, prepayment risk, and timing problems. While convenient for the issuer (and structurer), they normally transfer these risks right back to the former owner/originator of the assets via a back-to-back swap. It is very usual that the risks in these total-return swaps are never quantified, and thus the owner/originator could be in for a nasty shock in adverse environments.

If the transaction will include any swaps, then an International Swaps and Derivatives Association (ISDA) **master agreement,** which is the generic contract for all swap arrangements internationally, and the accompanying **ISDA schedule,** which details any changes to the ISDA master agreement will be needed. The financial details of how the swap will look will be provided in a separate **swap confirmation.** These contracts are both part of the collateral for the bond transaction, because the structure of the bond will depend on them. However, the counterparty providing the swap will also rely on the assets in the SPV to assure that the other side of the swap will be paid.

Counterparty Arrangements

In order to complete a securitization, there is a long list of duties that have to be taken by third parties and each duty will have to be described in a contract. The first and most important counterparty is the servicer and the terms of the agreement are normally in a **servicing agreement.** Unlike in the United States, where the convention is that the servicer "owns" an interest-only servicing strip, servicing in Europe is generally a contractual duty. Servicing fees vary widely in Europe, because there are no conventions, and in fact there are few third-party servicers. Servicing is most often performed by the originator/seller of the assets. Depending on the strength of the servicer, a **back-up servicer** may be required by rating agencies.

The next important counterparty is the **trustee**. The trustee is a third party who administrates the SPV, acting on behalf of the bondholders, to ensure that all the contracts that make up the securitization are properly enforced. The trustee will also act for the bondholders to make decisions. This role may be called different names, depending on the jurisdiction, and also may be divided into separate tasks. For example, there may be a separate **administration** or **management agreement**, where someone handles the day-to-day administration tasks and bookkeeping. There could also be a **supervisory company** or **bond agent**, whereby a company, most usually an accounting firm, holds the power of attorney to administer the securities on behalf of the secured parties in the transaction.

ABS may have fairly complicated structures, so there is often a **calculation agent** who is responsible for noting the incoming cash flows, as reported by the servicer, and making the appropriate calculations as to the payments that should be received by each class of bonds. Depending on the type of asset, there may be a **custodian agreement,** whereby a party will agree to the safekeeping of cash, documents, or securities on behalf of the bondholders. In RMBS, custodian duties regarding the loan documentation are normally performed by the servicer. If any cash is to be held in a bank account for any length of time, there may be a **guaranteed investment contract** that provides for a guaranteed rate of interest on the deposited funds. It is often the case that the custodian is the same as the GIC provider. GIC and custodian counterparties will generally have top investment-grade ratings for short-term liabilities. If there is a floating rate on the bonds, then there may be an **agent bank agreement**, whereby a bank has the official duty to quote the index rate such as EURIBOR on the bonds.

Bond Description

The entire structure of the collateral, counterparties, legal agreements, and the bond structure are described in the **offering circular** (also called selling memorandum or prospectus). The offering circular contains the **terms and conditions**, which is the legal contract between the issuer and the investors detailing how the bonds will work. The offering circular also contains background information on the assets. Normally, the version of the offering circular that is sent round to investors is called the "red herring." This circular is a draft version because there may be some small details that are not yet finalized. (See offering circular examples on the CD.)

Finally, the bond will have to be sold, which is provided for in a **subscription agreement** between the issuer and an investment bank. This investment bank is normally called the **lead manager** or **underwriter**. The term lead manager is really more appropriate these days, because bond issues are rarely truly underwritten. Underwriting implies that the investment bank will give the issuer a price and promise to purchase the bonds themselves if they cannot be sold to outside investors. Today, most bonds are sold on a best-efforts basis, which means that the price is not guaranteed, and indeed it is even possible that all the bonds will not be sold. Usually the lead manager will appoint a **syndicate**, that is, a group of banks to help sell the bond. The number of banks appointed will depend on the size of the deal to be sold. The syndicate is normally ranked in importance with **co-lead managers** being the second tier of the distribution syndicate; they have smaller amounts of the bond to sell and follow the instructions of the lead manager. **Co-manager** denotes the third tier of the distribution syndicate. If there are **joint lead managers**, that means that two or more banks have been appointed to jointly head the selling of the bond.

The **structurer** or **arranger** of the deal is the party that structures the deal, that is, that comes up with the financial structure of the bond, and "arranges" the bond, and manages all the different counterparties including the lawyers, rating agencies, and support roles. It is common that the lead manager takes these roles. However, some independent arrangers and larger issuers often arrange their own deals, and only appoint a lead manager to sell the deal.

Once the bonds are sold, the money from the collateral will have to be distributed to each individual bond investor. A **paying agent agreement** will normally take care of taking the funds from the issuer and sending them to the clearing agent with appropriate distribution instructions. A **clearing agreement** describes how the clearing agency, normally an organization such as Euroclear, will take the funds from the paying agent and distribute them to the appropriate investor accounts that may be scattered across the globe.

Accompanying all these agreements will normally be one or more **legal opinions** written by the law firm of the issuer. The legal opinion will give the lawyers' opinion on issues within the transaction. The purpose of the opinion is to clarify any areas that may be unclear in law and to confirm to all parties that the transaction will be implemented in the way everyone expects, in particular, with regard to a bankruptcy of the seller of the assets. **Auditors** normally have three different roles in a transaction. The first is to perform physical file audits prior to the issuance of the transaction and to issue a report of their findings. Second, the auditors act as advisors to entities on balance sheet and tax treatment of the securitization. Finally, all transactions will have an auditor appointed to audit the annual statements coming from the SPV. The final documents necessary for an ABS are the **rating letters** from the rating agency confirming its ratings on the bond.

Diversionary Tactics?

According to the Oxford English Dictionary (OED), a red herring refers to a smoked, salted, and dried herring that takes on a red color after being cured. In 1686, according to the OED, it was documented that red herrings were used in hunting by dragging them across the appropriate trail in order to put the dogs on the scent. Another version, not sanctified by the OED, is that escaped convicts would drag a dead herring across their own trails, to sidetrack and confuse the bloodhounds. Then, detective novels adopted the term whereby a red herring represents plot twists designed to take the reader off the scent of the person who really committed the crime. Regardless of the origin, it is clear, according to the OED, that by 1884, the term red herring was in wide use to describe an attempt to divert attention from the real question. In finance, the term red herring appears to have originated in the 1920s and refers to the preliminary information given to the potential investor before the real information is available. These preliminary prospectuses are normally marked with disclaimers in large *red* letters in order to alert investors that the information is not yet complete.

TIMING AND COSTS

A securitization is a fairly complicated transaction, involving a significant amount of due diligence, negotiation, and legal work. A first transaction from an originator can take anywhere from 3 months to 2 years to complete. If the assets are well documented with excellent quality computer data, the structure of the deal is fairly standard, and the jurisdiction has had previous deals with that asset type, then a first deal can move quite quickly. However, if the quality of the data is variable or the asset is new for the jurisdiction, the time to completion will be longer. Very often, there can be regulator issues, legal issues, or internal issues within the originator's organization that lengthen the time to completion.

Securitization is quite costly in terms of up-front and ongoing fees compared to other types of financing. The main variable is legal fees. Legal fees can quickly mount up in a securitization transaction, particularly if there are any new structuring or legal features in the transaction. Overcoming regulatory hurdles can also add greatly to the legal costs. The originator normally has to pay all the legal fees on the transaction, including all of the legal fees for all the counterparties.

TABLE 28.2 Typical Fee Ranges for Common Securitization Costs

Up Front	Upper	Lower
Legal fees	€ 250,000	€ 500,000
Auditor fees	€ 20,000	€ 50,000
Rating agency	2 basis points	4 basis points
Underwriter	25 basis points	200 basis points
Special purpose vehicle	€ 50,000	€ 50,000
Structurer and arranger	€ 100,000	€ 500,000
Listing fees	€ 5,000	€ 30,000
Ongoing (each year)		
Trustee	€ 10,000	€ 25,000
Auditor	€ 10,000	€ 20,000
Paying agent	€ 5,000	€ 10,000
Rating Agency × 2	€ 10,000	€ 10,000
Calculation Agent	€ 10,000	€ 20,000

Rating agencies tend to charge about 3.5 basis points of the principal amount of the transaction, usually with caps and floors. Structuring and arranging fees may be charged separately or may be included within the underwriting fee. Underwriting fees can vary greatly, from 30 basis points for a standard RMBS deal up to a few percent for more esoteric transactions.

The various counterparty roles will add some costs over the lifetime of the transaction. The largest cost is normally servicing. For a residential mortgage portfolio, this can range from about 15 to 30 basis points. The other types of counterparties tend to cost a few thousand euros a year each. Table 28.2 shows typical fee ranges for European securitization transactions for the basic roles. For a € 100 million transaction, which is the minimum threshold size for a public transaction, these costs add to the overall financing costs anywhere from about 15 to 50 basis points, assuming a 7-year bullet financing. Since these costs are, for a large part, fixed, the larger the transaction, the lower impact these costs will have on the final funding level.

EXERCISES

For the first three exercises, use the criteria data given in the Credit Enhancement Calculator on the CD.

Exercise 28.1 An application is made for a fixed-rate loan at an amount of € 200,000 for a house situated in the north of the Netherlands with a market value of € 250,000. The repayment of the loan will follow a linear pattern and the DTI of the person applying for the loan is 40. Calculate the required credit enhancement of the specific loan by following the different stages of the Credit Enhancement Calculator, based on these criteria.

Exercise 28.2   An application is made for a loan with a variable exchange rate at an amount of € 135,000 for a house situated in the south of the Netherlands with a market value of € 150,000. The repayment of the loan will be made as a bullet and the DTI ratio of the person applying for the loan is 50. Calculate the required credit enhancement of the specific loan by following the different stages of the Credit Enhancement Calculator, based on these criteria.

Exercise 28.3   An application is made for a loan with a variable exchange rate at an amount of € 175,000 for a house situated in the west of the Netherlands with a market value of € 325,000. The repayment of the loan will follow a linear pattern and the DTI ratio of the person applying for the loan is 30. Calculate the required credit enhancement of the specific loan by following the different stages of the Credit Enhancement Calculator, based on these criteria.

Exercise 28.4   Based on your understanding of how rating agencies work, what might their concerns be regarding the Dutch Savings mortgages, as described in Chapter 26?

Exercise 28.5   What might the rating agents be concerned about if you did not have a true sale of loans, but perfection based on triggers?

Exercise 28.6   What would the positive and negative characteristics of a credit wrap be? When might it be a good idea?

Bibliography

Ambrose, Brent W., and Sanders, Anthony B. "Commercial Mortgage Default and Prepayment Analysis." *Journal of Real Estate Finance and Economics* 26, no. 2–3 (March–May 2003): 179–196.

Ambrose, Brent W., and Warga, Arthur. "Measuring Potential GSE Funding Advantages." *Journal of Real Estate Finance and Economics* 25, no. 2–3 (September-December 2002).

Ames, Chris. *Introduction to Asset Backed Securities.* Lehman Brothers Fixed Income Mortgage and Asset Backed Securities, New York, July 1994.

Archer, Wayne, and Ling, David. "The Effects of Alternative Interest Rate Processes on the Valuation of Mortgage Securities." *Journal of Housing Research* 6, no. 2 (1995): 285–314.

Bartlett, William W. *The Valuation of Mortgage Backed Securities.* Irwin Professional Publishing, Burr Ridge, IL, 1994.

Bhattacharya, Anand K., and Fabozzi, Frank. *Asset Backed Securities.* Prudential Securities, New York, 1996.

Black, F., and Karasinski, P. "Bond and Option Pricing When Short Rates Are Lognormal." *Financial Analysts Journal* (July-August 1991): 52–59.

Blyth, S., and Uglum, J. "Rates of Skew." *Risk* (July 1999): 61–63.

Bond, Shaun A., Karolyi, G. Andrew, and Sanders, Anthony B. "International Real Estate Returns: A Multifactor, Multicountry Approach." *Real Estate Economics*, forthcoming.

The Bond Market Association. *Standard Formulas for the Analysis of Mortgage-Based Securities and Other Related Securities.* New York: TBMA, 2000.

Boudoukh, J., Richardson, M., Stanton, R., and Whitelaw, R. "Pricing Mortgage-Backed Securities in a Multifactor Interest Rate Environment: A Multivariate Density Estimation Approach." *Review of Financial Studies* 10 (1997): 405–446.

Buser, Stephen, Hendershott, Patric, and Sanders, Anthony B. "On the Determinants of the Value of Call Options on Default-free Bonds." *Journal of Business* 63, no. 1, p. 2 (January 1990): 33–50.

Buser, Stephen, Karolyi, Andrew, and Sanders, Anthony B. "Adjusted Forward Rates as Predictors of Future Spot Rates." *Journal of Fixed Income* (December 1996): 29–42.

Buser, Stephen, Hendershott, Patric, and Sanders, Anthony B. "Pricing Life-of-loan Rate Caps on Default-free Adjustable-rate Mortgages." *Journal of the American Real Estate and Urban Economics Association* (now *Real Estate Economics*) 13, no. 3 (Fall 1985): 248–260.

Buttimer, R. J., Hyland, D. C., and Sanders, A. B. "The Long-Run Performance of REIT IPOs." Working paper 2001–17, Dice Center for Financial Economics, The Ohio State University, 2002.

Chan, K. C., Hendershott, Patric, and Sanders, Anthony B. "Risk and Return on Real Estate: Evidence from Equity REITs." *AREUEA Journal* 18 (1990): 431–452.

Chan, K. C., Karolyi, A., Longstaff, F., and Sanders, A. "An Empirical Comparison of Alternative Models of Short-Term Interest Rates." *Journal of Finance* 47 (May 1992): 1209–1227.

Chan, S. H., Erickson, J., and Wang, K. *Real Estate Investment Trusts: Structure, Performance, and Investment Opportunities.* Oxford University Press, New York and London, 2003.

Davidson, Andrew, and Herskovitz, Michael. *Mortgage Backed Securities.* Probus Publishing, Chicago, IL, 1994.

Fabozzi, Frank J. *Mortgage Backed Securities.* Probus Publishing, Chicago, IL, 1987.

Fabozzi, Frank J. *The Handbook of Mortgage Backed Securities.* 5th ed. Probus Publishing, Chicago, IL, 1988.

Fabozzi, Frank J. *The Handbook of Fixed Income Securities.* Irwin Professional Publishing, Chicago, IL, 1997.

Fabozzi, Frank J. *The Handbook of Commercial Mortgage Backed Securities.* Frank J. Fabozzi & Associates, New Hope, PA, 1997.

Fabozzi, Frank J. *Handbook of Structured Financial Products.* Wiley, New York, 1998.

Fabozzi, Frank J., Ramsey, Chuck, Marz, Michael, and Ramirez, Frank. *The Handbook of Nonagency Mortgage Backed Securities.* Frank J. Fabozzi & Associates, New Hope, PA, 1997.

Fabrikant, Bruce, et al. *Moody's Approach to Rating Automobile-Backed Securitizations: The Driving Force.* Moody's Investor Service, Global Credit Research, August 1, 1995.

Hart, Judith. Mortgage Market Europe, Recent Trends and Their Likely Impact on the Mortgage Industry. Available at the Web site of the European Mortgage Federation, www.hypo.org.

Hogg, Robert V., and Craig, Allen T. *Introduction to Mathematical Statistics.* Macmillan Publishing Co., New York, 1978.

Hull, J. *Options, Futures, and Other Derivative Securities.* 4th ed. Prentice Hall, Englewood Cliffs, NJ, 2000.

Hypostat 1989–1990. A Statistical Survey on Mortgage and Property Markets in the European Union. Published by the European Mortgage Federation and available at www.hypo.org.

James, J., and Webber, N. *Interest Rate Modeling: Financial Engineering*, John Wiley & Sons, New York, 2000.

Karolyi, G. A., and Sanders, A. B. "The Variation in Economic Risk Premiums in Real Estate Returns." *Journal of Real Estate Finance and Economics* 17 (1998): 245–262.

Kau, James, Keenan, B. D., Muller, W., and Epperson, J. "Option Theory and Floating Rate Securities with a Comparison of Adjustable and Fixed Rate Mortgages." *Journal of Business* 66 (1993): 595–618.

Lehman Brothers. *The Lehman Brothers Mutual Fund Indices.* Lehman Brothers, New York, 1993.

Levin, A. "Deriving Closed-Form Solutions for Gaussian Pricing Models: A Systematic Time-Domain Approach." *International Journal of Theoretical and Applied Finance* 1, no. 3 (1998): 349–376.

Ling, David, and Naranjo, Andy. "The Integration of Commercial Real Estate Markets and Stock Markets." *Real Estate Economics* 27, no. 3 (Fall 1999): 483–515.

Ling, David, and Ryngaert, Michael. "The Predictability of Equity REIT Returns: Time Variation and Economic Significance. *Journal of Real Estate Finance and Economics* 20, no. 2 (March 2000): 117–136.

Ling, David, and Ryngaert, Michael. "Valuation Uncertainty, Institutional Involvement, and the Underpricing of IPOs: The Case of REITs." *Journal of Financial Economics* 43 (March 3, 1997), 433–456.

Peaslee, James M., and Nirenberg, David Z. *Federal Income Taxation of Securitization Transactions.* Frank J. Fabozzi & Associates, New Hope, PA, 2001.

Public Securities Association. *Standard Formulas.* Public Securities Association, New York, NY, 1990.

Prudential Securities. *Compendium of Prudential Securities Mortgage & Asset Backed Research.* Prudential Securities, New York, 1992.

Risk Publications. *Journal of Computational Finance.* Risk Publications, London, 1998.

Risk Publications. *Journal of Risk.* Risk Publications, London, 1998.

Sanders, Anthony B., "The Historical Behavior of REIT Returns: A Capital Market Perspective." *The Handbook of Real Estate Investment Trusts*, edited by R. Garrigan and J. Parsons. Irwin Publishing Co., Chicago, IL, 1997.

Sanders, Anthony B. "Government Sponsored Agencies: Do the Benefits Outweigh the Costs?" *Journal of Real Estate Finance and Economics* 25, no. 2–3 (September-December 2002).

Saunders, Anthony. *Financial Institutions Management*. Irwin Professional Publishing, Chicago, IL, 1997.

Stanton, R., Wallace, N. "Mortgage Choice: What's the Point?" *Real Estate Economics* 26 (1998): 173–205.

Wang, Ko, Chan, Su Han, Gau, George W. "Initial Public Offerings of Equity Securities: Anomalous Evidence Using REITs." *Journal of Financial Economics* 31, no. 3 (1992): 381–410.

Wilmott, P. *Derivatives*. John Wiley & Sons, New York, 1998.

Additional Resources

Asset Backed Securities Auto ABS, October 1999 (Credit Suisse First Boston).

Auto Loan Criteria, 2002 (Standard & Poor's Rating Services).

Faster than a Speeding Bullet? Prepayment Implications for MBS and Mortgage-Related ABS, (Moody's Investor Service, Structured Finance).

Manufactured Housing Collateral and Structural Aspects: A Solid Foundation, January 27, 1995 (Moody's Investor Service, Global Credit Research).

Manufactured Housing Criteria, January 2000 (Standard & Poor's).

Moody's Approach to Analyzing Home Equity Loans, March 8, 1996, (Moody's Investor Service, Global Credit Research).

Recent Developments Affecting Sub-Prime Home Equity Lenders, January 1999 (Moody's Investor Service, Global Credit Research).

Subprime Home Equity Industry Outlook, The Party's Over, October 1998, (Moody's Investor Service, Global Credit Research).

U.S. Residential Subprime Mortgage Criteria (Standard & Poor's Structured Finance).

General Web Sites

securitization.net	www.securitization.net
absnet	www.absnet.net
S&P	www.standardandpoors.com
Moody's	www.moodys.com
Fitch	www.fitch.com
Fannnie Mae	www.fanniemae.com
Freddie Mac	www.freddiemac.com
Ginnie Mae	www.ginniemae.gov
OFHEO	www.ofheo.gov

Mortgage and Banking Web Sites

BIS (Bank for International Settlements): www.bis.org
The European Mortgage Federation: www.hypo.org
The Swedish Bankers Association: www.bankforeningen.se
Council of Mortgage Lenders in the United Kingdom: www.cml.org.uk

Central Banks Web Sites

The European Central Bank: www.ecb.int
Austria: Oesterreichische Nationalbank, www.oenb.co.at
Belgium: Nationale Bank van België / Banque Nationale de Belgique,
     www.bnb.be
Denmark: Danmarks Nationalbank, www.nationalbanken.dk
Finland: Suomen Pankki, www.bof.fi
France: Banque de France, www.banque-france.fr
Germany: Deutsche Bundesbank, www.bundesbank.de
Greece: Bank of Greece, www.bankofgreece.gr
Ireland: Central Bank of Ireland, www.centralbank.ie
Italy: Banca d'Italia, www.bancaditalia.it
Luxembourg: Banque centrale du Luxembourg, www.bcl.lu
The Netherlands: De Nederlandsche Bank, www.dnb.nl
Portugal: Banco de Portugal, www.bportugal.pt
Spain: Banco de España, www.bde.es
Sweden: Sveriges Riksbank, www.riksbank.se
United Kingdom: Bank of England, www.bankofengland.co.uk
United States: Federal Reserve, www.federalreserve.gov

Periodicals

International Securitisation Report, Thomson Financial,
     www.securitisation.com.
Euroweek, www.euroweek.com
Structured Finance International, *Euromoney Institutional Investor*,
     www.ew-sfi.com

About the CD-ROM

INTRODUCTION

This CD contains supplemental information for *Securitization*. For each chapter, corresponding files may include answers to exercises, data, spreadsheets, or related information and documents. A listing of Web sites related to securitization is also included.

MINIMUM SYSTEM REQUIREMENTS

Make sure that your computer meets at least most of the minimum system requirements listed in this section. Otherwise you may have a problem using the contents of the CD.

For Windows 9*x*, Windows 2000, Windows NT4 (with SP 4 or later), Windows Me, or Windows XP:

- PC with a Pentium processor running at 120 Mhz or faster.
- At least 32 MB of total RAM installed on your computer; for best performance, we recommend at least 64 MB.
- Ethernet network interface card (NIC) or modem with a speed of at least 28,800 bps.
- A CD-ROM drive.

For Macintosh:

- Mac OS computer with a 68040 or faster processor running OS 7.6 or later.
- At least 32 MB of total RAM installed on your computer; for best performance, we recommend at least 64 MB.

USING THE CD WITH WINDOWS

To install the items from the CD to your hard drive, follow these steps:

1. Insert the CD into your computer's CD-ROM drive.
2. A window appears with the following options: Install, Explore, Links, and Exit.

   Install: Gives you the option to install the supplied software or the author-created samples on the CD-ROM.

   Explore: Enables you to view the contents of the CD-ROM in its directory structure.

   Links: A list of Web sites related to securitization.

   Exit: Closes the autorun window.

If you do not have autorun enabled, or if the autorun window does not appear, follow these steps to access the CD:

1. Click Start @> Run.
2. In the dialog box that appears, type *d*:\setup.exe, where *d* is the letter of your CD-ROM drive. This brings up the autorun window described in the preceding set of steps.
3. Choose the Install, Explore, or Exit option from the menu. (See Step 2 in the preceding list for a description of these options.)

USING THE CD WITH THE MAC OS

To install the items from the CD to your hard drive, follow these steps:

1. Insert the CD into your CD-ROM drive.
2. Double click the icon for the CD after it appears on the desktop.
3. Most programs come with installers; for those, simply open the program's folder on the CD and double click the Install or Installer icon. *Note:* To install some programs, just drag the program's folder from the CD window and drop it on your hard drive icon.

TROUBLESHOOTING

If you have difficulty installing or using any of the materials on the companion CD, try the following solutions:

■ **Turn off any antivirus software that you may have running.** Installers sometimes mimic virus activity and can make your computer incorrectly believe that it is being infected by a virus. (Be sure to turn the antivirus software back on later.)

■ **Close all running programs.** The more programs you are running, the less memory is available to other programs. Installers also typically update files and programs; if you keep other programs running, installation may not work properly.

■ **Reference the ReadMe:** Refer to the ReadMe file located at the root of the CD-ROM for the latest product information at the time of publication.

If you still have trouble with the CD-ROM, call the Wiley Product Technical Support phone number: (800) 762-2974. Outside the United States, call 1(317) 572-3994. You can also contact Wiley Product Technical Support at www.wiley.com/techsupport. Wiley Publishing will provide technical support only for installation and other general quality control items; for technical support on the applications themselves, consult the program's vendor or author.

To place additional orders or to request information about other Wiley products, please call (800) 225-5945.

Index

For information about the CD-ROM see the
About the CD-ROM section on page 533.

WILEY